Linux Security

Linux Security

Shadab Siddiqui

WITH NIIT

Premier
Press

ISBN: 1-931841-99-3

Library of Congress Catalog Card Number: 2002106501

Printed in the United States of America

02 03 04 05 BH 10 9 8 7 6 5 4 3 2 1

Premier Press, a division of Course Technology
2645 Erie Avenue, Suite 41
Cincinnati, Ohio 45208

Publisher:
Stacy L. Hiquet

Marketing Manager:
Heather Hurley

Project Editor:
Kathy Murray

Copy Editor:
Kathy Murray

Interior Layout:
LJ Graphics, Susan Honeywell

Cover Design:
Phil Velikan

Indexer:
Kelly Talbot

Proofreader:
Sandy Doell

About the Author

Shadab Siddiqui is an Instructional Designer with the Knowledge Solutions Business (KSB) division of NIIT, Inc. He is a Sun Certified Java Programmer. He has developed several Computer-Based Tutorials (CBTs) and Web-Based Tutorials (WBTs) and has written other books. He has developed learning materials covering various technical areas, such as Windows 2000 Networking, JSP, J2EE, Linux, and so on. These learning materials were developed to cater to the needs of different learners ranging from network administrators to programmers.

NIIT, a global training and software organization, offers customized and packaged multimedia educational software products and training, training needs identification (TNI), systems integration, software solutions (for business, engineering, and manufacturing), IT consulting and application software development to a range of audiences—both individuals and organizations.

The success of NIIT's courses lies in its unique approach to education. NIIT's Knowledge Solutions Business conceives, researches, and develops all the course material for a range of audiences. Each NIIT course has a definite aim. After finishing a course, the learner should be able to do a set of tasks.

Besides being a large software development and consulting division, NIIT has one of the largest learning material development facilities in the world. NIIT trains over 150,000 executives and learners each year in Information Technology areas using Stand-up Training, Video-Aided Instruction, Computer-Based Training (CBT), and Internet-Based Training (IBT). NIIT has been featured in the Guinness Book of World Records for the largest number of learners trained in one year!

NIIT has developed over 10,000 hours of Instructor-Led Training (ILT) and over 3,000 hours of Internet-Based Training and Computer-Based Training. Through the innovative use of training methods and its commitment to research and development, NIIT has been in the forefront of computer education and training.

NIIT has strategic partnerships with companies such as Microsoft, Computer Associates, AT&T, NETg, Sybase, Intersolv, and Information Builders.

Contents at a Glance

Contents

Introduction

This book provides you with comprehensive knowledge about Linux Security. The book is aimed at readers who are familiar with Linux concepts but now want to gain a solid foundation in Linux security features. It is assumed these readers already understand some Linux and networking concepts, such as network protocols, network servers, and so on. This book contains detailed information to help you fortify your Linux environment and provides questions that enable you to check your understanding at the end of key chapters.

Chapters 1 through 5 cover security basics in the Linux environment. These chapters give you an overview of Linux security, covering the precautions to be taken while installing and administering Linux. This part of the book also gives you an overview of the various authentication and encryption techniques you can use to protect your data.

Chapters 6 through 9 deal with securing networks in the Linux environment. Various kinds of possible network attacks are discussed in this part of the book, and you are given guidelines for preventing these attacks. Securing network servers—such as Apache Web server, FTP server, Sendmail, DNS, and SAMBA—is the core of this second part of the book.

Chapters 10 through 13 focus on preventing intrusion and data recovery. In these chapters, you are provided with an extensive list of signs of intrusions. You will learn to use various tools and security utilities to detect and avoid intrusion. Maintaining logs regularly is a good practice for system administrators. Logs can give you indications of methods used to attack your system, and at times, you can get information about the attacker as well. Chapter 12, "System Logs," educates you about using logs. In the last chapter of the book, I discuss the importance of making backups. You'll realize how important backups are if you ever lose data due to system crashes or other reasons. Various commercial and non-commercial tools that you can use to maintain backups are discussed in this chapter.

Finally, this book also includes several appendices. The appendices include best Linux practices and FAQs for Linux security. An appendix on the future of Linux also is included at the end of the book.

How to Use This Book

This book has been organized to facilitate your learning and give you a better grasp of the content covered here. The various conventions and special elements used in the book include:

- ◆ **Tips.** Tips have been used to provide special advice or unusual shortcuts.
- ◆ **Notes.** Notes give you additional information that may be of interest, but the information is not essential to performing the task at hand.
- ◆ **Cautions.** Cautions are used to warn you of possible disastrous results if you perform a task incorrectly.
- ◆ **New term definitions.** All new terms are italicized and then defined as a part of the text.

Chapter 1

Linux: An Overview

Origin of Linux

Linux is a UNIX-like operating system developed by Linus Torvalds, a student at the University of Helsinki in Finland. Linus was interested in Minix, and he decided to develop a system that exceeded Minix standards. Linus released the Linux Kernel Version 0.02 in 1991, and it was originally hosted on the Minix operating system. In 1994, Linux Kernel Version 1.0 was released.

 NOTE

Minix is a free UNIX-like operating system that is available with its source code. Features such as small size, micro kernel-based design, and good documentation make it suitable for people who want to run a UNIX-like system. Minix was designed by Andrew Tanenbaum for teaching operating system concepts for his book, *Operating Systems: Design and Implementation* (Prentice Hall, 1997).

Linux can be used for a wide variety of purposes, including:

◆ Networking
◆ Application development
◆ End-user platform

Linux has quickly become popular worldwide because of the free availability of its source code. A large number of software programmers have modified Linux source code to meet their individual needs. Thousands of programmers have contributed to the development of Linux. The free availability of Linux makes it a low-cost alternative to other expensive operating systems.

 NOTE

Linux's official mascot, the penguin, was selected by Linus Torvalds.

Let me begin by listing some of the advantages of the Linux operating system.

Advantages

Since its introduction, Linux has become immensely popular among various kinds of users. Numerous surveys conclude that Linux is among the fastest growing operating systems in the world today. I've listed some of the advantages that led to its popularity here:

◆ **Cost.** Many vendors freely distribute Linux; hence, there is no license charge. Some vendors do charge for Linux, but the price is nominal when compared to that of other operating systems.

◆ **Stability.** Linux is very stable due to the fact that patches for it are frequently released. Thousands of programmers have reviewed the source code to improve performance, eliminate bugs, strengthen security, and ensure stability. As a result, security problems in Linux tend to get resolved quickly. Patches are quickly available and are sometimes distributed across the Internet within hours of being detected. Fixes are often available before commercial vendors—such as Sun, HP, and IBM—even acknowledge a problem.

No other operating system has ever undergone the kind of extensive review that Linux has gone through. The stability of Linux has been tested by running some applications on it for years at a stretch. The same applications forced the computers to be rebooted often when run on other operating systems.

◆ **Support.** Support to counter Linux-related problems is free and readily available because those involved include commercial distributors, consultants, and a very active community of users and developers. You can contact *Linux users groups* (LUGs) mailing lists to resolve your queries. In addition, you will find extensive documentation available for ready reference. Another added advantage is that Linux is not locked in by a single vendor. The availability of its source code means that every user and support provider is able to get to the root of technical problems quickly and effectively. This contrasts with other operating systems, where people rely on the OS vendor for bug fixes.

◆ **Portability.** Most Linux systems are based on standard PC hardware, and Linux supports a wide range of PC devices. Linux was originally developed for 386/486-based PCs. Now, however, Linux supports a wide range of other computer types, including Alpha, Power PC, 680x0,

SPARC, ARMs, DEC Alphas, SUN Sparcs, M68000 computers, MIPS, Strong Arm processors, and system sizes ranging from PDAs to supercomputers.

◆ **Customization.** You can modify Linux for your hardware and software requirements. Therefore, you can configure Linux to your computer for optimum utilization. For example, Linux can run both the SMB protocol and AppleTalk.

◆ **Tools and Applications.** Linux has the tools and applications to cater to your various needs. Programs ranging from the Apache Web Server to the GIMP graphics editor are included in most Linux distributions. Most of these applications and tools are available free of cost.

Work is ongoing for creating highly stable Linux systems. Properly configured Linux kernels with suitably configured software commonly run for hundreds of days without any need for rebooting the computer.

NOTE

You can get more information about the popularity of Linux at the following sites:

◆ **www.linux-mag.com**

◆ **http://counter.li.org**

◆ **www.idc.com**

◆ **www.nwfusion.com**

◆ **http://linuxtoday.com**

Next, I'll explain the architecture of Linux.

Linux Architecture

Linux was based on the UNIX architecture. It is POSIX-compliant and supports most standards set for UNIX. Therefore, the basic architecture and many features of UNIX and Linux are the same. In fact, Linux often is considered another version of UNIX. The file system supported by Linux also is similar to the UNIX file system. Both have similar directory structures.

The UNIX-based architecture of Linux is illustrated in the Figure 1-1.

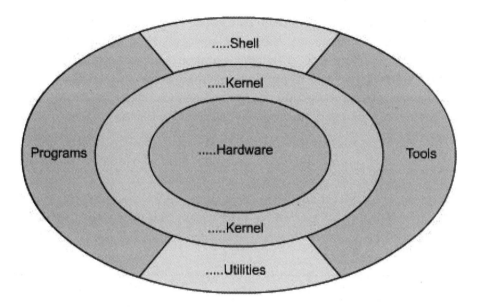

FIGURE 1-1 *The Linux architecture*

Because of these similarities, you can easily port UNIX applications on a Linux platform. Linux and the GNU C library used by it have been designed with application portability in mind. Linux also implements many features found in the *System V Interface Definition* (SVID) and *Berkeley Software Distribution* (BSD) variants of UNIX, but it does not necessarily adhere to them in all cases. In general, Linux has been designed to be compatible with UNIX implementations and to make application porting easier. In a number of instances, these applications have been improved and then implemented on the Linux operating system.

 NOTE

GNU is a recursive acronym for *GNU's Not UNIX* and is pronounced "guh-NEW." GNU is the output of the GNU project launched in 1984 to develop a UNIX-like operating system.

Let me next provide more detail on the free availability of Linux source code.

Linux - Open Source

Linux is developed under the GNU General Public License; therefore, its source code is freely distributable. Linux is said to have been developed over the Web because it has been seen by thousands of developers worldwide who have added to its features. These developers have tested Linux, reported bugs, and at the same time, contributed toward the elimination of these bugs. As a result, Linux has turned out to be a very stable system.

Eric Raymond has written an essay, "The Cathedral and the Bazaar," on the Linux development process. *Cathedral* and *Bazaar* are two different approaches for releasing software. In this essay, Raymond discusses the way Linux kernel development uses a *Bazaar* approach, in which code is released as quickly and as often as possible; thereby permitting extensive outside input that leads to rapid improvements.

 NOTE

Eric Raymond is a member of the Board of Directors of VA Linux Systems, which is a leading Linux hardware and systems company. He was the co-founder and ex-president of the Open Source Initiative, an educational organization that builds bridges between hacker communities and business communities with the aim of spreading the open source development method. To learn more about Eric Raymond, visit **tuxedo.org/~esr/resume.html**.

The code for applications following the Cathedral approach is more stable and released less often than the code released under the Bazaar approach. The Cathedral approach also offers less opportunity for people outside the core development group to contribute.

Projects with the Bazaar approach do not necessarily involve making code available to everyone at the design phase. Once the code has been debugged at the developer's end, however, it is reasonable to open the code to everyone so that more and more people can get involved in the process of finding and rectifying errors. This ensures that the errors are fixed.

You can use Linux as a server, as a workstation, and as a development platform for various applications. I'll now discuss the various roles that Linux can play.

Linux: A Server

Linux, like UNIX, is an excellent operating system for Internet servers, including Web, e-mail, and FTP servers. The vast networking capability of the Linux operating system makes it a prime candidate to be used as a server in any kind of networking environment. Linux supports all of the most common Internet protocols. Following is a list of some of the protocols supported by Linux:

◆ FTP

◆ SMNP

◆ HTTP

◆ POP

◆ SMTP

◆ Telnet

◆ SSH

◆ NNTP

Linux has already been widely used and tested on all of these listed protocols. Let me now discuss each of these protocols.

FTP

File Transfer Protocol (FTP) is one of oldest Internet protocols, and it is still being used extensively. FTP is a part of the Internet protocol suite that can be used to transfer files between two computers. FTP works in two modes: text and binary transfer mode. Many FTP servers such as WS-FTP are available for Linux. Using FTP, you can access files stored in the disk directory of a remote computer. FTP is used to do the following:

◆ Share files, which might include computer programs and data

◆ Indirectly or implicitly use remote computers

◆ Shield a user from variations in file storage systems among hosts

◆ Transfer data reliably and efficiently

SNMP

Simple Network Management Protocol (SNMP) is a network management protocol. It was developed in 1988 to provide a framework for network management. Some typical purposes for which SNMP can be used are these:

◆ Assigning addresses to devices

◆ Prioritizing communication

◆ Installing software on a network

◆ Managing printer queues

Over the years, SNMP has become the standard protocol for internetwork management. In the manager/agent model, which is adopted by the SNMP protocol, the processing capability resides on the management system. The management system is responsible for issuing messages such as `Get`, `GetNext`, and `Set`. You use these messages to obtain or store the value of variables. These messages are sent to the agent responsible for sending a response back to the management system.

HTTP Protocol

HyperText Transfer Protocol (HTTP) is the standard protocol used for transferring documents on the World Wide Web. HTTP is employed in the client/server architecture. After a successful connection is established between server and client, the client can send requests for resources, such as Web pages, on the server. The server then sends the requested resource back to the client. HTTP operates over TCP connections, usually at port 80, though this can be overridden and another port can be used.

POP Protocol

Post Office Protocol (POP) is a messaging protocol that enables users to access their mailboxes. The POP protocol is based on a client/server model. The messages are stored in the server. Users download these messages to their computer by using a POP client, such as Eudora. POP provides for user authentication by authenticating users through passwords. However, passwords are transmitted as clear text, which means that POP should be used very carefully because the password transmission method is not secure.

SMTP Protocol

Simple Mail Transfer Protocol (SMTP) is a messaging protocol responsible for delivering mail. It relays mail messages from an SMTP client to the SMTP server and from one SMTP server to another. In case of delivery failure of mail, the messages are queued up in the SMTP server. The SMTP server again tries to deliver these queued messages. Two popular SMTP servers for Linux are Sendmail and qmail.

Telnet Protocol

The *Telnet* protocol enables you to remotely log on to a computer on a network. The Telnet protocol is based on the client/server model. The computer that tries to connect to the server from a remote location is the client. On the other hand, the computer to which the request is being made and that allows establishment of the connection is the server. The connection between the two computers is established based on some pre-defined criteria, such as the terminal type to be used. The username you specify during the connection determines your access on the destination's computers files and directories.

SSH Protocol

The *Secure Shell* (SSH) is a protocol for encrypting TCP sessions over the Internet. The primary use of SSH is remote login. However, it also can be used as a cryptographic tunnel. This tunnel generated by the SSH can be used for various purposes, such as copying files, encrypting e-mail connections, and triggering the remote execution of programs.

Before establishing connection between two computers, SSH connects to the server, performs secret key negotiation between the two computers, and starts encrypting the session after successful negotiation. SSH uses asymmetric key pairs to implement its secure sessions. The asymmetric key pair consists of two keys: a private key and a public key. The private key is stored with the owner, and the public key is distributed freely across the network. The private and public key pair contains algorithms that complement each other. During authentication, the public and the private keys are matched. After successful authentication, the SSH client is allowed to log on without the need to supply a password.

NNTP

The *Network News Transport Protocol* (NNTP) is based on the request-response model. The news delivery is based on the broadcasting technology. Unlike the messaging protocols, NNTP is delivered to several hosts at a time rather than to a specific host. NNTP is used to send messages from newsgroups to a Linux computer and from users to the newsgroup. These messages are stored on a newsgroup or newsnet server. NNTP supports the processes of reading newsgroups, posting new articles, and transferring articles between news servers.

Networking Support in Linux

In today's environment, no operating system can be successful without efficient networking capabilities and support for easier network management. Linux provides you both these features. The use of the Internet is the backbone of the development efforts for the Linux OS. As a result, the support for networking was included during the development phase itself. In addition, due to the constant research and development activities being performed on Linux by various programmers, it has outperformed various existing operating systems. Linux provides full and seamless support for other operating systems, such as Macintosh, DOS, Windows, and OS/2.

Some of the advanced networking features of Linux are:

◆ Support for TCP/UDP/IP protocol suite

◆ A number of new features added to the kernel

◆ Support for *Quality of Service* (QoS)

◆ Firewall implementation by using `ipchains`

◆ VPN implementation by using *Generic Routing Encryption* (GRE) tunnels

◆ Advanced routing implementation using netlink sockets

Linux on a Desktop

Linux supporters claim that it's a perfect desktop replacement for Windows. Linux is a legitimate OS for normal desktop users, full-time Internet users, and others. It meets the requirements of most users. But, at times, some applications or tools might not be supported on Linux. For example, CAD programs such as AutoCAD might not be work as per the expectation.

Linux has many features that qualify it as a workstation. Linux supports the following:

◆ Multiuser workstations

◆ Web browsers (Mozilla/Konqueror/Netscape/Opera)

◆ Applications (such as word processing, spreadsheets, graphic applications, and games)

◆ Printers

◆ Plug-n-Play hardware devices

◆ X Windows GUI interface

◆ Thousands of other freely available software applications

Linux as a Development Platform

Linux also can be used as a development platform. It provides support for various programming and scripting languages, such as Perl, PHP, Python, C, C++, gtk, ASP, Java, and TCL. Linux supports compilers and other tools necessary to develop applications by using these languages. A brief description of some of these languages is given in the following list:

◆ **Perl.** Perl is a scripting language. Perl scripts can be used as CGI scripts and can be embedded in HTML code. Perl caters to a wide range of programming requirements. The language has been vastly tested and tried. The advantage of Perl is its string parsing abilities, and the drawback is that its source code appears complex to many.

◆ **Python.** Python is an interpreted, object-oriented language. Python scripts have a very well-defined structure and source codes are much simpler-looking than Perl. Some security concerns have been reported for Python, but that is true for every language.

◆ **PHP.** *HyperText Pre-Processor* (PHP) is a server-side scripting language and has gained tremendous popularity over the last few years. One of the reasons for this popularity is PHP's capability to manipulate datatypes and ease of use while interacting with databases. The simple source code and easy implementation on the Web has made PHP the best choice for performing many dynamic tasks on Web sites.

◆ **Java.** Java is the programming language that is based the concept of "write once, run anywhere." The *Java Virtual Machine* (JVM) enables Java programs to run on any machine. You just need to transfer the compiled Java code on the target machine. Linux supports Java, Servlets, JSP, applets, and related technologies. Servlets and JSP are used to create dynamic Web pages. The servlet and the JSP code are executed on the server. *Applets* are Java programs that are executed on the client browsers.

◆ **C/C++.** The C and C++ languages are so popular that they need no introduction for programmers. Linux supports compilers for these languages. For example, gcc is a compiler for the C language. Linux itself has been written in C/C++.

Summary

In this chapter, you learned about the features of Linux. Linux is an operating system with freely distributed source code. You learned how Linux can be used as a server, a workstation, and as an application development platform. You also learned about the protocols Linux supports, including FTP, Gopher, HTTP, IP, POP, SMTP, TCP, Telnet, SSH, and NNTP. You also learned about the networking features of Linux and how Linux can be used as a workstation. Finally, you looked at Linux's ability to be used as a development platform for languages, such as Perl, C, C++, and Java.

Chapter 2

Linux Security:
An Overview

In the modern world, electronic media are being used increasingly for communication and data storage. With the increase in electronic data exchange, the threat to shared data and information also has increased. The threat can be multifold, ranging from a competitor tracking communication to physical damage of the storage media.

This chapter provides guidelines to help you effectively counter these threats. In this chapter, I'll introduce the basics of security, the need for security, and the precautions you can take to secure data on your computer. I'll also discuss security for the Linux environment wherever applicable.

Need for Security

Today, millions of computers are connected to the Internet. People across the globe communicate, share business plans and goals, and store data on the network. Storing data on a network is risky because your business rivals always stand a fair chance of accessing this data.

For example, if you send data from a computer in Washington to a computer in Tokyo, the data may have to pass through several computers in order to reach its destination. This may give other users the opportunity to intercept and alter the data. Other users on your system may even maliciously modify the data.

Organizations are well aware of the importance for security of transactions, such as online shopping and banking, because the revenue of an organization depends on the security of the networks over which these critical transactions take place. However, security is equally necessary on a user's desktop or laptop computer. For example, your office computer may contain business information that may prove advantageous to your competitor if they somehow get their hands on it.

In a different scenario, losing information may cost you valuable time to retrieve or recreate it. Your home PC may contain information such as financial records, personal passwords for accessing your banking and investing online accounts, credit card numbers, private documents and e-mail, and other pieces of information that could be misused by any person to cause you financial losses. The data that is deleted due to intrusion or physical damage may even be irrecoverable.

No computer can be completely secure. Hackers are always on the lookout for ways to attack your system. However, you can make it difficult for someone to misuse your system. The average home Linux user doesn't have to make special efforts to keep the casual hacker at bay; but high profile Linux users need to take extra measures to secure their systems.

As an administrator, you should secure your system as much as possible. You should do a thorough analysis of the kind of security that your system and network require. You need to evaluate the threat to your systems, the vulnerability of your systems, the security holes in your systems, the estimated loss to your organization in case of an intrusion, and so on.

These three factors determine the level of security you need to implement:

◆ **Risk.** This is the risk that is involved in providing access to the users. You need to analyze the possibility of an intrusion. An intruder can inflict heavy damage to your system if he is able to obtain read and write permission to the file system. You might lose your data permanently.

◆ **Access.** You should have complete control over the kind of access that is provided to users. You should provide access judiciously. Only trusted users should be provided access. In addition, provide access to a user dependent upon his or her requirements. A user who doesn't need write access shouldn't be provided with it.

◆ **Vulnerability.** You should also do an analysis of the vulnerability of your system to attacks from users outside your local network. One way to protect data and ensure user privacy is to create and implement an effective security policy. The security policy you create should be such that users are easily able to comprehend it, and they shouldn't face any problem implementing it. The security policy should mention the permissions users have, the services a user can access, and so on. It is the responsibility of the system administrator to ensure that the policies are updated and implemented properly.

Intruders constantly attempt to attack your system. Their prime targets are the servers, dial-up accounts, and the Web sites. You should be aware of the techniques they might use. Intruders usually look for security holes in your system and networks. One of the common security holes is the presence of insecure accounts on your system. Once an intruder gets access to your system through an insecure account, he can hack other hosts if your system is connected to a network. There are several categories of intruders. They are categorized depending on their intentions and the damage they can cause.

The categories of the intruders are listed here:

- ◆ Curious intruders try to gather information, such as your system configuration and settings, the data that is stored on your system, and so on. The curious intruders don't intend to harm your system and data; their only purpose is to gain critical information stored on your system.

- ◆ Malicious intruders, unlike curious intruders, intend to damage your data and system. Once they gain access to a system, they will perform destructive activities, such as defacing Web pages, destroying system data, and so on. The purpose of these intruders is only destruction; they won't use the data on your system for their own benefit.

- ◆ Competitor intruders try to gain access to the data on your computer. They use this data for their business benefit and gain an edge over your business in the market. The purpose of their data access is to obtain your business-related data, analyze it, gain an insight into your future business plans, and use it for their own benefit.

- ◆ Borrower intruders lack resources that they need to perform their own activities. They intrude in your system to use your resources to fulfill their need.

- ◆ Leapfrogger intruders usually attack systems that are well-connected to other computers on the network. They try to attack and use resources on other computers in a network through a well-connected computer. Gateways are prime targets of such intruders.

In the wake of increasing Internet usage for communication and data exchange, it becomes essential for you to secure your system from attacks occurring via the Internet.

Security for the Linux environment can be categorized into four levels:

- ◆ Physical security
- ◆ Data security
- ◆ Network security
- ◆ Accounts security

In this chapter, I discuss each level of security in detail.

Physical Security

Physical security is the basic security that you need to implement. You need to consider factors such as physical accessibility of people to your system. Home users may not need to secure their computer physically. In an office environment, physical security of systems is more critical because they contain data sensitive to your business. In such an environment, you can take security measures, such as installing video surveillance and employing security guards.

The physical security you can provide to your system is based on security need and budget. For example, you will certainly not provide high physical security on a computer where only games are loaded. A computer with critical and confidential data will need high physical security. In an office environment, someone can easily get access to systems by simply walking to a user's desk and manipulating data.

Common Precautions for Physical Safety

You can take a number of measures to safeguard your PC equipment. Some methods are inexpensive and can be implemented easily, while others are expensive and more sophisticated. Here are a few of these measures:

- Use video surveillance at your workplace. The video cameras should be hidden and not easily noticeable.
- Store the backup media at safe places. If possible make copies of the backup and store them separately.
- Take care of your computer and other equipment while traveling.
- Lock the CPU cover to avoid theft of any part, such as motherboard or hard disk.
- Lock the equipment in a safe place when you leave.
- Install security alarms.
- Employ security personnel to protect your equipment.
- Restrict access to critical and expensive equipment. Use security measures, such as fingerprint scanners and voice identifiers.
- Buy computers and equipment that have built-in security features.
- Install the servers, such as gateways, that are most prone to attacks on separate computers.

I have listed above some of the precautions that you should take for physical security, but there's much more to physical security. Other aspects of physical security include:

◆ Computer locks
◆ BIOS security
◆ Boot Loader security
◆ xLock and vLock
◆ Detecting physical security compromises

Computer Locks

Using locks can prevent theft of hardware components of your system. If you leave your computer unlocked, thieves can open the CPU of your system and steal hardware pieces, such as motherboard and RAM chip. They might even damage your system beyond repair. In both cases, you lose your critical data as well as costly components. There are customized locks available in the market. Some computer manufacturers attach clasps with the CPU with which you can protect your system. You can secure your system by attaching a cable to these clasps. Thieves would need to cut the cable in order to get to the computer. This method is not foolproof, but it is helpful in discouraging thieves. You can use locks to safeguard your expensive equipment, such as Web cameras, CD Writer devices, and so on. Small devices can be placed in locked cabinets.

BIOS Security

The Basic Input/Output System (BIOS) is a program that determines how your computer starts. BIOS manages the communication between the operating system and the hardware devices attached to the computer. BIOS enables you to protect your computer. It does this by enabling you to specify a boot password. A user needs to provide this password in order to boot and log on to your system. However, the security provided by BIOS is very weak and can be easily breached because you can reset or remove the BIOS. Some BIOS makers provide default passwords with BIOS. These passwords are known to the hackers and they can easily boot your system if you haven't changed the default password. You also can configure BIOS so that it won't boot from floppy disks. Although protection through BIOS is not very secure, it can prove to be a deterrent. It will take more time for the attackers and there is high possibility of traces being left behind.

Boot Loader Security

You can set boot passwords for various Linux boot loaders. These passwords are not foolproof, however, and they will only delay the attacker. Intruders can bypass this password and boot the system. They can boot from floppies. To prevent intruders from employing this technique, disable booting from floppy on your system.

xlock and vlock

At times, you might have to leave your workstation. While you are away, anyone can come to your workstation and have a look at the document on which you are working. You can prevent this by locking your display console. The two programs that enable you to lock your console are *xlock* and *vlock*.

- ◆ `xlock` is an X display locker. `xlock` locks the display monitor of your computer. You need to provide a password to unlock the display monitor. `xlock` is available in all Linux distributions that support X.

- ◆ `vlock` locks the virtual consoles. It can be used to lock any or all of the virtual consoles on your computer. If you lock only a few consoles, you can continue to use other consoles. Locking your console will prevent someone from tampering with your work, but it does not prevent a person from doing the following:

  - Rebooting your computer
  - Accessing your computer from another computer on the network and causing problems
  - Switching out of the X Window System entirely and going to a normal virtual console login prompt

Detecting Physical Security Compromises

You should watch for various signs that hint at security breaches on your computer, and note the date and time your computer was rebooted. This can provide you a vital clue about the intrusion. Linux is very stable. You don't need to reboot a Linux computer often except in situations such as when you upgrade the OS or change the password. If you reboot the computer after changing the OS or upgrading the hardware, you will be well aware of the date and time you did that. Therefore, you can easily get an indication of intrusion if you notice that the computer was rebooted at an unusual time.

Check for physical signs of tampering, such as scratches or the shifting of the monitor or CPU from their original positions. Intruders often attempt to clean up any evidence of intrusion. They might modify the log files to delete entries caused by the attack. However, unless they are extremely careful, they will leave behind some evidence such as last modified timestamp of the log file. Therefore, if you suspect any intrusion, you should analyze the log file carefully. You also can maintain copies of log files at a different location and protect them. If you do not store logs in a protected environment, log data might be of little use because there is a high possibility of an intruder modifying it.

There's a daemon called syslog that can be used to log the activities on your computer. You can configure syslog to send data automatically to a central syslog server. However, the drawback of using syslog is that the log entries that it sends to the syslog server are sent as plain text. It is not encrypted. Therefore, any unauthorized user keeping a tab on your network can access the data that is being transferred. There's one more risk associated with using the syslog daemon. The syslog server doesn't verify the source of the log entry. It accepts log entries from any computer that claims to be a local host in the network. You should study the logs in the syslog server for these indications of intrusion:

- ◆ Unfamiliar log entries
- ◆ Unusual date and time entry in the log
- ◆ Logs suggesting that the computer was restarted or rebooted
- ◆ Logon attempts from unknown hosts

You have now looked at securing your system physically. Next I'll discuss how you can secure the data on your computer.

Data Security

Securing data is most critical for your business. The causes of data loss are many. You might lose data due to hard disk crash, virus attack, theft of hardware, or attack by intruders. One way to prevent data loss is to make regular backups. You can make backups on various storage media, such as tape, other hard disks, and cartridges. The choice of the backup media depends on the storage space that the data being backed up requires and the resources available to you. Data redundancy is another measure to prevent data loss. Data redundancy writes data onto several disks, which may be spread across drives. Identical data is copied to each drive.

This will ensure that even if one of the disks crashes, your data will be intact. Redundant Array of Inexpensive Devices (RAID) enables you to perform data redundancy rather inexpensively.

You should consider making more than one backup copy and storing the backups at different physical locations. Consider a situation where you have stored the backup data at your workplace, and some unfortunate event such as flood or earthquake occurs. In this case, you will end up losing your original data and backed up data. Storing backups at different locations will help you restore data in such situations.

Many organizations provide emergency business recovery services. These organizations provide services such as storing backup data at different physical locations and provide you computers and facilities in case your workplace becomes unusable.

You also can prepare a disaster recovery plan. This plan will contain details of how, when, and where the backup should be made and include the measures you need to take in order to protect that backup media and restore the data in case of any disaster. In addition to these items, the plan should mention how to continue running your business while your workplace is being repaired. The plan should enable you to perform all your business activities. The plan should be known to every concerned user and it should be open and regularly updated.

Many programs have the built-in feature of data recovery. If you have several servers on a network, you can configure the servers to back up data from one another. This will ensure that data is not lost in case one of the servers crashes.

 NOTE

Sometimes an unauthorized user can reboot your computer, resulting in loss of any unsaved data. To prevent this from happening, you can use the /etc/shutdown.allow file, which contains a list of usernames that are authorized to reboot the computer. Linux looks up this file when a user tries to boot the system by using the Ctrl+Alt+Del keys to determine whether the user has the authority to boot the system.

Secure Data Deletion

You make backups to prevent data loss. However, at times, you no longer use them but need to ensure that your business competitors or any other unauthorized user can't access that data. However, merely deleting a file does not ensure that an expert user cannot recover it. When you delete data, the reference data still exists in the memory until it is physically overwritten by other data. Even then, deleted files are potentially recoverable with sophisticated data recovery tools. To destroy sensitive data, you can use programs that will overwrite deleted files multiple times with dummy data. Of course, if the system is being scrapped or recycled, rather than resold, the surest method of preventing data from being recovered is to physically damage the hard disk beyond repair.

Data Encryption

The security measures discussed up to this point are helpful to a large extent in securing your data and PC and keeping intruders out. However, if an intruder is able to get access to your data even after you've adopted all these security measures, they can easily read and understand your data. One way to prevent this is to encrypt the critical data. You can encrypt the data that is stored on your computer as well as the data that is being transferred over a network.

Encryption is the process of converting data by applying some algorithm in such a way that it can't be read by anyone except the user who has the algorithm to reverse the algorithm that was applied earlier. The process of reversing encrypted data back to its original form is known as *decryption*. Encrypting data is particularly safe when you are transferring data over a network. Even if an intruder gets access to the data being transferred, he won't be able to use that data because he won't have the decrypting algorithm. Only users with the decryption algorithm will be able to use the data.

You'll learn more about encryption in Chapter 5, "Encryption and Authentication."

Next, we'll look at securing your network.

Network Security

In modern times, more and more people are connecting to the network, and an increasing number of organizations are moving toward network-centric business. Such businesses have become prone to attacks from intruders who want unauthorized access with varied intentions, such as business rivalry. A number of tools are available to help you with network security. Some of these tools are shipped with Linux operating systems.

You need to prepare for two kinds of security on a network: host-based security and network security. Host-based security is the most critical security area that system administrators need to implement. Ensuring host-based security involves securing your own and other systems on the network. This involves choosing strong passwords, securing the host's local network services, keeping logs, and upgrading programs. However, these tasks can become daunting when your network becomes larger than a few computers.

Network security is as necessary as host security. Network administrators should ensure that only authorized users access networks, build firewalls, use strong encryption, and ensure that all computers on the network are secure. The key to network security is to allow only those functions that users actually need and to make those functions as secure as possible. The following list provides some critical factors that are important for the smooth functioning of a network:

◆ Firewalls

◆ Secure protocols

◆ FTP security

◆ Modem security

◆ Windows networking

◆ Network monitoring

◆ Network configuration files

◆ Disable unnecessary and unauthorized services

◆ DNS security

◆ Network information service

I'll now discuss each of these in detail.

Firewalls

Each network includes some computers that are dedicated to the proper functioning of the network. The firewall is one such computer meant for the security of the network. Firewalls are used to separate an organization's intranet from the Internet. Firewalls are used to check the communication between computers in different networks. Let me first explain the terms related to firewalls. These are as follows:

◆ Bastion host

◆ Router

◆ Demilitarized Zone

◆ Proxy

Bastion Host

A *Bastion host* is a computer used to control access between an organization's intranet and the Internet. The Bastion host usually runs a Linux-like operating system. These hosts are configured so that they perform only the task for which they are meant. All other unnecessary and unutilized services are turned off.

Router

A *router* is a computer meant for connecting networks together. Routers also handle additional functions, such as managing the traffic on the networks they connect.

Demilitarized Zone (DMZ)

A *DMZ* is a host or a small network within a network. It acts as a neutral zone; that is, it is neither trusted nor distrusted. It is usually placed between an intranet of an organization and the outer network. It prevents users from outside the network from directly accessing data on computers within a network. The host on the DMZ network receives requests from the internal users and then creates a session for these requests.

Proxy

A *proxy* server is a server that acts as an intermediary between the Internet and a user. A computer that has the ability to fetch documents from the Internet might be configured as a proxy server, and other computers on the intranet might be configured to be proxy clients. Therefore, when proxy clients need to access resources on the Internet, they make a request to the proxy server. The proxy server then uses the URL provided by the proxy client, fetches the resource from the Internet, and then passes it to the proxy client. In this way, all hosts on the intranet are able to access resources on the Internet without being directly connected to the Internet.

Access servers, such as firewalls and gateways, should be configuring after much thought. These servers act as entry points to your network. Therefore, hackers try first to gain access to these servers, because once they get access to these servers, they get access to all the hosts on the networks.

There are three basic types of firewalls:

- ◆ Application gateways
- ◆ Packet filters
- ◆ Hybrid systems

These are discussed in the next three sections.

Application Gateways

The application or proxy gateways act as a proxy server in the network. The software that enables the application to run as a proxy server runs at the application layer of the OSI Model. By default, the application gateway blocks the traffic between the local network and the Internet. They need to be configured in order to allow traffic to pass through.

Packet Filtering

Packet filtering is a technique whereby routers have *Access Control Lists* (ACL) turned on. You can use ACL to enforce security policy in a network. ACL determines the kind of access you allow computers over the Internet or other networks to have to your internal network and vice versa. If ACL is not turned on, a router will pass all traffic sent to it without any restrictions.

Packet filtering requires less overhead than application gateways. Therefore, packet filtering techniques work faster than the application gateways.

The packet filtering technique uses either the transport or the session layer of the OSI Reference Model. The usage of lower levels enables it to support new applications. This support for new applications comes automatically. However, the disadvantage of using packet filters is that you cannot determine the source of the packets. To overcome this disadvantage, you can use different techniques to identify the source of the packet filters. One of the methods is to use different layers of packet filters for local networks or Internet.

Hybrid Systems

Many vendors are developing systems that provide advantages of both application gateways and packet filtering techniques. The application gateway is secure, whereas the packet filtering technique is faster and flexible. In these systems, application gateways approve the new connections requests. The packet filtering ensures that the packets belonging to the authenticated connection pass through.

You should regularly review the access policies, security, and services running on the system. The system should run only the services necessary to perform the desired tasks. If you have configured a firewall on the system, you should not use it as a mail server, Web server, and so on. Here are some of the checks you need to perform while configuring a firewall:

- ◆ Disable the services that are no longer required.
- ◆ Disable the system from using the routing packets by stopping the IP Forwarding service.
- ◆ Use the latest version of the software that runs the firewall. A policy for firewalls should be in place. The policy should specify the action to be performed for preventing attacks.
- ◆ Access to the system and network management utilities should be restricted.
- ◆ You should check the status of your system and network at regular intervals. Any unusual activity might be a sign of an intrusion.

Take every care while configuring firewalls because they act as an entry point to your network. The firewalls are more prone to intrusion attacks. Make sure that you review your firewall policies before the configuration and at regular intervals.

Prevent Spoofing

A computer can imitate another host on a network by using the same host name, which means that it can pretend to be a trusted computer on your network.

You can stop this by modifying system files on the host computers in your network. The hosts should be configured to turn off the source routing. The incoming packets to your network should be filtered properly. This will ensure that the source IP address of any of the packets is not the same as that of any host on your network. If any such packet is found, it should be discarded.

Secure Protocols

You should use secure protocols on your network. These are two secure protocols that you can use:

♦ SSH

♦ SSL

These protocols are described in the following sections.

SSH

Secure Shell (SSH) protocol is used for securing remote access connections over IP networks. SSH protocol secures data by encrypting it when it is transmitted over the network. The SSH program has made remote management of network hosts over the Internet possible. SSH is designed to be a complete replacement for Telnet programs and `rlogin`, `rsh`, and `rcp` commands.

SSL

Secure Socket Layer (SSL) protocol was developed by Netscape to provide privacy and reliability between two communicating applications. The SSL protocol runs above TCP/IP and below other higher-level protocols, such as TELNET, FTP, or HTTP. SSH enables data encryption, authentication of server and client, and message authentication.

SSL is a layered protocol. It has two major layers: the SSL Handshake Protocol and the SSL Record Protocol. The SSL Handshake Protocol creates secure communication between the client and the server. The SSL Record Protocol encapsulates information of higher level protocols. The benefits of using SSL include cryptographic security, reliability, interoperability, extensibility, and efficiency.

FTP Security

The guidelines you should follow regarding FTP security are listed here:

◆ When not needed, disable the FTP service. As per your requirements, you can disable the entire service or provide access to some selected users.

◆ The /etc/ftpusers file contains the list of users who do not have access to the FTP service. This file should be maintained and monitored regularly.

◆ Maintain a log of the FTP-related activities.

◆ The access permission you assign to FTP users should be as restrictive as possible. The write permissions shouldn't be given to the directories unless it is a must.

Modem Security

If you are using a modem to connect to the Internet, you should configure a password for security reasons. A user getting access to the Internet will have to provide this password in order to get through. To do this:

◆ Configure the /etc/d_passwd file.

◆ Verify that passwords are not guessable.

◆ Do not assign the same password to more than one user.

◆ Disable the account when the user no longer needs access.

◆ Log out users after disconnecting.

Windows Clients

Networks normally include Microsoft clients that most probably use either Net BIOS or other insecure networking protocols. NetBIOS is the protocol that publishes share names, user names, and host names on the network. It is advisable to disable NetBIOS for Windows workstations. In situations where you need NT servers in the network, you should have two NICs in the NT server. One NIC should be outbound through TCP/IP and one should be internal. After configuring NICs, you can disable NetBIOS binding to TCP/IP. This will prevent intruders from accessing your network through TCP/IP. Once intruders get access to your network through TCP/IP, they can easily obtain critical information about your network. In addition to performing these tasks, you also should consider blocking ports 137 to 139 on routers and firewalls.

Network Monitoring

Monitor your network closely and regularly. You should be aware of the status of your network so that you can detect any kind of intrusion. Monitoring also helps you detect abnormal system activities, such as high system load, increased disk use, slower network, unfamiliar processes, etc. Many tools are available for network monitoring. Some tools, such asKSermon, Sysmon, and NetSaint, were developed for other platforms first and then ported to Linux.

Disable Unnecessary and Unauthorized Services

By default, Linux might run several services. These services offer a wide range of services to the users. You should switch off the services that you do not require. Running unnecessary services poses a risk of unauthorized users accessing these services and harming your system. Computers on your network running unauthorized services can provide an opportunity for a hacker to gain access to the system. You should create and implement a policy to scan the ports of the hosts on your network. The port scanning helps you detect security holes in your network. It is common practice among intruders to look for vulnerable ports in a network. There are several scanning tools that help you in this task.

Domain Name Service Security

The monitoring and regular updating of DNS information in your network is critical for network security. The DNS information of the hosts on your network helps you monitor the network and ensure security. In case an intruder tries to connect to your network, you can recognize him by checking the DNS entry of his host. If there is no corresponding DNS entry, it indicates an unauthorized host. Various services are available to assist you in denying the connectivity permissions to the unauthorized hosts. These services look up the DNS entries to authenticate hosts.

Network Information Service

Network Information Services (NIS) is a distributed access system in which every host on the network that an NIS client accesses a central server called the *NIS master* for access permission. NIS is a generic client/server database system. It shares account information contained in various database files, such as the /etc/passwd and /etc/group files over a network.

NIS maintains a centralized password database that is accessible over a network. This eases the administrative concerns associated with multiple hosts and users. Without NIS, the user's account would have to be maintained on each host. Maintaining account information on a large number of computers may cause problems. For example, you wouldn't be sure that the change of password on one host is reflected on other hosts. Every host on the network is configured to use the NIS server for its security instead of using its own local password database.

Account Security

Account security involves securing and maintaining accounts of various users on your computers and networks. In the Linux environment, accounts are created for different users and groups, and each account has certain access rights and permissions associated with it. Accounts of high-profile users, such as administrators, would have more access rights than a normal user.

Linux systems support two types of users:

◆ Root users

◆ Normal users

The root users have all the administrative rights for the system. The root users are responsible for performing all the administrative tasks, such as creating partitions, installing and upgrading software, creating user accounts, and so on. On the other hand, normal users are the users who use the services provided by your system. The root users assign the required permissions to the normal users. These permissions are set in the home directories that are created for each user. A user cannot access the home directory of another user.

You should be very careful while you are logged on as a root user. Consider a situation in which you accidentally delete some critical system files. Therefore, you should log in as root only when you need to perform root-specific tasks. For performing the routine tasks, you should log on as a normal user.

Password Security

When selecting passwords, it is important to select ones that are not easy to guess. A company should have standard guidelines for passwords. You should not use common words as passwords because hackers easily guess those common words. There are programs available to test password security by trying the thousands of words available in the dictionary. If the password is a word found in the dictionary, your security is rendered useless.

You should encourage users on your network to change passwords at regular intervals. You should try to hack the passwords of the hosts on your network to ensure that passwords are strong enough. Configure the accounts to be disabled after a specified number of unsuccessful login attempts. This will discourage hackers who are trying to get through your system by guessing your password.

Many vendors supply systems with default passwords. Most hackers are aware of these default passwords. You can eliminate the problem of default passwords by changing the default password when allotting systems to users. You can create unique default passwords for each system before distributing them to users and then ask users to change the passwords.

The /etc/passwd file contains your system passwords. To prevent someone from breaking into the file, create shadow passwords. *Shadow passwords* are used to protect system passwords by making the file containing the shadow passwords readable only by the root operator. Shadow passwords replace with asterisks the encrypted password in the passwd file. Moving the passwords to the shadow makes it less likely that the encrypted password can be decrypted because only the root user has access to the shadow file. To see whether you have shadow passwords enabled on your system, use the command:

```
ls /etc/shadow
```

If the file has not yet been created, you receive the following message:

```
ls /etc/shadow: No such file or directory
```

If you are using or planning to use shadow passwords, you can use the pwconv and pwunconv utilities that are part of the Shadow Suite of tools. The pwconv utility will create the shadow file if it does not exist. If the shadow file does exist, pwconv synchronizes it with passwd by adding to the shadow file any passwords that are not there and deleting those that are no longer in the passwd file. The pwconv utility also updates any password aging information. The pwunconv utility allows you to remove shadow passwords and restore passwd to its original state.

The command passwd is the default command used to change passwords in UNIX and Linux systems. It generally supports minimal checking of user passwords. It might not support password aging. *Password aging* is the requirement that users change their passwords after a specified period. For example, the version of passwd included in Sun Solaris supports password aging and makes the following checks:

◆ Minimum length, which the administrator can specify. Only the first eight characters are considered for the purpose of authentication.

◆ Must contain at least two letters in any case and one number or symbol.

◆ Cannot be the user's login name, the reverse of the name, or any circular shift of that name.

◆ New passwords must have at least three characters that are different from the old password.

You can set up passwords for LILO and screen savers as well. If you configure passwords for LILO, you are prompted to specify that password during the boot time. The lilo.conf file is used to configure the LILO password. However, this method is not secure if you have multiple operating systems installed on your computer. An intruder can boot to the other operating system on your computer that does not have the booting password configured.

You can protect your data from being displayed to the other users by setting a screen saver. The screen saver blocks the display of your monitor after a specified inactivity period. You also can configure a password for the screen saver. You need to provide this password in order to view the display again. This method is useful for those users who frequently walk away from their workstation.

You can specify passwords for hardware devices as well. There are two such types of passwords:

◆ Power On Password (POP)

◆ Privileged Access Password (PAP)

The POP is configured in the CMOS of the computer. POP requires users to specify the configured password before booting the computer. The PAP password stores passwords in nonvolatile memory. If a hacker is able to break the POP password and boot your computer, he is prompted for the PAP password. You should be extra careful with this, because there is no way to crack the PAP password. If you forget the PAP password, you system will not be of any use. If you forget the POP password, however, you can reconfigure it by using the PAP password.

Some hard drives are available that can be configured to demand passwords. This password is needed before you start using the drive. You won't be able to use the drive unless you provide the password. However, this ensures that the data on the drive is untouched because no one other than the person with the password can get access the files on the drive.

The account security can be implemented for three categories of users. These are as follows:

◆ Root accounts

◆ Guest accounts

◆ User accounts

I'll now discuss each of these categories in detail.

Root Accounts

Root users are the most powerful users in Linux systems. They have the rights to perform all the administrative tasks. This means that you need to be careful when you assign root accounts to users and also when you are logged in as a root user yourself. It is easiest to track changes and security violations when very few people have root access. Here are some guidelines regarding root account security:

◆ The passwords to the root accounts should be very strong. They should be known only to trusted users.

◆ You should log on to the root shell only when it is a must. Log out of the root shell as soon as you finish your work.

◆ Only the root should be assigned UID 0.

◆ The non-root accounts should not have any write permissions in the root directory.

◆ The temporary files of the root account should be in directories that provide read and write access to other accounts.

You should always log out of the root shell immediately after performing the root-specific tasks. You should be extremely careful while you are in the root shell. Even a small mistake made by root users could be disastrous for the whole system. The less time you are on with root privileges, the safer your system will be. Several tricks to avoid compromising your Linux system when logged in as root are as follows:

◆ When in doubt about the usage of a particular command that can damage your system, get the complete information about the command from the manual page. If possible, run the commands with the options that will not damage your system.

◆ Even if you have the privilege of a root user, you should log on to the root account only when it is required. For example, you need to perform some administrative tasks. While performing the routine tasks, if possible, you should log on as a normal user. The su command can be used to temporarily switch to the root account. You need to provide the root login name and root password while using the su command. The syntax of the su command is shown here:

```
su [option]…..[user] [arg]…
```

NOTE

If no user is specified, the default user is root.

◆ The root users shouldn't use the rexec tools. These are the prime targets of the hackers. The root users also shouldn't have the .rhosts file created for themselves.

◆ The terminals from where the root users can log on are listed in the securetty file. You shouldn't modify the content of this file.

SUDO

sudo can be used to provide users root access to the Linux system. However, the root access provided to them is restricted depending upon their requirements. The disadvantage of sudo is that you can perform only limited tasks. For example, mounting and removing various media on your system, restarting a server, and adding new users. sudo prompts you for a password before allowing root access. In addition, a program such as /bin/cat can be used to overwrite files. This could allow root to be exploited. Therefore, sudo can be considered as a means for accountability.

Guest Accounts

The guest accounts are created for temporary users and for users who are not regular users of your networks. However, the users should be the trusted ones. You should monitor these accounts regularly. Delete any guest accounts no longer in use. You also can set an expiration period for guest accounts. In addition, you can configure the password of guest accounts to expire after a specified period. The password assigned to the guest accounts should be strong.

User Accounts

Here are some guidelines for working with user accounts:

- Do not share the user accounts.
- Accounts no longer in use should be deleted. In addition, you should consider disabling login to well-known accounts. These accounts do not require interactive login.
- Assign strong passwords to the accounts in your network.
- The non-regular users, such as the guest accounts, should have restricted shell.

User accounts should be provided with the minimal required privileges. These privileges should be sufficient to enable the user to perform all the required tasks. Here are some precautions you should take:

- The permissions and rights should be assigned carefully.
- Identify the time and place from which the user needs to logon.
- Use a standard pattern for assigning usernames in your network. This helps in management tasks.
- You shouldn't create a common user account for several users in your network. This creates problems with accountability.

Here are some guidelines for monitoring and ensuring user accounts security:

- You should regularly maintain the logs of activities in your system and network. Analyze the log periodically.
- Create a backup policy to backup the critical data at regular intervals. The back up copies should be stored at safe locations.

◆ The bandwidth of your network should be maintained for smooth functioning. An unusual drop in bandwidth might be an indication of some unauthorized activity in your network.

◆ The disk space that is available on servers and hosts should be monitored. There are some viruses that use all the free disk space, leading to computer crashes.

◆ Use the Intrusion Detection tools in your network judiciously. Administrators should be well informed on how to use these tools.

Let me now discuss the measures for maintaining and ensuring security based on user accounts: using logs, securing the file system, and setting umask.

Using Logs

Logs are a means to track the activities going on in your system and on the network. You ensure that logging is enabled in your personal system and both servers and workstations on the network. Log files are generally located in /var and/or /var/log directories. These log files can be used to detect evidence of both successful and failed attempts, and even to track the intruders. In addition to enabling logging, you should save copies of important log files to other servers so that a smart intruder cannot simply change the logs to cover his tracks. For devices such as routers and switches that generate large quantities of system log records, keep copies of the logs on the same subnet as the device and periodically forward copies to a centralized server. This could help experts spot a series of seemingly unrelated events that, when taken together, would identify an attack.

In addition, you can configure /etc/syslog.conf for easier analysis of potential security exposures. On one hand, you can set it up to send system logging information to specific files. On the other, you can restrict access to log directories and files.

You should check logs periodically and randomly. Check the logs when an unexpected event, such as a system reboot, occurs. You can use the tail command on the log files to check entries at the end of the file so that you do not have to go through all the entries of the log file. In fact, you might want to write a short script that runs the tail command against each log file and writes all the results to one output file so that you can scan the latest logs at once. Alternatively, you can use a tool like Logcheck to simplify the process of identifying suspected security breaches.

Log files can grow quite large, especially on servers. To prevent a log file from filling up all available space in your data partition and crashing your system, either limit the files to a maximum size or move the log files to a separate partition containing only log files.

Securing the File System

You can restrict a user's access to files by setting the file system security. The read and write permissions for the system files and directories should not be provided to all the users and groups. The permissions on system files and directories should be granted as per the user requirements. You need to ensure that unauthorized users are not able to view or modify the files in the Linux system. You can assign access permissions to users and groups on the files and directories.

UNIX manages access control on files and directories according to three permissions: read, write, and execute. You can assign file-level and directory-level permissions to users, owners, groups, and others. These permissions are listed here:

◆ The read permission enables you to view and read the contents of a file. You cannot modify or delete the file.

◆ The write permission enables you to modify a file by adding or deleting contents of the file. You also can move the files in a directory.

◆ The execute permission enables you to run the binary code or shell script.

If you need to share a system with other users, you can assign permissions to other users depending upon the level of need and trust. You should identify and grant the exact degree of authority users will need.

Preparing and planning the file system before putting your systems on line can help to protect the systems and the data stored on them. Here are some issues you need to address:

◆ The SUID or the SGID programs should not be executed from the home directories of the users. This can be done by using the nodev and noexec options on the home directories. These options prevent the execution of these programs.

◆ If you are using NFS to export the file system, access to the /etc/exports file should be very restrictive. Similarly, the umask settings for file creation should be restrictive.

◆ The records containing user login details, such as time and place of logon, are stored in the /log/wtmp and /run/utmp files. You should check these files to look for the logon attempts of intruders.

◆ The SUID and SGID permissions to users and groups to files in your system should be provided as per their requirements. Misuse of these permissions can harm your system. This is because these permissions grant special privileges to the users. Using the SUID programs to gain entry in your system is a common practice among hackers. Therefore, you should monitor these permissions regularly. You can change the SUID and SGID permissions by using the chmod command. You can restore the permissions if necessary, however. The syntax of the chmod command is as follows:

```
chmod [ugoa..] [+-=] [rwx…]
```

The [uogoa] option in the preceding syntax determines the permission to be set for the user who owns the file (u), users in the file's group (g), other users not in the file's group (o), and all users (a). The [+-=] options are used to add or remove the permissions. You can assign permissions (+), remove permissions (-), or specify the only available permissions (=). The read (r), write (w), and execute (x) are permissions assigned to users or groups. The read, write, and execute permissions can be numerically represented by the numbers 4, 2, and 1, respectively. Therefore, 6 would represent read (4) and write (2) permissions. Consider this command:

```
chmod 664 test.txt
```

This command is equivalent to the following command:

```
chmod u+rw g+rw o+r test.txt
```

◆ The files that have write permissions for all the users can prove to be a major security hole in your network. The hackers can easily modify these files and use them to harm your system. You should look for such files in your system and remove the global write permissions on these files. Here is the command to search for those files:

```
root# find / -perm -2 ! -type 1 -ls
```

◆ Look for files in your system that have no ownership. There is a possibility that these files might have been dropped in your system by the hackers. You can find such unowned files with the following command:

```
root# find / -nouser -o -nogroup -print
```

◆ The .rhosts file is used by the remote users to log on to your systems. This file should be securely configured as per your requirements. You can locate the .rhosts file by executing the following command:

```
root# find /home -name .rhosts -print
```

◆ The permission on the system files should be assigned as per your requirements. Assigning read or write permissions to unauthorized users might cause problems.

Setting umask

The umask command can be used to set the file creation mode. The permissions attached with the file system are very critical from the security point of view. The read or write permissions should be assigned carefully. The settings you specify through the umask command apply to all users. This is because these settings are saved in the /etc/profile file. The umask is the octal complement of the file mask. You can calculate the mask by deleting the desired mask from 777. If you provide umask of 777, no user will have the read, write, or execute permission. The umask of the root should be 777. Doing this will disable read, write, and execute permission for other users. The permission for a user or group can be changed by the chmod command.

Table 2-1 gives the description of various file permissions as obtained by executing the ls -l command.

Table 2-1: File Permissions

Permission	Description
-r―――――	Allows read access to the owner of the file.
―w―――――--	Allows the owner to modify or delete the file.
――-x―――――	Enables the owner to execute the program.
――-s―――――	Execute with effective User ID.
―――――――s-	Execute with effective Group ID.
-rw―――――T	Disable the update of the last modified time. This kind of permission is usually required for swap files.

Table 2-2 gives the description of various directory permissions as obtained by executing the ls -1 command.

Table 2-2: Directory Permissions

Permission	Description
dr———	Enables you to list the contents of the directory. However, you cannot read the file attributes.
d—x———	Enables you to enter the directory and use it in full execution paths.
d———x-t	Prevents files from being deleted by others with write access. This permission is usually used on /tmp.

 NOTE

◆ System files should be owned by the root.

◆ System files normally are created in the mode 640. You can change this mode as per your requirements.

◆ Users and groups other than root should not have write permission on the system files.

I've discussed various measures and actions that you can take to implement physical, network, and account security. At times, however, intruders might get smarter than you think and breach the security. You should be able to detect the intrusion and bring the security back in place by plugging the security holes. Therefore, intrusion detection is our next topic of discussion.

Summary

In this chapter, you looked at various security aspects of the Linux environment. We discussed the need for security in standalone as well as network environments. You looked at some of the common precautions and steps to be taken to keep intruders at bay.

Security in the Linux environment can be configured at four levels: Physical, Data, Network, and Accounts. You can ensure physical security by applying measures such as computer locks, BIOS, and Boot Loader security. You also learned how to detect physical security compromises. You can ensure data security by thorough measures, such as effective backup, data encryption, and securely deleting data. Network security depends on the firewalls, secure protocols, and so on, which you use in a network. You can secure the accounts of various types of users by assigning strong passwords, and protect security by assigning files and directory permissions judiciously only to the users who need them.

You learned how to ensure security at each level. I also discussed various signs indicating possible intrusion detection and the methods to overcome the intrusion. Other aspects of Linux security are covered exhaustively in this book in the chapters to come.

Check Your Understanding

Multiple Choice Questions

1. What is the function of vLock?

   a. It locks some or all of the virtual consoles in your Linux computer.

   b. It locks the booting up of your computer by a user.

   c. It locks the display and requires a password.

   d. It locks the computer if the user enters incorrect passwords three times.

2. The chmod 664 test.txt command is equivalent to which of the following commands?

   a. chmod u+rw g+rw o+r test.txt

   b. chmod u-rw g+rw o-r test.txt

   c. chmod u+rw g-rw o-r test.txt

   d. chmod u-rw g-rw o-r test.txt

3. To prevent unauthorized users from rebooting your computer, you can use the _____ file, which contains a list of usernames that are authorized to reboot the computer.

   a. /etc/shutdown.allow

   b. /bin/ shutdown.allow

   c. /etc/ allow.shutdown

   d. /bin/shutdown.allow

4. _____ is a computer used to control access between an organization's intranet and the Internet.

   a. Bastion hosts

   b. Router

   c. DMZ

5. NIS does not share information contained in the _____ file over a network.

   a. /etc/passwd

   b. /etc/group

   c. /etc/shadow

   d. /etc/allow

6. To password protect LILO using Red Hat Linux, you can use the _____ utility.

   a. linuxconf

   b. sudo

   c. pwconv

   d. unpwconv

7. The _____ utility creates the shadow file if it does not exist.

   a. linuxconf

   b. sudo

   c. pwconv

   d. unpwconv

8. _____ prevents anyone from booting the computer without entering the password.

   a. POP

   b. PAP

   c. shadow

   d. passwd

9. The _____ and _____ files contain the login records for all users on your system.

   a. /var/log/wtmp

   b. /var/run/utmp

   c. /var/run/usrlog

   d. /var/log/utmp

Short Questions

1. You are a network administrator. You are performing a security check for intrusion detection on the server. One of the guidelines for the check requires you to search for unowned files that have no owner or belong to no group. Give the command to search for such files.

2. You need to suggest to the Chief Technical Officer (CTO) of your organization how the organization should go about securing its network. Briefly describe the role and advantages of the SSH and SSL protocols that make it a feasible option for implementing network security.

Answers

Multiple Choice Answers

1. `vlock` locks some or all of the virtual consoles in your Linux computer.

2. The `chmod 664 test.txt` command is equivalent to `chmod u+rw g+rw o+r test.txt` because read is equivalent to 4 and write is equivalent to 2.

3. `/etc/shutdown.allow` contains a list of user names that are authorized to reboot the computer.

4. Bastion hosts control access between an organization's intranet and the Internet.

5. NIS does not share information contained in `/etc/allow` file over a network.

6. `linuxconf` can be used to password protect LILO.

7. The `pwconv` utility creates the shadow file if it does not exist.

8. POP prevents anyone from booting the computer without entering the password.

9. The files that contain the login record for users are /var/log/utmp and /var/run/utmp.

Short Answers

1. `root# find / -nouser -o -nogroup -print`

2. Secure Shell (SSH) protocol is used for securing remote access connections over IP networks. SSH protocol secures data by encrypting when it is transmitted over the network. The SSH program has made remote management of network hosts over the Internet possible.

   Secure Socket Layer (SSL) protocol provides privacy and reliability between two communicating applications. The SSL protocol runs above TCP/IP and below other higher level protocols, such as TELNET, FTP, or HTTP. SSH enables data encryption, authentication of server and client, and message authentication. The benefits of using SSL include cryptographic security, reliability, interoperability, extensibility, and efficiency.

Chapter 3

In this chapter, you learn about the various Linux distributions available. You also look at the different installation media for the Linux operating system. In addition, you learn about the partition and file system in Linux and find out how Linux installations can be automated by using the Kickstart facility.

Linux Distributions

Various Linux distributions are available, such as Debian, Red Hat, Caldera, and SuSE. Each of these distributions is aimed at a different type of user.

The core of all Linux distributions is the kernel. Most system and administrative software that comes with different Linux distributions is freely available, and can be ported between various UNIX platforms.

You need to consider all your requirements, such as intended use, before selecting a distribution. You can seek advice from the Linux community through various Linux mailing lists, such as `caldera-users-digest` and `debian-user`. In addition, you can refer to the comparison report of various Linux distributions that is available at **http://www.distrowatch.com**. You also can ask for help and advice from people who have installed Linux.

I'll now discuss the following Linux distributions:

- Red Hat
- MandrakeSoft
- Caldera
- Debian
- Corel
- SusE

Red Hat

Red Hat was established in 1994 by Bob Young and Marc Ewing. Red Hat is a leader in the development, deployment, and management of the Linux operating system. Red Hat solutions cover the Red Hat Linux operating system, developer and embedded technologies, training, management services, and technical support. They also provide open source solutions for Internet infrastructure devices ranging from embedded devices to Web servers.

Red Hat makes the source code of its products available to everyone. Developers who use the software can work on the source code of the software and improve it. Red Hat delivers its open source innovation to its customers through an Internet platform called *Red Hat Network*.

MandrakeSoft

In November 1998, several Linux enthusiasts had an online discussion and founded MandrakeSoft. MandrakeSoft's strategy is to promote Linux for users of all levels, ranging from beginners to experts and from individuals to corporate users. It provides a wide range of services, such as improved software and hardware and a package manager developed for the Linux environment.

MandrakeSoft, with its Linux-Mandrake distribution, has become an international mode of reference in open source software and Linux. Several factors, such as open source for Linux and the availability of the Linux-Mandrake distribution in more than 40 languages, have contributed to the company's growth.

Linux-Mandrake currently includes more than 2,300 applications in its distribution. It provides a distribution that is easy to install and use. In addition, Linux-Mandrake is fast and reliable. Linux-Mandrake products include the operating system, related programs, installation tools, full documentation, and technical support.

Caldera

Caldera is based in Orem, Utah, and has a worldwide presence with 20 offices spread across 18 countries, including the U.S., Germany, the U.K., Brazil, South Africa, and some Asian countries. Caldera's infrastructure extends to 82 countries and has over 15,000 resellers worldwide. Caldera was the first Linux company to create the Linux Value Added Resellers (VAR) channel.

Caldera enables the development, deployment, and management of unified Linux and UNIX platform solutions for business through its OpenLinux, OpenUNIX, and SCO OpenServer product lines and services. Caldera solutions combine the performance, scalability, and confidence associated with UNIX and the flexibility associated with Linux. Therefore, Caldera provides an integrated solution for small-to-medium businesses, retail operations, telecommunications, and other vertical markets. Caldera solutions are divided into two business lines: *Platform Business Line* and *Services Business Line.*

◆ **Platform Business Line.** The platform business line supports Caldera Volution, which is a collection of Caldera server, development tools, and management products. Caldera Volution provides a platform for application development and administration and management of Caldera Linux and UNIX operating systems.

◆ **Services Business Line.** The services business line is responsible for providing a wide range of services on the Caldera platform. The services range from management products to application development.

Debian

The Debian project was founded by Ian Murdock on August 16, 1993. When Ian started this project, the concept of free Linux distribution was new. Ian wanted the Debian project to be a distribution whose source would be made freely available. The creation of Debian was sponsored by the Free Software Foundation's (FSF) GNU project for one year—from November 1994 to November 1995. It started as a small group of software hackers and gradually grew to become a large, well-organized community of developers and users.

The Debian distribution is open for contribution from every developer and user. The features of Debian are listed here:

◆ The only non-commercial Linux distribution.

◆ The strong dependency between its packages ensures consistency in upgrades.

Debian includes over 3,950 packages. The Debian GNU/Linux distribution is the primary product of the Debian project. The distribution contains kernel and various pre-packaged software applications. The Debian distribution supports multiple processor types, such as Intel i386 and above, PowerPC, IBM S/390, Sparc, and Hitachi SuperH.

Debian motivated the formation of Software in the Public Interest, Inc. (SPI), which is a New York-based, non-profit organization. SPI helps companies in development and distribution of hardware and software.

SuSE

SuSE Linux is one of the world's leading providers of complete solutions based on Linux. SuSE also provides Linux deployment solutions.

SuSE provides a wide range of consultation, technical, and other services to its customers. It has the largest open-source solutions development team.

Now that you are familiar with the different types of Linux distributions, I'll discuss the installation of Red Hat Linux using various installation media.

Installing Red Hat Linux

In this section, you'll look at the various media you can use to install Red Hat Linux. You can install Red Hat Linux by using one of the following media:

◆ CD-ROM

◆ NFS

◆ Hard drive

◆ FTP

CD-ROM Installation

One media you can use to install Red Hat Linux distribution is CD-ROM. To install the Red Hat Linux installation from CD-ROM, follow these steps:

1. Select the Local CD-ROM option from the list of installation types, and then click OK. When you are prompted for the type of drive; specify whether you have an SCSI, IDE/ATAPI, or proprietary CD-ROM drive.

2. Select the SCSI card from the list that is displayed at selection of the SCSI drive. After you select the SCSI card, you will be asked whether you want to select AUTOPROBE or SPECIFY OPTIONS for the SCSI card.

3. Choose AUTOPROBE. This causes the program to scan for your SCSI card and, when the card is found, enable the SCSI support. The installation program now locates the Red Hat CD-ROM and proceeds with the installation.

NFS Installation

For the NFS installation, you need an existing Linux computer that can support and export an ISO-9660 file system. Otherwise, you need to mirror one of the Red Hat distributions with the directory tree. You need to export the /RedHat directory to the computers on the network where the Red Hat Linux will be installed. This computer must be on an Ethernet network, because you cannot perform an NFS installation through a dial-up link.

Some important steps during the NFS installation are listed here:

1. Select the Ethernet card. This ensures that the appropriate driver is loaded.
2. Select the appropriate card from the list that is displayed.
3. At times, your computer might stop responding. In this case, press Ctrl+Alt+Del to restart the computer.
4. The system then searches for the card. Upon successful detection of the card, you are prompted to provide some information, such as TCP/IP details, NFS server name, network, gateway address, and the DNS server.
5. In the last screen, specify the NFS server name. You also need to specify the path of the directory that contains the Linux distribution.

Hard Drive Installation

During a hard drive installation, the root directory of the partition, which will contain the Red Hat distribution, must have the /RedHat directory. On the primary Disk Operating System (DOS) partition, the path to /RedHat should be C:\RedHat. You can get the Red Hat distribution from either a CD-ROM or an FTP server.

In an MS-DOS file system, you do not have to ensure that the package.rpm names are truncated. You need to make sure that the /RedHat/base directory contains the required files copied from the CD-ROM or FTP server. You should also ensure that the package.rpm files are present in the /RedHat/RPMS directory. Now you can install or upgrade from the partition. You will need to insert an additional disk if you haven't selected to support PCMCIA.

FTP Installation

You also can install Red Hat Linux through the FTP server. To install Linux through an FTP server, you need to specify the FTP server and the path. If you are installing Linux through the FTP server over the Internet, it might take a while because the /RedHat/RPMS directory is huge. If you get disconnected, you will need to start the installation all over again. Therefore, it is advisable that on networks with low bandwidth, you should first copy the installation files to the hard drive and then perform the Linux installation from there.

FTP installation is similar to the NFS installation. You will need to specify the Ethernet card and other information, such as TCP/IP details of your computer, FTP server name, directory path, and so on. You can either provide your own FTP server that has a Red Hat Installation or enter the Red Hat directory and one of the the Red Hat mirror sites. Select a server that is closest to your location and is processing the fewest number of requests. If your hardware is not detected, you might need to specify manually the hardware available on your computer.

For the FTP installation, you need a single floppy disk and a server with all the files. Simply mirror the directory structure you need and then make it accessible through an FTP server, after providing your username and password. The files should be read-only, and no write permissions should be given.

FTP installations also can be automated with the Kickstart utility. (For more information, see the section, "Automated Installation: Kickstart," later in this chapter.) In addition, you can perform customized installation by removing unwanted packages. The FTP servers should be secure. If you are using a public FTP server, make sure that the Web site is listed as a secure server in the main distribution Web site.

Customizing FTP, NFS, or Hard Drive Installation

Customizing the list of packages available for installation is an option while you are installing the system by using FTP, NFS, and your hard drive. You can copy the files from the CD-ROM to the hard drive and install Linux from there with the customized package list. To install from an FTP or NFS server, you need to have root access to the servers on the network.

You might need to perform a customized installation in some situations; for example, when you are installing Red Hat Linux via FTP over a low-bandwidth connection. To customize the installation, you need to do the following:

1. Obtain the /base/comps file, which provides you with a list of packages that a full installation normally includes.

2. Download from /base/comps the packages you want to install.

3. Edit the /base/comps file so that it contains the entry for the packages that you need to install. The already installed RPM packages should be specified in this file.

4. The kernel detects the hardware attached to the computer during system boot.

5. A message appears, asking whether you have a color screen, and then the Welcome screen is displayed to you. Click the OK button to continue.

6. Next, you are prompted for the PCMCIA support.

7. After you select the option to support PCMCIA, a screen is displayed where you need to specify the type of installation that you need to perform. After selecting the installation type, the installation wizard will guide you through the normal installation process.

The comps file

The Red Hat installation program uses the /RedHat/base/comps file to determine which packages are available in the /RedHat/RPMS directory for each category of the package to be installed. The file is organized into various categories of packages. The comps file can be used across different versions of Red Hat Linux because it contains only the package name part of the package.

Users need all the software packages listed in the Base section of the file. You can customize other sections to your need. For example, there are three types of networked stations:

◆ Plain

◆ Management

◆ Dial-up

You need to ensure that the packages are listed in the appropritae category.

Installation of a package on your computer might depend on the availability of other packages on your system. You need to ensure that package dependencies are met. When an RPM package is built, RPM tries to determine which packages must be installed for a package to be functional. For example, if you have user access to your NFS server on an existing Red Hat Linux computer, one way to determine package dependencies is to telnet or log on to it and query the package for dependencies.

The `libc` and `termcap` packages form a part of the `base` system of the Linux operating system. Therefore, you must make sure that the `libc` and `libtermcap` packages are present so that you can install `bash`. After you install the entire `base` system, you can start the system.

Verifying Package Integrities

An attacker can create RPMs that appear very much like a genuine package. Finding the MD5 sums of the files in trusted locations is very difficult. Typically, all RPM distribution files are signed, which makes it easy to verify their correctness. Some packages are not signed, however, which makes it very easy for an unauthorized person to change packages at a distribution site and go unnoticed. An unauthorized person need not even modify or add files to the package to cause the problem. Instead, the person needs only to add a pre/post installation malicious script, which runs with root privileges and is capable of corrupting the system. Therefore, users must ensure that the RPMs they are downloading are signed. They must also, if possible, verify MD5 checksums.

Trojan Infected CDs/Distributions

Anyone with a CD writer can access the public distribution Web sites of Linux distributions and burn installation CDs. Also, in accordance with the General Public License, they can make modifications in these Linux distributions and further distribute them. On the pretext of helping you, malicious distributors may give you CDs that are infected with Trojans. Therefore, it is more secure to buy original distribution CDs or make installation CDs on your own. If you download a modified Linux distribution accessible on the net, keep in mind that many FTP search programs may find that the server has a mirror and can download files from there. It is best to only download from verified servers.

Automated Installation: Kickstart

RedHat Linux has a utility called Kickstart. Kickstart allows you to automate most of the RedHat Linux installation steps. These are some of the steps you can automate:

- Selecting the language
- Configuring network
- Selecting the type of keyboard
- Installing boot loader
- Partitioning disks
- Creating file systems
- Selecting Mouse
- Configuring X window server
- Selecting time zone
- Selecting the packages

If you have installed Linux, you know that these steps are essentially the most important steps involved in the manual installation of a RedHat Linux system. Kickstart enables you to script the installation process by specifying the installation information in a configuration file.

After completing the installation process, you can specify a list of shell-level commands, which will be executed by Kickstart. You also can automatically install extra software that is not distributed as part of RedHat Linux and carry out other tasks that you might need to do to get a fully operational system.

There are two approaches to Kickstart installation:

- The first approach is to copy the configuration file of the Linux to a RedHat boot floppy.
- The second approach is to use a regular boot floppy to boot the computer. After doing that, you can obtain the config file for Kickstart from the network.

These two approaches are meant for different types of networks. For a network with a DHCP server, no individual IP addresses need to be defined in the Kickstart configuration files. Therefore, if a network has a DHCP server, the Kickstart boot floppy can contain the config file. If each computer on the network has to be configured with a fixed IP address, you should use a regular installation floppy and manually add the IP address.

In both cases, you will need the following:

◆ Intel (i386) class computers

◆ Kickstart `config` file

◆ RedHat boot disk

◆ DNS entries for the IP addresses

The config File

If you want to fetch the `config` file over the network, you will have to export it through NFS. This is the only access method supported by the current version of Red Hat. The `config` file allows you to specify a different NFS server. You can configure the IP address either statically or dynamically through BOOTP/ DHCP server.

The `config` file has three main sections:

◆ System info

◆ RedHat packages

◆ Post-installation shell commands

More information on the `config` file is available in the `misc/src/install/ ks.samp` and `doc/README.ks` files. These files are available under the i386 RedHat distribution directory.

Some of the available directives in the `config` file are listed here:

◆ **Lang.** This directive configures the language for Linux.

◆ **Network.** This directive configures the network options.

◆ **NFS.** This directive specifies the NFS server.

◆ **Keyboard.** This directive specifies the keyboard type.

◆ **Zerombr.** This directive clears the MBR and removes the boot loader from the disk.

◆ **Clearpart.** This directive clears the existing partitions.

◆ **Part.** This directive partitions the hard disk.

- ◆ **Install.** This directive makes a fresh installation of RedHat Linux.
- ◆ **Mouse.** This directive sets the mouse to be used.
- ◆ **Timezone.** This directive sets the time zone.
- ◆ **Rootpw.** This directive sets initial root password.
- ◆ **Lilo.** This directive installs the LILO boot loader.
- ◆ **%packages.** This directive installs the software packages.
- ◆ **%post.** This directive executes the post-installation shell commands.
- ◆ **Cdrom.** This directive performs installation from CD-ROM.
- ◆ **Device.** This directive specifies details of devices connected with the computer.
- ◆ **Upgrade.** This directive upgrades an existing installation.
- ◆ **Xconfig.** This directive configures the X Windows server, graphics card, and monitor.

Packages to Install

The %packages directive indicates the beginning of the packages section in the config file. The packages to be installed on the computer are specified in this section of the kickstart file. You can install individual packages by specifying the name of their RPM, and you can install groups of packages by specifying their group names.

The list of packages that can be installed is available in the file RedHat/base/comps, which is part of the Red Hat distribution. The RedHat/base/comps file contains package groups. A package group contains a list of related packages. The %packages section expects either a package group name, which is preceded by the @ symbol, or individual package names. You don't have to specify the package version, the release number, and the platform in the kick-start file. An abbreviated version of the RedHat/base/comps file is listed here:

```
1 Base
perl
mkbootdisk
linuxconf
gd
ldconfig
```

```
chkconfig
ntsysv
mktemp
setup
setuptool
filesystem
MAKEDEV
SysVinit
alpha: aboot
apmd
ash
at
end
0 Printer Support
chkfontpath
lpr
mpage
rhs-printfilters
end
```

The group list in the RedHat/base/comps file begins with the number 0 or 1, followed by a group name. The keyword end marks the end of the group. The groups marked by 1 are installed by default. An administrator can define new groups or modify existing ones by modifying the RedHat/base/comps file. Editing the RedHat/base/comps file offers another means of customizing Red Hat Linux installation.

There are a number of groups defined by default in a file called base/comps, under the RedHat distribution's top-level directory. Some of the groups are listed here:

◆ X Windows system
◆ Base
◆ Mail/WWW/News tools
◆ DOS/Windows connectivity
◆ Printer support
◆ Graphics manipulation
◆ File managers

◆ Web server

◆ DNS server

◆ SMB (Samba) connectivity

◆ C Development

◆ Development libraries

◆ C++ development

◆ X development

◆ IPX/Netware(tm) connectivity

◆ Anonymous FTP/Gopher server

◆ Postgres (SQL) server

◆ Network management workstation

◆ Emacs with X windows

◆ Extra documentation

Post-Installation Shell Commands

This section does not have any direct equivalent in the manual installation process. Here, I specify a sequence of shell-level commands that should be executed when the main installation is over. The %post directive signifies the beginning of this section in the Kickstart config file, as shown in the following code snippet:

```
%post
ln -s /etc/rc.d/init.d /etc/init.d
ln -s /etc/rc.d/rc.local /etc/rc.local
ln -s /usr/bin/md5sum /usr/bin/md5
ln -s /usr/bin/perl /usr/local/bin/perl
chmod ug-s /bin/linuxconf
mkdir /var/tmp/tmp
perl -spi -e 's!image=/boot/vmlinuz-.*!image=/boot/vmlinuz!' /etc/lilo.conf
rm /etc/rc.d/rc*.d/*sendmail
```

Linux Installation from Kickstart

Start the computer on which you want to install Linux by using your RedHat boot floppy as usual, but type linux ks instead of pressing the Return (or Enter) key at the SYSLINUX prompt. By using Kickstart, you can automate the normal steps involved in a RedHat installation. This means that you might see dialog boxes that appear during manual installation. These dialog boxes are displayed only when Kickstart cannot identify what to do next. It is likely that your network interface may not be detected automatically, and you may be prompted for its IRQ and I/O address space.

You can check the progress of Kickstart by switching between the listed virtual consoles using these key combinations:

◆ Alt-F1—Installation dialog

◆ Alt-F2—Shell prompt

◆ Alt-F3—Install log (messages from install program)

◆ Alt-F4—System log (messages from kernel and so on)

◆ Alt-F5—Other messages

Mounting boot/supp Disks

The RedHat boot disk, `boot.img`, is in the MS-DOS format and uses the SYS-LINUX program to start. The supplementary disk, `supp.img`, is a Linux ext2 file system. If you have support for the `loopback` file system in your Linux kernel, you can mount these files in your file system and gain unauthorized access to them:

```
# mkdir -p /mnt/boot /mnt/supp
# mount -o loop -t msdos boot.img /mnt/boot
# mount -o loop supp.img /mnt/supp
```

Now you should be able to see and manipulate the files on the boot and supplementary disk under `/mnt/boot` and `/mnt/supp`, respectively. The older versions of `mount` might not support the `-o loop` option. In this case, you will need to configure the `loopback` device explicitly for each file. You also might need to use the `-t ext2` option explicitly when mounting the `ext2` file system. If you are using the latest Linux distributions, however, you need not worry about the lack of support for the `-o` option.

Linux Partitions

Hard drives are divided into one or more partitions, which are sections of the hard drive set aside for some operating system to use. The concept of a partition allows you to have a dual boot mechanism. For example, you might have MS-DOS running on one partition on your hard drive and Linux on another.

Master Boot Record (MBR) is the first cylinder, the first head, and the first sector of the disk. The boot record is used to boot the system, and the partition table contains information about the location and size of your partitions.

Partitions are of three types:

◆ Primary

◆ Extended

◆ Logical

The primary partition type is the one most used. A drive supports a maximum of four primary partitions. The partition table size is limited, however. The extended partition can be used to overcome this limit. The extended partitions act as containers for logical partitions. Extended partitions do not hold any data. A single extended partition can cover the entire drive.

Within this partition, you can create several logical partitions. However, you might have only one extended partition for each drive. Extended partitions should cover the entire drive only when the disk is not to be used for booting. Extended partitions have an address inside /dev. In Linux although extended partitions have drive labels assigned to them, extended partitions themselves cannot be mounted. However, once logical partitions are created in extended partitions, individual logical partitions can be mounted.

Resizing Current Partitions

If your hard drive currently is taken up by partitions for other operating systems, you need to delete and resize these partitions to allocate space for Linux. There is no safe or reliable way to resize an existing partition without deleting it. An interesting experiment is however being carried out by the GNU community at www.gnu.org/software/parted/. In any case, before repartitioning your drive, you should back up your system. After you have repartitioned the drive, you can reinstall your original software..

Here are the two commands you can use for managing the partitions:

◆ fdisk.

◆ cfdisk.

In the sections that follow, I discuss each of these commands in detail.

fdisk

You use the fdisk command to create and manipulate partition tables. The fdisk command is used with DOS type partitions. In addition, it is also compatible with BSD or SUN type disk labels. The volume headers should not be covered by any partition. If you do this, the partition table will be lost.

You can have numerous partitions in a DOS type partition table. In sector 0, there is space for a description of four partitions, called *primary partitions*. One of these can be an extended partition. The four primary partitions get numbers ranging from 1 to 4. Logical partitions start with the number 5.

The geometry specifies the number of heads and the number of sectors for each track. The fdisk command will automatically try to get the disk geometry. This is not necessarily the physical disk geometry; however, this is the disk geometry that MS-DOS uses for the partition table. If you have only Linux on your computer, you shouldn't have any problem. On the other hand, if multiple operating systems are installed on your computer, you should run the fdisk command from the operating systems other than Linux. You should do this to create at least one partition.

When you start Linux, the operating system tries to obtain information about the disk geometry by reading the partition table. The partition table is checked for the integrity for its entries. This happens when the partition table is printed. The check is done to ensure that the logical start and end is the same as that of the physical start and end. The check also ensures that the starting and ending points of the partition is the cylinder boundaries. This may not be necessary for the first partition.

cfdisk

The cfdisk command is used for partitioning the hard disk drive. To write to the partition table, cfdisk needs the geometry of the disk. If the disk is not accessed by other operating systems, you can safely accept the defaults that cfdisk selects.

I'll now explain the geometry used by the cfdisk command. First, the partition table is examined to determine the geometry used by the previous program that changed it. If the partition table is empty, contains garbage, or does not reveal a consistent geometry, the kernel is referred.

The cfdisk command reads the current partition table from the disk drive. An error message is generated in case it is unable to do so. The error message also can be displayed due to incorrect geometry information. You also can solve this problem by using the -z option of the cfdisk command. The -z option ignores the partition table.

The main display consists of four sections:

◆ **Header.** This section contains the program name and the version number. In addition, it contains the disk drive and geometry information.

◆ **Partition.** This section displays the current partition table.

◆ **Command Line**. This section contains the available commands.

◆ **Warning Line.** This section contains information, such as the warnings to be displayed.

The current partition is highlighted with a reverse video or an arrow, if the -a option is given. All partition-specific commands apply to the current partition.

The fdisk command can create either primary of logical partitions. The file system of the partition is displayed in the file system type section. If the file system is not known, the Unknown value and the hex value of the file system get displayed. The Unusable value is displayed for the file system type when all the primary partitions are used. The partition size is displayed in the size field. If the partition is not aligned on cylinder boundaries, an asterisk is displayed after the size.

Given here is a list of the commands available:

◆ **bb.** This command toggles the bootable flag of the current partition. The toggling of the bootable flags enables you to select the primary partition.

◆ **dd.** This command deletes the current partition.

◆ **gg.** This command changes the disk geometry.

◆ **hh.** This command prints the help screen.

◆ **mm.** This command maximizes disk use of the current partition.

◆ **nn.** This command creates a new partition from free space. If the partition type is primary or logical, a partition of primary or logical type is created. On the other hand, if the partition type is Pri/Log, you are prompted for the partition type that you want to create.

◆ **pp.** This command prints the partition table to the screen or to a file.

◆ **qq.** This command quits the program.

- ◆ **tt.** This command changes the file system type on the partitions.
- ◆ **uu.** This command changes the units of the partition size display.
- ◆ **WW.** This command writes a partition table to disk. This command might destroy the existing data on the disk. Therefore, you should use this command judiciously. While running this command, you are prompted for the confirmation.
- ◆ **??.** This command prints the help screen.

 TIP

You can enter all commands in either uppercase or lowercase letters.

Boot Loader Installation

To start your Red Hat Linux computer without a boot disk, you need to install a boot loader. Two of the commonly used boot loaders are *GRand Unified Bootloader* (GRUB) or *LInux LOader* (LILO). Introduced with Red Hat Linux 7.2, GRUB is a software boot loader that can be used to start Red Hat Linux on your computer. It also can start other operating systems, such as Windows 9x.

If you do not install a boot loader during Linux installation, you need to have a boot disk or a third-party boot loader, which will boot the RedHat Linux system. When you decide to install a boot loader, you must first determine where it should be installed. The boot loader can be installed at two locations:

- ◆ The Master Boot Record
- ◆ The first sector of your root partition

Master Boot Record (MBR)

MBR is automatically loaded by the BIOS during system startup. When you install boot loader in MBR, the boot loader can take control of the boot process during boot itself. Therefore, it is recommended to install boot loader at MBR. However, as an exception, you shouldn't install boot loader at MBR when the MBR is configuring to start another operating system. On computers where only Linux is installed, install boot loader on MBR.

The First Sector of the Root Partition

As you read earlier, you shouldn't install boot loader at MBR when the MBR is configured to load operating systems other than Linux. In such situations, you should consider installing boot loader in the first sector of the root partition. The boot loader can be configured to boot RedHat Linux.

GRUB

GRUB is a boot loader that can load a variety of open source operating systems and proprietary operating systems. GRUB is designed to address the complexity of starting a computer.

One of the important features of GRUB is flexibility. GRUB interprets file systems and kernel executable formats. You can load the kernel simply by specifying its file name and the drive where the kernel resides. To let GRUB know the drive and the file name, you can either type them in manually, using the command-line interface, or use the menu interface. You can easily select the OS to boot through the menu interface. GRUB loads a preexisting configuration file to allow you to customize the menu interface.

The goals of GRUB are listed here:

- ◆ Basic functions should be straightforward for end-users.
- ◆ Rich functionality to support kernel experts and designers.
- ◆ Backward compatibility for booting FreeBSD, NetBSD, OpenBSD, and Linux. GRUB supports proprietary kernels, such as DOS, Windows NT, and OS/2, through a chain-loading function.

In addition to these requirements, GRUB has the following features:

- ◆ Recognizes multiple executable formats
- ◆ Supports non-multiboot kernels
- ◆ Loads multiples modules
- ◆ Loads a configuration file
- ◆ Provides a menu interface
- ◆ Has a flexible command-line interface
- ◆ Supports multiple file system types
- ◆ Supports automatic decompression

♦ Accesses data on any installed device

♦ Is independent of drive geometry translations

♦ Detects all installed RAM

♦ Supports the Logical Block Address mode

♦ Supports network booting

♦ Provides alternative boot loaders

Apart from using GRUB or LILO, you can use the following options to boot Linux computers:

♦ **LOADLIN.** You can load Linux from MS-DOS by using `LOADLIN`. If you have a SCSI adapter, you need a copy of the Linux kernel and an initial RAM disk for LOADLIN to be available on an MS-DOS partition. You can do this by starting Linux through an alternate method and then copying kernel to an MS-DOS partition. LOADLIN is available from `ftp://metalab.unc.edu/pub/Linux/system/boot/dualboot/` and associated mirror sites.

♦ **SYSLINUX.** `SYSLINUX` is an MS-DOS program that is very similar to `LOADLIN`. It also is available from `ftp://metalab.unc.edu/pub/Linux/system/boot/loaders/` and associated mirror sites.

♦ **Some commercial boot loaders.** You also can load Linux by using commercial boot loaders. Examples of commercial boot loaders are System Commander and Partition Magic. You can buy System Commander from `www.v-com.com/product/sc7_ind.html`. Partition Magic can be bought from `www.checkmark.com.au/PartitionMagic.htm`.

LILO

The LILO program, written by Werner Almesberger, is the most commonly used boot loader for Linux. LILO can be used to boot various kernels. LILO stores the kernel configuration information in a text file. The majority of the Linux distribution has LILO as the default boot loader. In addition, LILO is quite flexible.

In a typical configuration, a boot prompt will be displayed shortly after you start your computer. The boot prompt will be displayed for some time to enable you to select the appropriate operating system. If you do not provide any input, LILO starts the default operating system. When LILO boots the system, it uses BIOS calls to load the Linux kernel off the disk. This means that the kernel should be accessible by the BIOS.

If you need to exceed the 1024 cylinder limit for the /boot option, you should use the LBA32 option of LILO. If you have a system that supports the LBA32 extension for starting operating systems above the 1024 cylinder limit, you should place your /boot partition above this limit. If the installation program has not already detected this extension from your BIOS, you should select this option.

LILO does not read the file system during booting. The pathnames in lilo.conf are resolved during the installation time. This happens when the /sbin/lilo file is invoked. During installation, the program builds the tables that list some sectors. These sectors are used by the files that load the operating system, which means that these files should be in a partition that is accessible by BIOS. The files are usually located in the /boot directory. Therefore, only the root partition of your Linux system needs to be accessed through the BIOS.

You need to reinstall the loader whenever any modification is made to the LILO setup. The LILO should be reinstalled when you recompile the kernel. The lilo.conf file has a boot= directive. This directive tells LILO about the location of the primary boot loader. The location can be either of these two:

◆ MBR
◆ Root partition of Linux

If more than one OS is installed on your computer, you should install LILO to the root partition. If you do this, you should specify the root partition as bootable. This can be done by using the fdisk command (with -a option) and the cfdisk command (with -b option).

You may install LILO to MBR even if you already have another operating system installed there. For example, if you have installed Windows NT 4.0 as the first operating system on your computer, NT's boot loader will be placed into MBR. Therefore, when you install Linux to MBR, LILO rewrites the NT's boot loader. Now when you start the computer, you will not be able to boot NT. You can solve this problem by editing the /etc/lilo.conf file and adding a new entry for NT. When you restart your system, there will be a new added NT entry under the LILO menu.

The linear keyword available in the lilo.conf file helps you solve the disk geometry related problems. The linear keyword directs the LILO to use the linear sector addresses. Otherwise, LILO uses the sector, head, or cylinder tuples. The linear keyword delays the conversion of linear sector addresses to 3-D addresses till the runtime.

 NOTE

If you have more than one hard disk and Linux uses only some of them, you can configure BIOS so that they are detected. This will cause quick detection of disks and therefore, Linux will boot faster.

During boot process, the LILO prompt is displayed to you. You can view the configuration option available in LILO by pressing the Tab key. While booting Linux kernel, you can specify various command-line arguments that are acceptable by kernel. A few command-line arguments are given in the following list:

◆ **root.** This enables you to specify the Linux kernel to mount as root a partition different from the one appearing in /lilo.conf.

◆ **init.** This enables you to execute a command other than /sbin/init, as specified on the command line.

◆ **A number.** This enables init to run at the specified run level.

SMP Motherboards

If you are using an SMP motherboard, two files are created by the installation program: /boot/grub/grub.conf and /etc/lilo.conf. The entry created depends on the boot loader you have installed.

The grub.conf file has the following entries:

◆ Red Hat Linux (Kernel version)
◆ Red Hat Linux (Kernel version-SMP)

The Red Hat Linux (Kernel version-SMP) boots by default. You also can boot the Red Hat Linux (kernel version). However, this should be done when there is some problem with the SMP kernel. This allows you to retain all functionality. In contrast, the entries in lilo.conf will be Linux and Linux-up. Linux will boot by default. If you have trouble with the SMP kernel, you can select to boot the Linux-up entry instead. A sample entry of the lilo.conf file is given here:

```
boot=/dev/sda
map=/boot/map
install=/boot/boot.b
prompt
timeout=50
linear
default=linux
image=/boot/vmlinuz-xxxxxsmp
        label=linux
        read-only
        root=/dev/sda6
image=/boot/vmlinuz-xxxxxxxxxxxb
        label=linux-up
        read-only
        root=/dev/sda6
```

Linux File Systems

In the Linux file system, every resource in your system is considered a file. Even the devices are considered to be files. Some of the device files are listed here:

◆ **/dev/dsp.** This file represents the Digital Signal Processor and acts as an interface between the software that produces sound and the sound card.

◆ **/dev/fd0.** This file represents the first floppy drive. If you have several drives, they will be numbered sequentially.

◆ **/dev/fb0.** This file represents the first framebuffer device. A *framebuffer* is an abstraction layer between software and graphics hardware. Therefore, applications need not identify the hardware. They need to know only how to communicate with the framebuffer driver's Application Programming Interface (API).

◆ **/dev/hd[a-d].** This file is the master IDE drive on the primary IDE controller. The drive /dev/hdb is the slave drive on the primary controller. The drives /dev/hdc and /dev/hdd are master and slave devices on the secondary controller. Each disk is divided into partitions. Partitions 1 through 4 are primary partitions and partitions 5 and above are logical partitions, inside extended partitions.

◆ **/dev/ht0.** This file represents the first IDE tape drive. Subsequent drives are numbered ht1, ht2, and so on.

◆ **/dev/js0.** This file is the first analog joystick. Subsequent joysticks are numbered js1, js2, and so on. Digital joysticks are called djs0, djs1, and so on. These are character devices.

◆ **/dev/lp0.** This file is the first parallel printer device. Subsequent printers are numbered lp1, lp2, and so on.

◆ **/dev/loop0.** This file is the first loopback device. *Loopback* devices are used for mounting file systems that are not located on other block devices, such as disks. For example, if you want to mount an iso9660 CD-ROM image without burning it to CD, you need to use a loopback device. This is usually transparent to the user and is handled with the mount command.

◆ **/dev/md0.** This file is the first metadisk group. *Metadisks* are related to Redundant Array of Independent Disks (RAID) devices. Metadisk devices are block devices beginning at 0 and numbered sequentially.

◆ **/dev/mixer.** This file is part of the Open Sound System (OSS) driver. It is a character device.

◆ **/dev/null.** This file is like a black hole to which you can only send data. This data is never seen again. Anything sent to /dev/null will be permanently deleted. This can be useful if, for example, you want to run a command but not have any feedback appear on the terminal. It is a character device.

◆ **/dev/psaux.** This file is the PS/2 mouse port. This is a character device.

◆ **/dev/pda.** These files represent parallel port IDE disks. Their names are similar to the disks on internal IDE controllers (/dev/hd*). They are block devices. The first device is /dev/pda. Partitions on this device are found by adding the partition number to the minor number of the device.

◆ **/dev/pcd0.** This file is a parallel port CD-ROM drive. These are numbered from 0 onwards. All are block devices on major node 46. The drive /dev/pcd0 is on the minor node 0, with subsequent drives on minor nodes 1, 2, 3, and so on.

◆ **/dev/pt0.** This file is a parallel port tape device. Tapes do not have partitions; therefore, these are numbered sequentially. They are character devices on the major node 96. Minor node numbers start from 0 for /dev/pt0, 1 for /dev/pt1, and so on.

◆ **/dev/parport0.** This file is a raw parallel port. Most devices attached to parallel ports have their own drivers. This is a device to access the port directly. It is a character device.

◆ **/dev/random or /dev/urandom.** These files are kernel random number generators. The generator /dev/random is a non-deterministic generator, which means that the value of the next number cannot be guessed from the preceding ones.

◆ **/dev/zero.** This device file returns 0 every time you read from this device. This can be useful when, for example, you want a fixed-length file but do not care for its contents.

Be careful when dealing with file systems in Linux. You should take the following precautions:

◆ Never store files in the root directory, and never create new directories in the root directory unless you cannot do without them.

◆ Use your home directory (/home/<username>) to store data. You can create subdirectories to organize data.

◆ Directory and file names under Linux are case-sensitive. If you make a capitalization error in typing a directory or file name, the case sensitivity can cause problems, such as missing files.

Setting up partitions for Linux is very similar to setting up partitions for other operating systems, such as MS-DOS. To create your Linux partitions, use the Linux version of the fdisk program. After you create the partitions, you can create file systems on them. This allows the partitions to be used by the Linux system.

Introduction to the Linux File System

Linux uses a single hierarchical file system layout. It uses the same inverted-tree type directory hierarchy as UNIX. There's a root directory at the top and other directories are spread out below the root. The / is the root of the directory structure in Linux.

In the Linux file system, you need to mount a partition or a device to be able to use it. This might not be the easiest way to gain access to partitions and devices, but it offers great flexibility.

The directory Listing of / is given here:

- ◆ bin/
- ◆ etc/
- ◆ lost+found/
- ◆ proc/
- ◆ tmp/
- ◆ boot/
- ◆ home/
- ◆ mnt/
- ◆ root/
- ◆ usr/
- ◆ dev/
- ◆ lib/
- ◆ opt/
- ◆ sbin/
- ◆ var/

Each of these directories is discussed in detail in the upcoming sections.

/dev(Devices)

In Linux, a device resides in a file. Devices in Linux fall under two categories: character and block. *Character devices* are those in which input is read one character at a time. Examples of character devices are the keyboard, mouse, and serial port. *Block devices*, such as the hard drive and CD-ROM drive, read and write information in blocks of characters. For block devices, you need to know the block size for I/O operations. Drivers under Linux are specified by two numbers—a major and a minor number. The major number identifies the type of device, and the minor number identifies an interface specific to that device. All device files are stored in the /dev directory.

Some of the common files in the /dev directory are listed here.

- **audio.** Sound card
- **audio1.** Second sound card
- **cdrom@.** Link to CD-ROM
- **console.** System console
- **cua[0-3].** Serial ports (COM 1-4)
- **dsp.** Digital speaker
- **dsp1.** Second digital speaker
- **fd@.** Link to the primary floppy drive
- **fd0.** Auto detecting primary floppy
- **fd1.** Auto detecting secondary floppy
- **hd[a-h].** IDE hard drive MBRs
- **hd[a-h][1-15].** IDE hard drive partitions
- **kmem.** Kernel virtual memory access
- **lp[0-2].** Parallel printers
- **mem.** Physical memory access
- **modem@.** Link to modem device
- **mouse@.** Link to mouse device
- **null.** Null device
- **psaux.** PS/2 mouse
- **pty[p-za-e][0-f].** Pseudo-terminal masters
- **random.** Random number generator
- **rtc.** Real-time clock
- **sd[a-g].** SCSI hard drive MBRs
- **sd[a-g][1-15].** SCSI hard drive partitions
- **sg[a-h].** Generic SCSI devices
- **sndstat.** Sound card status information
- **stderr@.** Standard error file descriptor
- **stdin@.** Standard in file descriptor
- **stdout@.** Standard out file descriptor
- **tty.** Current tty device

- **tty0.** Current virtual console
- **tty[1-63].** Virtual consoles
- **ttyS[0-63].** Serial ports
- **tty[p-za-e][0-f].** Pseudo-terminal slaves
- **urandom.** Faster, less secure random number generator
- **zero.** Source of nulls

Here are some guidelines regarding file systems to follow while you are creating partitions:

- Put on separate partitions file systems on which users have write permission.
- Put on separate partitions file systems with critical system components or configurations.
- Consider mounting some partitions with system binaries as read-only and mounting /bin/, /sbin/, and /etc/ separately. Test the partitions before using them in a production environment.

More guidelines for assigning permissions on various directories in the Linux file systems are listed in Table 3-1.

Table 3-1: Guidelines for Assigning Permissions to Directories

Directory	nodev	noexec	nosuid	read-only
/	yes	yes	yes	yes
/boot/	yes	yes	yes	yes
/bin/	yes	no	no	ok
/dev/	no	yes	yes	no
/etc/	yes	yes	yes	no
/home/	yes	good idea	yes	no
/lib/	yes	no	yes	ok
/mnt/	yes	good idea	good idea	ok
/opt/	yes	no	no	no
/root/	yes	no	no	no
/sbin/	yes	no	no	ok
/tmp/	yes	yes	yes	no
/usr/	yes	no	no	ok
/var/	yes	yes	yes	no

/lib (System Libraries)

The /lib directory contains shared object libraries needed by system-critical programs, such as rm and ls, which make system and library calls. Libraries occasionally are updated with new features. As a result, there are two different versions of libraries: major and minor. New libraries that are backward compatible with previous versions have the same major version number, but a higher minor number. Libraries not backward compatible get a new major number.

Here are some of the libraries contained in /lib:

◆ **libc.so.** This is a C programming library. This contains code for all system calls and all library calls.

◆ **ld-linux.so.** This contains shared objects for Linux utilities.

◆ **libdl.so.** This contains dynamic linking functions.

◆ **libm.so.** This contains math functions.

◆ **libncurses.so.** This contains functions that support character-based graphics.

◆ **libcrypt.so.** This contains cryptologic functions.

/sbin (System Admin Binaries)

The /sbin directory holds system administration and maintenance binaries. These tools generally are used only by the root user. Some of the programs that you may need to make your system operational are discussed in the following section.

Disk Fixers

Disk fixers programs are used to manage partitions and file systems. Some of these disk fixers are listed here:

◆ **fdisk.** This is used for changing your partition tables.

◆ **fsck.** This is the file system integrity checker.

◆ **mkfs.** This makes a file system on a partition.

◆ **lilo.** This tells MBR where to find the systems files. LILO stores its working files in /boot.

Hardware Detectors

Hardware detector tools are used to detect various hardware devices on your system. Some of these tools are discussed here:

- **pnpdump.** This checks for any Plug-and-Play peripherals.
- **isapnp.** This configures PnP cards.

Network

Some of the network tools include these:

- **ifconfig.** This is used to add or remove a network interface.
- **route.** This manipulates your kernel IP routing table.

Modules

These are some of the modules for performing kernel-related activities:

- **insmod.** This inserts a kernel module.
- **lsmod.** This lists kernel module.
- **rmmod.** This removes kernel module.

General System Admin

Some of the general administrative tools are listed here:

- **init.** This creates processes from a script stored in the file /etc/inittab.
- **pidof.** This finds the process ID of a running program.
- **shutdown.** This shuts down the system.

/bin (Useful Binaries)

The /bin directory holds programs that make the system usable. However, the programs in the /bin directory aren't absolutely necessary to keep the system running. These utilities are listed in the next section.

Shells

Shell can be one of the following:

- ◆ ash.
- ◆ bash.
- ◆ csh.
- ◆ sh.
- ◆ tcsh.
- ◆ zsh.

File System Manipulation

The /bin directory contains many file system utilities. Some of the utilities are listed in Table 3-2.

Table 3-2: File System Utilities

cat	chgrp	chmod	chown
cp	dd	df	echo
grep	gunzip/gzip	ln	ls
mkdir	mknod	more	mount
mv	pwd	rm	rmdir
sync	tar	touch	umount
vi	zcat		

Process Handlers

The /bin directory contains utilities to manage various processes. Some of these utilities are these:

- ◆ **kill.** This terminates a process.
- ◆ **nice.** This runs a program with modified scheduling priority.
- ◆ **ps.** This reports process status.

/etc (System Configuration)

The /etc directory contains the configuration files of various programs. Some of the config files in the /etc directory are listed here:

- ◆ **X11/.** This is the X Windows config directory.
- ◆ **aliases.** This is the aliases file for sendmail.
- ◆ **bashrc.** This file contains system-wide functions and aliases for bash.
- ◆ **crontab.** This file contains tables for driving crond.
- ◆ **csh.cshrc.** This file contains systemwide functions for csh users.
- ◆ **exports.** This file contains information about the NFS file systems being exported.
- ◆ **fstab.** This file contains the static file system information.
- ◆ **group.** This file is the user group file.
- ◆ **hosts.** This file contains the list of known hosts to shortcut nameserver lookups.
- ◆ **hosts.allow, hosts.deny.** These files are access control files for network operations.
- ◆ **inetd.conf.** This is the config file for inetd.
- ◆ **inittab.** This file is the config file for init.
- ◆ **ld.so.conf.** This file contains the list of library directories for ldconfig to check.
- ◆ **lilo.conf.** This is the lilo config file.
- ◆ **motd.** This file contains message of the day.
- ◆ **passwd.** This file contains information about the system password.
- ◆ **profile.** This file contains the systemwide environment setup.
- ◆ **resolv.conf.** This file is the hostname resolver configuration file.
- ◆ **services.** This file contains the network services list.
- ◆ **skel/.** This is the skeleton directory for adding new users.
- ◆ **sysconfig/.** This directory contains (RedHat) additional system config files.

/proc (Linux Profiling & Tuning)

The /proc directory is an interface to the kernel data structures. Most of the files in this pseudo file system are read-only. This directory contains subdirectories representing the running processes on the system. Each of these subdirectory is named by the process ID of the process that it represents. Each subdirectory contains these files and subdirectories:

- ◆ **cmdline.** This holds the command line for the process.
- ◆ **cwd.** This is a link to the current working directory of the process.
- ◆ **environ.** This contains the process environment.
- ◆ **exe.** This is a link to the binary that is executed.
- ◆ **fd.** This is a subdirectory containing one entry for each file that the process has opened. The entry is named by its file descriptor and is a symbolic link to the actual file.
- ◆ **maps.** This is a file that contains the currently mapped memory regions and their access permissions.
- ◆ **mem.** The mem file points to the memory of the process that accesses it.
- ◆ **stat.** This contains the status information about the process.

Other files and directories in /proc include:

- ◆ **cpuinfo.** This is a collection of CPU and items that are dependent on system architecture. The only two common entries are CPU and BogoMIPS. CPU shows the CPUs that are currently in use. BogoMIPS is a system constant, which is calculated during kernel initialization.
- ◆ **devices.** This is a text listing of major numbers and device groups.
- ◆ **dma.** This is a list of registered ISA Direct Memory Access (DMA) channels in use.
- ◆ **filesystems.** This is a text listing of the different file system types that were compiled in the kernel.
- ◆ **interrupts.** This is used to record the number of interrupts per IRQ on the i386 architecture.
- ◆ **ioports.** This is a list of currently registered Input-Output port regions that are in use.
- ◆ **kcore.** This file represents the physical memory of the system.

◆ **kmsg.** This file can be used instead of the syslog system call to log kernel messages.

◆ **ksyms.** This file holds the symbol definitions used by modules(x) tools.

◆ **loadavg.** This gives the number of jobs in the run queue averaged over 1, 5, and 15 minutes. This number is the same as the load average numbers given by uptime and other programs.

◆ **meminfo.** This is used by free to report the amount of free and used physical and swap memory on the system. It also reports the amount of shared memory and buffers used by the kernel.

◆ **modules.** This is a text list of the modules that have been loaded by the system.

◆ **net/.** This contains various net pseudo-files that give the status of some part of the networking layer.

◆ **pci.** This is a listing of all PCI devices found during kernel initialization and their configuration.

◆ **scsi/.** This is a directory of the SCSI mid-level pseudo-file and various SCSI low-level driver directories that give the status of some part of the SCSI IO subsystem. The SCSI low-level directories contain a file for each SCSI host in this system. These files contain ASCII structures and also are readable with cat. You also can write to some of the files to reconfigure the subsystem or switch certain features on or off.

◆ **self.** This directory refers to the process that accesses the /proc file system. It is identical to the /proc directory, named by the process ID of the same process.

◆ **stat.** This contains kernel and/or system statistics.

◆ **sys/.** This directory contains files and subdirectories corresponding to kernel variables. These variables can be read and modified by using the /proc file system.

◆ **version.** This file identifies the current kernel version.

/tmp (Temporary Storage)

If you are uncompressing an application, but the combined size of the zip file and the uncompressed data is too large for your file system, you need some scratch space for storing the temporary data. The /tmp directory is meant to be used as temporary storage space. It is usually deleted to keep the system clean. Therefore, you should not leave important files in this directory because its contents are highly variable.

/var (Variable File Storage)

The /var directory holds files that are variable in size, time, or content. It is usually split into other directories, based on the kind of files in those directories. The other directories may include the following:

- ◆ **catman.** This directory contains subdirectories with preformatted manual pages.
- ◆ **games.** This directory stores games-related files.
- ◆ **lib.** This directory is used for storing information about various applications. The `locate` utility stores its lookup table here.
- ◆ **lock.** The programs that need temporarily to lock files put the files here.
- ◆ **log.** This directory stores system logs.
- ◆ **run.** Various processes ids and other miscellaneous information are stored here.
- ◆ **spool.** This directory contains spools for various applications, each of which has its own subdirectory. The most common programs that spool files are `mail` and `lpd`.
- ◆ **tmp.** This directory stores temporary information about the running programs.

/root and /home/user (Home Directories)

The /root directory is the home directory for the super user root. It usually contains files and tools that concern system administrative tasks. This directory has read privileges only for the root user and other administrative accounts. Each user has a username and a directory in /home. The users can place any kind of files here and set up permissions to determine exactly to whom they want to allow access to their data.

/mnt (Temporary Mount Point)

The /mnt directory is a temporary mount point. Sometimes, it has subdirectories for different types of file systems.

/lost+found (Lost and Found)

The /lost+found directory is used for storing files that the file system cannot identify when it cleans up the file system. If you lose some data unexpectedly, look for it in this directory.

/usr (Applications)

The /usr directory is meant for storing applications. The /usr directory typically includes the following subdirectories:

- ◆ **lib/.** This directory contains application-specific libraries.
- ◆ **sbin/.** This directory contains binaries that are not critical to system operation, but without which the system's functionality would be greatly reduced. For example, some binaries available in this directory are crond, lpd, edquota, makewhatis, and traceroute.
- ◆ **bin/.** Most application binaries reside in this directory.
- ◆ **etc/.** This directory contains config files for applications.
- ◆ **tmp/.** This directory is a temporary storage for your applications.

In addition, /usr has directories that do not have systemwide counterparts. Some of these directories are listed here:

- ◆ **X11 or X11R6/.** This directory represents the X windowing application hierarchy.
- ◆ **dict/.** This directory contains a dictionary.
- ◆ **doc/.** This directory contains documentation for the applications in /usr/bin.
- ◆ **games/.** This directory contains game programs.
- ◆ **include/.** This directory contains files for software development.
- ◆ **info/.** This directory is used by the info command. The info command can be used instead of man, for some applications.

- ◆ **man/.** This directory contains man pages.
- ◆ **src/.** This directory contains source code for applications. The Linux kernel is stored here.

The /usr/share directory contains the data that you can share across various applications. The /usr directory can contain various utilities, such as awk, emacs, gettext, lyx, and vim. Additionally, the directory can contain the subdirectories listed here:

- ◆ afterstep/
- ◆ automake/
- ◆ games/
- ◆ icons/
- ◆ magic
- ◆ terminfo/
- ◆ zoneinfo

Some information and applications are specific to a single network of computers, however. For example, you need different applications to run the office and home versions of LAN. The /usr/local directory provides storage for this information. The /usr/local directory generally is a complete file system. Therefore, the /usr/local directory will probably include the bin, etc, games, include, info, lib, man, sbin, and src directories. Sometimes, shared and proprietary configuration files are located in the /usr/local/share directory. People also store applications like a Web server under www, or a database under mysql.

Summary

In this chapter, you learned about various Linux distributions, such as Red Hat, MandrakeSoft, Caldera, Debian, Corel, and SuSE. Next, you learned about the different installation methods of Linux. You can install Linux via CD-ROM, NFS, hard disk drive, and FTP. You also can automate the installation process by using the Kickstart feature. Using Kickstart, you can automate tasks such as language, keyboard, time zone, package, and mouse selection.

Next, you looked at the file system and drive partitioning in Linux. You learned about `fdisk` and `cfdisk` tools, which are used to manage partitions in your system. I discussed in detail two popular boot loaders: LILO and GRUB. LILO is the most commonly used boot loader for Linux. LILO can boot various kernels. It stores the kernel-related information in a plain text file. You can use LILO to boot MS DOS, Linux, FreeBSD, and so on. GRUB is a boot loader that can load a wide variety of free operating systems and proprietary operating systems with chain loading. GRUB is designed to address the complexity of starting a personal computer.

Finally, you explored the file system of Linux. The / is the root directory of the file system. The root directory contains several standard directories. These standard directories, and the content of each directory, were considered in detail.

Check Your Understanding

Multiple Choice Questions

1. The Red Hat installation program uses the _____ file to determine the packages that are available in the `/RedHat/RPMS` directory for each category of package to be installed.

   a. `/RedHat/comps`

   b. `/RedHat/comp`

   c. `/RedHat/base/comps`

   d. `/RedHat/base/comp`

2. The _____ and _____ packages form a part of the base system of Linux operating system.

   a. `libc`

   b. `termcap`

   c. `lib`

   d. `termpack`

3. Select the three main sections of the `config` file.

   a. System info

   b. RedHat packages

   c. Post-installation shell commands

   d. Pre-installation shell commands

4. The list of packages that can be installed is available in the _____ file.

   a. `/RedHat/base/comps`

   b. `/RedHat/comps`

   c. `/RedHat/base/packages`

   d. `/RedHat/packages`

5. During Kickstart installation, which key combination will you use to view the system log console?

   a. Alt+F1

   b. Alt+F2

   c. Alt+F3

   d. Alt+F4

6. Which directory contains the man pages?

   a. `/etc`

   b. `/dev`

   c. `/bin`

   d. `/usr`

7. Which directory contains `mount` and `umount` utilities?

   a. `/etc`

   b. `/dev`

   c. `/bin`

   d. `/usr`

Answers

Multiple Choice Answers

1. The Red Hat installation program uses the /RedHat/base/comps file to determine the packages that are available in the /RedHat/RPMS directory—for each category of package to be installed.

2. The libc and termcap packages form a part of the base system of the Linux operating system.

3. The three main sections of the config file are system info, RedHat packages, and post-installation shell commands.

4. The list of packages that can be installed is available in the /RedHat/base/comps file.

5. During Kickstart installation, the Alt+F4 key combination is used to view the system log console.

6. The /usr directory contains the man pages.

7. The /bin directory contains mount and umount utilities.

Chapter 4

Linux
Administration

The job of an administrator, in relation to system and network administration, can be briefly described as follows:

◆ Managing users and groups on a host and network.

◆ Installing, uninstalling, and upgrading software packages.

◆ Configuring services and applications on a server or network.

◆ Monitoring network performance.

◆ Troubleshooting of system and network problems, and disaster recovery.

In this chapter, you will learn about various commands and tools that are critical for the proper administration of a Linux computer. The Linux OS comes with a large number of tools for system administrators' use. In this chapter, I discuss some of these tools to show you the various administrative tools available for configuring a server.

General Administration

You need to know some basic commands to manage your computer, users, and programs. Based on the tasks performed by an administrator, some aspects of administration of a Linux computer are listed here:

◆ Searching information

◆ System diagnostics

◆ Process control

◆ Daemon control

◆ Linuxconf

◆ Webmin

In this section, I'll discuss each of these aspects.

Searching for Information

At times, you need to search for specific files—such as files modified after a particular date—to generate statistical representations, and so on. The search command provided by Linux can be used effectively for extracting such information from the system. Some of the commands used by administrators for this purpose are grep, find, slocate, finger, which, whereis, and updatedb.

find

The find command searches for files in a directory and its subdirectories. This command searches the directory tree by evaluating an expression.

The syntax of the find command is as follows:

```
Find [path] [expression]
```

The [path] argument specifies the directory where the files matching the [expression] will be searched. If the path is not specified, the current directory is used for searching files. Similarly, if no expression is given, the expression -print is used, which prints the output on the screen. The find command exits with status 0 if all files are searched successfully. If an error occurs, a value greater than 0 is returned. For example, to search for all the files with the .txt extension in the current directory, you execute the following command:

```
find *.txt
```

Similarly, to find all the files in the root directory that were accessed in the last three days, you execute the following command:

```
find / -atime 3
```

You can use the find command to search for a file that might be created as a result of unauthorized user activity or some virus activity. In case of intrusion detection, this command can also be used to detect the files modified during a specific period.

grep

The grep command prints lines that match a specified pattern. You can specify different patterns by using the options available for the grep command. You can use the grep command to search for some specific strings in the log files. Thus, you can identify any unexpected entries in the log files. These entries could be created as a result of intrusions, virus attacks, or any other security breach. Two variant programs of the grep command, egrep and fgrep, are also available. The egrep command is the same as the grep -e command, and the fgrep command is the same as the grep -f command. The -e option of the grep command is used to search for specific patterns, while the -f option is used to search specified patterns from the selected file.

Input to the grep command can be provided in the form of a file name, output from another command, or directly as a parameter. The grep command accepts a number of parameters to perform search on the input data. The syntax of the grep command is shown here:

```
grep [options] [search_text] [filenames]
```

Some important parameters of the grep command are listed here:

◆ **-n.** This parameter returns the line(s) containing the search phrase along with the line number.

◆ **-v.** This parameter returns output that does not contain the search phrase or word.

◆ **^<word>.** This parameter returns all the lines starting with <word>.

◆ **<word>$.** This parameter returns all the lines ending with <word>.

slocate

The slocate (secure locate) command is the security-enhanced version of the GNU locate command. Secure locate provides a secure way to index and search quickly for files on your computer. It uses incremental encoding to compress its database to search faster. The command also stores file permissions and ownership details of files so that users will not be able to view files they do not have access to. The syntax of the slocate command is as follows:

```
slocate [options] [path] [search_string]
```

finger

The finger command displays information about the user. The following list tells you about the options of the finger command and the user information it displays.

◆ **-s.** This option displays the user's login name, real name, terminal name, write status, idle time, login time, office location, and office phone number. Login time is displayed as month, day, hours, and minutes. Unknown devices, as well as non-existent idle and login times, are displayed as single asterisks.

◆ **-l.** This option shows a multi-line format output that displays all information described for the -s option. This option also displays details of the user's home directory, home phone number, login shell, mail status, and the contents of the .plan, .project, and .forward files from the user's home directory.

Suppose that you have created a user named John, and you want to view his user information. To do so, you can execute the following command:

```
finger -ls john
```

The output of the preceding command looks like this:

```
Login: john                    Name: (null)
Directory: /home/john          Shell: /bin/bash
Never logged in.
No mail.
No Plan.
```

The `finger` command, when used by unauthorized users, can reveal user information. Therefore, its usage should be restricted.

which

The `which` command shows the full path of shell commands. This command takes one or more arguments. For each of the command's arguments, it prints to `stdout` the full path of the executables. These are executed when the arguments are entered at the shell prompt. The `which` command searches for an executable or script in the directories listed in the environment variable, `PATH`, using the same algorithm as `bash` (1). This command can be useful in detecting trojans. An administrator can find the exact location of the trojan that is present in the memory. This tool can also help to verify the correct location of files for a particular service.

For example, execute the following command:

```
which which
```

The output of the command is displayed here:

```
which    alias ¦ /usr/bin/which —tty-only —read-alias —show-dot —show-tilde
/usr/bin/which
```

whereis

The `whereis` command locates the binary, source, and manual page files for a command. The supplied names are first stripped of leading pathname components and any trailing extension. `whereis` then locates the desired program in a list of system directories in your Linux computer.

If you execute the following command:

```
whereis which
```

the following output is displayed:

```
whereis: /usr/bin/whereis
```

updatedb

The `updatedb` program updates the `slocate` database. `Updatedb` is simply a link to `slocate`, which implies the `-u` option.

An example of the usage of `updatedb` is displayed here:

```
updatedb -uv
```

System Diagnostics

Various commands are available for system diagnostics. These commands enable you to obtain information about your computer—for example, the amount of disk space being used. Some system diagnostics commands are `df`, `du`, `free`, `ipcs`, `tload`, `runlevel`, and `vmstat`. These commands are explained in detail in this section.

df

The df command is used to generate a report on disk space usage. The df command displays the amount of disk space available on the file system. If you do not provide any file name, the df command displays the space available on the mounted file systems. Disk space is shown in 1K blocks by default, unless the environment variable POSIXLY_CORRECT is set, in which case 512-byte blocks are used.

The syntax of the df command is as follows:

```
df [options] [filesystems] [files]
```

In the syntax, filesystems is the name of the device on which the file system resides, the directory on which the file system is mounted, or the relative path name of a file system. The files parameter specifies a file or a directory that is not a mount point.

The output of the df -a command is displayed as you see here:

Filesystem	1k-blocks	Used	Available	Use%	Mounted on
/dev/hda1	3028552	2703660	171048	95%	/
none	0	0	0	-	/proc
usbdevfs	0	0	0	-	/proc/bus/usb
none	0	0	0	-	/dev/pts
automount(pid505)	0	0	0	-	/misc

du

The du command reports the amount of disk space used by the specified files or directories. The syntax of the command is as follows:

```
du [OPTION] [FILE]
```

With no arguments, the du command reports the disk space for the current directory. Normally, the disk space is printed in units of 1024 bytes, but this can be overridden. Following is a sample output of the du command:.

```
4        ./.bash_logout
4        ./.bash_profile
4        ./.bashrc
```

```
_ _ _ _ _ _ _ _
_ _ _ _ _ _ _ _
_ _ _ _ _ _ _ _ .
32      ./e -{NAME} as the format string. To
12      ./name and  distribution  information  in
32      ./talled package named <package_name>.
24      ./grep.txt
6144    .
```

free

The free command displays the amount of free and used memory in your computer. This command displays the total amount of free and used physical and swap memory in the computer—as well as the shared memory and buffers being used by the kernel.

The syntax of the free command is given here:

```
free [options]
```

The output of the free -b command is displayed below:

	total	used	free	shared	buffers	cached
Mem:	129781760	125329408	4452352	108756992	16285696	28430336
-/+ buffers/cache:	80613376	49168384				
Swap:	108339200	5545984	102793216			

ipcs

The ipcs command provides information on Inter Process Communication (IPC) facilities for which the calling process has read access.

The syntax of the ipcs command is shown here:

```
ipcs [options]
```

The -i option allows a specific resource ID to be specified. Only information on this ID will be printed. Resources can be specified as follows:

◆ -m for shared memory segments

◆ -q for message queues

◆ -s for semaphore arrays

◆ -a for all

The output format can be specified using these options:

◆ -t for time

◆ -p for pid

◆ -c for creator

◆ -l for limits

◆ -u for summary

The output of the ipcs -a command is displayed here:

```
——— Shared Memory Segments ————
key             shmid     owner     perms     bytes      nattch      status
0x00000000      8193      root      777       196608     2           dest
0x00000000      11266     root      777       196608     2           dest
0x00000000      29699     root      777       196608     2           dest
0x00000000      32772     root      777       196608     2           dest
0x00000000      410629    root      777       196608     2           dest
0x00000000      218119    root      777       196608     2           dest
0x00000000      221192    root      777       196608     2           dest
——— Semaphore Arrays ————
key             semid owner    perms     nsems      status
——— Message Queues ————
key             msqid owner    perms     used-bytes      messages
```

runlevel

The `runlevel` command is used to find the current and previous system `runlevel`. *Runlevels* are stages when various features and services become available in Linux. This command first reads the system utmp file to locate the `runlevel` record, and then prints the runlevel. By default, the system utmp file is `/var/run/utmp`. If there is no previous system `runlevel`, `N` is printed instead. The usage of the `runlevel` command is as follows:

```
runlevel
```

init

You use the `init` command to change the `runlevels` in Linux. Information about the `runlevel` settings can be found in the `/etc/inittab` file. An abstraction of this file is given here:

```
# Default runlevel. The runlevels used by RHS are:
#    0 - halt (Do NOT set initdefault to this)
#    1 - Single user mode
#    2 - Multiuser, without NFS. This is same as runlevel 3, if your computer is
not connected to a network.
#    3 - Full multiuser mode
#    4 - unused
#    5 - X11
#    6 - reboot (Do NOT set initdefault to this)
#
id:5:initdefault:
# System initialization.
si::sysinit:/etc/rc.d/rc.sysinit
# Things to run in every runlevel.
ud::once:/sbin/update
# Trap CTRL-ALT-DELETE
ca::ctrlaltdel:/sbin/shutdown -t3 -r now
# When our UPS tells us power has failed, assume we have a few minutes
# of power left.  Schedule a shutdown for 2 minutes from now.
# This does, of course, assume you have powered installed and your
# UPS connected and working correctly.
pf::powerfail:/sbin/shutdown -f -h +2 "Power Failure; System Shutting Down"
```

```
# If power was restored before the shutdown kicked in, cancel it.
pr:12345:powerokwait:/sbin/shutdown -c "Power Restored; Shutdown Cancelled"
# Run gettys in standard runlevels
1:2345:respawn:/sbin/mingetty tty1
2:2345:respawn:/sbin/mingetty tty2
3:2345:respawn:/sbin/mingetty tty3
4:2345:respawn:/sbin/mingetty tty4
5:2345:respawn:/sbin/mingetty tty5
6:2345:respawn:/sbin/mingetty tty6
```

The syntax for changing the runlevel is shown here:

```
init <runlevel_number>
```

Services start at certain runlevels when the computer is switched on. When the boot process is complete, all services that are defined in the /etc/inittab file should start at appropriate runlevels. The initdefault action in the inittab file determines the runlevel that should be entered after system boot. The sysinit action is executed during the system boot before any boot or bootwait entries. This command saves administrators a lot of effort and time spent on restarting computers during troubleshooting and disaster recovery.

tload

The tload command presents the average system load in graphical mode. This command prints to the specified terminal a graph of the current average system load. The -scale option allows a vertical scale to be specified for the display, which means that a smaller value represents a larger scale, and vice versa. The -delay option sets the delay (in seconds) between graph updates. The syntax of the tload command is displayed here:

```
tload [-V] [-s scale] [ -d delay ] [tty]
```

The output of the tload command is printed to the specified [tty].

vmstat

The vmstat command reports virtual memory statistics. This command reports information about processes, memory, paging, block IO, traps, and CPU activity. The first report produced by this command gives all averages since the last reboot.

The syntax of the vmstat command is as follows:

```
vmstat [-n / -V] [delay] [count]
```

In the syntax, the -n option causes the header to be displayed only once. The -V option displays the version information, delay specifies the number of seconds between updates, and count is the number of updates.

The output of the vmstat command is displayed here:

procs						memory	swap		io		system		cpu		
r	b	w	swpd	free	buff	cache	si	so	bi	bo	in	cs	us	sy	id
0	0	0	5392	3492	15268	29108	0	0	0	1	113	18	0	0 100

Process Control

Some of the commands used to control processes running on a Linux computer are fuser, kill, killall, ps, pstree, and top.

fuser

The fuser command displays the process IDs (PIDs) of processes by using the specified files or file systems. The fuser command, when executed, will display a letter after each file in the output. These letters indicate the access of the files. The letters that you can use for access types are listed here:

- ♦ c denotes the current directory.
- ♦ e denotes the executable that is being run.
- ♦ f denotes that it is an open file.
- ♦ r denotes that the file is the root directory.
- ♦ m denotes that the file is mapped or shared.

The fuser command returns a non-zero return code if none of the files specified are accessed—or in case of a fatal error.

kill

The kill command is used to terminate a process. The kill command sends a signal to the process that it needs to kill. The command must also include the Process IP(pid) of the application that needs to be terminated. If somehow the kill command fails to terminate an application, then the more forceful -9 signal can be used to terminate the application forcefully. `kill` is a forceful way to terminate a process. If you do not specify a signal with the `kill` command, the TERM signal is sent. The processes that don't catch this signal are killed by the TERM signal. Programs similar to `kill` are available in modern shells.

killall

The `killall` command kills processes by name. This command sends a signal to all running processes. If no signal name is specified, SIGTERM is sent. Signals can be specified either by name or by number. For example, a signal specified by name can be written as -HUP, and a signal specified by number can be -1. HUP and 1 are the same. Signal 0 can be specified only by number. If you specify a slash with the command, it will kill the process that is executed from a specified file. The `killall` command will return a non-zero value if no process is killed.

ps

The `ps` command is used to identify the status of a process. This command gives information such as the process ID and the TTY number of the current process. The output of the `ps` command is displayed here:

```
PID      TTY          TIME      CMD
13238    pts/1        00:00:00  bash
13415    pts/1        00:00:00  ps
```

pstree

The `pstree` command displays a tree of processes. Running processes are displayed as trees. The tree is rooted at either `pid` or `init`. If you specify a username with the command, the processes owned by that user are displayed. The output of the `pstree` command is displayed here:

```
init-+-apmd
     |-atd
     |-automount
     |-crond
     |-deskguide_apple
     |-gdm-+-X
     |       `-gdm---gnome-session
     |-gmc
```

```
¦-gnome-name-serv
¦-gnome-smproxy
¦-gnome-terminal-+-csh——mc
¦                    `-gnome-pty-helpe
¦-gpm
¦-httpd——8*[httpd]
¦-identd——identd——3*[identd]
¦-kflushd
¦-khubd
¦-klogd
¦-kpiod
¦-ksnapshot——csh
¦-kswapd
¦-kupdate
¦-lockd——rpciod
¦-magicdev
¦-mdrecoveryd
¦-6*[mingetty]
¦-miniserv.pl——3*[miniserv.pl]
¦-netscape-commun——netscape-commun
¦-panel
¦-portmap
¦-rhnsd
¦-rpc.statd
¦-sawfish
¦-sendmail
¦-sshd
¦-syslogd
¦-tasklist_applet
¦-xfs
`-xinetd——in.telnetd——login——bash——pstree
```

top

The top command displays the most CPU-intensive tasks. This command provides a continuously updated list of processes. The top command can sort the running tasks based on the CPU, memory usage, and runtime required. In addition, it enables you to manipulate processes through an interactive interface.

The output of the top command is displayed here:

```
11:24am  up 3 days, 14:45,  4 users,  load average: 0.00, 0.00, 0.00
77 processes: 75 sleeping, 1 running, 1 zombie, 0 stopped
CPU states:  0.0% user,  1.1% system,  0.0% nice, 98.8% idle
Mem:   126740K av,  123612K used,    3128K free,  111060K shrd,   12684K buff
Swap:  105800K av,    5392K used,  100408K free                   30460K cached
```

PID	USER	PRI	NI	SIZE	RSS	SHARE	STAT	%CPU	%MEM	TIME	COMMAND
13417	amit	8	0	1048	1048	816	S	0.5	0.8	0:04	top
13455	root	16	0	1048	1048	816	R	0.5	0.8	0:00	top
1	root	0	0	420	412	364	S	0.0	0.3	0:04	init
2	root	0	0	0	0	0	SW	0.0	0.0	0:00	kflushd
3	root	0	0	0	0	0	SW	0.0	0.0	0:00	kupdate
4	root	0	0	0	0	0	SW	0.0	0.0	0:00	kpiod
5	root	0	0	0	0	0	SW	0.0	0.0	0:01	kswapd
6	root	20	-20	0	0	0	SW<	0.0	0.0	0:00	mdrecoveryd
61	root	0	0	0	0	0	SW	0.0	0.0	0:00	khubd
387	root	0	0	596	596	496	S	0.0	0.4	0:00	syslogd
397	root	0	0	776	772	368	S	0.0	0.6	0:00	klogd
412	rpc	0	0	508	504	416	S	0.0	0.3	0:00	portmap
428	root	0	0	0	0	0	SW	0.0	0.0	0:00	lockd
429	root	0	0	0	0	0	SW	0.0	0.0	0:00	rpciod
439	rpcuser	0	0	724	724	612	S	0.0	0.5	0:00	rpc.statd
454	root	0	0	424	420	360	S	0.0	0.3	0:00	apmd
505	root	0	0	572	572	472	S	0.0	0.4	0:00	automount

User Management

Managing users is certainly high on the to-do list of system administrators. You might need to add, modify, and delete users from your computer or networks. Before I discuss the actual commands to perform these tasks, I talk about a few files and directories that contain general user information.

◆ **/etc/defaults/useradd.** This file contains the default settings of a new user. The content of the useradd file is as follows:

```
# useradd defaults file
GROUP=100
HOME=/home
INACTIVE=-1
```

```
EXPIRE=
SHELL=/bin/bash
SKEL=/etc/skel
```

◆ **/etc/login.defs.** This file contains the default logon details for a new user. The content of the login.defs file is as follows:

```
# *REQUIRED*
#   Directory where mailboxes reside, _or_ name of file, relative to the
#   home directory.  If you _do_ define both, MAIL_DIR takes precedence.
#   QMAIL_DIR is for Qmail
#
#QMAIL_DIR        Maildir
MAIL_DIR          /var/spool/mail
#MAIL_FILE        .mail
# Password aging controls:
#
#         PASS_MAX_DAYS   Maximum number of days a password may be used.
#         PASS_MIN_DAYS   Minimum number of days allowed between password changes.
#         PASS_MIN_LEN    Minimum acceptable password length.
#         PASS_WARN_AGE   Number of days warning given before a password expires.
#
PASS_MAX_DAYS   99999
PASS_MIN_DAYS   0
PASS_MIN_LEN    5
PASS_WARN_AGE   7
#
# Min/max values for automatic uid selection in useradd
#
UID_MIN                   500
UID_MAX                 60000
#
# Min/max values for automatic gid selection in groupadd
#
GID_MIN                   500
GID_MAX                 60000
#
# If defined, this command is run when removing a user.
# It should remove any at/cron/print jobs etc. owned by
```

```
# the user to be removed (passed as the first argument).
#
#USERDEL_CMD     /usr/sbin/userdel_local
#
# If useradd should create home directories for users by default
# On RH systems, we do. This option is ORed with the -m flag on
# useradd command line.
#
CREATE_HOME     yes
```

- ◆ **/etc/group.** This file contains the computer group information for all groups of users.
- ◆ **/home.** This directory specifies the home directory for each user.
- ◆ **/etc/skel.** This directory forms the blueprint for all new users. Whenever a new user is created, this is the initial directory structure that is created for the user's home directory.

Now you're ready for the commands that help you manage users and groups. Some of these commands are listed here:

- *   useradd
- *   usermod
- *   userdel
- *   groupadd
- *   groupdel
- *   groupmod

The following sections discuss each of these commands in detail.

useradd

The useradd command is used to create or update new user information. The syntax of the useradd command is as follows:

```
useradd [-c comment] [-d home_dir] [-e expire_date] [-f inactive_time] [-g ini-
tial_group] [-G group[,...]] [-m [-k skeleton_dir] ¦ -M] [-p passwd] [-s shell] [-u
uid [ -o]] [-n] [-r] login
useradd -D [-g default_group] [-b default_home] [-f default_inactive] [-e
default_expire_date] [-s default_shell]
```

The second syntax uses the -D option. When you execute the useradd command in the second syntax, a new user is created with the values specified with the command. Some default values are provided by the system. Depending on the command line options, the details of the new user account are entered into the system files as needed, the home directory is created, and initial files are copied. The version of this command that is provided with Red Hat Linux, creates a group for each user added to the system, unless the -n option is given.

An example of the useradd command is given here:

```
useradd -p user$123 David
```

This example creates a user named David and sets the user's password.

usermod

The usermod command is used to modify a user account. The syntax for the usermod command is given here:

```
usermod [-c comment] [-d home_dir [ -m]] [-e expire_date] [-f inactive_time] [-g
initial_group] [-G group[,...]] [-l login_name] [-p passwd] [-s shell] [-u uid [ -
o]] [-L¦-U] login
```

Remember that while executing the usermod command, you cannot change the username of the currently logged users. You should also ensure that there is no running process owned by the user whose user account details are being changed.

userdel

The userdel command is used to delete a user account and related files. The syntax for the userdel command is shown here:

```
userdel [-r] login
```

The userdel command modifies the system account files and deletes the entries that refer to the given login. The named login must exist.

This command will not allow you to delete an account if the user is currently logged in. You must first kill any running processes that belong to the account you are deleting. If the user to be deleted is an NIS client, you cannot remove any Network Information Service (NIS) attributes of the user from your computer. This must be performed on the NIS server.

The command to delete the user, David, is given here:

```
userdel -r David
```

groupadd

The `groupadd` command creates a new group. The syntax for the `groupadd` command is as follows:

```
groupadd [-g gid [-o]] [-r] [-f] group
```

When you execute this command, a new group with the details specified with the command is created. The new group will be updated in the system files as needed.

groupdel

The `groupdel` command is used to delete a group. The syntax for the `groupdel` command is shown here:

```
groupdel group
```

This command modifies the system account files, deleting all entries that refer to that group. You must manually check all file systems to ensure that no files remain with the named group as the file group ID.

groupmod

The `groupmod` command is used to modify a group. You can modify attributes of a group, such as the group ID and the group name. The syntax for the `groupmod` command is as follows:

```
groupmod [-g gid [-o]] [-n group_name ] group
```

This command modifies the system account files to reflect the changes that are specified on the command line.

You have seen various commands to manage users and groups. The information regarding users is stored in the /etc/skel directory. This directory contains files that determine the user settings.

You can view the content of the /etc/skel directory by executing the following command:

```
ls -la /etc/skel
```

The following output is displayed:

```
total 40
drwxr-xr-x    4 root     root        4096 Feb 27 21:27 .
drwxr-xr-x   57 root     root        4096 May 11 14:55 ..
-rw-r—r—      1 root     root          24 Aug 22  2000 .bash_logout
-rw-r—r—      1 root     root         230 Aug 22  2000 .bash_profile
-rw-r—r—      1 root     root         124 Aug 22  2000 .bashrc
-rw-r—r—      1 root     root         688 Aug 25  2000 .emacs
drwxr-xr-x    3 root     root        4096 Feb 27 21:21 .kde
-rw-r—r—      1 root     root         321 Aug 14  2000 .kderc
-rw-r—r—      1 root     root        3651 Aug 15  2000 .screenrc
drwxr-xr-x    5 root     root        4096 Feb 27 21:21 Desktop
```

The /etc/.bash_profile file stores the local system configuration for bash, which controls the environment variables and programs that are run when bash is executed. These environment variables and functions are specific only to the currently logged on user and they do not affect other users. This file is executed immediately after the global configuration file /etc/profile. Unlike the /etc/profile file, which affects all users except csh derived shells, /etc/.bash_profile affects only the user who is running bash.

The command to view the .bash_profile file is as follows:

```
cat /etc/skel/.bash_profile
```

The content of the .bash_profile file is displayed:

```
# .bash_profile
# Get the aliases and functions
if [ -f ~/.bashrc ]; then
        . ~/.bashrc
fi
# User specific environment and startup programs
PATH=$PATH:$HOME/bin
BASH_ENV=$HOME/.bashrc
USERNAME=""
export USERNAME BASH_ENV PATH
```

Daemon Control

In Greek mythology, *daemon* means supernatural being. In Linux, daemons are invisible programs that run in the background. A daemon is not attached to any terminal, because no output on the screen is expected from it. The common functions of daemons are to do the following:

◆ Serve other client programs

◆ Publish information as required by other programs

◆ Assist other programs in accessing a resource on the computer

◆ Enable two individual programs to communicate with each other

A user might never need to know about a daemon. But, for an administrator, knowledge of daemons is critical.

Daemons can be invoked by using any of the following methods:

◆ `rc` script at boot time

◆ `init` method at boot time

◆ `inetd` daemon

◆ `tcpd`

Daemons are usually associated with a network port. A network port is an isolated channel through which a particular daemon sends or receives information. For example, an http daemon will have the port 80 attached to it. Therefore, if an http server is attached to port 80, and a domain, for example, `www.abc.com` is hosted on it, typing `http://www.abc.com` or `http://www.abc.com:80` would display the same output in the Web browser.

Some default ports have been assigned to various daemons, as given here:

◆ HTTP to port 80

◆ Post office protocol (POP) to port 110

◆ Simple Mail Transfer Protocol (SMTP) to port 25

◆ File Transfer Protocol (FTP) to port 21

◆ Telnet to port 23

The `/etc/service` file should contain information about the ports and daemons on your system.

The purpose of a daemon is to serve the system while working in the background. A mechanism exists that allows daemons to start and shut down without human intervention. This is accomplished by the `inetd` daemon, which is a special daemon that monitors the ports of a computer. The `inetd` daemon invokes the appropriate daemon, according to the schedule. The `/etc/inetd` file has information about all the daemons that are under the control of `inetd`.

You can set new daemons to work under `inetd` by adding the appropriate fields in `/etc/inetd`. The file has seven fields to configure various aspects of the daemon:

- **Service.** This is the name of the daemon. This name should also be listed in the list of services, defined in `/etc/services` file.
- **Socket_type.** This can be one of the following values:
  `dgram, raw, rdm,` and `seqpacket.`
- **Protocol.** This specifies the protocol the daemon will use. All available protocols are listed in `/etc/protocols`.
- **Wait/nowait.** This field is either `wait` or `nowait`. This field is used for the datagram sockets only. If a datagram server frees the datagram socket after connecting to a peer, the `nowait` value is used. The `nowait` value indicates that the socket is free to receive messages. The `wait` value is used for the datagram servers that process all incoming datagrams on the socket.
- **User.** This field specifies the username under which this daemon will run. Each daemon is associated with a user name. The access permissions for the user also apply to the daemon.
- **Program.** This is the name of the executable file of the daemon.
- **Argument.** This contains the command line arguments that are passed to the server when the command is executed.

There are many daemons available in standard Linux distributions. Descriptions of some of the important daemons are given here:

- **fingerd.** This daemon maintains information that can be retrieved using the `finger` command.
- **gated.** This daemon provides services for routing protocols.
- **gdc.** This daemon controls the gated daemon.
- **syslogd.** This daemon maintains a log for the system.

◆ **klogd.** This daemon listens to messages from the kernel and prioritizes and processes OS messages.

◆ **lpd.** This daemon services line printer requests.

◆ **mountd.** This daemon controls NFS-mounted drives.

◆ **named.** This is an Internet Domain Name Service (DNS) daemon. This daemon is used to provide name resolution services.

◆ **identd.** This daemon services all programs that require TCP/IP identification protocol.

◆ **imapd.** This daemon controls remote mail access.

◆ **inetd.** This daemon invokes other daemons as listed and configured in the `/etc/inetd.conf`.

◆ **pppd.** This daemon controls Point-to-Point protocol communications.

◆ **rexecd.** This daemon handles remote execution of commands.

◆ **rlogin.** This daemon provides services that allow users to login to the system from a remote location.

◆ **rcmd.** This daemon provides assistance in execution of commands given from remote locations.

◆ **rshd.** This daemon also provides assistance in execution of commands given from remote locations.

◆ **talk.** This daemon enables communication between users.

◆ **telnetd.** This daemon serves telnet clients.

◆ **tftpd.** This daemon services `tftp` requests.

◆ **ftpd.** This daemon services requests from the `ftp` clients.

Linuxconf

Linuxconf is a sophisticated administration system for the Linux operating system. With this system, you can perform almost all administrative tasks. You can configure the following items by using Linuxconf:

1. Networking (client)

    ◆ Basic TCP/IP setup

    ◆ Routing

    ◆ DNS location

- ◆ NIS client
- ◆ IPX (Novell setup)
- ◆ PPP and SLIP dialout

2. Networking (server)
   - ◆ Boot services: RARP and DHCP
   - ◆ DNS
   - ◆ IP Aliasing
   - ◆ NFS
   - ◆ Mail
   - ◆ Uucp

3. User account
4. File systems (partitions)
5. Boot mode
   - ◆ LILO
   - ◆ Boot runlevel

Linuxconf also can be run from the command line. You need to execute the `Linuxconf` command at the command prompt. Linuxconf has several aliases, which allows you to enter directly into one of its functional areas. These include the following:

- ◆ **domainname.** Prints and sets the NIS domain name.
- ◆ **dnsconf.** Displays the main menu of the DNS configure program.
- ◆ **fixperm.** Ensures that the critical files and directories have proper ownership and permissions.
- ◆ **fsconf.** Displays the file system's configuration menu.
- ◆ **hostname.** Prints and sets the hostname.
- ◆ **Linuxconf.** Activates Linuxconf's main menu.
- ◆ **passwd.** Allows you to change your password or the password of other users, if you are the root user.
- ◆ **netconf.** Directs you to the networking submenu of Linuxconf.
- ◆ **userconf.** Takes you directly to the user configuration menu.
- ◆ **The WWW Interface.** Allows you to operate Linuxconf from a Web browser. To do this, type the following address in the address bar:

```
http://<computer_name>:98/
```

The menu structure is the same across all three interfaces: command line, GUI, and the Web browser interface. The advantage of the Web interface is that you can set bookmarks to permit rapid movement to specific configuration screens.

When you execute Linuxconf at the command prompt, the Linuxconf interface, shown in Figure 4-1, is displayed.

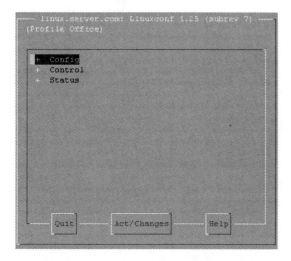

FIGURE 4-1 *The Linuxconf interface.*

As shown in Figure 4-1, the main menu displays the following items:

◆ Config

◆ Control

◆ Status

The following section discusses these menu items one by one.

Config

The options in the Config menu are listed here:

- ◆ Networking
- ◆ User accounts
- ◆ File systems
- ◆ Miscellaneous services
- ◆ Boot mode

These submenus are displayed in Figure 4-2.

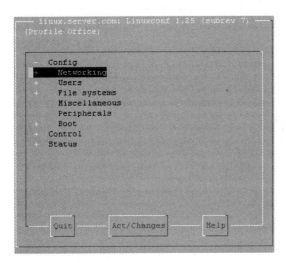

FIGURE 4-2 *The Config menu.*

The Networking submenu provides you with options for configuring your network. The options of the Networking submenus are shown here:

- ◆ **Client tasks.** The Client tasks submenu enables you to specify basic host information and details of the DNS server that will be used to resolve IP addresses.

◆ **Routing and gateways.** The Routing and gateways submenu allows you to configure the routing options for your Linux computer. The screen to specify the default gateway and enable IP routing is displayed in Figure 4-3.

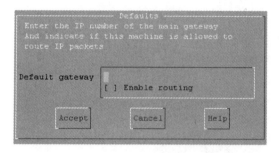

FIGURE 4-3 *The default gateway and routing screen.*

◆ **Host name search path.** The Host name search path submenu allows you to specify the order in which the name services, such as NIS and DNS, will be probed (see Figure 4-4).

FIGURE 4-4 *The Name service access screen.*

◆ **Network Information service.** The Network Information service submenu enables you to specify the NIS domain and NIS server. The screen
to configure the network information service is displayed in Figure 4-5.

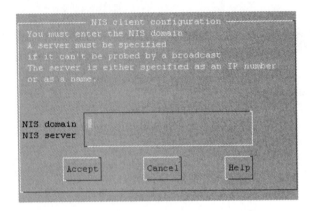

FIGURE 4-5 *The NIS client configuration screen.*

◆ **Remote mail servers (fetchmail).** This enables you to configure mail
servers. The screen for configuring the mail server is displayed in
Figure 4-6.

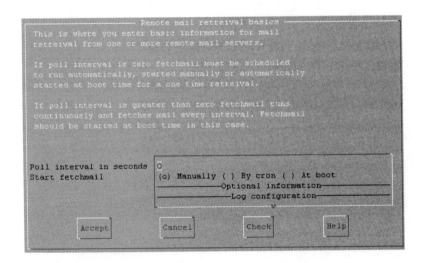

FIGURE 4-6 *The Remote mail retrieval basics screen.*

◆ **Server tasks.** Server tasks enable you to configure export file systems and IP aliases for virtual hosts. The screen for specifying IP aliases is displayed in Figure 4-7.

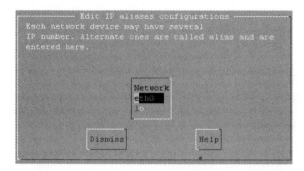

FIGURE 4-7 *The Edit IP aliases configurations screen.*

◆ **Misc.** This selection allows you to specify information about other hosts and networks. It also allows you to specify which networks or hosts are allowed to access Linuxconf to configure your computer.

The options within the User Accounts menu (refer to Figure 4-2) are displayed in Figure 4-8.

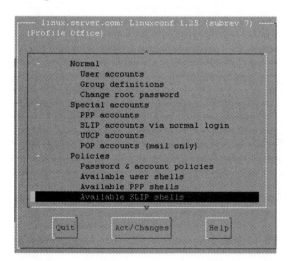

FIGURE 4-8 *The Options within User Accounts submenu.*

The User Accounts submenu provides you with options to configure and manage user accounts. The options in the user accounts submenu are as follows:

◆ **Normal.** This option allows you to add, modify, or delete users and groups. It also allows you to change the root password. The screen for managing groups is displayed in Figure 4-9.

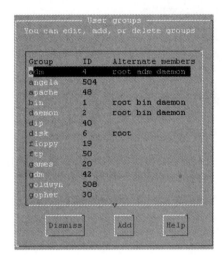

FIGURE 4-9 *The User groups screen.*

◆ **Special Accounts.** This option allows you to manage Point-to-Point Protocol (PPP), Serial Line Internet Protocol (SLIP), Unix-to-Unix Copy Protocol (UUCP), and Post Office Protocol (POP) accounts.

◆ **Policies.** This option enables you to configure password and account policies for users. After the password policy is set, a user will not be able to set a password that does not fulfill the requirements of the password policy. This option also allows you to manage user, PPP, and SLIP shells. The Password/Account setting policies screen is displayed in Figure 4-10.

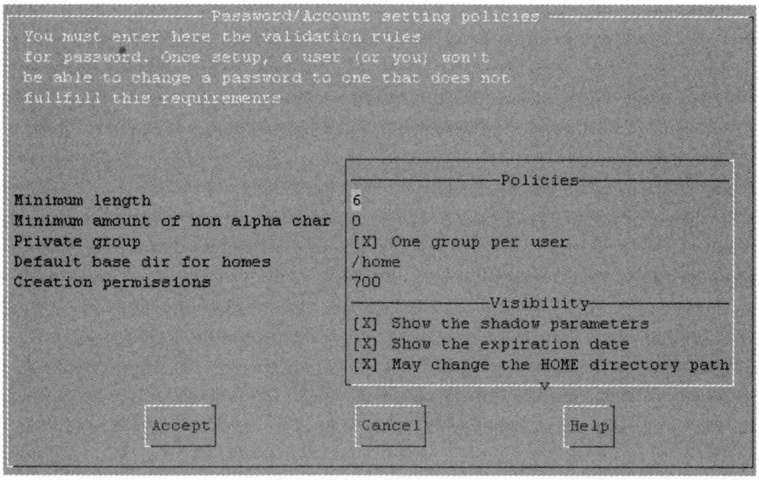

```
───────────── Password/Account setting policies ─────────────
You must enter here the validation rules
for password. Once setup, a user (or you) won't
be able to change a password to one that does not
fulfill this requirements


                                    ┌─────────────Policies─────────────
Minimum length                      │ 6
Minimum amount of non alpha char    │ 0
Private group                       │ [X] One group per user
Default base dir for homes          │ /home
Creation permissions                │ 700
                                    ├─────────────Visibility───────────
                                    │ [X] Show the shadow parameters
                                    │ [X] Show the expiration date
                                    │ [X] May change the HOME directory path
                                    │              v

        ┌────────┐        ┌────────┐        ┌────────┐
        │ Accept │        │ Cancel │        │ Help   │
        └────────┘        └────────┘        └────────┘
```

FIGURE 4-10 *The Password/Account setting policies screen.*

The Files systems submenu enables you to manage various drives and devices mounted on your computer. It also allows you to check file permissions. The options in the File systems submenu are displayed in Figure 4-11.

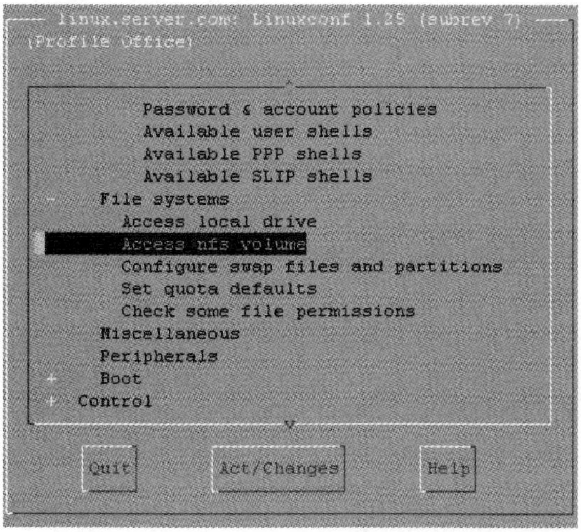

```
──── linux.server.com: Linuxconf 1.25 (subrev 7) ────
(Profile Office)

                              ^
            Password & account policies
            Available user shells
            Available PPP shells
            Available SLIP shells
  -    File systems
            Access local drive
   █        Access nfs volume
            Configure swap files and partitions
            Set quota defaults
            Check some file permissions
       Miscellaneous
       Peripherals
  +    Boot
  +  Control
                              v

        ┌──────┐    ┌─────────────┐    ┌──────┐
        │ Quit │    │ Act/Changes │    │ Help │
        └──────┘    └─────────────┘    └──────┘
```

FIGURE 4-11 *The options in the File systems submenu.*

Boot mode enables you to configure the boot options for your computer. The options in the boot mode are displayed in Figure 4-12.

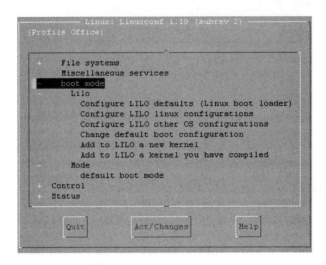

FIGURE 4-12 *The options in boot mode.*

Control

The options in the Control menu are used to configure various settings in your computer. These options are displayed in Figure 4-13.

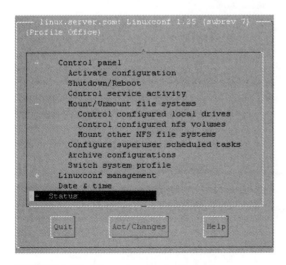

FIGURE 4-13 *The options in the Control menu.*

Status

The Status option displays various messages and logs generated when you are using your computer. The options in the Status menu are displayed in Figure 4-14.

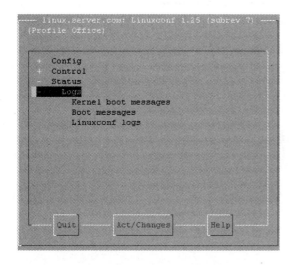

FIGURE 4-14 *The options in the Status menu.*

The screen in Figure 4-15 displays the kernel boot messages.

```
------------------------- Kernel boot messages -------------------------

  Linux version 2.4.7-10 (bhcompile@stripples.devel.redhat.com) (gcc versio
  BIOS-provided physical RAM map:
   BIOS-e820: 0000000000000000 - 000000000009fc00 (usable)
   BIOS-e820: 000000000009fc00 - 00000000000a0000 (reserved)
   BIOS-e820: 00000000000e0000 - 0000000000100000 (reserved)
   BIOS-e820: 0000000000100000 - 0000000007f00000 (usable)
   BIOS-e820: 00000000feea0000 - 0000000100000000 (reserved)
  Scanning bios EBDA for MXT signature
  On node 0 totalpages: 32512
  zone(0): 4096 pages.
  zone(1): 28416 pages.
  zone(2): 0 pages.
  Kernel command line: auto BOOT_IMAGE=linux ro root=301 BOOT_FILE=/boot/vm
  Initializing CPU#0
  Detected 498.497 MHz processor.
                              v
                        Dismiss
```

FIGURE 4-15 *The Kernel boot message screen.*

RedHat Package Manager

The RedHat Package Manager (rpm) is a powerful and flexible package manager. You can use rpm to build, install, query, verify, update, and uninstall various packages. A package consists of an archive of files. The package also contains other information, such as name, version, and description of the package. The syntax for rpm to install a package is shown here:

```
rpm -i [install_options] <package_file>
```

The syntax to upgrade a package by using rpm is as follows:

```
rpm -u [install_options] <package_file>
```

The preceding command will upgrade a package already installed on the computer. When the command is executed, the previous versions of the package are removed from the computer. The <package_file> in the preceding command can be specified as an FTP server or an HTTP URL. The package will be downloaded from the specified location before installation starts.

You can obtain information about a package by using the -q option of the rpm command:

```
rpm -q [query_options]
```

The format in which the packet will be printed can be specified.

You also can verify a package by using the rpm manager. The rpm manager verifies a package by comparing the details of the already installed package with the original package stored in the rpm manager. Packages are also verified by comparing the size, MD5 sum, permissions, type, owner, and group of each file. The syntax for an rpm command to verify a package is as follows:

```
rpm -v ¦ -y ¦ —verify [verify-options]
```

The general form of an rpm signature check command is shown here:

```
rpm —checksig <package_file>
```

The preceding command will check the PGP signature of package <package_file> to ensure its integrity and origin. PGP configuration information is read from configuration files. After you do this, you can build a package by issuing the following command:

```
rpm -[b¦t]O [build-options] <package_spec>
```

In the preceding syntax, you use the -b argument if a spec file is being used to build the package. Similarly, you use the -t argument if rpm needs to check in a gzipped tar file for the spec file to be used. The second argument, O, specifies the stages of building and packaging to be done.

Administration Utilities

Numerous administrative utilities are available for managing and maintaining a Linux computer. In this section, I discuss the following utilities:

◆ YaST

◆ Sudo

◆ Super

YaST

Yet Another Setup Tool (YaST) is a command line graphical interface that provides a user-friendly approach to many administrative tasks of Linux administration. However, it does not have the ability to restrict user access, which makes it useful for minimizing errors and allowing users to administer their systems. Unlike Linuxconf, YaST is not network aware, which means that you must log into each computer you want to manage.

Sudo

Superuser do (Sudo) allows a system administrator to give users, or groups of users, the ability to run commands as root users. Its features are listed here:

◆ Sudo restricts the commands a user can execute.

◆ Sudo logs details of each command being executed. When used along with syslogd, the system log daemon, Sudo can be configured to log all commands to a central host as well as to the local host. Sudo also can be configured to log all the attempts, whether successful or unsuccessful, of the commands being executed. In addition, sudo can also log errors generated while executing the command. These events are logged in the syslog (3) file. However, this log file is changeable.

◆ Sudo uses timestamp files to implement a timeout system. Users, upon invoking Sudo, are prompted for their password. Upon validation, they are granted a ticket for five minutes. This timeout is configurable at compile-time. Each subsequent Sudo command updates the ticket for another five minutes.

◆ The configuration file of Sudo, sudoers, is set up in such a manner that the same sudoers file may be used on many machines. This allows for central administration. However, the flexibility to define a user's privileges on a per-host basis is still available.

Sudo allows a user to execute a command as the superuser, as specified in the sudoers file. The uid and gid of the user are set to match those of the superuser, as specified in the passwd file. The /etc/sudoers file contains the list of authorized users. Sudo uses this file to validate users. If a user not listed in this file tries to log on, an error message is generated.

By default, Sudo requires that users be authenticated with a password. The authentication password is normally the user's password, not the root password. After a user has been authenticated, a timestamp is updated and the user can use Sudo without a password for a permitted period of time. The prompt for password will also time out if the user's password is not entered within five minutes, unless it's overridden by a modification in the sudoers file. You can update the default timestamp by running the sudo command with the -v flag.

 NOTE

An e-mail message will not be sent if an unauthorized user tries to run Sudo with the -l or -v flags.

Sudo accepts the following command line options:

◆ **-V.** The -V (version) option is used to print the version number of Sudo. When executed by the root user, the -V option prints a list of defaults.

◆ **-l.** The -l (list) option is used to list the commands that are allowed or restricted for a user.

◆ **-L.** The -L (list defaults) option is used to display a list of the default parameters.

◆ **-h.** The -h (help) option is used to print a usage message.

◆ **-v.** The -v (validate) option is used to update the user's timestamp and, if necessary, prompts for the user's password. This extends the Sudo time-out for another five minutes or the time configured in the sudoers file.

◆ **-k.** The -k (kill) option is used to validate the user's timestamp. You need to specify a password if you run Sudo after specifying this option.

◆ **-K.** The -K (sure kill) option is used to remove a user's timestamp. This option does not require a password.

◆ **-b.** The -b (background) option is used to tell Sudo to run a command in the background.

◆ **-p.** The -p (prompt) option is used to override the default password prompt. You can also customize the password prompt.

◆ **-c.** The -c (class) option is used to run a specified command by the specified login class. The class argument can be a class name or a single dash (-) character. The class name is defined in the /etc/login.conf file. The command should be run as root if you specify an existing user.

◆ **-a.** The -a (authentication type) option is used to validate users with different authentication types. The authentication type to be used for a user is mentioned in the /etc/login.conf file.

◆ **-u.** The -u (user) option is used to run a specified command as a user other than the root user. Use #uid if you want to specify a uid instead of a username.

◆ **-s.** The -s (shell) option is used to run the shell specified by the SHELL environment variable.

◆ **-H.** The -H (HOME) option is used to set the HOME environment variable to the homedir of the specified user.

◆ **-P.** The -P (I) option is used to store the unmodified group vector of a user. The group vector is initialized to the groups to which the specified user belongs.

◆ **-S.** The -S (stdin) option is used to accept a password from standard input devices.

Super

Super is a tool that can be used to give users and groups varied levels of access for system administration. In addition to giving access to users, you can specify access time and the level of access to scripts. The access level you give is critical. For example, giving `setuid` access to ordinary commands could create unexpected consequences. Debian ships with super, and there are rpms available in the contrib directory. This is a powerful tool, but it requires a significant amount of effort to be implemented properly. The primary distribution site for super is `ftp://ftp.ucolick.org/pub/users/will/`.

Remote Administration

An administrator who manages only one server can afford to use the local administration tools alone, but a network administrator who has to manage many client computers and other hosts on a network cannot do without remote administration tools. You might need to remotely manage your Linux computer and other hosts of your network. Remote administration tools even allow an administrator to see the remote computer's desktop in a virtual window. There are many tools and utilities available to assist you in maintaining your system from a remote location. I discuss the following remote administration tools in this section:

◆ VNC
◆ Webmin
◆ cfengine

VNC

Virtual Network Computing (VNC) is a remote display system that enables you to view a computing desktop environment—not only on the computer where it is running, but also from a remote location.

Users use a VNC viewer to view Linux environments that are running on different computers. The computer running the Linux environment can be at a remote location. Some of the features of VNC are listed here:

◆ State is not stored at the VNC viewer. This means that you can shift to VNC viewers on different computers, reconnect to your desktop, and complete the task you were performing. All the information about the tasks that you were performing will be intact.

◆ VNC is a small and simple utility. It's about 150KB in size and can be stored and run from a floppy disk.

◆ No installation is needed.

◆ It is platform-independent. The VNC protocol is portable to any platform.

◆ VNC is shareable. Many VNC viewers can share a desktop.

◆ It is free. It is distributed under the terms of GNU Public License.

The VNC protocol is used to connect the VNC viewer and server. This is a protocol for remote access to GUIs. The VNC protocol is based on the remote framebuffer (RFB) model. Therefore, the framebuffer is updated on the VNC viewer. It is supported by almost all operating systems and applications.

VNC protocol has been designed to make very few demands from clients. It can be used with a variety of hardware. The implementation of the VNC clients has been simplified.

You can run Xvnc servers for various users at a time. Each user is represented by a VNC desktop. These desktops resemble an X display. In X display, there's a root window containing several X applications.

Connection Setup and Shutdown

When a connection between the VNC client and VNC server is established, the server requests authentication from the client by using a challenge-response scheme. In the challenge-response scheme, users are prompted for a password. The password provided by the user is verified and the server and client start exchanging information. The connection between the server and the client is stateless.

The VNC protocol uses port 59xx, where xx is the display number of the server. For example, a VNC server running on a computer with display number 1 will use the port 5911 for listening to the clients. You also can configure the remote VNC server as running on your local host. This can be done by configuring the port number, which the server uses to listen to the client, on the remote server.

Securing VNC

As discussed in the preceding section, VNC uses a challenge-response system to provide user authentication. The password is not sent over the network for authentication. Once the connection is established, however, the communication between the viewer and server is unencrypted. Therefore, any unauthorized user can easily gain access to the data being exchanged. To ensure security, you should tunnel the VNC protocol through a secure channel, such as SSH.

SSH encrypts the data that is being transferred by using the public key encryption. SSH is freely available for the Linux platform. It provides you a secure shell that displays a login window to a remote computer.

Compression

In addition to securing VNC, SSH can compress the data that is sent between the VNC server and the VNC client. This is particularly useful if the link between your computer and the server is slow. It can be helpful on a fast link where encryption happens. The encryption process takes some time, and it can slow down the link. Therefore, using SSH can help make up the time that is spent in encryption.

Webmin

Webmin is a Linux administration tool that provides you a Web-based interface for performing the administrative tasks. It provides you access to the administrative modules that are responsible for the maintenance and running of your Linux computer.

Beginners appreciate Webmin because it can manage almost all administrative tasks from a single location. You do not have to memorize or write down executable commands with numerous options and long file paths.

Installation

Webmin is a collection of CGI scripts. By default, Webmin is run on port number 1000. However, you can specify another port number during installation. Webmin supports distributions such as Red Hat, Solaris, Debian, SCO, and Mac OS X.

Every service or program on your Linux computer is connected through a set of modules. If the application you want to control from Webmin is not supported, you can build a new module for that application.

Webmin is distributed under the BSD license. However, if you build modules for it, the modules can be distributed under any license you choose. Therefore, Webmin is available to the Linux community for upgrades and modifications. You can download Webmin from `www.webmin.com/webmin`.

Webmin Interfaces

To access Webmin, you need to go to the IP address and the port number that you specified during installation. The default is 10000. For example, you can open the Webmin application by entering the following in the address bar of the Web browser:

```
http://<computer_name>:10000
```

You will be prompted for your login name and password. After authentication, the Webmin interface will be displayed. The Webmin interface is displayed in Figure 4-16.

FIGURE 4-16 *The Webmin interface.*

The Webmin interface has several tabs that provide access to various Webmin modules:

◆ The System tab manages tasks within the computer or server environment, such as disk quota, NIS, PAM, syslog, adding users, managing cron, managing NFS and changing boot services, processes, and restarting the machine.

◆ The Servers tab enables you to manage various servers on your Linux computer. The Servers tab of Webmin is displayed in Figure 4-17.

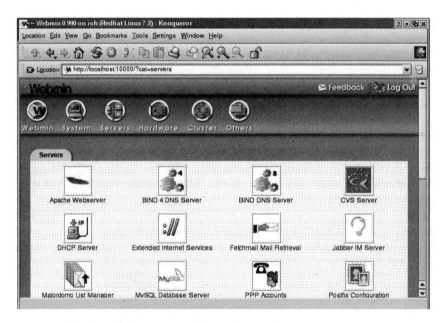

FIGURE 4-17 *The Servers page of the Webmin interface.*

◆ The Networking group enables you to specify ipchains. In addition, it enables you to manage permissions of network utilities such as ping, traceroute, whois, and dig.

◆ The Hardware tab handles hardware-related tasks. In this tab, you will find information about disk partitions, system time, network interface configurations, LILO, RAID, and so on.

Webmin has some built-in security features. You need to specify username and password before you are allowed to use Webmin. It supports SSL. You can limit users to the domains they or their groups own in the DNS module.

Webmin is not very safe because it is a Web-based tool. However, using a firewall can greatly reduce the risks of attack.

```
ipfwadm -I -a accept -P tcp -S 10.0.0.0/8 -D 0.0.0.0/0 10000
ipfwadm -I -a accept -P tcp -S this_is_some.trusted.host -D 0.0.0.0/0 10000
ipfwadm -I -a deny -P tcp -S 0.0.0.0/0 -D 0.0.0.0/0 10000
```

Webmin also can be firewalled using IPCHAINS:

```
ipchains -A input -p all -j ACCEPT -s 10.0.0.0/8 -d 0.0.0.0/0 10000
ipchains -A input -p all -j ACCEPT -s this_is_some.trusted.host -d 0.0.0.0/0 10000
ipchains -A input -p all -j DENY -s 0.0.0.0/0 -d 0.0.0.0/0 10000
```

cfengine

The `cfengine` tool is the result of a research project started in 1993 that was designed to help system administrators solve problems such as managing permissions for files and users in a large network. `cfengine` is a very high-level policy language, in which a single statement can result in hundreds of operations being performed on multiple hosts.

The `cfengine` tool manages the systems by using a high-level policy language. `cfengine` sets up and maintains BSD and System-5-like operating systems attached to a TCP/IP network.

`cfengine` enables you to create a centralized configuration system. You can use this system to manage configuration of the hosts in your network. To configure the hosts based on this system, an interpreter parses the master file. The configuration of each host is then checked. Any deviations from the defined configuration are fixed automatically. You do not need to mention host names. Instead, you can refer to the properties, which distinguish hosts from one another. It is a useful tool for managing old junk files and for making scripts to manage the access rights and permissions on your files. `cfengine` also contains a text editing language that can be used to edit text files.

Originally, `cfengine` was meant only for root users. However, it is increasingly being used by ordinary users as a scripting language.

`cfengine` focuses on a few key functions that are handled rather poorly from scripts. You can specify how your network should be configured from a single configuration file. `cfengine` then parses your file and executes the instructions. While executing the instructions, it generates warnings or fixes errors.

Some of the tasks that can be automated with `cfengine` are listed here:

◆ Mounting file systems

◆ Editing text files

◆ Checking and configuring the network interfaces

◆ Creating and maintaining symbolic links

◆ Managing junk files

◆ Checking and setting the permissions and ownership of files

◆ Executing user scripts and shell commands

Summary

In this chapter, you looked at the various aspects of Linux administration. I discussed several commands for information search, systems diagnostics, and process and daemon control. You looked at the output of some of these commands.

Linuxconf is a sophisticated administration system for the Linux operating system. In this chapter, you explored the numerous options to manage client, server, users, and file systems available in Linuxconf.

This chapter also discussed `rpm`, which is a powerful and flexible package manager. You can use `rpm` to build, install, query, verify, update, and uninstall various packages.

At times, you need tools and utilities to remotely manage your Linux computer and other hosts on your network. Three such tools—VNC, Webmin, and `cfengine`—were discussed in this chapter. VNC is a remote display system, which enables you to view a computing desktop environment. Webmin provides a Web-based interface with various modules. These modules communicate directly with standard programs and services on your Linux computer. `cfengine` builds systems with a declarative language and is used for setting up and maintaining BSD and System-5-like operating systems attached to a TCP/IP network.

Check Your Understanding

Multiple Choice Questions

1. Which of the following is the default port for SMTP?

   a. 110

   b. 25

   c. 21

   d. 23

2. Which command will generate the following outputs?

```
procs                          memory    swap        io     system         cpu
r  b  w   swpd   free   buff  cache  si  so    bi    bo   in    cs  us  sy  id
0  0  0   5392   3492  15268  29108   0   0     0     1   113    18   0   0 100
```

   a. vmstat

   b. finger

   c. df

   d. free

3. Linuxconf main menu contains which of these options?

   a. control

   b. config

   c. status

   d. settings

4. Which of the following enables you to manage user accounts?

   a. control

   b. config

   c. status

   c. settings

5. _____ is a remote display system that enables you to view a desktop environment not only on the computer where it is running but also from a remote location.

a. Webmin

b. Yast

c. cfengine

d. Yast

Short Questions

1. Edward, the system administrator, needs to access the Webmin through the Web browser. Which command does he need to execute? In addition, briefly discuss the following interfaces provided by Webmin:

◆ System

◆ Servers

2. List some of the tasks that can be automated by cfengine.

Answers

Multiple Choice Answers

1. The default port for SMTP is 25.

2. The given output is obtained by executing the vmstat command.

3. The options in the Linuxconf main menu are config, control, and status.

4. The config menu provides you the option to manage the user accounts.

5. VNC is a remote display system that enables you to view a desktop environment not only on the computer where it is running but also from a remote location.

Short Answers

1. The command to run Webmin from the Web browser is to enter the following address in the address bar:

   ```
   http://<computer_name>: 10000
   ```

   System interface: The System tab manages tasks within the computer or server environment, including disk quota, NIS, PAM, syslog, adding users, managing cron, managing NFS and changing boot services, processes, and restarting the machine.

   Servers interface: The Servers tab allows you to manage servers, such as Apache, BIND, DHCP, sendmail, Squid, and so on.

2. Some of the tasks that can be automated by using cfengine are listed here:

   ◆ Check and configure the network interface.

   ◆ Edit text files.

   ◆ Make and maintain symbolic links, including multiple links from a single command.

   ◆ Check and set the permissions and ownership of files.

   ◆ Manage junk files which clutter the system.

   ◆ Mount file systems systematically and automatically.

   ◆ Check for the presence of important files and file systems.

   ◆ Control execution of user scripts and shell commands.

Chapter 5

**Encryption and
Authentication**

ncryption and *authentication* are methods you use to secure your data and establish the identity of users and clients. Encryption secures data by converting it into a form that is hard to understand. On the other hand, authentication establishes the identity of users and clients and ensures that only authorized users are allowed access to data. In this chapter, you'll look at the various encryption and authentication methods that make your Linux environment secure and learn about the tools available for encrypting data and authenticating users in Linux.

Encryption

Encryption is the process of converting data into a form that is not easy to read. The original data is called *plain text,* and the encrypted data is called *cipher text.* There are simple or sophisticated methods of encryption. The simple encryption includes substituting, rotating, and scrambling letters. The sophisticated cipher includes applying complex algorithms to letters, words, or phrases.

You can convert the cipher text back to plain text through the decryption process. To recover the plain text from the cipher text, you use the decryption key. The *decryption key* is another algorithm that reverses the effect of the algorithm that was applied to convert the plain text to the cipher text.

The encryption process is also known as *cryptography.* There are two main types of cryptography:

◆ Single key cryptography
◆ Public key cryptography

The following sections discuss each of these in detail.

Single Key Cryptography

Single key cryptography is also known as *symmetric key cryptography.* In this type of cryptography, the encryption and decryption of data takes place with the use of a secret key. The sender, as well as the receiver, should have the secret key.

Several secret key algorithms have been developed. Some of them discussed in this chapter include:

♦ Data Encryption Standard (DES)

♦ Triple Data Encryption Standard (3DES)

♦ International Data Encryption Algorithm (IDEA)

Data Encryption Standard

DES is a secure method for data encryption that uses a secret key to encrypt data. The secret key is extremely difficult to break. With this method, more than 72 quadrillion encryption keys can be generated and used. This method uses private key cryptography, in which both the sender and the receiver use the same private key to encrypt and decrypt data.

DES applies a 56-bit key to each 64-bit block of data. Although this is considered a strong level of encryption, many companies use triple DES, which applies three keys in succession.

 NOTE

DES originated at IBM in 1977 and was adopted by the U.S. Department of Defense. DES is specified in the ANSI X3.92 and X3.106 and in the Federal FIPS 46 and 81 standards.

Triple Data Encryption Standard

3DES is another form of DES encryption. Three 64-bit keys are needed to form an overall length of 192 bits. The 3DES encryption breaks the secret key into three sub-keys and pads the keys, if necessary, so that they are each 64 bits long. The data is encrypted with the first key and then decrypted with the second key. This decrypted data is again encrypted with the third key.

The procedure for encryption is the same as with regular DES, but is repeated three times. This makes the 3DES encryption more secure than the DES encryption; however, it is slower than DES.

International Data Encryption Algorithm

IDEA is a symmetric block cipher developed by Xuejia Lai and James Massey of the Swiss Federal Institute of technology. IDEA, which is designed to facilitate both software and hardware implementation, provides a high level of security with easy implementation. Due to its strength and reliability, IDEA is now used worldwide in many banking and industry applications.

IDEA encrypts data in 64-bit blocks with a 128-bit key. The 64-bit data block is divided into four 16-bit sub-blocks. Each of these blocks undergoes eight rounds of operations. In each round of operation, the XOR algorithm is applied. After that, they are added and multiplied with one another and with 16-bit sub-blocks of data. These functions are combined to produce complex encrypted data that is very difficult to analyze.

Public Key Cryptography

The public key cryptography uses a pair of keys instead of a single key for the encryption and decryption process. In this process, one key is used for encryption, and the other key is used for decryption. This process is known as *asymmetric cryptography* because both the keys are required to complete the process and both the keys are based on different algorithms.

In the public key cryptography, one of the keys is freely distributed to the users. This key is called the *public key* and is used for encryption. The other key, called the *private key*, is used for the decryption purpose and is kept with the owner. The data that is encrypted with the public key can be decrypted only with the corresponding private key. Conversely, data encrypted with the private key can be decrypted only with the corresponding public key. The most popular algorithm of asymmetric encryption is the RSA encryption.

RSA Encryption

RSA encryption is based on asymmetrical cryptography. The RSA encryption algorithm uses very large prime numbers to generate the public and private keys. The usage of large numbers makes it almost impossible to calculate the original keys. RSA-based encryption schemes encrypt a symmetrical key using the public key. The data is then encrypted by using the symmetrical key, which uses a faster algorithm. The symmetrical key is randomly generated. Therefore, the only way to get it is to use the private key to decrypt the RSA-encrypted symmetrical key. The use of large numbers to generate the public and private keys makes this encryption algorithm very slow.

Hashing Functions

A *hash function* is a conversion technique that takes input and returns a string, which is called a *hash value*. The hash function converts the string into a form that is irreversible. Hashing is different from encryption in the sense that the encrypted data can be decrypted, but once hashing is applied to data, it can't be converted back to the original form. Some of the basic requirements of a hash function are listed here:

◆ The input can be of a variable length.

◆ The output has a fixed length.

◆ The hash value should be easy to compute.

◆ The conversion should be one way only. This means that you cannot derive the original value from the hash value.

A well-known hash function is message digest (MD).

Message Digest

Professor Ronald L. Rivest of MIT has created three MD algorithms. These are as follows:

◆ **MD2.** In this algorithm, the message is first padded so that its length is divisible by 16 bytes. A 16-byte checksum is then appended to the message, and the hash value is computed on the resulting message. This was developed in 1989.

◆ **MD4.** In this algorithm, the message is padded to ensure that its length, plus 64-bits, is divisible by 512 bits. A 64-bit binary representation of the original length of the message is then concatenated to the message. The message is processed in 512-bit blocks, and each block is processed in three distinct rounds. This was developed in 1990.

◆ **MD5.** MD5 was developed by Rivest in 1991. It is basically the same as MD4, but includes more security features. This algorithm consists of four distinct rounds, which have a slightly different design from that of MD4. Message-digest size, as well as padding requirements, remain the same as those in MD4.

MD5 is an algorithm used to verify data integrity. MD5 verifies data integrity through the creation of a 128-bit message digest. It is intended for use with digital signature applications, which require data to be compressed by a secure method before being encrypted with a secret key. According to the MD5 standard, it is nearly impossible to produce the same output with different data when the MD5 algorithm is applied.

Although the three algorithms have similar structures, MD2 is optimized for 8-bit machines. The other two algorithms, MD4 and MD5, are optimized for 32-bit machines. The MD5 algorithm is an extension of MD4, which is fast, but not absolutely secure. In comparison, MD5 is not quite as fast as the MD4 algorithm, but it offers much more reliability for data security.

Apart from encryption, another way to protect your data is to restrict the access of users to your systems. Only authenticated users should be allowed access. *Lightweight Directory Access Protocol* (LDAP) is one method available for authentication. The next section discusses LDAP.

LDAP

LDAP is a client-server protocol for accessing a directory service. A directory service is similar to a database, but contains more descriptive and attribute-based information. Directory services can be local or global, providing access to a restricted set or a wider group of users. There are many different ways to provide a directory service, and different methods allow different kinds of information to be stored in the directory. They also specify how the information can be referenced, queried, and updated.

In Linux, the daemon for the LDAP directory server is called `slapd`. The `slapd` daemon runs on different UNIX platforms. Another daemon called `slurpd` performs replication between LDAP servers. The `slurpd` daemon enables the server to take the benefits of caching and manage concurrency with databases.

NOTE

The slurpd daemon is responsible for replication between LDAP servers.

The command for running slapd is shown here:

```
/usr/local/etc/libexec/slapd [<option>]*
```

In the given command, the <option> can be replaced by any of the following options:

- **-f.** This option is used to specify an alternate configuration file for the slapd daemon.

- **-n.** This option is used to specify the service name that will be used for logging and other purposes.

- **-l.** This option is used to specify the local user for the syslog facility.

- **-u user and -g group.** These options are used to specify the user and group.

- **-r.** This option is used to specify a run-time directory.

- **-d.** This option is used to set the slapd debug level to a specified level. To access the LDAP service, the LDAP client first must authenticate itself. If the client authentication is successful, the server checks whether the client has the required permissions for accessing the requested service. This process is called *access control*.

In LDAP, three types of authentication are supported:

- **Anonymous.** In this type of authentication, the client is treated as the anonymous one.

- **Simple.** In this type of authentication, the fully qualified name of the client and the password is sent in clear-text format to the LDAP server for authentication. This mechanism is not very secure because the password is sent as clear-text.

- **SASL Authentication.** *Simple Authentication and Security Layer* (SASL) specifies a challenge-response protocol in which data is exchanged between the client and the server. The challenge-response protocol is used for the authentication and establishing a security layer on which subsequent communication will be carried out.

This section discussed authentication by LDAP. Another common method involves using passwords. Linux has the password suite, which implements authentication through passwords.

Password Suite

On a Linux system, the user information and passwords are stored in the /etc/passwd file. The password is encrypted by using the hashing technique. The encrypted password and the value with which the password was encrypted are both stored in the /etc/passwd file. The benefit of storing the encrypted password is that it is very difficult to obtain the original password. Therefore, even if someone manages to steal your /etc/passwd file, the person cannot decrypt the passwords. At most, an attempt can be made to guess the original password and then confirm it by first calculating a hash for it and then comparing it to the one in the /etc/passwd file. More about such attacks is discussed in Chapter 7, in the "Word List or Dictionary Attacks" section.

When a user tries to log on:

1. First, the password hash is retrieved from the passwd file.
2. Next, the password provided by the user is encrypted.
3. Then, the encrypted form of the password provided by the user is matched with the encrypted password retrieved from the passwd file.

Storing encrypted passwords in the passwd file is not completely safe. Hackers can use techniques, such as dictionary attacks, to obtain passwords. Storing the value used to encrypt the password in the passwd file is also risky, because unauthorized users can easily obtain it once they get access to the passwd file. In addition to the passwords, the /etc/passwd file also contains information such as user and group IDs, which are used by many system programs. Therefore, the /etc/passwd file must have read access for applications that use Linux authentication directly. If you deny the read access, the ls -l command displays user IDs instead of usernames.

Following is a sample output of the ls -l command:

```
-rwxr-xr-x    1    0      root        2828  Aug 31   2000 arch
-rwxr-xr-x    1    0      root       64924  Aug 31   2000 ash
-rwxr-xr-x    1    0      root      384232  Aug 31   2000 ash.static
```

-rwxr-xr-x	1	0	root	10460	Jul 12 2000	aumix-minimal
lrwxrwxrwx	1	0	root	4	Feb 27 21:14	awk -> gawk
-rwxr-xr-x	1	0	root	5780	Jul 13 2000	basename
-rwxr-xr-x	1	0	root	512540	Aug 22 2000	bash
lrwxrwxrwx	1	0	root	4	Feb 27 21:14	bash2 -> bash
lrwxrwxrwx	1	0	root	3	Feb 27 21:15	bsh -> ash
-rwxr-xr-x	1	0	root	9588	Aug 31 2000	cat
-rwxr-xr-x	1	0	root	14972	Aug 25 2000	chgrp
-rwxr-xr-x	1	0	root	16732	Aug 25 2000	chmod
-rwxr-xr-x	1	0	root	15676	Aug 25 2000	chown

In the preceding output, notice that the third column has the value 0, which is the UID for the root user.

One drawback associated with the password suite is that it is not secure. Users have read permission to the passwd file, which could prove to be a security hole. You can solve this problem by using Shadow suite. The Shadow suite helps you secure your passwords more efficiently.

Shadow Suite

The Shadow suite stores the passwords to another file: /etc/shadow. No user has the read permission for the *shadow* file. Only the root user has read and write access for the file. Moving the passwords to the /etc/shadow file prevents hackers from gaining access to them.

The Shadow suite enables you to do the following:

◆ Set logon defaults by using the configuration file, /etc/login.defs

◆ Manage users and groups

◆ Manage passwords and accounts

You should not use the Shadow suite in the following situations:

◆ User accounts are not stored in the computer.

◆ The computer is using Network Information Services (NIS) to receive usernames and passwords or supply them to other machines on the network.

◆ The computer is used by terminal servers to verify users via Network File System (NFS), NIS, or some other method.

◆ The computer runs other software that validates users, and there is no Shadow version available.

Sample output of the passwd file when the Shadow suite is installed is displayed here:

```
root:x:0:0:root,9810541423,9810541423,913091830219:/root:/bin/csh
user1:x:506:506::/home/user1:/bin/bash
john:x:507:507::/home/john:/bin/bash
```

Notice that the format of the entries in the passwd file is as follows:

```
[username]:[passwd]:[UID]:[GID]:[full_name]:[directory]:[shell]
```

In the preceding format,

◆ [username] is the logon name of the user.

◆ [passwd] is the encoded password of the user.

◆ [UID] is the user ID.

◆ [GID] is the group ID of the user.

◆ [full_name] is the full name of the user.

◆ [directory] is the home directory of the user.

◆ [shell] is the logon shell of the user.

You'll now look at the sample entries in the /etc/shadow file:

```
root:$1$YgmpAbXE$9h3ghaSqjZYOrMt8ZNwBN1:11767:0:99999:7:::
user1:*$9h3ghaSqjZsdYW34OrMtytU8ZNwCPNM:11818:0:99999:7:::
john:AbXE$9hYutopjZYOrMhiAswHJTZNwBNPuR:11821:0:99999:7:::
```

Notice that the format of the entries in the /etc/shadow file is as follows:

```
[username]:[passwd]:[last]:[may]:[must]:[warn]:[expire]:[disable]:[reserved]
```

In the preceding format,

◆ [username] is the username.

◆ [passwd] is the encoded password.

◆ [last] is the number of days, since Jan 1, 1970, that the password was last changed.

◆ [may] is the number of days before password can be changed.

◆ [must] is the number of days after which password must be changed.

◆ [warn] is the number of days before password is to expire that the user is warned.

◆ [expire] is the number of days after the password expires that account is disabled.

◆ [disable] is the number of days since Jan 1, 1970 that the account is disabled.

◆ [reserved] is a reserved field.

The passwords in the shadow file are normally encrypted by using the *crypt encryption* function. The crypt function is the password encryption function that is based on the DES algorithm.

Shadow Suite Versions

Several versions of Shadow suite are available. These are listed here:

◆ Shadow-3.3.1 was the first version released.

◆ Shadow-3.3.1-2 is a Linux-specific patch that contains some further enhancements to the Shadow-3.3.1 version.

◆ Shadow-mk was specifically packaged for Linux.

◆ Shadow-4.0.0.14 is the latest version of the Shadow suite.

However, there are security problems within the login program of the Shadow versions 3.3.1, 3.3.1-2, and shadow-mk. These versions do not check the length of a logon name. This causes the buffer to overflow, which can lead to computer crashes. This buffer overflow might also allow an account holder on the system to use this buffer, and the shared libraries, to gain root access. This makes computers with these versions of Shadow suite vulnerable.

The Shadow suite package uses the following naming convention:

shadow-YYMMDD.tar.gz

In the preceding syntax, YYMMDD is the issue date of the suite.

The Shadow suite can be obtained from the following sites:

- ftp://ftp.icm.edu.pl/pub/Linux/shadow/shadow-current.tar.gz
- ftp://iguana.hut.fi/pub/linux/shadow/shadow-current.tar.gz
- ftp://ftp.cin.net/usr/ggallag/shadow/shadow-current.tar.gz
- ftp://ftp.netural.com/pub/linux/shadow/shadow-current.tar.gz

 CAUTION

You should *not* use a version older than shadow-960129, because earlier versions also have the logon security problem discussed previously.

Shadow Suite Content

The Shadow suite contains replacement programs for su, login, passwd, newgrp, chfn, chsh, and id. I'll now discuss each of these.

su

The su command allows one user to temporarily become another user. The syntax of the su command is as follows:

```
su [OPTION] [USER [ARG]]
```

Following is the list of options supported by the su command:

- -l, —login
- -c, —command=COMMAND
- -f, —fast
- -m, —preserve-environment
- -s, —shell=SHELL
- —help
- —version

By executing the su command, the user and group ID of the current user is changed to that of the USER. If no USER is given, the superuser is used. If USER has a password, su prompts for the password. If the su command was given by a normal user and the person knows the root password, the Linux prompt changes from a $ prompt to a # prompt, suggesting that the user is now the root user. This command is especially useful during telnet sessions.

login

The `login` command is used during the logon process. If you do not give any argument with the `login` command, you are prompted for the username.

If restrictions have been specified in the /etc/usertty file, these restrictions must be met. Otherwise, the logon will be denied and a syslog will be generated. For root users, the logon details must be present in the /etc/securetty file. After this, the system will request a password from the user. You can configure the number of failed attempts after which the user will be denied access.

passwd

The `passwd` command updates a user's authentication token. The syntax of the `passwd` command is given here:

```
passwd [-k] [-l] [-u [-f]] [-d] [-S] [username]
```

The descriptions of the arguments of the `passwd` command are as follows:

- ◆ **-k.** This option is used to indicate that only the expired passwords should be updated.
- ◆ **-l.** This option can be used only by a root user to lock a specified account.
- ◆ **-u.** This option can be used only by a root user to unlock a specified account.
- ◆ **-d.** This option is a quick way to disable a password for an account. It will set the named account as `passwordless`.
- ◆ **-S.** This option displays information about the status of the password for a given account to a root user.

newgrp

The `newgrp` command is used to change the user's group. The `newgrp` command also changes the group identification of its caller. After you use the `newgrp` command to change to a new group, you remain logged on and continue using the current directories. However, your access permissions to various files and directories depend on the permissions given to the new users. The syntax of using the newgrp command is shown here:

```
newgrp [group]
```

chfn

The chfn command is used to change a user's information, such as a user's real name and work and home phone number, stored in the /etc/passwd file. The information is displayed by using the finger command. The syntax of using the chfn command is given here:

```
chfn  [ -f]   [ -o]   [ -p]  [ -h]  [ -u]  [ -v ]  [ username ]
```

The arguments of the chfn command are as follows:

- ◆ -f. Used to specify the full name of the user
- ◆ -o. Used to specify the office room number of the user
- ◆ -p. Used to specify the office phone number of the user
- ◆ -h. Used to specify the home phone number of the user
- ◆ -u. Used to display the usage of the chfn command
- ◆ -v. Used to display the version information of the chfn program

chsh

The chsh command is used to change the logon shell. If a shell is not specified on the command line, chsh prompts for one. The chsh command will accept the full pathname of any executable file on the system. However, it will issue a warning if the shell is not listed in the /etc/shells file. The syntax of the chsh command is given here:

```
chsh [ -s]  [ -l ]  [ -u ]  [ -v ]  [ username ]
```

The arguments of the chsh command are as follows:

- ◆ -s. The -s option is used to specify the logon shell.
- ◆ -l. The -l option lists all the available shells.
- ◆ -u. The -u is used to print the help.
- ◆ -v. The -v option is used to display the version information.

id

The `id` command prints the user ID and group ID of a specified user or the current user. The syntax of the `id` command is displayed here:

```
id [option] [username]
```

The values accepted by the argument option are as follows:

- ◆ **-g.** Prints the group ID.
- ◆ **-G.** Prints the supplementary groups.
- ◆ **-u.** Prints the user ID.
- ◆ **-help.** Displays the help.
- ◆ **-version.** Displays the version information.

The Shadow suite package also contains new programs, such as `chage`, `newusers`, `dpasswd`, `gpasswd`, `useradd`, `userdel`, `usermod`, `groupadd`, `groupdel`, `groupmod`, `groups`, `pwck`, `grpck`, `lastlog`, `pwconv`, and `pwunconv`. Additionally, the `lib-shadow`.library is included for writing and compiling programs that need to access user passwords. There is also a configuration file for the `login` program, which is installed as `/etc/login.defs`.

chage

The `chage` command is used by the root user to specify when users must change their password. Only the root user can use the `chage` command. The syntax of the `chage` command is given here.

```
chage [-m] [-M] [-d] [-I] [-E] [-W] user
```

The arguments of the `chage` command are as follows:

- ◆ **-m.** This option specifies the minimum number of days a user has to change the password.
- ◆ **-M.** This option specifies the maximum number of days for which the password is valid.
- ◆ **-d.** This option sets the value of `lastday` as the number of days since January 1st, 1970 when the password was last changed.
- ◆ **-I.** This option is used to set the number of days of inactivity after a password has expired, before the account is locked.

◆ -E. This option is used to set the expiration date of the user account.

◆ -W. This option is used to set the number of days of warning before a password change is required.

newusers

The newusers command is used to update and create new users or groups in a batch. It reads username and password pairs from the passwd file, which is normally the standard password file. This information is used to update a group of existing users or to create new users. The syntax of the command is as follows:

```
newusers [ new_users ]
```

gpasswd

The gpasswd command is used to manage the /etc/group file. Various syntaxes of the gpasswd command are as follows:

```
gpasswd group
gpasswd -a user group
gpasswd -d user group
gpasswd -R group
gpasswd -r group
gpasswd [-A user,...]  [-M user,...]  group
```

The arguments of the gpasswd command are discussed here:

◆ The -a option is used to add a user to a group.

◆ The -d option is used to delete a user from a group.

◆ The -r option is used to remove the group password.

◆ The -A option is used to define group administrator(s). Only the system administrators can use this option.

◆ The -M option is used to define members and has all rights of group administrators and members.

groups

The `groups` command prints the groups to which a user belongs. The syntax of the `groups` command is shown here:

```
groups [option] [user_name]
```

pwck

The `pwck` command is used to verify the integrity of password files. This command validates the entries in the `/etc/passwd` and `/etc/shadow` files.

This command checks whether the entries in these files have the correct number of fields, a unique username, a valid user and group identifier, a valid logon shell, and a valid home directory. The syntax of this command is as follows:

```
pwck [-r] [passwd shadow]
```

The `/etc/passwd` and `/etc/shadow` files are the default files to be validated. You can specify other files in the `passwd` and `shadow` arguments. The `pwck` is interactive; it prompts for inputs if any invalid entry is found. However, you can make it non-interactive by using the `-r` option. The `-r` option causes the command to run in the read-only mode. All questions regarding the changes, if invalid entries are found, are answered in negative.

grpck

The `grpck` command verifies the integrity of the group files. This command checks the entries in the `/etc/group` and `/etc/gshadow` files to ensure that they have the proper format and valid data in each field. The command checks each entry for the correct number of fields, a unique group name, and a valid list of users in the group. The syntax for the command is shown here:

```
grpck [-r] [group shdow]
```

lastlog

The `lastlog` command formats and prints the contents of the log file, `/var/log/lastlog`, created during the last logon. It prints the logon name, port number, and the last logon time from the `lastlog` file. The syntax of the `last-log` command is given here:

```
lastlog [-u uid] [-t days]
```

The `-u` option causes only the logon name to be printed. The `-t` option will print recent logons—to the number of days. If the user has never logged on, the message `**Never logged in**` is printed. A sample output of the command is given here:

```
Username        Port    From          Latest
root            pts/2   :0            Tue May 14 11:15:16 +0530 2002
bin                                         **Never logged in**
daemon                                      **Never logged in**
adm                                         **Never logged in**
lp                                          **Never logged in**
user1           tty2                  Mon Mar 18 14:55:02 +0530 2002
David           tty3                  Mon Mar 18 14:56:05 +0530 2002
John            tty4                  Wed Mar 20 14:12:49 +0530 2002
```

pwconv and pwunconv

The `pwconv` and `pwunconv` commands operate on the normal and shadow password files, `/etc/passwd` and `/etc/shadow`. The `pwconv` command creates the `/etc/shadow` file with the information from `/etc/passwd` file. Information, such as username, password, and password expiration details, is taken from the `/etc/passwd` file.

If the `/etc/shadow` file already exists, running the `pwconv` command triggers the following tasks:

- Entries in the `/etc/passwd` file, which don't exist in the `/etc/shadow` file, are added to the `/etc/shadow` file.

- Entries in `/etc/shadow` file, which are not present in `/etc/passwd` file, are removed from the `/etc/shadow` file.

- Password details for entries that exist in both the files are copied from the `/etc/passwd` file to the `/etc/shadow` file.

Installing Shadow Suite

You can install the Shadow suite two ways. First, you can install it by using the following syntax of `rpm` command, as you see here:

```
rpm -i <package_name>
```

The other installation method involves steps categorized like this:

- ◆ Pre-installation steps
- ◆ Installation steps

Pre-Installation Steps

The pre-installation steps are listed here:

1. First, you need to obtain the archive file for the Shadow suite from a mirror site. The package you obtain is in the `tar` format, compressed using gzip. To unpack the package, you need to type:

   ```
   tar -xzvf shadow-current.tar.gz
   ```

 NOTE

The package should be unpacked to the `/usr/src/shadow-`*YYMMDD* directory.

2. Next, you need to copy the `Makefile` and the `config.h` file. To copy these files, issue the following commands:

   ```
   cp Makefile.linux Makefile
   cp config.h.linux config.h
   ```

3. Make backup copies of the original programs. The programs that you need to backup are `/bin/su`, `/bin/login`, `/usr/bin/passwd`, `/usr/bin/newgrp`, `/usr/bin/chfn`, `/usr/bin/chsh`, and `/usr/bin/id`. In addition, backup the `/etc/passwd` file.

4. Execute the following command to compile the executables in the package:

   ```
   make all
   ```

Installation Steps

The installation process is listed here:

1. Be sure that you have a bootable disk with you. This disk may be required if the system stops responding during installation.

2. Manual pages for the programs that are part of the Shadow suite will not be replaced by the Shadow suite package. These pages are not updated automatically during the Shadow suite installation and need to be removed. Some of the manual pages that you need to remove are listed here:

   ◆ /usr/man/man1/chfn.1.gz

   ◆ /usr/man/man1/chsh.1.gz

   ◆ /usr/man/man1/login.1.gz

   ◆ /usr/man/man1/passwd.1.gz

   ◆ /usr/man/man1/su.1.gz

   ◆ /usr/man/man5/passwd.5.gz

3. Execute the following command to install the program and the manual pages of the Shadow suite:

   ```
   make install
   ```

4. Run the pwconv command. This command will create two files, /etc/npasswd and /etc/nshadow, from the /etc/passwd file. Rename these files as /etc/passwd and /etc/shadow files, respectively. You should ensure that the file permissions and ownerships are correct.

5. Upgrade the programs that'll need access to the passwords. Some such programs are adduser, wu_ftpd, ftpd, pop3d, xlock, xdm, and sudo. You should upgrade these programs so they support the Shadow Suite.

Apart from LDAP and Shadow suite, another authentication mechanism is PAM. I am now going to discuss PAM in detail.

Pluggable Authentication Modules (PAM)

Traditionally, users of UNIX-based systems are authenticated by the password encryption method. The password provided by the user is encrypted using a specific value. The encrypted password is then matched with another encrypted password stored in a file. If both encrypted forms of the passwords match, the user is authenticated.

After a user is authenticated, various privileges are granted to the user, based on the UID. This UID is used by the system to determine the user's permissions for services and applications. However, these methods are vulnerable to attacks from hackers. There are many tools and applications available to make your system secure. One such tool is *Pluggable Authentication Modules* (PAM) for Linux. PAM is a suite of shared libraries that allows the system administrators to determine the way in which users will be authenticated.

PAM enables you to switch between authentication schemes. PAM aims to separate development of privileges granting software from the development of secure and appropriate authentication schemes. This is possible because PAM provides a library of shared functions that an application can use to authenticate users. This library is configured with the /etc/pam.conf file, or the /etc/pam.d directory. The /etc/pam.d directory contains various configuration files for PAM. The modules that are used to authenticate users are located in the /usr/lib/security directory and are loaded dynamically.

Linux PAM supports four types of modules:

- ◆ **Authentication.** This module provides two aspects of user authentication. First, it establishes the identity of the user by directing the applications to accept passwords or other identity details from the users. Next, the module grants permissions and group membership to the user.

- ◆ **Account.** This module performs account management. It can be used to perform tasks, such as granting permission for files and directories based on the time and day configured, maximum number of users allowed to logon at a time, and so on.

- ◆ **Session.** This module manages tasks, such as maintaining logs and other information, after a session is established with a user. The session module works until the session remains active.

◆ **Password.** This module is required for updating the authentication token associated with the user.

The module that PAM calls for an application is determined by the configuration file. An application's configuration file is stored in the /etc/pam.d/ directory. The pam.conf is the configuration file for PAM, which is discussed in the next section.

The /etc/pam.conf File

PAM can be configured in the /etc/pam.conf file or the /etc/pam.d directory. I'll now discuss the structure of the pam.conf file. The general entry in pam.conf has the following format:

```
[service-name]   [module-type]   [control-flag]   [module-path]   [arguments]
```

Each of these arguments is discussed in the subsequent sections.

[service_name]

This argument specifies the service or the application associated with the given configuration entry. By using this parameter, you can select services, such as ftpd, rlogind, and su.

It is difficult to create an entry for all the services and applications that exist on your system. A general entry in pam.conf can be created to determine the default authentication scheme for services and applications other than those specified in the file. For the general entry, the [service_name] parameter will be OTHER, which can be written either in upper- or lowercase. If an entry already exists for a service or an application, the OTHER entry will be ignored.

[module_type]

This argument can have one of the four listed values:

◆ auth (for authentication module)

◆ account (for account module)

◆ session (for session module)

◆ password (for password module)

[control_flag]

The control_flag specifies the action to be performed on success or failure of modules. Modules of similar type are stacked over one another and they are assigned priority by the control_flags. The execution order of these modules is specified in the /etc/pam.conf file. The earliest listed entries will be executed first.

The syntax of the control flag is displayed here:

```
[value1 = action1 value2 = action2]
```

This syntax gives the administrator greater control over the user authentication process.

In the preceding syntax, value1 or value2 can have the following values:

◆ Success

◆ open_err

◆ symbol_err

◆ service_err

◆ system_err

◆ buf_err

◆ perm_denied

◆ auth_err

◆ cred_insufficient

◆ authinfo_unavail

◆ user_unknown

◆ maxtries

◆ new_authtok_reqd

◆ acct_expired

◆ session_err

◆ cred_unavail

◆ cred_expired

◆ cred_err

◆ no_module_data

◆ conv_err

- ◆ `authtok_err`
- ◆ `authtok_recover_err`
- ◆ `authtok_lock_busy`
- ◆ `authtok_disable_aging`
- ◆ `try_again`
- ◆ `ignore`
- ◆ `abort`
- ◆ `authtok_expired`
- ◆ `module_unknown`
- ◆ `bad_item`
- ◆ `default`

The default value can be used to set the action for those return values that are not explicitly defined.

The `action1` or `action2` parameters of the control flag can have the following six values:

- ◆ `ignore`
- ◆ `ok`
- ◆ `done`
- ◆ `bad`
- ◆ `die`
- ◆ `reset`

A positive integer, n, also can be specified as the action to indicate that the next n modules of the current type need to be skipped. This parameter enables the administrator to develop a sophisticated stack of modules with different paths of execution.

[module_path]

This argument represents the pathname of the dynamically loadable object file, which is normally the pluggable module. If the path name starts with a /, it is assumed to be a complete pathname. Otherwise, the module path that is specified is appended to the default path, `/usr/lib/security`.

[arguments]

Arguments are passed to a module when it is invoked. Valid arguments are usually optional and are specific to any given module. Invalid arguments are ignored by a module. However, while encountering an invalid argument, the module writes an error to syslog (3).

So far, you have looked at the format of the pam.conf file. PAM can be configured in another way—by using the configuration files in the /etc/pam.d/ directory. The format of the files in the /etc/pam.d/ directory is similar to that of the pam.conf file, as given here:

```
module-type   control-flag   module-path   arguments
```

The only difference between the structure of the pam.conf file and the files in the /etc/pam.d/ directory is that the [service_name] is not present in the latter. This is because the name of the service is assigned to the configuration file. For example, the /etc/pam.d/login file contains the configuration for the logon service. The content of the /etc/pam.d/login file is displayed here:

```
auth       required    /lib/security/pam_securetty.so
auth       required    /lib/security/pam_stack.so service=system-auth
auth       required    /lib/security/pam_nologin.so
account    required    /lib/security/pam_stack.so service=system-auth
password   required    /lib/security/pam_stack.so service=system-auth
session    required    /lib/security/pam_stack.so service=system-auth
session    optional    /lib/security/pam_console.so
```

This method of configuration has a number of advantages over the single file approach. I've listed some of these advantages here:

- ◆ It is easier to maintain.
- ◆ Parsing is quicker.
- ◆ Read access to Linux-PAM configuration files can be limited.
- ◆ Package management is simpler.

Kerberos

Kerberos is a network protocol designed to provide authentication by using secret key cryptography. It has been designed to provide security from hackers, as well as any users with doubtful intentions within your network. Kerberos was created at Massachusetts Institute of Technology (MIT) as a solution to the authentication problems in your network.

The Kerberos authentication process is listed here:

1. First, a client requests a ticket from the Key Distribution Center (KDC).
2. A Ticket Granting Ticket (TGT) is created by the KDC for the client. The TGT is encrypted by using the client's password. This encrypted TGT is then sent back to the client.
3. Upon receipt of the TGT, the client decrypts the TGT by using his password. The client is authenticated if he is able to decrypt the TGT successfully.

The TGT expires after a specified time. A client can obtain multiple TGTs, which gives permission for various services to the client. The requesting and granting of tickets is transparent to the user. Kerberos uses the single-sign-on system, which means that you need to supply your password only once per session.

I'll now discuss some aspects of the Kerberos authentication system:

◆ Kerberos Principal
◆ Ticket Management
◆ Password Management

Kerberos Principal

The Kerberos *principal* is an identity to which a ticket can be granted. This identity can be a user or a service. A Kerberos principal is divided into three parts: primary, instance, and realm.

◆ **Primary.** The primary is the first part of the principal. For a user, a principal is the username.

◆ **Instance.** The instance is an optional part that qualifies the primary. The instance is separated from the primary by a slash (/). For users, the instance is usually `null`. However, sometimes a user might have an additional principal. For example, the principal `user1@abc.com` is different from the principal `user1/admin@abc.com`. Both will have different sets of passwords and permissions.

◆ **Realm.** The realm is usually the domain name to which the client belongs.

Ticket Management

Usually, the Kerberos is built into the `login` program. Clients or services get the ticket automatically when they logon. The ticket is destroyed when clients exit the application. Kerberos has built-in ability for ticket management. You can perform the following ticket management tasks by using Kerberos:

◆ Obtain Tickets

◆ View Tickets

◆ Destroy Tickets

Obtaining Tickets

If you are using the Kerberos V5 `login` program, a ticket is issued automatically when you logon. However, if you are using a different logon program, you need to explicitly obtain the ticket. The `kinit` program also is used to obtain new tickets, in case your old tickets expire.

The syntax of the `kinit` program is given here:

```
Shell% kinit [options] [optional_realm]
```

[options] can have these values:

◆ **f.** This option is used if you want to create a ticket that can be forwarded to another host.

◆ **l.** This option is used to specify a life line for the ticket. Tickets are provided for a default lifeline, after which they expire. If you want to obtain a ticket with a life line different from the default life line, you should use the `l` option.

The [optional_realm] is used if you need to obtain a ticket for a user on a realm different from the default realm.

Viewing Tickets

You can view the tickets available to you by using the klist program. The syntax of the klist program is as follows:

```
Shell% klist
```

The format of the output is given here:

```
Ticket cache: /tmp/file1
Default principal: user1@abc.com

Valid starting      Expires           Service principal
XX/XX/XX            XX/XX/XX          XXXXXX
```

In the format given above, the critical parts of the output, which have been highlighted in bold, are explained:

- ◆ **Ticket cache.** Specifies the location of the ticket file.
- ◆ **Default principal.** Specifies the default Kerberos principal.
- ◆ **Valid starting.** Specifies the date and time of the starting period when the ticket is valid.
- ◆ **Expires.** Specifies the date and time of expiration of the ticket.
- ◆ **Service principal.** Describes the primary and the instance of the TGT.

You can use the -f option to view the flags that apply to your tickets. These flags are as follows:

- ◆ **F.** Ticket can be forwarded.
- ◆ **f.** Ticket has been forwarded.
- ◆ **P.** Ticket is proxiable.
- ◆ **p.** Ticket is proxy.
- ◆ **D.** Ticket is postdateable.
- ◆ **d.** Ticket has been postdated.
- ◆ **R.** Ticket is renewable.
- ◆ **i.** Ticket is invalid.

Destroying Tickets

You should destroy tickets when you don't need them. This will prevent their misuse by unauthorized users. You can use the kdestroy program to destroy your tickets. If kdestroy is unable to locate or destroy any ticket, it will generate an error message.

Password Management

Password is the only authentication mechanism used by Kerberos to establish a client's identity. If malicious users get access to your password, they can be authenticated and manipulate your data. Therefore, it is important to select a good password and keep it secure. You also should change passwords frequently.

Changing Passwords

To change the Kerberos password, you can use the kpasswd program. The program will prompt you for the old password. The old password is needed to ensure that you are the valid user. After password verification, you are prompted to enter the new password twice. An error message will be displayed if there is any mismatch in the new passwords that you have entered. The syntax for using the kpasswd program is as follows:

```
Shell% kpasswd
```

Granting Access to Your Account

At times, you need to give access to your account to different users. To provide access without giving your password to other users, you can create a .k5login file in your home directory. This is a text file, which might exist in the home directory. It contains a list of the principals who have permission to log onto the account. The listed principals can log on and use the account without any restrictions. However, other users should have Kerberos tickets in their respective Kerberos realms.

Summary

In this chapter, you looked at the different encryption and authentication techniques used to make the Linux environment secure. You can use two types of encryption for data security: single key encryption and public key encryption. In addition to encryption, hashing also can be used to secure the data. *Hashing* is a technique in which a string is converted to an irreversible form. You learned about the most popular hash function, MD5. Authentication restricts a user's access to the critical data on your system and network. The authentication mechanisms that I discussed in detail in this chapter are LDAP, Shadow Suite, Kerberos, and PAM.

Check Your Understanding

Multiple Choice Questions

1. Which configuration file allows you to set logon defaults?

   a. `login.defs`

   b. `passwd`

   c. `shadow`

   d. `logon.defs`

2. Which of the following tasks are triggered when you run the pwconv command while the /etc/shadow file exists?

   a. Entries in the `/etc/passwd` file, which don't exist in the `/etc/shadow` file, are added to the `/etc/shadow` file.

   b. Entries in `/etc/shadow`, which are not present in `/etc/passwd`, are removed from the `/etc/shadow` file.

   c. Entries in `/etc/shadow`, which are present in `/etc/passwd`, are removed from the `/etc/passwd` file.

   d. Password details for entries that exist in both the files are copied from the `/etc/passwd` file to the `/etc/shadow` file.

    3. Select the modules supported by Linux PAM.

       a. Authentication

       b. Shadow

       c. Session

       d. Password

    4. Execute the command to view the tickets.

    5. Execute the command to change the Kerberos password.

Short Questions

    1. Edward is unable to understand to format of an entry in the pam.conf file. Explain the format to him.

    2. Briefly discuss these secret key algorithms:

       • DES

       • 3DES

       • IDEA

    3. Discuss the PAM modules.

Answers

Multiple Choice Questions

1. The logon.defs file allows you to set logon defaults.

2. The tasks that are triggered when you run the pwconv command and the /etc/shadow are as follows:

   a. Entries in /etc/passwd, which don't exist in the /etc/shadow file, are added to the /etc/shadow file.

   b. Entries in /etc/shadow, which are not present in /etc/passwd, are removed from the /etc/shadow file.

   d. Password details for entries that exist in both files are copied from the /etc/passwd file to the /etc/shadow file.

3. The modules supported by Linux-PAM are authentication, session, and password.

4. The command to view the tickets is as follows:

```
Shell% klist
```

5. The command to change the Kerberos password is given here:

```
Shell% kpasswd
```

Short Answers

1. The general entry in the pam.conf file has the following format:

```
[service-name]    [module-type]    [control-flag]    [module-path]    [arguments]
```

The [service_name] argument specifies the service or the application associated with the given configuration entry. By using this parameter, you can select services such as ftpd, rlogind, and su.

The [module_type] argument can have one of the four listed values:

- auth
- account
- session
- password

The [control_flag] argument is used to specify the response of the PAM library in events of success or failure of the module with which it is associated. The keywords that you can assign are listed here:

- Required
- Requisite
- Sufficient
- Optional

The [module_path] argument represents the pathname of the dynamically loadable object file, which is normally the pluggable module.

The [arguments] arguments are a list of tokens that are passed to the module when it is invoked.

2. **DES**

   DES is a method for data encryption that uses a secret key, which is extremely difficult to break, to encrypt data. DES applies a 56-bit key to each 64-bit block of data. This method uses the private key cryptography, where both the sender and the receiver use the same private key to encrypt and decrypt data.

   3DES

   3DES takes three 64-bit keys to form an overall key length of 192 bits. The data is encrypted with the first key and decrypted with the second key. This decrypted data is again encrypted with the third key. The 3DES encryption breaks the secret key into three subkeys and pads the keys, if necessary, so that they are each 64-bit long. The 3DES encryption is more secure than the DES encryption.

   IDEA

   IDEA is a symmetric block cipher designed to facilitate both software and hardware implementation. It was developed to provide a high level of security with ease of implementation. IDEA encrypts data in 64-bit blocks with a 128-bit key. The 64-bit data block is divided into four 16-bit sub-blocks. Each of these sub-blocks undergoes eight rounds of operations where the XOR algorithm is applied on the sub-blocks. This results in a very complex value, which is very difficult to analyze.

3. Linux PAM supports four types of modules:

- **Authentication.** This module first establishes the identity of the user by directing the applications to accept passwords or other identity details from the users. After that, the module grants permissions and group membership to the user.

- **Account.** This module is responsible for account management. It can be used to perform tasks, such as granting permission for files and directories based on the time and day configured, the maximum number of users allowed to log on at a time, and so on.

- **Session.** This module manages tasks, such as maintaining logs and other information after a session is established with a user. The session module works until the session remains active.

- **Password.** This module is required for updating the authentication token associated with the user.

Chapter 6

Network Basics

A network is a communication system that helps computers interact with each other. To enable this interaction, certain rules must be followed. These rules are known as *protocol*. A protocol is nothing but a set of rules or formats that are followed to create a means of effective communication between two or more computers. It is very difficult to build a protocol that is sufficient to cater to various kinds of applications and computers. Therefore, the need for a common platform that supports protocols at various levels of communication arises. Such a platform is the OSI reference model.

In this chapter, I discuss the different layers of the OSI reference model. You will also learn in greater detail about the important layers of network security. Finally, the last section of the chapter covers topics that are relevant to system administrators.

Open Systems Interconnection (OSI)

The OSI reference model is an open set of definitions that presents a common technical framework for standardization of communication. This framework provides an infrastructure that is sufficient to place mandatory and optional components of effective communication in place.

The OSI reference model is divided into several layers. Each layer provides a plug-in space to various components involved in networking. The layers of the OSI reference model are illustrated in Figure 6-1.

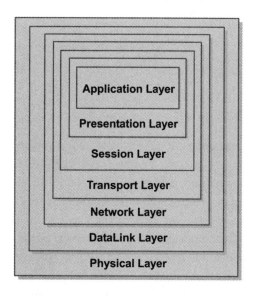

FIGURE 6-1 *OSI reference model.*

The layers of the OSI reference model are as follows:

- Physical layer
- DataLink layer
- Network layer
- Transport layer
- Session layer
- Presentation layer
- Application layer

In the following sections, I explain each of these layers.

Physical Layer

The physical layer is essentially the hardware support layer for networking equipment. This layer provides electrical and functional characteristics to initialize, maintain, and deactivate physical network links. Network links send bit streams of data and understand information only in the form of individual bits. The cabling used in a network is an example of a component that operates in the physical layer of the OSI model.

The physical layer takes care of the following components in a network:

◆ Transmission medium

◆ Means of signaling

◆ Timing and clocks

◆ Synchronous serial communication

Network security is not limited to intrusions; it also involves choosing the right type of hardware while setting up your network. Therefore, though the physical layer might not seem to be a very important part in a secure network, you can't overlook it. For example, poor quality cabling might save initial infrastructure costs, but in the long run, it can lead to data loss even in the best protocols, such as the User Datagram Protocol (UDP), and cause severe network performance problems with other reliable protocols. Therefore, you should always use standardized networking equipment and avoid bizarre configurations for your network—even if investing in standard networking components pushes the networking budget a little higher.

Data Link Layer

The data link layer is the second basic layer of the OSI model. It provides a functional and procedural medium for the exchange of data between network entities. This layer understands data in the form of characters and enables you to initialize and maintain data link connections. An example of a component that functions in this layer of the OSI model is the standard of the Institute of Electrical and Electronic Engineers (IEEE), the IEEE 802.3 or Ethernet. Ethernet is a widely accepted standard for LAN, and it can accommodate up to 1024 nodes. If the distance is greater, the High-Level Data Link Control (HDLC)-based networks are used.

Network Layer

The network layer is an important layer from the point of view of a network administrator. This layer encapsulates most upper layers of the OSI model and provides point-to-point interaction between the two networking components in the upper layer. Some components of this layer, such as IP, Routers, and ICMP, are important for network security. These components are discussed in the following sections.

Internet Protocol

Internet Protocol (IP) operates in the third layer of the OSI model and provides encapsulation facilities to protocols that operate in the higher levels of the model. An example of this is shown in Figure 6-2.

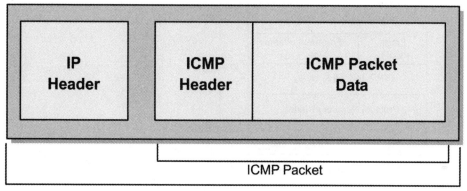

FIGURE 6-2 *Encapsulation of an ICMP packet within the IP protocol.*

The IP protocol uses datagrams to communicate over a packet-switched network. In a packet-switched network, every packet of data that is traveling through a network is treated as a separate entity. The packet contains a header information section, which contains the address of the recipient, and other important details about the data within the packet. Intermediate systems, such as routers (discussed in the next section) use this header information to forward the packet to the correct path or return an error message if the packet cannot be forwarded. An IP datagram is depicted in Figure 6-3.

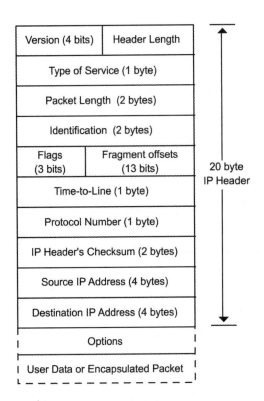

Version (4 bits)	Header Length
Type of Service (1 byte)	
Packet Length (2 bytes)	
Identification (2 bytes)	
Flags (3 bits)	Fragment offsets (13 bits)
Time-to-Line (1 byte)	
Protocol Number (1 byte)	
IP Header's Checksum (2 bytes)	
Source IP Address (4 bytes)	
Destination IP Address (4 bytes)	
Options	
User Data or Encapsulated Packet	

20 byte IP Header

FIGURE 6-3 *Structure of an IP datagram.*

Following is the structure of the IP packet header:

◆ **Version.** This is the version of the IP.

◆ **IP Header Length.** This field contains the size of the IP header. Note that this field contains only the length of the IP header and not the combined length of all headers that may be encapsulated inside the IP packet.

◆ **Type of Service.** This field is usually set to zero and defines the "quality" of service that is expected from a network.

◆ **Packet Size.** This field contains the total size of the packet, which is the sum of the size of the header and the size of actual data.

◆ **Identification.** This is a 2-byte number that is used by recipient computers to arrange fragmented data packets before merging them. More information on packet fragmenting and merging can be found in the "Routers" section of this chapter.

◆ **Flags.** This is a combination of three bits that inform the intermediate systems about the fragmenting feasibility for a packet. The field also contains the Don't Fragment (DF) flag of the IP packet.

◆ **Fragmentation Offset.** This is a 13-bit byte count that starts from the first byte of the original packet (the packet before any fragmentation). This counter helps the end system, or the recipient computer, to confirm correct re-assembly of the packet.

◆ **Time To Live.** This field contains an 8-bit number of hops that a packet can sustain. A packet can be routed only up to a certain number of times, which is specified in this field. This is done to avoid a scenario in which a packet continues to hop infinitely inside a network. Every time a packet is passed through a network, this number is decremented by the router.

◆ **Protocol.** This field specifies the type of packet that is encapsulated inside the IP packet. A specific number represents each higher level, encapsulated protocol type. For example, if the packet being carried is an ICMP packet, the value of this field is 1. Similarly, if the packet is a TCP packet, the value of this field is 6.

◆ **Header Checksum.** This field is a checksum number that can inform the recipient or an intermediate system whether the IP header is corrupted. End recipients or intermediate systems discard packets if the checksums are wrong. The checksum is initially inserted by the sender of the packet and can be updated by every intermediate system if any changes (such as fragmentation) are made to the packet.

◆ **Source Address.** This is the IP address of the original sender of the packet. This field can be dangerously modified to spoof the identity of the sender during a network attack. More on this topic is discussed in the "IP Spoofing" section of Chapter 7, "Network Attacks."

◆ **Destination Address.** This is the IP address of the final recipient of the IP packet.

◆ **Options.** The options are almost never used. If they are used, however, the size of the IP header can be increased.

Routers

Routers are computers or gadgets that do not directly store usernames or act as a server or a client. Routers operate at the Network Layer 3 (L3) of the OSI model. They forward data to the intended recipient. Routers may be used to connect two or more IP networks or to connect an IP network to an Internet connection. Although routers need not know the information being sent through them, they might modify certain aspects of the information to enable information packets to reach the correct destination.

A router, in physical terms, consists of a computer with a minimum of two network interface cards. Both these network cards should support IP. A router receives a packet from each interface and forwards the received packets to an appropriate output network interface. All packets received by the router have DataLink layer (L2) protocol headers. The router removes these headers and adds a new DataLink Layer header to the packet. After the new header is added to the packet, it can be transmitted using the appropriate network interface.

A router reads the network layer header or IP header information before it can decide the following:

◆ Should the packet be forwarded?

◆ Which network interface should the packet be forwarded to?

A series of steps is involved in routing a packet. These steps are shown here:

1. The router receives a packet.
2. The packet's header information is extracted.
3. The destination IP address of the packet is extracted.
4. If the size of the packet is larger than the Maximum Transfer Unit (MTU) and the packet's header information has a Don't Fragment (DF) flag set, the packet is discarded. A message of failure is sent to the original sender of the packet.
5. If the size of the packet is larger than the MTU but the DF flag is not set, the packet is broken down into smaller fragments.
6. The best path for the packet is found by searching the routing table stored inside the router.
7. If the size of the original packet is larger than the MTU, the small fragments are dispatched through the appropriate network interface. Otherwise, the packet is forwarded to its destination address.
8. The packet fragments are collected at the destination and reassembled.

Routing tables have the same format as the tables in network bridges and switches. The difference is that routers are identified by the IP addresses of computers instead of MAC hardware addresses.

The routing table is nothing but a list of known IP destination addresses and the associated network interfaces that can be used to reach the destinations. Routers also have a provision for a default network interface. This interface may be used for all addresses that are not mentioned in a routing table. Routers also provide packet filters. The packet filter simply discards unwanted packets, which can cause an unnecessary overload on networks. The filter can be used as a firewall, and unsupported protocols can be blocked outside the router. Such a firewall, to some extent, can provide basic security to prevent unauthorized users from entering a network using remote computers.

The basic purpose of a router is to forward packets from one IP network to another IP network. A router determines the broadcast IP destination of a network from the logical AND of an IP address and its associated subnet mask. If a router isn't configured properly, a serious security threat can occur when a packet is sent to a network broadcast address. If a large number of packets is forwarded, your network might face the problem of network overload.

Routers are often used to connect different types of networks. A router can connect networks that use totally different link methodologies. For example, an HDLC link can connect a WAN to an Ethernet-based LAN, as shown in Figure 6-4.

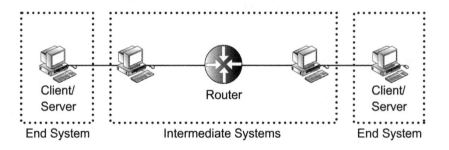

| Client/ Server | | Router | | Client/ Server |
| End System | | Intermediate Systems | | End System |

FIGURE 6-4 *Role of routers in a network.*

The important thing to note here is that each of these networks has a different MTU. This is due to the fact that optimization levels for packet sizes are different for the two networks. Therefore, whenever a packet comes from the network that has a bigger MTU and needs to go to the network with a smaller MTU, the router will fragment the packet according to the norms of the destination network. IP packet fragmentation is illustrated in Figure 6-5.

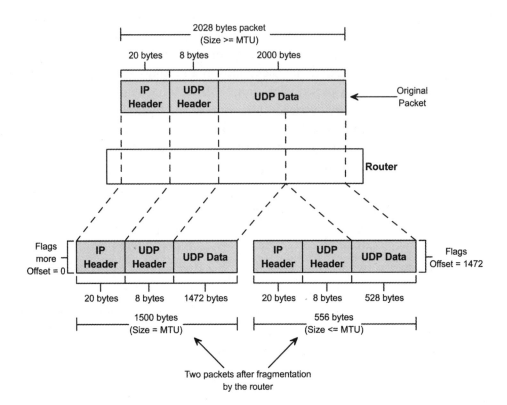

FIGURE 6-5 *IP packet fragmentation.*

Important roles, such as that of a mediator, make routers an integral part of an Internet configuration. These roles also make a router susceptible to hacking attacks.

With many computers accessing the Internet, associated protocols require a network error reporting mechanism to determine better routes in reaching a destination. Internet Control Message Protocol (ICMP) fulfills this need. Next, I first explain ICMP and then proceed to the vulnerabilities that exist in the protocol.

Internet Control Message Protocol

All routers and servers on the Internet provide the ICMP service. ICMP is an error reporting protocol that is used to inform the source computer about any problems occurring with a data packet during transit or upon reaching the destination. Problems, such as the destination server not responding, the destination host being too busy, the IP packet header being corrupted, and so on, are all handled by ICMP. ICMP is also the first medium that is tested after setting up a network. Therefore, administrators use this protocol frequently to verify the sound state of a network server. Consider the example shown in Figure 6-6 to understand the workings of an ICMP service.

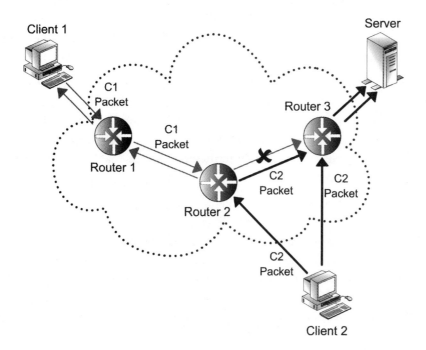

FIGURE 6-6 *An ICMP ECHO request and response.*

You see the following items in Figure 6-6:

1. A client computer, Client1, sends a request to Server1.

2. The router, Router1, receives this packet and forwards it to Router2.

3. Router2 receives this packet and realizes that the packet is too large to enter the next network and has a DF flag set on it.

4. Router2 calls the ICMP server and sends a message back to Client1 stating the problem.

5. In another instance, a second computer, Client2, sends a request for a connection to Server1.

6. The packet is received by Router2 and forwarded to Router3.

7. Router3 sends the packet to Server1, and the operation is completed without requiring ICMP.

Although ICMP can generate many types of messages, the above example uses two messages—an ECHO request and an ECHO reply. The request that was sent to Router1 and Router2 by Client1 was the ECHO request. The error response that Router2 returned was the ECHO reply. ICMP packets are sent in encapsulated form, using the IP protocol for transmission over the Internet.

The Network layer IP is responsible for ensuring reliability in any transaction made over the Internet. Reliability is achieved by specifying a destination address in each packet that is being transmitted. The source address is set as the IP address of Client1, which generates the ICMP echo request. The IP protocol type is set to ICMP, which indicates to every intermediate system that the packet is to be handled only by the remote end system's ICMP server program.

It is possible that a packet sent by Client1 does not reach Server1, and yet no ICMP message is received by Client1. Such a situation can occur when Router1 forwards the packet to Router2 and breaks down. Router2 rejects the packet, and an ICMP ECHO reply is generated and dispatched to Client1. However, since Router1 is no longer functional, the request never reaches Client1. Another important point to note is that no acknowledgements are sent for ICMP messages. This would be ludicrous, because an infinite exchange of packets can overload all network lines between the two computers.

 NOTE

Although the IP protocol is responsible for reliable communication, IP isn't a reliable protocol. This is simply because network hardware itself can't be relied upon. The purpose of the ICMP protocol is only to provide feedback to the source computers and not to ensure the reliability of the IP protocol.

The ping application is the client interface to the ICMP server. A ping application is the easiest method to verify the operational status of another computer. A ping application can also be used with parameters to collect information about various other attributes of performance. You could test the performance of the end computer or of the route that is connecting the two computers. Performance is determined by measuring the time taken by a packet to complete a return trip from the client, to the server, and back to the client.

Transport Layer

The fourth layer in the OSI reference model is the transport layer. This layer facilitates data transfer between two end systems by encapsulating the data packet within the network layer data packet. Two important components of the transport layer are TCP and the UDP protocol, which are discussed in detail in this section.

TCP

TCP is a connection-oriented and reliable transport protocol. A connection-oriented protocol implies that two hosts, wanting to communicate with each other, must first establish a connection before actual data exchange can take place. In TCP, a connection is established using a three-way handshake. TCP assigns sequence numbers to every packet in each segment, and all data received is responded to with an acknowledgement to the sender. TCP hides perplexing network details from the upper layers of the IP protocol.

Information Fields in a TCP Packet

A typical TCP packet contains the following six information fields along with actual data:

- **Synchronize Sequence Numbers (SYN).** This field is valid only during the three steps involving the handshake. The sequence number is read by the receiving host and is stored as the client computer's first sequence number. TCP sequence numbers are 32-bit numbers, ranging from 0 to 4,294,967,295(2 ^ 32). Every packet of data that is exchanged between two computers using a TCP connection is sequenced.

- **Acknowledgement (ACK).** This field is generally set. The `acknowledgement number` field in the TCP header contains the assumed value of the next sequence number. This field is also an acknowledgement of the data received in the previous packet.

- **Reset (RST).** This field informs the other computer that the connection has been dropped and all memory structures have been flushed.

◆ **Urgent (URG).** This field informs the other computer to process data on a priority basis.

◆ **Push (PSH).** This field informs the other computer to pass the data to the concerned application as soon as possible instead of putting the data in the queue. This flag is generally set in interactive connections, such as Telnet, rlogin, and some chat applications.

◆ **Finish (FIN).** This field informs the other computer that the transmission of data is complete, but the host is still open to accepting data.

User Datagram Protocol (UDP)

The US Department of Defense (DoD) developed UDP for use with IP. Unlike TCP, which first tries to establish a reliable connection with the server, UDP works on the concept of "best-effort mechanism." However, UDP is an unreliable protocol for communication because of the following reasons:

1. No error is generated for lost data packets.

2. No error is generated for duplicate packets.

3. No assurance is provided that a packet has reached the destination safely.

In simpler terms, UDP is a one-way protocol—what is sent from the client is gone for good. The client will never hear any further information about this packet.

Although some reliability is provided in UDP, the end recipients reject packets that are corrupted during transit. It's the responsibility of the upper layer application to check such loss. In addition, because no packet acknowledgement is required in UDP, the network load is reduced to a certain extent.

The packet structure of UDP is very simple, as shown in Figure 6-7.

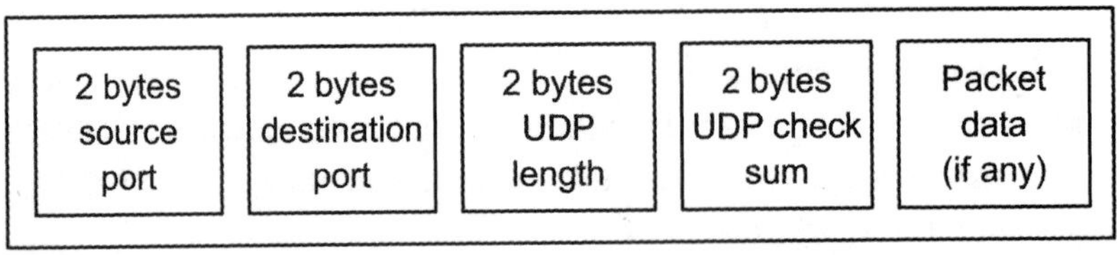

2 bytes source port	2 bytes destination port	2 bytes UDP length	2 bytes UDP check sum	Packet data (if any)

FIGURE 6-7 *Structure of a UDP packet.*

The UDP header consists of four fields, each two bytes in length:

◆ Source Port

◆ Destination Port

◆ UDP Data Length

◆ UDP Checksum

UDP is unsuitable for many applications, although the simplicity of the protocol gives performance advantage to those applications that do not require much reliability. An example of such an application is one that pertains to streaming video and audio content.

What Are Ports?

Port is a term that is used often in networking. Regardless of whether your computer is online or offline, your computer has a number of open channels to which various programs or other computers can connect. These channels are known as *ports*. Obviously, if your computer isn't connected to a network, only the local program will be able to access these ports. Once a computer is online, however, anyone on the network can execute a client program on their remote computer to connect to these ports.

Ports are channels created between two computers for the exchange of information. A computer can have many open ports for receiving connection requests. For example, a server that has HTTP, SMTP, POP, FTP, and Telnet services can have five open ports. The default port numbers of HTTP, SMTP, POP, FTP, and Telnet are 80, 25, 110, 21, and 23, respectively. These ports are not hardware components, but are like virtual stations within your computer's memory. All computers have them, including the server you dial to access the Internet.

When a computer is turned on, a number of ports are virtually created. These remain open and search for programs that are running on remote or local computers. This process is known as *listening*. If another computer wishes to connect to a port on your computer, it can do this in two ways: by being offered a port address to connect to, or by scanning available open ports.

Sometimes, your computer willingly gives a port number to another computer to make a connection. At other times, the other computer might just guess or try one of the universally known port numbers. However, hackers might also choose to run a port scan through your computer from a remote location. A *port scanner* is software that allows a user to search all ports that a server is listening to. When such a program is used, the user simply has to type the IP address of the desired computer, and the scanner presents a complete report of all ports that are being listened to by the host computer.

 NOTE

Port scanners are of two types: *stealth* and *normal*. Stealth port scanners are less effective in finding open ports, but they can hide from intrusion detection systems, firewalls, and an ISP's administrative staff. Normal scanners, on the other hand, provide more information about open ports in a server and are used by administrators because they do not need to hide within their own network.

Session Layer and Presentation Layer

The session layer is the fifth layer in the OSI model, and it offers a channel to session-based services, such as:

◆ **Telnet.** Telnet is a protocol that can be used to perform remote logins and operate a remote computer from a virtual terminal.

◆ **FTP.** FTP is used for transferring files between two connected computers.

Both these protocols maintain user sessions from the time they log on to the time they log out. The session layer supports a feature that helps in structuring response dialogues between computers. This feature allows two-way simultaneous or alternative cross-network operations.

The presentation layer supports a common syntax and provides conversion facilities from one type of network to another. This layer also permits computers to be referenced by their names, rather than by their difficult-to-remember addresses. The presentation layer defines how applications should use a network. An example of a component that operates in this layer is the SMB protocol. The SMB protocol provides naming facilities and file sharing features in Windows and UNIX-based networks, using appropriate servers.

Application Layer

The application layer is the uppermost layer in the OSI model. This layer is used directly by applications. Data belonging to this layer cannot generally travel in a network on its own and requires encapsulation by another layer to reach the destination.

The application layer can be considered the cause of the existence of all other layers of the OSI model. The other layers in the OSI model carry the application layer data. All services in a server send application layer data packets. Similarly, all client programs exchange data using this protocol. This layer does all the actual work and is supported by the other layers. Some programs that operate in this layer are

- ◆ E-mail servers and clients, such as sendmail
- ◆ Web servers and clients, such as Apache
- ◆ DNS servers, such as Bind

We will be discussing each of these servers in detail in the coming chapters.

Summary

In this chapter, you learned about the different layers of the OSI model and their roles in a network. In this chapter, I discussed the data link, network, transport, session, presentation, and application layers of the OSI reference model. You will find these basic fundamentals in all networking technologies that use the Internet.

Check Your Understanding

Multiple Choice Questions

1. What is an ICMP ECHO request?

    a. A method of establishing a TCP connection.

    b. A method to transfer files from one computer to another over an IP network.

    c. A method to determine the network operational status of another computer.

    d. A method to broadcast a data packet to all the computers in a network.

2. Which of the following is the correct expansion of the acronym UDP?

    a. Universal Datagram Protocol

    b. Unreliable Data Protocol

    c. Unlimited Data Protocol

    d. User Datagram Protocol

3. What is the minimum number of network interface cards that a router should have?

    a. 1

    b. 2

    c. 4

    d. 16

Short Questions

1. Why is TCP a reliable protocol?

2. What is packet encapsulation?

Answers

Multiple Choice Answers

1. **c.** ICMP ECHO request is a method to determine the network operational status of another computer.

2. **d.** UDP stands for User Datagram Protocol.

3. **b.** A router should have a minimum of two network interface cards.

Short Answers

1. TCP uses a two-way communication system for data transfer. Whenever a data packet is sent from one computer to another, the recipient sends an acknowledgement receipt back to the sender. This method is a confirmation for the original sender that the communication was successful. This mechanism makes TCP a reliable protocol.

2. A particular data packet can travel only in the layer that it is meant for. If an application layer packet needs to travel in an IP-based network, the application layer packet must be encapsulated inside an IP packet. Encapsulation is the process of enclosing the upper layer data packet inside a lower layer protocol's packet header.

Chapter 7

Network Attacks

Vulnerabilities on the Internet can put governments, businesses, and individual users at risk. No one could have imagined that the Internet would grow to become the huge, complex, and dynamic structure of interconnected networks that it is today. The Internet has no clear boundaries and no central command control.

When the Internet was designed, security was not the main concern. The aim of the Internet was to be an open-ended system with distributed control and responsibility. Further, users on the Internet were expected to have mutual trust.

Security issues are still not well understood and are not given high priority by software developers, network managers, or even end users. Therefore, it is difficult to ensure the integrity, availability, and privacy of information, especially on the Internet.

In addition, the Internet is virtual, not physical. This means that it has no geographic status, location, or well-defined boundaries. Conventional rules of physical security are impossible to apply on the Internet. Instead, new technologies and innovative thinking are required to understand the working and the vulnerabilities of the Internet.

With the development of security services, intruders also are becoming organized. Intruders discover vulnerabilities within weeks of the release of software. Moreover, intruders prefer to use the open-architecture approach. Highly sophisticated and user-friendly intruder tools are being developed and distributed over the Internet. Even though a user might simply download these tools to experiment with hacking, he or she could inadvertently fall into a trap and become a victim of an attack.

The Internet is growing at a very rapid pace. Networks have become interconnected and the intrusion tools have become advanced, which means that the security of your machine depends more on the security of other computers than on your own.

To begin with in this chapter, I give an overview of network attacks, different kinds of attackers, possible motives of attacks, possible vulnerabilities, and basic measures to avoid network attacks. Proceeding further, I discuss various types of attacks in detail.

Definition of an Attack

An attack is an attempt to do one of the following on a known or unknown network or server:

◆ Undermine or adversely affect performance

◆ Retrieve secret information

◆ Destroy or replace information

◆ Illegally use resources

◆ Restrict or prevent a legitimate user from accessing resources

The moment a computer on your network is connected to the Internet, it opens a window to your local network that all users on the Internet can peer through. Most visitors to your network will not be interested in window-shopping. However, a few visitors might try to view data that you do not intend to make available for public use. Some visitors, who experiment just for the satisfaction, might attempt to force the window open and sneak in. The results of this "sneaking" can range from mere embarrassment to serious data loss for an organization. For example, you might discover one fine morning that the content of all Web sites on your server has been replaced with obscene messages. Another serious loss can be a case in which your server has been unreachable for the last 12 hours or more, and all your confidential data has been stolen and wiped off your system.

Even though the threats mentioned here have been around for some time, there is no software available that is invulnerable to all attacks. The maxim is that every software product has bugs or security holes. Some of them have been discovered and exploited. The rest are waiting to be discovered. Internet development cannot stop out of fear of network attacks, however. Services also cannot be denied to legitimate users fearing a security threat.

The sole aim of having network security is to keep strangers out. Yet, the basis of bringing a server online is to provide to the world a controlled method of accessing your network. Drawing the line between controlled access and uncontrolled access can be difficult. For example, a poorly configured Ping Server Internet Control Message Protocol (ICMP) can compromise even a very carefully planned firewall security system. Similarly, a poorly configured firewall system can make a Web server impossible to use.

An attack can be launched from anywhere at any time. Your information can be attacked when data is about to be dispatched, when data is being transmitted, or when data is being received. Therefore, end users as well as administrators need to take precautions against network attacks.

Who Is an Attacker?

As already discussed in earlier chapters, a typical computer network has three types of users: administrators, normal users, and outsiders. Following is a description of each of these users:

◆ **Administrators.** An administrator of a network or a computer is a user who has the maximum authority to access or modify the network or the computer. The administrator has access to all the resources of the computer and the network. An administrator creates users, applies security updates, and determines security policies for the network. The administrator also is responsible for ensuring that nothing goes wrong on the network and can access it at all times. This means that the administrator does not need to attack his network. Instead, attackers would be normal users or outsiders who are trying to become the administrators of the network.

◆ **Normal users.** A normal user is any user who has been provided a username and a password and has the authority to log on to a server or a network. This type of user generally has limited access permissions to the server. For example, permissions for disk space in the user's home directory, FTP access, access to e-mail, access to Telnet, SSH, and so on are restricted. Permissions granted to a normal user depend on the security policy of a particular network.

◆ **Outsiders.** An outsider is a person who is unknown to the server or the network and who does not have permissions to log on the server or the network. Similarly, access to services such as Anonymous FTP, open relay SMTP, ICMP, and HTTP also are provided to an outsider. The degree of access provided to these services varies in each network.

Motives behind an Attack

You can never quite determine the exact motive of an attack. However, there are a few common reasons for an attack, which are discussed below:

◆ **Undermine or adversely affect the performance of a computer.** A personal grudge, an inadvertent mistake, or frustration can provoke an attacker to unleash an attack on your system. A few examples of attacks that adversely affect the performance of a server are flooding, spamming, and Distributed Denial of Service (DoS) attack. The details of these attacks are covered in the section, "External Attacks," later in this chapter.

◆ **Retrieve secret information.** In such attacks, the attacker wants some confidential information that might be available on your computer. Such attacks are generally dictionary- or word list-based password or brute force password attacks. More information on these attacks can be found in the "Password Attacks" section.

◆ **Destroy or replace information.** An attacker who fails to retrieve information from your network might just destroy whatever information is available. The attacker might launch a password attack or exploit the known vulnerabilities in a program installed on your computer.

◆ **Illegitimately use computing resources.** An attacker trying to send e-mail messages randomly might use your SMTP server to relay those e-mail messages. Or he may run a program on your computer to collect data from the Internet, process it, and send it to some other location.

◆ **Restrict a legitimate user from accessing resources.** In these attacks, the attacker targets your computer and deploys Trojans on your system. These Trojans might disallow users from accessing resources on their computers.

Types of Attacks

A network can be attacked from within or without. These are referred to as *internal* and *external* attacks, respectively. In this section, I describe both these types of attacks in detail.

Internal Attacks

Internal attacks are generally initiated from within a server or a network. They may be used to reduce the performance of a server or gain unsolicited access to a network or a server. Examples of such attacks are password file brute forcing and Trojan attacks. Let's examine some of these attacks in detail.

Trojans

The Trojan legacy dates back to a Greek myth of a wooden horse in which a dangerous army was hidden inside what appeared to be a magnificent gift. Trojans behave in a similar manner. In layman terms, Trojans are malicious programs that appear to be nice utilities or games but have a malicious intent. For example, an executable cartoon file that you download to show your child might contain a program to destroy all the data on your disk.

A Trojan is harmless if it's stored on your disk but isn't accessible for execution. However, a problem arises when you run a Trojan. A Trojan, when executed, might display nothing and return you back to the prompt or display a confusing error message. If the program is really a Trojan, you could be in for trouble. A powerful Trojan could give more control to a hacker than the administrator. Trojans could run in the background just like a daemon. Unlike the good daemon, however, the Trojan will serve the attacker instead of the administrator.

The more severe impact of Trojans is that Trojans facilitate hackers who wouldn't have bothered to peep into your system. There are numerous programs available on the Internet that search Trojan-infected servers. Any person with such a scanner program can make the fullest use of Trojans.

It doesn't take a mastermind hacker to get into a Trojan-infected computer. People who are likely to break into your computer using Trojans aren't nuclear scientists or hardened cyber criminals. Usually, they are enthusiasts who think hacking a computer is an achievement to display their might. Many such crackers have just a little more knowledge than the administrator of the hacked server. Firstly, the hacker knows that the system is infected, and secondly, the hacker knows how to use the Trojan!

Single-user operating systems have been threatened by Trojans for a long time. In a multi-user environment like Linux, however, the damage can be significantly contained if proper precautions are taken.

CAUTION

All administrators should remember this: " Never run an unknown executable as root."
To go a step further, never log on as root unless you need to for a specific purpose.

Having talked about Trojan attacks, I will now discuss the types of Trojans;
namely Remote Access Tools (RAT), Password Retrievers, Key loggers, and Trojans based on known protocols.

Remote Access Tools

A RAT (Remote Access Tools) Trojan runs a daemon-like service on your computer. The daemon enables the attacker to connect to your computer and execute
any command on your system. Even when you scan the services running on your
server, the Trojan would probably be listed with a description, such as "required by
Linux kernel," so that a novice administrator would never turn it off.

Most Trojans aren't self-propagating. Therefore, unless you run a program with
incorrect permissions, a Trojan won't cause trouble. When you run the program,
however, you automatically trigger the Trojan. The Trojan would copy itself at a
safe location, rename itself to hide its identity, and add itself in the middle of the
/etc/services file.

Every RAT Trojan runs on a particular port (like a daemon). Therefore, by searching for a specific open port, a Trojan scanner can find the presence of a RAT Trojan. As a result, Trojan scanners can help systems administrators find the presence
of Trojans on their computers.

Password Retrievers

Passwords retrievers are Trojans that run in the background and illegally hog system resources by trying to recover passwords for user accounts that are installed
with Linux. Such Trojans are easier to detect because they show up as a lot of
activity in various log files and the running process list.

Key Loggers

Key loggers are also daemons that record every incoming character. These logs can be sent by e-mail or published to attackers. Key loggers don't simply record the data typed on the console. Powerful Trojans may log even those characters that were typed on Telnet terminals, VNC sessions, rlogin sessions, and so on.

In addition to logging commands and typed characters, a key logger can log all content read, written, or displayed during a user's session. For example, key loggers can log the output of the following line:

```
cat    /etc/passwd
```

The preceding command could facilitate an active Trojan to log the contents of the entire `passwd` file and inform a hacker about the accounts that are not shadowed. These accounts can later be brute forced to recover original passwords and gain access to the server. I discuss password-retrieving tools attacks later in this chapter, in the section "Password Attacks."

Trojans Based on Known Protocols

Trojans based on known protocols are not very difficult to detect but can cause serious damage. Such Trojans will install themselves as though they are known services. For example, a Telnet-based Trojan can delete your currently installed Telnet server and redefine all links to point to itself. The Trojan also will retain the name of the service as "Telnet Server" to avoid detection. In addition, the Trojan can hook port 23, which is the default port for Telnet. Whenever a user tries to log on, the user's access information will be stored or sent to the offender. These Trojans are easier to detect and eliminate. You should examine the Telnet server logs for the period of inactivity to find the file that was used by the Trojan to store information. After you find the file, reinstalling the original Telnet server can solve the problem. Similar types of Trojans can operate on FTP, SMTP, POP, and other commonly used protocols.

Password Attacks

Most Linux distributions store passwords as hashes. As already discussed in Chapter 5, "Encryption and Authentication," hashes cannot be reverted back to their original form. You also learned that in hash-based authentication, hashes of input passwords are compared with stored hashes. However, this doesn't mean that you can freely distribute your hashed passwords and expect that no one will be able to reverse engineer them. If your passwords are not shadowed and an attacker manages to extract the /etc/passwd file from your system, he or she can try to recover passwords from this file.

The /etc/passwd file stores usernames and hashed passwords along with other related data. If the hashes cannot be used to recover original passwords, an attacker can use programs to calculate the hashes of word lists and compare them with the stored hashes to find the correct password. A single computer might take too long to compare hashes, especially if the word lists are huge. Therefore, an attacker may use the resources in vulnerable hosts that run in parallel to speed up the attack several times.

Password attacks can be studied in four broad categories. The method of guessing or retrieving passwords is different in each category. The categories are listed here:

◆ Word List or Dictionary Attacks
◆ Brute Force Attacks
◆ Word List and Brute Force Attacks combined
◆ Internal Flood Attacks

Let me explain each of the above-listed categories in detail.

Word List or Dictionary Attacks

Word list or dictionary attacks are made on the /etc/passwd file. A program uses dictionaries or word lists that could store an exhaustive list of possible passwords. Many hacking tools that use word lists and dictionaries are freely available for downloading on the Internet. The hacking tool reads each word in the file and computes a hash for it. This hash is then compared with the one in the /etc/passwd file for each account. The process is time-consuming, but bad passwords are recovered easily. Therefore, good passwords are critical to keep your system secure. You can learn more about good passwords in the next chapter.

Brute Force Attacks

Brute force attacks are not based on any word lists or dictionaries. Instead, these attacks are based on password criteria. Brute force programs try to guess a password in a sequential manner based on the criteria provided. For example, a typical criterion set for a password could be one of the following:

◆ Password minimum length = 2

◆ Password maximum length = 2

◆ Password can contain alphabets = Yes

◆ Password can contain numeric = No

◆ Password is case-sensitive = Yes

The preceding criteria instructs the attacker program to compute hashes for all words starting from aa to ZZ.

This process takes much more time than word list attacks but can be used to guess passwords even if they are not bad passwords. Brute force attacks are highly effective if many computers are used in parallel to search for passwords. Such attacks also generally target specific accounts instead of all the accounts on a system because otherwise

POPULAR PASSWORD ATTACKERS

There are many password-cracking tools freely available for download. Here are a few exceptionally popular tools:

◆ **Crack.** Crack is a perl script that uses the dictionary approach as well as the brute force approach to crack passwords. The program is quite fast and can be run on multiple hosts simultaneously with the help of rsh or other related utilities. Crack requires a wordlist for efficient password guessing. The program also tries several combinations of passwords by using a simple logic to crack badly chosen passwords. For example, some of the methods employed by this script check lowercase and uppercase options for password, repeat usernames, and add two to three digit numbers at the end of usernames. The script is freely available for download on the Internet and can be useful for administrators also—because it can help them find weak passwords before someone else finds them.

◆ **John the Ripper.** This is probably the most popular password-attacking tool available on the Internet. The program is freely available for download and can be used on both Windows and Linux platforms. The program uses complex algorithms to speed up the guessing process and can crack DES encryption-based passwords.

◆ **Xcrack.** Xcrack is also a perl script, like Crack, and uses a word list to attack the /etc/passwd file. The script is a lightweight password attacker and doesn't do much guesswork. Instead, it simply tries to generate word list hashes and compare them with the user's password. The program isn't too effective but works fine for exceptionally bad passwords.

the task would be time-consuming. For example, they can target default users that are created with the standard installation of Linux.

Word List and Brute Force Attacks Combined

The two types of attacks discussed above, Trojans and password attacks, can be combined to improve the effectiveness of an internal attack. Most users use passwords that contain text and numeric characters, such as "danger34," and assume that they are good passwords. However, a combined wordlist and brute force attack can extract these types of passwords easily. These programs make use of wordlists, as well as a criterion. The main advantage of this kind of attack is that many low-probability passwords, which might not be used by users, are bypassed.

Internal Flood Attacks

Internal flood attacks make use of loopholes that go unchecked by an administrator. Authenticated users of a server carry out these attacks to exploit the errors committed by an administrator. For example, a common mistake committed by administrators is to keep user log files on the boot partition of Linux. Recursive and frequent requests to a service by a user can cause the log files to become very huge and eventually choke the server. Such attacks can also be caused if users' home directories are on the boot partition. In addition, some users with no disk quota can run the simplest shell scripts to fill space on the partition and cause a computer to stop responding.

Internal floods also can be initiated by sending an exceptionally high number of e-mail messages or other kinds of requests to remote servers. These requests can overload the server substantially.

External or Network Attacks

External attacks are perpetrated from outside the computer. These attacks generally aim at reducing the performance of a server or pushing the server to a limit at which point it breaks down and can then be used to gain access to data. In most cases, the attacker has very limited or no authorized access to the victim computer. There are many types of external attacks:

- ◆ Common Gateway Interface (CGI) attacks
- ◆ Denial of Service

♦ E-mail Bombing

♦ E-mail Spamming

♦ Spoofed/Forged E-mail

♦ TCP SYN Flooding and IP Spoofing

The following sections discuss each of these attacks in detail.

CGI Attacks

CGI is a mechanism through which a browser is allowed to communicate with the programs running on a Web server. The phrase CGI means:

♦ **Common.** Something that is widely available, regardless of the platform or software used by people.

♦ **Gateway.** A method by which two devices or components, such as a Web browser and a server, communicate.

♦ **Interface.** A "front end" for the server that is running in the background. For example, when an HTML form is filled and submitted, a CGI script might be submitting data to the server and then to another destination.

CGI is a powerful feature for Web servers, it enables Web servers to display information to the users. In addition to this, CGI utilizes the computing abilities of the computer. A Web server that supports CGI gives users a certain amount of control over what the Web server displays.

Careful implementation of CGI programs can make a Web server more versatile. Web sites can deliver dynamic information, interactive pages, user-friendly Web interfaces, and several other features. However, careless use of CGI can cause a major security hole in a server. Each Web server uses a username for its operations. CGI scripts are potential security threats even when you run your Web server as "nobody." A subverted CGI script running as "nobody" still has sufficient privileges to collect and reveal system-critical data or examine the network information that could later be used to compromise the host computer. A poorly written CGI application can hand over unlimited control to the Web user. Therefore, a system administrator who doesn't worry about CGI security should expect abuse of his network infrastructure, network downtime due to malicious attacks, and loss of confidential data.

CGI scripts and applications should be written with the same care and attention given to Internet servers because each CGI script is a gateway to the server. The problem with CGI scripts is that each script presents its own set of exploitable bugs. CGI scripts can present security threats in two ways:

◆ They may intentionally or unintentionally display secret information about the host system that can help attackers break in.

◆ Hackers can trick CGI scripts that allow user input from a Web interface. Hackers may use special commands from within HTML forms to execute arbitrary commands on the server.

A disadvantage of CGI applications that accept data is that they can be tricked by hackers to execute any command they want. The security vulnerability arises because many command interpreters understand special characters differently. If a hacker formats special characters correctly and submits them to poorly written CGI applications, the submission might result in damage. A malicious Web user could include operating system commands in HTML text fields and enclose them in the back ticks (`) character, which is used to pass complete commands in shell scripts and also is recognized by languages like Perl.

For example, a hacker can construct a form and set the `formname` field as:

```
'`cat /etc/passwd` bighack@illegal.org #'
```

This form input might prove to be a critical security hole. In case a programmer doesn't perform a check on the form inputs, this can harm the data or show undesirable results.

CGI applications that do not perform sanity checks for data pertaining to user input can be crashed through a Web browser. For example, suppose that an HTML form accepts data using the `GET` method and submits it to a CGI program. This CGI program can be crashed by putting lots of junk text in text fields. Because the `GET` method appends variables to a URL, if too much data is entered, it can cause buffer overflows in CGI applications or even result in a crash of CGI programs.

DoS Attacks

The phrase of the times in the hacking world is *DoS*, short for Denial of Service. This attack does exactly what the name suggests— it denies access to a service to the legitimate users of a computer. DoS attacks have become a very dangerous weapon in Internet warfare.

A DoS attack can do the following damage:

- Flood network and block legitimate network traffic
- Disrupt communication between two computers and prevent everyone from accessing a service
- Prevent an authorized user from accessing a service on the computer
- Choke all services on a specific system

Denial of service attacks are simple to implement and can be very effective. An attacker tries to choke a service by giving it more tasks than it can handle. For example, if you have a Web server capable of accepting or publishing 5,000 pages per second, a DoS attack might send 50,000 fake requests. This means that many genuine page view requests would be denied permission due to an overloaded server. The server might even stop responding and freeze. Typically, DoS attacks are targeted at easily accessible targets, such as HTTP servers, routers, or network gateways.

DoS service attacks have been successfully used against some bandwidth-abundant network servers, such as Yahoo and MSN. The attacks caused the servers to stop their services for a short period of time. A well-planned DoS attack can bring down even the most resource-abundant servers on the Internet.

A DoS attack can be used in combination with Trojans to multiply the attack strength. An attacker can arrange a group of Trojan computers to attack the victim. The underlying statement in DoS attacks is that the actual request that is sent to the victim computer by the offender is a common request, but the number of such requests is so high that the server is unable to handle them. Also, the server cannot easily differentiate between attack requests and genuine user requests resulting in Denial of Service.

A more dangerous aspect of a DoS attack is that the attacker needs to send a very small amount of data. This data gets so amplified by the time it reaches the victim computer that even a high-end bandwidth server cannot handle it. This kind of DoS uses Internet Address spoofing along with other techniques.

DoS attacks can be precisely targeted at particular services on a network. To make DoS attacks effective, the nonrenewable or scarce resources of a computer might be identified and targeted. DoS attacks can be classified into three categories, based upon their targets:

◆ Those that exploit scarce or non-renewable resources

◆ Those that destroy or alter the target network's system configuration

◆ Those that try to cause physical damage to network hardware

Before you get into the details of these DoS attacks, you need to understand IP spoofing.

IP Spoofing

IP spoofing is a way of hiding your identity on a network. Any computer can hide its original identity using public proxy servers. Most protocols, such as TCP, are two-way communication protocols. Many attacks on the Internet use the reliability aspect of two-way protocols against the servers that employ these protocols.

A proxy server is a kind of storage buffer between your computer and a Web site on the Internet you are accessing. The Web site doesn't necessarily need to use the HTTP protocol. A Web site can be an anonymous FTP server, a POP mail server, an SMTP or IMAP server, and so on. The main functional difference between using a proxy and not using a proxy is that when you have a proxy server between your computer and the end resource, a reply to your request doesn't come to you directly; it comes to the proxy server first, and from there, it is relayed to you.

Proxy servers employ a well-known concept of caching. Caching is nothing but a way of locally storing frequently accessed data. A proxy can store files locally. As a result, whenever a user requests these files, instead of downloading them from the Web site, the proxy server simply checks whether the documents are up-to-date and furnishes them from local storage. This mechanism of proxy servers can effectively enhance the performance of a network.

Many Web sites record IP addresses of their visitors to track their movements through pages and monitor visitor trends. Your visit to each page can be logged into a database and used later to generate demographic data or gather information about you.

A solution was developed to prevent Web sites from extracting information about your identity. The solution came up in the form of *public proxy* servers. These public proxy servers are free and open to everyone on the Internet. There are a large number of public proxy servers available in many countries. Some of these require a user to log on to a Web site while others allow anonymous proxy usage. To obtain a list of free proxy servers on the Internet, try searching for *public proxies* or *free proxies*.

An anonymous HTTP proxy server does not forward the HTTP header variable HTTP_X_FORWARDED_FOR to the Web site that a user is visiting. This ensures privacy to the visitor because the Web site could not have logged your IP address.

Other high-end anonymity HTTP servers block a few more headers from reaching Web sites. For example, HTTP_X_FORWARDED_FOR, HTTP_VIA and HTTP_PROXY_CONNECTION variables can be blocked to provide anonymity. This ensures that the destination Web site doesn't even know that you are being redirected via a proxy.

 NOTE

Installing a public proxy for your browser is fairly simple. Correct proxy server information needs to be entered into the browser configuration options. However, take care while using a proxy. Many proxy servers that claim anonymity are actually transparent servers that reveal everything to the end Web site.

Opaque proxy servers show your IP address as nothing or unknown. To find out if your proxy is opaque or transparent, visit www.all-nettools.com/tools1.htm and take the Proxy test. If it displays the message, Proxy server detected, your proxy is ineffective and others can access information about you.

There are proxy services available on the Internet that give you total control over the traffic that is exchanged between your computer and the destination Web site. A feature that can be helpful in IP spoofing is a search option that allows you to choose the fastest anonymous proxy for the Web site that interests you and check the degree of your anonymity. A good anonymous server should allow you to block cookies, modify request headers, and inspect all information sent out by your browser and modify any part of it.

Having examined the concept of IP spoofing, let me get back to our discussion on DoS attacks. DoS attacks that work on the TCP protocol use IP spoofing to hide their original identity. If IP spoofing is not used, SYN attacks and ICMP ECHO attacks will not be possible. Also, the offender will be at risk of being listed in the server logs of the victim computer. The following sections examine these attacks in detail.

DoS Attacks that Exploit Scarce or Nonrenewable Resources

Computers and networks require certain resources to function at full capacity. Some of these resources, such as bandwidth, can be increased to a certain extent by using instant burst mechanisms.Other resources are nonrenewable, however, such as CPU time, memory, and, in some cases, disk space.

DoS attacks target these resources to bring a network to a halt. These attacks can be in the form of flooding infinite recursive programs or propagating self-replicating scripts. These attacks generally employ very basic methodology to crash a computer. For example, a Flood attack can occur when the attacker tries to send continuous e-mail messages to or from the victim server. An example of an infinite recursive attack could be two e-mail accounts in a victim computer that have auto responders or support for ICMP ECHO and reply packets.

Another example could be a self-replicating script that evolves in an infinite loop and keeps generating its copy and executing it. I discuss each kind of attack in more detail later in this chapter, in the section "Viruses and Worms."

DoS Attacks on Network Bandwidth

An attacker can flood the entire bandwidth available on a computer, preventing all legitimate users from accessing that system. Such an attack can be launched by sending ICMP ECHO packets or UDP ECHO packets to the victim computer. If mounted on a one-to-one basis, the attack can be controlled very easily, but when clusters of unconcerned computers are forced to be a part of this attack, the victim computer can be paralyzed within minutes.

To make such an attack possible, the attacking program should have the following capabilities:

◆ The attacker's computer should be able to spoof its original identity. Otherwise, the attack on the intermediary computers would backfire on the attacker himself.

◆ The attacker program should be able to search computers on the Internet that support ICMP or UDP ECHO packets to increase the strength of the attack several times.

In DoS attacks on network bandwidth, the intruder sends to a server fabricated UDP packets that connect its ECHO service to the service on another computer. The forged packets contain the false source address of the victim computer. The two services together create an extremely high volume of packets. The result is that the two computers, the intermediate and the victim, consume all available network bandwidth between them, which means that all other computers on the network have difficulty with communication. When such attacks are targeted between many computers on the same network, the impact of the attack can be devastating.

DoS Attacks on a Network without Consuming the Bandwidth

A Denial of Service attack can cause a system to deny access to legitimate users without actually invading the victim system or choking its bandwidth. The concept might sound very strange. The explanation lies in the basics of TCP/IP protocols and the way operating systems handle them. Such DoS attacks create many "half-open" connections in the victim server.

Before explaining the attack, let me first give you an overview of how a TCP connection is established between two computers. TCP establishes a connection between two computers using a three-stage mechanism. Suppose that computer X, which has a client program, wants to establish a connection with computer Y, which has a server program. The process by which the two computers can establish a connection is depicted in Figure 7-1.

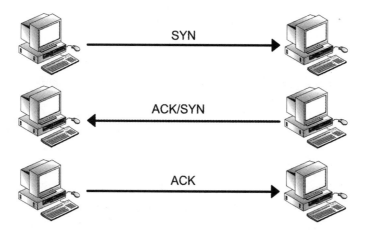

FIGURE 7-1 *Establishing a TCP connection.*

As depicted above, the following steps are involved in creating a TCP connection:

1. X ———SYN———>   Y
2. X <—-SYN/ACK—-   Y
3. X ——-ACK———->   Y

Let me explain each of these steps:

◆ **STEP 1.** The client informs the server that it requires a connection by setting the SYN flag to on. The only purpose of the SYN flag is to inform the server about the state of the flag. The client computer also replies to the server that the sequence number field is valid. Therefore, the server must check the SYN and note it. The sequence number field in the TCP header is set to its ISN Initial Sequence Number (ISN).

◆ **STEP 2.** The server receives this segment and responds back with its own ISN; therefore, the SYN flag is set to on. The server also sends back an acknowledgement (ACK) as a receipt of the client's first segment. The value of this ACK is client's ISN+1.

◆ **STEP 3.** The client receives the acknowledgement (ACK) for its data as well as the server ISN.

If these three steps complete successfully, the connection is established and data transfer may begin.

When a DoS attacker computer initiates Step 1, however, the scenario changes significantly. During Step 2, a space is allocated for the client computer to store the details of the connection. In Step 1, while sending SYN to the server, the attacking computer spoofs its address and sends a request for a connection with a wrong source address. In the second step, the server computer sends the SYN-ACK packet to the wrong address. This wrong address must be a non-existent address; otherwise, the attack will not be effective for reasons I explain later. The server, however, is now in the middle of a nowhere situation. The server is still waiting for the final Step 3 ACK packet, which will never come. This is a half-open connection as displayed in Figure 7-2.

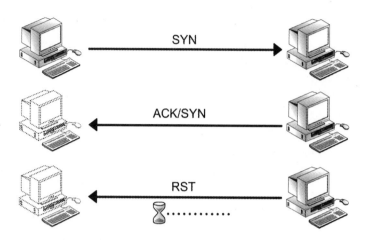

FIGURE 7-2 *Half-open connection.*

There is a data structure in the system memory of the server. This data structure describes all those connections that have not yet been approved or disapproved by the server. Each such data structure is of a finite size and occupies space in system memory. Too many half-open connections can fill this space. When this space eventually gets filled, the server will not accept any new connections, resulting in Denial of Service.

Every server generally has a timeout for each pending connection. This means that after a while, half-open connections will be thrown off the system memory, which also helps the victim computer recover a bit. But a continuously running attack can cause a huge gap in the victim server's performance. In a multi-server coordinated attack, the victim computer will have more spoofed requests coming in than the ones that are expiring.

Therefore, the DoS attack results in a server that denies access to legitimate users even without invading the system or choking its bandwidth. The computer might crash or stop responding due to the lack of free space. The force and strength with which a hacker is attacking your computer is not affected by the bandwidth that the hacker is using. The hacker uses the kernel data structures to establish incomplete network connection. As a result, intruders can attack even from a dial-up connection.

Let us now go back to a point that we left unfinished earlier—the need for the spoofed address to be a non-existent address. This is necessary because if the address exists, the computer that receives the SYN/ACK packet will return an RST packet to the victim computer. We already discussed that in the TCP information fields, the RST field is sent a flag that contains a connection termination message. When the segment containing the RST field reaches the victim computer, system memory for that address would be freed. If many or all fake addresses are reachable, the effect of the attack will be minimized.

If the address does not exist, the IP part of the TCP/IP combination will use ICMP to inform TCP that the computer that had generated the initial SYN is unreachable. However, TCP would consider these errors to be momentary and leave their resolution to Internet Protocol. IP will continue to try and reroute the packets until it finally reaches the conclusion that the host actually doesn't exist. By this time, several more spoofed requests would have reached the server.

An example of a DoS attack using half connections is depicted in Figure 7-3.

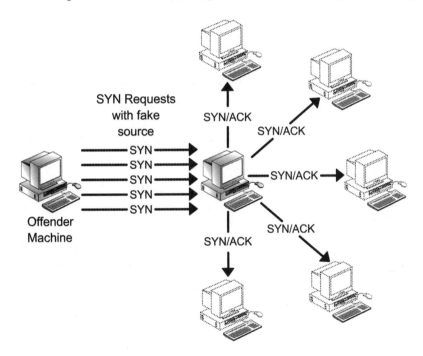

FIGURE 7-3 *A DoS attack using half connections.*

In this illustration, X is the offending computer, Y is the victim server, and Z is a non-existent address that was faked by X. The following sequence of interactions takes place between X, Y, and Z:

1. X sends many connection requests to Y that contain a fake address, Z.
2. Y sends an ACK response to each connection request, but the ACK replies are sent at the Z address. Because Z is a non-existent address, no one actually receives the requests.
3. Y keeps trying to send the packets through alternate routes and finally decides to send the terminate connection request (RST).

By this time, many more connection requests come from X. Eventually, Y exhausts all available memory to accommodate fake connections. Whenever a connection is timed out and an RST request is sent, more connection requests are sent from X, and Y is paralyzed.

The source of the SYN packets is unreachable. Therefore, the location of the system from where the attacks are being originated is unknown. The victim computer has no method to find the true source of the packets because the network forwards packets based on the destination addresses.

DoS Attacks on Target Network's System Configuration

An improperly configured computer may be vulnerable to attacks that not only render the computer useless but also may modify critical configuration files to gain further access to the computer. Such attacks can alter routing information for your network routers and make your entire network inaccessible.

In addition, many sites have certain schemes as part of their security policies to deny an account access after a certain number of failed logon attempts. A typical setup locks out an account after three to five failed logon attempts. An intruder may use this concept to his benefit and try bogus attempts to log on using many user accounts; the server will eventually deny access to these users even when they themselves try to log on. Hackers can prevent even root users from using the systems. It would be time-consuming for the administrators to be able to log on again to the system. To overcome such situations, administrators should have an alternate logon plan.

Hackers might cause harm to your network by blocking it by sending unexpected data. The best example of such an attack is the Ping of Death attack.

Ping of Death Attacks

Ping of Death is a brute force DoS attack that makes use of a kernel bug in many operating systems. Many modern operating systems are still vulnerable to this kind of attack. It is possible to crash or reboot a remote computer by sending a ping of a certain size. This is a serious problem, mainly because it can be reproduced very easily from a remote computer. The more severe aspect of the attack is that the attacker doesn't need to know anything about the victim computer other than the IP address, which implies that if an attacker chooses to ping random remote computers on the Internet, many will crumble down. Many operating systems, including Linux, have come up with patches for this kind of attack, but a lot of vulnerable operating systems still exist (in particular, Windows 95).

This attack exploits a bug in many ICMP servers that cannot handle packets greater than 64Kb in size (65,536 bytes, to be precise). The default size of a ping packet is only 64 bytes. Theoretically speaking, an IP packet of 65,536 bytes is invalid, but practically it is possible due to the fragmenting abilities of routers. The problem occurs at the time of reassembling fragments into the original packet. It overflows the buffer on some ICMP servers, causing a reboot, kernel panic, or hang on various operating systems.

Most genuine ping interfaces will not allow packets over 64Kb to be sent. However, because writing an ICMP client interface is not difficult, you can find numerous malicious implementations of the ping interface on the Internet.

 NOTE

RFC-791 defines the structure of an IP packet. According to these definitions, a unit IP packet cannot exceed the size of 65,535 bytes (that is, $2^{16}-1$). This is the maximum packet size and is inclusive of header information. The header has a default length of 20 bytes when no special parameters are used to alter the packet. Packets that are bigger than the maximum size must be broken down into smaller chunks and later on assembled into the original form. For Ethernet complaint devices, the MTU is typically 1,500.

An ICMP ECHO request is encapsulated within an IP packet and it includes 8-byte ICMP header information. Therefore, the structure of an IP packet that encapsulates the ICMP ECHO request can be broken down as follows:

- 20-bytes IP header
- 8-bytes ICMP ECHO header
- xx-bytes data in the ping packet

The sum of these packet components cannot exceed 65,535 bytes. Therefore, essentially, the ping packet size (excluding the header) can't be more than 65,507 bytes.

As already discussed, it is possible to send larger packets using the fragmentation abilities of intermediate computers. The fragmentation concept relies on an offset value in each fragment to determine the position of each fragment at the time of reassembly. Therefore, it is possible to combine an offset with an appropriate fragment size so that the sum of the offset and the size becomes greater than 64Kb on the last fragment. The recipient computer can't start reassembling a packet unless and until all its fragments have been received. This creates the possibility of an overflow of 16-bit internal variables in recipient computers, which can lead to system crashes, reboots, kernel panics, and so on.

An interesting thing to note is that ping isn't the only program that uses IP datagrams. The root cause lies in the basic low-level IP protocol and, therefore, can be exploited by any service that can send an IP packet. A few examples of such services are TCP, UDP, Telnet, HTTP, and so on. To put it clearly, any port you listen to on your server is open to such an attack. Even those ports that are not listened to are vulnerable!

Blocking the ping program or somehow disabling ICMP cannot bring a solution to the above problem. The correct solution would be applying an available patch to your kernel if it hasn't been already patched.

To determine whether your system is vulnerable, you can ping your computer. If you computer reboots, hangs, or displays a "kernel panic" message, you should find a patch immediately. If a patch isn't available yet, which is highly unlikely, you can consider blocking fragmented pings. This will allow your common 64-byte ping to work while blocking all pings bigger than the MTU of your link.

Smurf DoS Attack

The "smurf" attack is a more recent type in the category of network-level attacks against hosts. Smurf denial-of-service attacks use fabricated ICMP ECHO request packets and direct them to IP broadcast addresses.

As already discussed, ICMP is used to provide feedback on errors to the sender computer. You can use ICMP to determine the functionality of a computer on the network. The ICMP ECHO request packets are sent to the remote computer. On receipt of the request packets, the remote computer sends back the ICMP reply packets. I have already discussed an implementation of this mechanism in the ping application. You can send a packet to a single computer or broadcast it to the computers in a network. If you send a packet from a computer within a local network and it is addressed to the IP broadcast address of a network, the packet is delivered to all the computers on the network. On the other hand, if the packet is sent from a computer outside the local network, the packet is broadcasted to all the computers on the network.

A network broadcast address sets the destination to the network part and then fills each position of the host part of the address with a binary 1. For example, the IP broadcast address for the network 10.0.0.0 is 10.255.255.255. If your network has a class A subnet network of 256 subnets, the IP broadcast address for the 10.50 subnet would be 10.50.255.255. A broadcast response also can be generated from network addresses with all zeros in the host portion, such as 10.50.0.0.

A few other examples are given in Table 7-1.

Table 7-1: Examples of Determining Broadcast IP for Networks

IP Address	Subnet Mask	Network Number	Host Part Network	Broadcast Address
9.9.9.9/10	255.0.0.0	9.0.0.0	9.9.9	9.255.255.255
179.133.7.10/24	255.255.255.0	179.133.7.0	10	179.133.7.255
119.6.255.2/16	255.255.0.0	119.6.0.0	255.2	119.6.255.255

A smurf attack sends an ICMP ECHO request packet to the IP broadcast addresses of various networks to increase the impact of the strike on the victim computer. The offensive computer generally sends these packets from outside intermediate networks. There are three bodies involved in a smurf attack: the offensive computer or the attacker, intermediate networks, and the target victim. The attack propagates in such a way that sometimes the intermediate networks not targeted by the attacker become partial victims of the attack.

The attack progress can be broken down as follows:

- ◆ **STEP 1.** The attacker computer sends an ICMP ECHO request to an IP broadcast address of a network (the intermediate network). This ICMP ECHO request apparently has a source IP address of the target victim computer.
- ◆ **STEP 2.** All computers on the network receive this ICMP request.
- ◆ **STEP 3.** On receiving this request, each computer on the network generates an ICMP ECHO reply response and sends it to the source IP address.

◆ **STEP 4.** A huge amount of network traffic is generated, and the victim computer is caught unaware with bulks of ICMP ECHO reply packets.

A side effect of this kind of attack also is felt by the intermediate networks. Severe network congestion occurs when ICMP ECHO reply packets are being generated and dispatched all over a network.

When such an attack is organized using multiple intermediary networks, the impact of the attack multiplies. An important feature about this kind of attack is that the attacker uses much less bandwidth than the amount of bandwidth that gets congested. This is due to the amplification of junk content that was created by the intermediary networks.

Figure 7-4, which depicts a smurf attack, should give you a better understanding of how the attack actually takes place on the Internet.

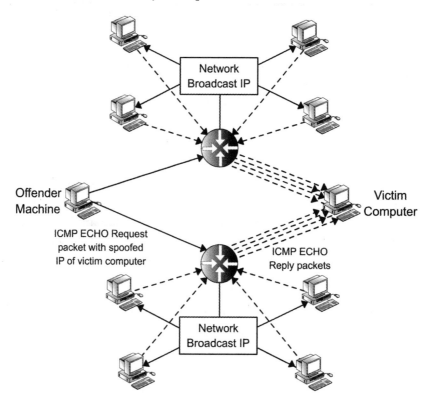

FIGURE 7-4 *A "smurf" attack.*

As shown in Figure 7-4, an attacker sends two ICMP ECHO requests (pings) to the IP broadcast addresses of two networks simultaneously. Both the packets contain spoofed IP addresses of the victim computer. All hosts on both the networks will receive the ICMP ECHO request and respond by sending an ICMP ECHO reply. Therefore, the traffic is multiplied by the number of hosts that respond. If the intermediate networks are multi-access broadcast types, potentially thousands of computers could reply to each packet.

A similar attack, "fraggle," sends UDP packets to generate such traffic. The main targets of such attacks are IRC servers because they use UDP many times. Two parties affected by this kind of attack are the intermediary networks and the victim computer. The intermediary networks are affected because they generate high traffic and the victim computer is affected because it receives multiple amounts of such traffic.

E-Mail Bombing and Spamming

E-mail bombing happens when abusers repeatedly send identical or very similar e-mail messages to a particular address. *E-mail spamming* is a variant of bombing and refers to sending e-mail messages to many users simultaneously. Directing these e-mail messages to mailing lists that have a large number of subscribers can increase the magnitude of the attack.

The e-mail messages that are sent contain fake origin or "return-to" addresses. Therefore, when the recipient replies to the mail, the mail server is not able to reach the bogus address, resulting in the SMTP server leaving the message in the pending queue. The SMTP server continuously tries to send the message every few seconds, until it finally decides to trash the message.

E-mail bombs may be targeted against specific mail addresses that need only a trigger to start a mail war among them. Suppose that there are several e-mail addresses that have auto-responders or vacation messages set. Let's say an attacker prepares a list of 10 such mail addresses. The attacker then sends several e-mails, where recipient and sender attributes are chosen from these 10 mail addresses. Upon receiving the mail, the recipient mailbox will send an auto-reply to the sender, who again sends an acknowledgement message back to the original recipient. When this happens between more than two mail addresses, huge amounts of unnecessary network traffic can be generated. This grows exponentially as the number of target e-mail accounts increases. Although methods have been developed to counter such attacks, many mail servers are still open to them.

E-mail spamming is very difficult to contain because a user with a valid e-mail address can send e-mail messages to any other valid e-mail address, newsgroup, mailing list, or bulletin board service. It also is very difficult for a computer to judge whether the e-mail is a spam or a genuine message.

When a large number of e-mail messages are directed to or through a single site, the site may suffer a Denial of Service attack due to overloaded network connections or system crashes. As a result of multiple postings and related log file entries, bandwidth and disk space is wasted.

E-Mail Spoof Attacks

E-mail spoofing is defined as disguising the identity of the sender to retrieve some crucial information from the victim. The victim receives an e-mail message that appears to have come from one source when it actually was sent from another source. E-mail spoofing is technically a low-level attack, which attempts to fool the person accessing an account instead of fooling a computer. Spoof attacks attempt to trick the e-mail recipient into releasing sensitive information, such as user passwords, and so on.

A few commonly used tricks take the following form:

◆ An e-mail message appears to have come from your system administrator, asking you to tell your account password to make some urgent modifications in your profile, and so on.

◆ An e-mail message is received from an administrator telling a user to change his password to a particular string or face account deactivation.

◆ An e-mail message arrives claiming to be from a person in authority, requesting users to send them a copy of a password file or other sensitive information.

The basis of the attack lies in the fact that SMTP doesn't have provisions for authenticating the e-mail sender. If proper precautions are not taken, any unauthorized person can use your SMTP server to relay spoofed e-mail messages.

Viruses and Worms

In Linux and other UNIX-based systems, security controls are a fundamental part of the operating system. This precisely means that most users except root aren't allowed to perform tasks freely on the computer. An ordinary user has very limited access, and therefore, a virus-infected file that comes into the system using the user's log on session does not have much data to corrupt.

Of the very rare Linux viruses, a popular one is called *bliss*. This is a decent virus that comes with an uninstall option! The virus can't affect the system unless it's run as `root`.

Although viruses aren't bothersome to Linux users, worms are widely prevalent in UNIX-based systems. Ever since the first breakout of the wild Morris Internet worm that caused panic the world over, worms have been appearing often. The Internet worm has exploited the vulnerability of the sendmail package. Newer, advanced Linux worms exploit minor mistakes in `imapd`, `sendmail`, WU-FTPD, and other daemons.

The reason for the success of worms is that they rely on instant explosions and don't host themselves; they just continue to explode and multiply forever. In addition, unlike DoS and other forms of hacking attacks, worms do not target specific computers. A worm's target is "every" computer that is connected to the infected network. The effectiveness of a worm is highest when network servers are not up–to-date with security patches. Their attack strength fades out gradually as security patches become available and people upgrade their software.

Worms are scripts that replicate themselves. Unlike viruses, however, they do not alter other executable programs. Also, worms are different from Trojans because they don't need to be triggered by users. Worms are closed programs or scripts that spread themselves using networks, attack systems, or other programs without changing them in any way. They typically use networks to accomplish this. The worm that reportedly gained access to more than 6,000 UNIX systems flooded the Internet with so many access requests that it became unusable. However, such worms are no longer as common as they once were.

Tools Used for Attacking Networks

Network tools are sophisticated software applications that are widely available on the Internet. These tools are packaged with user-friendly interfaces. As a result, even a novice can use them to attack another computer. These tools also take assistance from various other reachable computers that have the same tools installed. Such tools are called *distributed-system attack* tools. Offenders can involve a large number of tool installations and use the resources on those computers to focus all of them to attack one or more victim computers or networks. In this section, I explain some of these tools and explore how they can be used for attacking networks.

Trinoo

Trinoo is software that can be used to hurl coordinated DoS attacks against remote servers. The tool allows a user to launch a coordinated UDP flood to the victim computer, which results in DoS to its legitimate users due to connectivity overload. As the tool is widely used, it is able to strengthen the attack. A typical Trinoo attack team can include a few servers and a large number of client computers on which the Trinoo daemon is running.

The tool is very easy to use, and an attacker using it doesn't need to be a networking guru. An offending computer can instruct one of many Trinoo servers to open a DoS attack against a particular computer. After the attack is opened, the Trinoo master server searches for as many client Trinoos as possible and directs them to UDP flood one or more IP addresses of the victim computer.

A typical Trinoo attack can be divided into four steps:

1. An intruder connects to the master on port `27665/tcp` and provides attack details.

2. A master connects to many daemons on port `27444/udp`.

3. Multiple daemons propagate UDP floods to the target computers with random destination ports. The binary for the Trinoo daemon contains IP addresses for one or more Trinoo masters.

4. The daemon announces the availability of Trinoo upon its execution. The daemon does this by sending a UDP packet that has the string `*HELLO*`. This string is sent to the Trinoo master's IP address.

The Trinoo master stores a list of known daemons in an encrypted file named `..` (dot-dot). This file and the master binary are stored in the same directory. You can configure the Trinoo master so that it sends requests to the daemons to determine the daemon's availability. Daemons respond to these requests by sending UDP packets back to the Trinoo master. The UDP packets contains the string `PONG`.

Trinoo operates on a set of standards, a few of which are known and have been listed in Table 7-2.

Table 7-2: Standards for Operating Trinoo

Application	Type	Port
Trinoo Master Server	TCP	27665
Trinoo Master Server	UDP	31335
Trinoo Daemon	UDP	27444

Before an attack can be announced by the master server to other Trinoo client daemons, an attacker requires a password to connect to a master Trinoo server. Trinoo doesn't separately maintain a password database for attackers. Instead, it maintains encrypted passwords hidden within the main executable. The master server listens on the port 27665 on TCP to allow an attacker to connect to the Trinoo service. Another master server runs on the port 31335 on UDP, but this master listens only to Trinoo client computers. Trinoo client daemons run on the port 27444 on UDP.

There are a variety of Trinoo variants available on the Internet today. Some are known to implement IP spoofing for Trinoo clients, while others are simple flooders. Even without IP spoofing, the attack comes simultaneously from many computers. Finally, Trinoo daemons and masters disguise themselves under many names but the most commonly used ones are ns, http, rpc.trinoo, rpc.listen, trinix, rpc.irix, and irix.

Tribe Flood Network (TFN)

TFN attack is an advanced DoS attack tool that can initiate coordinated DoS attacks from one or more sources to one or more destinations. Tribe Flood Attack supports many methods of attack in addition to the UDP floods supported by Trinoo. TFN also supports TCP SYN floods, ICMP ECHO request floods, ICMP-directed broadcast DoS attacks, and spoofing of IP addresses.

A TFN network can employ hundreds of TFN clients and masters to initiate an attack against a particular computer. TFN provides a command-line interface to send various commands to TFN daemons. TFN masters communicate with TFN daemons by encapsulating the commands within ICMP ECHO reply packets. Two bytes of binary values are embedded in the ID field and the parameters are embedded in the data portion. Using TFN isn't as easy as using Trinoo, but with a few trials, intermediate network users can determine ways of controlling TFN.

In order to use TFN, the TFN master requires an attacker to provide a list of daemon IPs. The TFN program cannot search a network for client daemons automatically. However, other independent utilities are available on the Internet to do this search. TFN networks have reportedly supported automated update mechanisms and the remote copying of files.

Summary

The utility of a server is directly proportional to the number of features available on it. Unfortunately, the vulnerability of a machine also is directly proportional to the number of features that a server provides to its legitimate users. In this chapter, you learned about the various vulnerabilities that exist in modern networks. You also learned how small loopholes in basic network protocols can be exploited to create havoc in platforms that are presumably very secure. Network attack tools are becoming exceptionally organized and intelligent. In today's potentially hostile networking environment, certain measures can be taken to make an intruder's task very difficult.

In Chapter 10, "Linux Network Defense and Intrusion Detection," I discuss network defense strategies, security policies, firewalls, and various other tools that can assist administrators in preventing attacks and recovering a network when it is under attack.

Check Your Understanding

Multiple Choice Questions

1. A dictionary-based brute force attack targets which component of a network or computer?

   a. Bandwidth of a network

   b. Password file of a computer

   c. Memory of a computer

   d. None of the above

2. Which of the following correctly defines a CGI script?

   a. A daemon or service that continuously runs in the background

   b. An application that connects various services running in a computer to trusted networks

   c. A hardware component that connects two different networks

   d. A script that can add dynamic functionality to Web pages

3. Trinoo is an example of:

   a. A word-list or dictionary based attack.

   b. A SYN Flood Attack

   c. A UDP based DoS Attack

   d. A DoS attack that exploits vulnerability in the ICMP client/server transit mechanism

4. Which of these services on the server handles a ping request from the client?

   a. Hyper Text Terminal Protocol Server

   b. File Transfer Protocol Server

   c. Post Office Protocol Server

   d. Internet Control Message Protocol Server

5. Smurf attack fabricates the ICMP ECHO request so that the source IP in the packet becomes:

    a. The IP of an intermediary network

    b. The victim computer

    c. A non-existent IP address

Answers

Multiple Choice Answers

1. **b.** A dictionary-based brute force attack targets the password file of a computer.

2. **d.** CGI is a script that can add dynamic functionality to Web pages.

3. **c.** Trinoo is a UDP-based DoS attack.

4. **d.** The ICMP service handles a ping request from a client.

5. **b.** The source IP address becomes the victim computer because all the ICMP ECHO reply packets are directed towards it. Therefore, the source receives a large number of data packets in reply to just a single broadcast ICMP ECHO request.

Chapter 8

Apache Web Server

The Apache Web server is the most widely used Web server on the Internet. It hosts more than 50 percent of the Web sites in the world. The first version of Apache was developed by a group of volunteer programmers in 1995 and was based on the httpd Web server of NCSA. Apache was known as the patchy server, because it was developed from existing NCSA code, plus various patches. Apache has become the world's most popular Web server because of these characteristics:

- Sophisticated features
- Efficient performance
- Security features
- Module Plug-in support
- Free availability

A group of volunteer programmers, known as the Apache Software Foundation, is involved in the development of the Apache server. In addition, programmers throughout the world can contribute to its development, because the source code is freely available. Apache was originally developed for the UNIX operating system, but is now available for platforms such as Linux, OS/2, and Windows.

You can choose to install the Apache Web server while installing Red Hat Linux. However, if you did not install Apache during the installation process, you can install it later by using the `rpm` program or by compiling the Apache source distribution. Once installed, Apache has the following directories:

- **/etc/httpd/conf/.** This directory contains all Apache configuration files. Some of the configuration files include `httpd.conf`, `access.conf`, and `srm.conf`.
- **/var/www/html/.** This is the default location for the CGI programs and HTML files. If you change the default location, the configuration files need to be updated accordingly.
- **/usr/sbin/.** This directory contains the executable programs. The programs can be critical server executables or utilities, such as the `htpasswd` program. The `htpasswd` program is used for creating and updating the user authentication files.

- ◆ **/var/log/http/.** This directory contains the server log files. There are two log files by default: `access_log` and `error_log`.
- ◆ **/etc/rc.d/.** This directory stores the daemon startup scripts. The scripts are usually located in the `init.d` directory within this directory. The scripts in this directory are executed automatically at boot time.
- ◆ **/usr/doc/ and /usr/man/.** These directories store the help and manual files for Apache.

You know that the `/etc/httpd/conf` directory contains some important configuration files for the Apache server. The directives in these files determine the configuration of the Apache server. The following list describes the three most important configuration files:

- ◆ **httpd.conf.** This file contains directives that control the operation of the server daemon.
- ◆ **srm.conf.** This file contains directives for controlling the specification of the documents provided to the clients by the server. Server settings, which affect how requests are serviced and how the results are formatted, also are defined in this file.
- ◆ **access.conf.** This file defines the server settings that affect the types of services allowed and the conditions for allowing these services.

In later versions of Apache 1.3.4, the configuration files for Apache are stored in single file, `httpd.conf`. The other files are present but they are there for purely historical reasons. These files contain only the comment entries. You should put all the configuration details in the `httpd.conf` file.

The httpd Daemon

The `httpd` daemon, which runs as a stand-alone daemon process, is the Apache server program. The Web server can be run in the stand-alone mode or by the `inetd` server. You can invoke the `httpd` daemon by using the Internet daemon, `inetd`. The main configuration file for the `httpd` daemon is the `httpd.conf` file. This `httpd` service controls the Web server and the HTTP services in Linux. The main script for starting and stopping the Web server is presented in the `httpd` file in the `/etc/rc.d/init.d` directory.

When run in the stand-alone mode, the `httpd` daemon creates a pool of child processes to handle requests. To stop the daemon, you need to send a TERM signal to the initial parent process. The process ID (PID) of this process is written to a file, as given in the configuration file. This file is usually the `/var/run/httpd.pid` file.

Here is an example of the `httpd` daemon running in the stand-alone mode:

```
cat /var/run/httpd.pid
830
ps -aux ¦ grep httpd
root       830  0.0  0.1 10724  184 ?        S    13:09   0:00 /usr/sbin/httpd -
apache     846  0.0  1.5 10852 1988 ?        S    13:09   0:00 /usr/sbin/httpd -
apache     847  0.0  1.4 10816 1780 ?        S    13:09   0:00 /usr/sbin/httpd -
apache     848  0.0  1.4 10816 1784 ?        S    13:09   0:00 /usr/sbin/httpd -
apache     849  0.0  1.4 10816 1784 ?        S    13:09   0:00 /usr/sbin/httpd -
apache     850  0.0  1.5 10852 1988 ?        S    13:09   0:00 /usr/sbin/httpd -
apache     851  0.0  1.4 10816 1784 ?        S    13:09   0:00 /usr/sbin/httpd -
apache     852  0.0  1.4 10816 1784 ?        S    13:09   0:00 /usr/sbin/httpd -
apache     853  0.0  1.4 10816 1784 ?        S    13:09   0:00 /usr/sbin/httpd -
root      2515  0.0  0.4  1520  604 pts/2    S    16:22   0:00 grep httpd
```

In the preceding example, note the output of the first command, `cat /var/run/httpd.pid`. It displays the PID of the parent httpd daemon. The next command displays all the running `httpd` daemon processes. You can start the `httpd` daemon service by using the `httpd` script present in the `/etc/rc.d/init.d` directory.

The `httpd` daemon should not be run as root userid. A better idea is to create a new user and define that user in the `user` directive in Apache's main configuration file, `/etc/httpd/conf/httpd.conf`. This directive tells Apache to run under that user. Apache will have all the permissions that this user has been granted. Therefore, this user should not have access to files that are not meant for public use.

The user directive also can be used inside the `<virtualhost>…</virtualhost>` block. This means that only CGIs for this host would have a different `userid` for execution. The directive can be used like this only if the `suEXEC` wrapper feature is enabled on Apache. The `suEXEC` wrapper is discussed in detail in the next section.

Some administrators prefer to run the httpd daemon as the nobody user. This option has its own advantages and disadvantages. The main advantage is that Apache will have very limited access, and the security threat will be minimized. A disadvantage is that some utilities that allow distributed permission systems, like suEXEC, will be more difficult to implement.

suEXEC

suEXEC is a utility in Apache that allows CGIs to be executed under usernames different from the user who runs Apache's parent thread. It allows different users on a server to have different levels of permissions while executing CGI scripts. If all CGI scripts are run under a single username, that user has the potential to access the cgi-bin/ directories of other users on the system. To get rid of this problem, suEXEC can be enabled. Enabling this feature would mean that all users who have CGI files will run under their own userids. The advantage to this is that access permissions of every CGI file will be limited to the extent of the user who wrote the CGIs.

The httpd.conf File

The httpd.conf file is the configuration file for the Apache server. It is a text file and has numerous configuration options. These options can be configured by adding, commenting, un-commenting, and deleting the options present in it. This file is based on the configuration files of the NCSA server that were originally developed by Rob McCool.

Editing the Apache configuration file is the most common method used for configuring the Apache server. However, only the experienced Web server administrators should do this. New users might find it difficult to understand the options specified in this file.

Directives

Before examining the options present in the httpd.conf file, you should be familiar with the concept of directives. The httpd.conf file uses directives to configure the Apache Web server. Directives follow a specific syntax, similar to a programming language. However, directives can't be called commands and they don't operate like programming languages. Directives can be referred to as instructions to the Apache server that help Apache behave in a particular manner and locate the resources to be used. Directives don't control the actions of Apache, however. An Apache Web server administrator should be able to understand the purpose and usage of Apache directives to perform Web administration tasks effectively.

Directives can be classified into two categories:

◆ Core directives
◆ Directives supplied by add-on modules

I will briefly discuss these types of directives before we begin examining the sections and options of the `httpd.conf` file.

Core Directives

As the name suggests, core directives are the most critical directives for the Apache Web server. These directives are compiled into the Apache executable code and are available by default. No special configuration is required. The core directives are essential for Apache Web server to function properly.

Directives Supplied by Add-on Modules

There are numerous add-on modules that can be used with the Apache Web server. When you install these add-on modules, they make directives available to the Apache server. This means that the Web server administrator can use these directives only when the corresponding add-on module is added.

Layout of the httpd.conf File

The configuration directives in the `httpd.conf` file are grouped into three sections. These sections make it convenient for you to locate the configuration options while editing the `httpd.conf` file. These sections are as follows:

◆ The Global Environment section
◆ The Main server configuration section
◆ The Virtual Hosts section

The Global Environment Section

This section contains directives that globally affect the functioning of the Apache Web server. These directives are essential for the overall operation of Apache. The directives presented in this section determine how the Apache server processes will be controlled.

The ServerType Directive

The ServerType option can be configured with two modes: inetd or standalone. The inetd mode is used only when you install Apache on Linux or UNIX platforms. The extract from the httpd.conf, where the ServerType directive, is specified as follows:

```
# ServerType is either inetd, or standalone.  Inetd mode is only supported on
# Unix platforms.
#
ServerType standalone
```

Do not tamper with the ServerType option. The default value for this option is standalone.

The ServerRoot Directive

The ServerRoot directive is used to specify the location where the following important files will be located:

◆ Configuration files
◆ Error files
◆ Log files

The location you specify in the ServerRoot directive to store the configuration, error, or log files could be the local file system or a Network File System (NFS). If you choose to use a location on the local file system, you need to specify the directory path in this directive, as follows:

```
# ServerRoot: The top of the directory tree under which the server's
# configuration, error, and log files are kept.
#
# NOTE!  If you intend to place this on an NFS (or otherwise network)
# mounted filesystem then please read the LockFile documentation
# (available at <URL:http://www.apache.org/docs/mod/core.html#lockfile>);
```

```
# you will save yourself a lot of trouble.
#
ServerRoot "/usr/local/apache"
```

 NOTE

I've taken extracts of these directives from the http.conf file from my Linux computer. The values of the directives might be different in the http.conf file of your Linux computer, depending on the kind of installation you have performed.

The path in the ServerRoot directive should be specified with care.

The LockFile Directive

The LockFile directive is used to specify the path for the lockfile. A lockfile is used when Apache is compiled by using either of these two options:

- USE_FCNTL_SERIALIZED_ACCEPT
- USE_FLOCK_SERIALIZED_ACCEPT

You should leave the value of this directive as default. However, if the lockfile is located on an NFS mounted file system, the default path of the lockfile should be changed accordingly. A sample LockFile directive is given here:

```
# The LockFile directive sets the path to the lockfile used when Apache
# is compiled with either USE_FCNTL_SERIALIZED_ACCEPT or
# USE_FLOCK_SERIALIZED_ACCEPT. This directive should normally be left at
# its default value. The main reason for changing it is if the logs
# directory is NFS mounted, since the lockfile MUST BE STORED ON A LOCAL
# DISK. The PID of the main server process is automatically appended to
# the filename.
#
#LockFile /usr/local/apache/logs/httpd.lock
```

In the preceding extract, the path for the lockfile is set as /usr/local/apache/logs/httpd.lock. If you are using the standard installation of Apache, the path would ideally be /var/run/httpd.lock.

The PidFile Directive

Whenever Apache is started, a PID is allocated to it. The PID is then stored in a file. You use the `PidFile` directive to specify the path for the file that stores the PID of the Apache Web server. However, this file is used only if you have configured the value of `ServerType` directive as standalone. A sample `PidFile` directive is given:

```
# PidFile: The file in which the server should record its process
# identification number when it starts.
#
PidFile /usr/local/apache/logs/httpd.pid
```

In the preceding extract, the path set for the PID file is `/usr/local/apache/logs/httpd.pid`. If you are using the standard installation of Apache, the path should be `/var/run/httpd.pid`.

The ScoreBoardFile Directive

The `ScoreBoardFile` directive is used to specify the location for the `httpd.score-board file`. This file stores information regarding the internal server processes. It determines how the parent and child processes, which are invoked by the Apache Web server, communicate with each other:

```
# ScoreBoardFile: File used to store internal server process information.
# Not all architectures require this.  But if yours does (you'll know because
# this file will be  created when you run Apache) then you *must* ensure that
# no two invocations of Apache share the same scoreboard file.
#
ScoreBoardFile /usr/local/apache/logs/httpd.scoreboard
```

In the preceding extract, the path specified for the `ScoreBoardFile` directive is `/usr/local/apache/logs/httpd.scoreboard`.

The `ScoreBoardFile` directive need not be configured for all architectures. To identify whether the architecture you are using requires the `ScoreBoardFile` directive, perform the following steps:.

◆ Start the Apache server.
◆ Search for the file named `httpd.scoreboard`.

If you find this file, it means that your architecture requires that the `ScoreBoardFile` directive be configured. If you are using the `ScoreBoardFile` directive, you should ensure that no more than one instance of Apache is using this file at a given time.

The ResourceConfig and AccessConfig Directives

The `ResourceConfig` and the `AccessConfig` directives are used to store the path for the `srm.conf` and `access.conf` files, respectively. These files were used with versions of Apache prior to 1.3.4. For later version of Apache, it was recommended that all directives be stored in a single file.

Although, srm.conf and access.conf files are not required any more, they are still a part of the Apache distribution. These files contain only comments and you can safely get rid of them by specifying /dev/null as the filename for the Resource-Config and AccessConfig directives. Doing this will ignore these directives. Consider the following extract:

```
# In the standard configuration, the server will process httpd.conf (this
# file, specified by the -f command line option), srm.conf, and access.conf
# in that order.  The latter two files are now distributed empty, as it is
# recommended that all directives be kept in a single file for simplicity.
# The commented-out values below are the built-in defaults.  You can have the
# server ignore these files altogether by using "/dev/null" (for Unix) or
# "nul" (for Win32) for the arguments to the directives.
#
#ResourceConfig conf/srm.conf
#AccessConfig conf/access.conf
```

In the preceding extract, notice that the `ResourceConfig` and the `AccessConfig` directives are commented by default.

 NOTE

If you specify a directory as a value for these directives, the Apache Web server will parse all files present in the specified directory. Apache assumes that the files within the specified directory are the configuration files. Therefore, in order to avoid a situation where all the stray files in the specified directory are loaded as configuration files, you should keep the specified directory empty.

The Timeout Directive

The Timeout directive specifies the time lapse for which Apache will wait before sending a timeout message. The value specified in this directive specifies the time taken to do the following:

◆ Receive a GET request.

◆ Receive a POST or PUT request.

◆ Send TCP packets as responses to a request.

```
# Timeout: The number of seconds before receives and sends time out.
#
Timeout 300
```

The default value set for this directive is 1200 seconds in Apache versions prior to 1.2.

The KeepAlive Directive

The KeepAlive directive is used to specify whether Apache should allow persistent connections. HTTP/1.1 uses a mechanism called *persistent connections*. Persistent connections allow the client to establish multiple connections at a given time, resulting in faster download.

```
# KeepAlive: Whether or not to allow persistent connections (more than
# one request per connection). Set to "Off" to deactivate.
#
KeepAlive On
```

By default, the value for the KeepAlive directive is set to On. The On value means that Apache will allow the use of persistent connections. However, if you do not want to use persistent connections, you can set the value to Off.

The MaxKeepAliveRequests Directive

You can specify the maximum number of requests that are allowed per connection. This is needed if you have enabled support for the KeepAlive directive. You can use the MaxKeepAliveRequests directive to specify the number of maximum requests that can be sent to the server for each connection. A numeric value can be assigned to this directive, to specify the maximum number of allowed requests. If the number 0 is specified, unlimited requests are allowed. If you are using persistent connections, it is advisable that you set the value of this directive, so that it can handle several requests at a time.

A sample `MaxKeepAliveRequests` directive is given here:

```
# MaxKeepAliveRequests: The maximum number of requests to allow
# during a persistent connection. Set to 0 to allow an unlimited amount.
# We recommend you leave this number high, for maximum performance.
#
MaxKeepAliveRequests 100
```

The default value for this directive is `100`, which means that 100 requests will be allowed per connection. To improve performance, this value can be set to a higher number.

You should consider the performance and availability of resources while allowing `KeepAlive` connections. Every operating system has a maximum number of simultaneous TCP connections that are allowed. Therefore, the number of `MaxKeepAliveRequests` should be set so that the performance is not adversely affected, and there is excess load on the server.

The KeepAliveTimeout Directive

The `KeepAliveTimeout` directive is used to specify the amount of time after which Apache will be ready to receive the next consecutive request from a client.

```
# KeepAliveTimeout: Number of seconds to wait for the next request from the
# same client on the same connection.
#
KeepAliveTimeout 15
```

By default, the time specified for this directive is `15` seconds, which means that a KeepAlive connection will close if a new client connection request is not received in 15 seconds.

The MinSpareServers and the MaxSpareServers Directive

The `MinSpareServers` and `MaxSpareServers` directives are used to specify the minimum number of servers and the maximum number of processes that will be idle and waiting for requests at a given time. The number specified in these directives does not determine the maximum number of clients that can connect to an

Apache server at a given time. The spare server's parameter should be left unaltered, unless the network traffic of your site is high. Sample `MinSpareServers` and `MaxSpareServers` directives are given here:

```
# Server-pool size regulation.  Rather than making you guess how many
# server processes you need, Apache dynamically adapts to the load it
# sees —- that is, it tries to maintain enough server processes to
# handle the current load, plus a few spare servers to handle transient
# load spikes (e.g., multiple simultaneous requests from a single
# Netscape browser).
#
# It does this by periodically checking how many servers are waiting
# for a request.  If there are fewer than MinSpareServers, it creates
# a new spare.  If there are more than MaxSpareServers, some of the
# spares die off.  The default values are probably OK for most sites.
#
MinSpareServers 5
MaxSpareServers 10
```

The default value for the `MinSpareServers` directive is 5, and the `MaxSpareServers` directive has the value of 10. If the number of idle servers is less than the specified amount, the Apache server automatically creates child processes until it reaches the minimum specified limit. The maximum limit is specified to keep a check on the number of child processes invoked. If the number of child processes exceeds the limit specified in the `MaxSpareServers` directive, the parent process automatically kills the excess processes.

The StartServers Directive

The `StartServers` directive allows you to specify the number of child processes that will be created during startup. However, Apache considers the server load before deciding how many child processes should be running at any given time. Therefore, you might not need to edit the value specified in this directive, and you can safely leave the default option for this directive unaltered.

```
# Number of servers to start initially —- should be a reasonable ballpark
# figure.
#
StartServers 5
```

In the preceding extract, the default value assigned to the StartServers directive is 5. This means that 5 child processes will be automatically created at start time.

The MaxClients Directive

The MaxClients directive helps you specify the maximum number of clients that can connect simultaneously at any given time:

```
# Limit on total number of servers running, i.e., limit on the number
# of clients who can simultaneously connect —· if this limit is ever
# reached, clients will be LOCKED OUT, so it should NOT BE SET TOO LOW.
# It is intended mainly as a brake to keep a runaway server from taking
# the system with it as it spirals down...
#
MaxClients 150
```

In the preceding extract for the MaxClients directive, the default value is 150. This means that, at any given time, Apache will not handle more than 150 simultaneous connections. If there are more connections, they get queued. The number of queued connections depends on the ListenBacklog directive.

The MaxRequestsPerChild Directive

The MaxRequestsPerChild directive is used to specify the maximum number of requests that a child process will handle:

```
# MaxRequestsPerChild: the number of requests each child process is
# allowed to process before the child dies.  The child will exit so
# as to avoid problems after prolonged use when Apache (and maybe the
# libraries it uses) leak memory or other resources.  On most systems, this
# isn't really needed, but a few (such as Solaris) do have notable leaks
# in the libraries. For these platforms, set to something like 10000
# or so; a setting of 0 means unlimited.
#
# NOTE: This value does not include keepalive requests after the initial
#       request per connection. For example, if a child process handles
#       an initial request and 10 subsequent "keptalive" requests, it
#       would only count as 1 request towards this limit.
#
MaxRequestsPerChild 0
```

The default value set for this directive is 0, which means that the child process will never die.

The Listen Directive

The Listen directive is an important directive which can be configured to enhance performance and ensure security. This directive can be configured so that Apache listens to IP addresses and ports other than the default ones. You can specify the port number or a combination of both IP interface and port number. The Listen directive also can be used to specify more than one IP interface and port. In this case, the server will respond to all the specified IP interfaces and ports. For example,

```
# Listen: Allows you to bind Apache to specific IP addresses and/or
# ports, in addition to the default. See also the <VirtualHost>
# directive.
#
#Listen 3000
#Listen 12.34.56.78:80
```

You can use the Listen directive as an alternative to the BindAddress and Port directives. However, it is advisable to use the Port directive because Apache generates certain URLs that point to your server. These URLs will work only when the Port directive is used.

The LoadModule Directive

The LoadModule is an important directive used to add new modules to your Apache installation. This directive consists of the module and the filename. The syntax for using this directive is as follows:

```
LoadModule sample_module modules/mod_sample.so
#sample is the name of a module
```

The following is a sample extract of the httpd.conf file, which shows a few entries made to the LoadModule directive:

```
# Dynamic Shared Object (DSO) Support
#
# To be able to use the functionality of a module which was built as a DSO you
# have to place corresponding `LoadModule' lines at this location so the
```

```
# directives contained in it are actually available _before_ they are used.
# Please read the file http://httpd.apache.org/docs/dso.html for more
# details about the DSO mechanism and run `httpd -l' for the list of already
# built-in (statically linked and thus always available) modules in your httpd
# binary.
#
# Note: The order in which modules are loaded is important.  Don't change
# the order below without expert advice.
#
# Example:
# LoadModule foo_module libexec/mod_foo.so
LoadModule vhost_alias_module libexec/mod_vhost_alias.so
LoadModule env_module         libexec/mod_env.so
LoadModule config_log_module  libexec/mod_log_config.so
LoadModule mime_magic_module  libexec/mod_mime_magic.so
LoadModule mime_module        libexec/mod_mime.so
LoadModule negotiation_module libexec/mod_negotiation.so
LoadModule status_module      libexec/mod_status.so
LoadModule info_module        libexec/mod_info.so
LoadModule includes_module    libexec/mod_include.so
LoadModule autoindex_module   libexec/mod_autoindex.so
LoadModule dir_module         libexec/mod_dir.so
LoadModule cgi_module         libexec/mod_cgi.so
LoadModule asis_module        libexec/mod_asis.so
LoadModule imap_module        libexec/mod_imap.so
LoadModule action_module      libexec/mod_actions.so
LoadModule speling_module     libexec/mod_speling.so
............ ............ ............ ............ ............
............ ............ ............ ............ ............
```

The preceding extract shows that the LoadModule directive is used to specify which modules need to be loaded.

The AddModule Directive

The AddModule directive is used to re-populate the list of modules. Modules specified in the LoadModule section should also have a corresponding AddModule entry:

```
#   Reconstruction of the complete module list from all available modules
#   (static and shared ones) to achieve correct module execution order.
#   [WHENEVER YOU CHANGE THE LOADMODULE SECTION ABOVE UPDATE THIS, TOO]
ClearModuleList
AddModule mod_vhost_alias.c
AddModule mod_env.c
AddModule mod_log_config.c
AddModule mod_mime_magic.c
AddModule mod_mime.c
AddModule mod_negotiation.c
AddModule mod_status.c
AddModule mod_info.c
AddModule mod_include.c
AddModule mod_autoindex.c
AddModule mod_dir.c
AddModule mod_cgi.c
AddModule mod_asis.c
AddModule mod_imap.c
AddModule mod_actions.c
AddModule mod_speling.c
.........more lines here........
```

This is a small extract of `AddModule` entries.

The ExtendedStatus Directive

The `ExtendedStatus` directive is used to specify whether the extended status information for each request should be tracked. Configuring this directive is useful if you have already enabled the status module in the server:

```
# ExtendedStatus controls whether Apache will generate "full" status
# information (ExtendedStatus On) or just basic information (ExtendedStatus
# Off) when the "server-status" handler is called. The default is Off.
#
#ExtendedStatus On
```

In the extract, the default value for this directive is `On`. By default, the entry is commented.

Main Server Configuration Options

The default Apache Web server is the main server. The Main server configuration section consists of all the directives that are used to define the parameters used by the main server.

The Port Directive

The `Port` directive is used to specify the port number on which Apache will listen to client requests:

```
# Port: The port to which the standalone server listens. For
# ports < 1023, you will need httpd to be run as root initially.
#
Port 80
```

You can view the port allocation in the `/etc/services` file in a Red Hat Linux system. Keep the following points in mind while configuring the `Port` directive:

◆ The server will listen to the port number specified in the `Port` directive, but only when a port number is not specified in the `Listen` or `BindAddress` directives.

◆ The `Port` directive is used to set the environment variable named `SERVER_PORT`. This environment variable is used for *Common Gateway Interface* (CGI) and *Server Side Includes* (SSI).

◆ Sometimes, you will want to use SSL for secure transmission of data. In this case, you will need to specify the port number that will be used by *Secure Hypertext Transfer Protocol* (HTTPS). This port number is ideally 443 and is specified with the `Listen` directive as shown here:

```
## When we also provide SSL, we have to listen to the
## standard HTTP port (see above) and to the HTTPS port
##
<IfDefine HAVE_SSL>
Listen 80
Listen 443
</IfDefine>
```

The `<IfDefine>` and `</IfDefine>` directives are used to check whether SSL support is required.

The User and the Group Directive

The User and Group directives are used to store the default user information that runs Apache. For example,

```
# If you wish httpd to run as a different user or group, you must run
# httpd as root initially and it will switch.
#
# User/Group: The name (or #number) of the user/group to run httpd as.
#  . On SCO (ODT 3) use "User nouser" and "Group nogroup".
#  . On HPUX you may not be able to use shared memory as nobody, and the
#    suggested workaround is to create a user www and use that user.
#  NOTE that some kernels refuse to setgid(Group) or semctl(IPC_SET)
#  when the value of (unsigned)Group is above 60000;
#  don't use Group www on these systems!
#
User www
Group www
```

The ServerAdmin Directive

The ServerAdmin directive is used to specify an e-mail address. This e-mail address belongs to the server administrator and can be used to contact the server administrator if the client is facing a problem:

```
# ServerAdmin: Your address, where problems with the server should be
# e-mailed.  This address appears on some server-generated pages, such
# as error documents.
#
ServerAdmin root@localhost.localdomain
```

The ServerName Directive

The ServerName directive specifies the server name. This name is used when redirection of URLs is created. If you don't specify a server name at the time of installation, the value localhost is used by default. For example,

```
# ServerName allows you to set a host name which is sent back to clients for
# your server if it's different than the one the program would get (i.e., use
# "www" instead of the host's real name).
#
```

```
# Note: You cannot just invent host names and hope they work. The name you
# define here must be a valid DNS name for your host. If you don't understand
# this, ask your network administrator.
# If your host doesn't have a registered DNS name, enter its IP address here.
# You will have to access it by its address (e.g., http://123.45.67.89/)
# anyway, and this will make redirections work in a sensible way.
#
# 127.0.0.1 is the TCP/IP local loop-back address, often named localhost. Your
# machine always knows itself by this address. If you use Apache strictly for
# local testing and development, you may use 127.0.0.1 as the server name.
#
#ServerName localhost.localdomain
```

If you want to specify a domain name other than localhost, be careful about the name that you specify. The domain name specified in the `ServerName` directive should be a valid and registered DNS name. Preferably, the domain name should be in the following format:

```
servername.domainname
```

The DocumentRoot Directive

The `DocumentRoot` directive is used to specify the document root of a Web server. The document root is where all Web-related files are stored:

```
# DocumentRoot: The directory out of which you will serve your
# documents. By default, all requests are taken from this directory, but
# symbolic links and aliases may be used to point to other locations.
#
DocumentRoot "/var/www/html"
```

The default value assigned to the `DocumentRoot` directory is `/var/www/html`. However, you can specify an alternate location when you compile Apache.

The <Directory> and </Directory> Directives: Configuration for the / Directory

The `<Directory>` and `</Directory>` directives are used to enclose other directives. These directives are applicable only to the directory specified in the `<Directory>` directive.

```
# Each directory to which Apache has access, can be configured with respect
# to which services and features are allowed and/or disabled in that
# directory (and its subdirectories).
#
# First, we configure the "default" to be a very restrictive set of
# permissions.
#
<Directory />
    Options FollowSymLinks
    AllowOverride None
</Directory>
```

In this extract, notice that within the opening <Directory> tag, the directory /
(root) is specified. The root directory is the top level directory of the Linux file
system. All directives specified in <Directory> and </Directory> will only apply
to the root directory.

Within the <Directory> and </Directory> directives, two more directives named
Options and AllowOverride are specified. The Options directive is used to specify the features that will be available for the specified directory. When the Options
directive is set to the FollowSymlinks value, it indicates that the server will follow
the symbolic links in the specified directory.

The AllowOverride directive is used to specify which options specified in the
.htaccess file can be overridden. The .htaccess file is used for specifying access
rights and authentication services to users. When the value for the AllowOverride
directive is set to None, all .htaccess files are ignored.

The <Directory> and </Directory> Directives: Configuration for the Document Root Directory

The next portion of the httpd.conf file is used to configure the <Directory>
directive for the document root directory.

```
# Note that from this point forward you must specifically allow
# particular features to be enabled - so if something's not working as
# you might expect, make sure that you have specifically enabled it
# below.
#
#
# This should be changed to whatever you set DocumentRoot to.
```

```
#
<Directory "/var/www/html">
#
# This may also be "None", "All", or any combination of "Indexes",
# "Includes", "FollowSymLinks", "ExecCGI", or "MultiViews".
#
# Note that "MultiViews" must be named *explicitly* —- "Options All"
# doesn't give it to you.
#
    Options Indexes FollowSymLinks MultiViews
#
# This controls which options the .htaccess files in directories can
# override. Can also be "All", or any combination of "Options", "FileInfo",
# "AuthConfig", and "Limit"
#
    AllowOverride None
#
# Controls who can get stuff from this server.
#
    Order allow,deny
    Allow from all
</Directory>
```

In the preceding extract:

◆ Two values are specified for the Options directive. The first value,
  Indexes, displays a directory listing all the contents of the document
  root directory if no default Web page is specified. The Indexes option
  should not be used. Displaying the contents of the document root would
  mean showing the visitor the entire directory structure of a website,
  including those directories that you do not want the user to see.
  Although directories can be protected individually using .htaccess files
  etc, a better practice in system administration is always to allow access
  only to those sections where it is required, and block everything else
  rather than the opposite, which is to protect what is to be protected and
  leave everything else accessible.

◆ The AllowOverride None option indicates that the .htaccess file will be
  ignored.

◆ The Order directive is used to specify the default access state of the specified directory. This directive is also used to specify the order in which the Allow and Deny directives will be used.

The UserDir Directive

When a user accesses the Web server from a client computer, a directory is appended to the user's home directory. The UserDir directory is used to specify the name of this directory.

```
# UserDir: The name of the directory which is appended onto a user's home
# directory if a ~user request is received.
#
<IfModule mod_userdir.c>
    UserDir public_html
</IfModule>
```

As you can see in the preceding extract, the UserDir directive is assigned the value public_html. Also notice that the IfModule directive has been used. The IfModule directive is a conditional directive. In other words, all conditional directives are included in the IfModule directive.

The configuration lines from the following extract need to be uncommented if you want to implement user control on UserDir directories. While enabling this directive, the directive should never be enabled for the root user as it can inadvertently lead to root user's home directory access. The directive should instead be enabled for selective users if at all required. The following is an example:

```
Control access to UserDir directories.
# for a site where these directories are restricted to read-only.
#
#<Directory /home/*/public_html>
#     AllowOverride FileInfo AuthConfig Limit
#     Options MultiViews Indexes SymLinksIfOwnerMatch IncludesNoExec
#     <Limit GET POST OPTIONS PROPFIND>
#         Order allow,deny
#         Allow from all
#     </Limit>
#     <LimitExcept GET POST OPTIONS PROPFIND>
#         Order deny,allow
```

```
#        Deny from all
#    </LimitExcept>
#</Directory>
```

The DirectoryIndex Directive

The DirectoryIndex directive specifies which resources should be searched in the Web server when the client specifies a slash (/) at the end of the directory name. You have the option of specifying one or more file names with the DirectoryIndex directive. If only one file name is specified, the local URL points to this file, and its contents are displayed. However, if several files are specified, the server returns the content of the first file that it finds in the directory. If you haven't specified any resources or files and the Indexed option is set, the server returns its own directory listing.

```
# DirectoryIndex: Name of the file or files to use as a pre-written HTML
# directory index. Separate multiple entries with spaces.
#
<IfModule mod_dir.c>
    DirectoryIndex index.html
</IfModule>
```

In the preceding extract, several files are specified as a part of the DirectoryIndex directive. The Indexed option should not be using while securing Apache.

The AccessFileName Directive

AccessFileName is an important directive, used to access control and ensure security. In addition, the AccessFileName directive is used to specify a name of the file that will be checked in each directory, before allowing access to the resources of the directory. The syntax for the AccessFileName directive is shown in the following code sample:

```
# AccessFileName: The name of the file to look for in each directory
# for access control information.
#
AccessFileName .htaccess
```

The preceding extract from the httpd.conf file indicates that the AccessFileName directive is assigned the value .htaccess.

The CacheNegotiatedDocs Directive

The `CacheNegotiatedDocs` directive allows the proxy to cache the content-negotiated documents. Doing this enables clients behind the firewall to extract the cached documents and, as a result, save time and bandwidth.

```
# CacheNegotiatedDocs: By default, Apache sends "Pragma: no-cache" with each
# document that was negotiated on the basis of content. This asks proxy
# servers not to cache the document. Uncommenting the following line disables
# this behavior, and proxies will be allowed to cache the documents.
#
#CacheNegotiatedDocs
```

The UseCononicalName Directive

The canonical name is the primary name used by a Web server. However, there might be situations in which you want to specify more than one hostname for your Web server. This can be achieved by creating aliases to the existing canonical names. The `UseCanonicalName` directive allows you to specify whether you want to use the canonical name for your server.

```
# UseCanonicalName:  (new for 1.3)  With this setting turned on, whenever
# Apache needs to construct a self-referencing URL (a URL that refers back
# to the server the response is coming from) it will use ServerName and
# Port to form a "canonical" name.  With this setting off, Apache will
# use the hostname:port that the client supplied, when possible.  This
# also affects SERVER_NAME and SERVER_PORT in CGI scripts.
#
UseCanonicalName On
```

The TypeConfig Directive

The `TypesConfig` directive sets a location for the configuration file that contains details about the MIME types. These details include the mapping of file extensions to the associated content type. It is advisable not to change the MIME type configuration file.

```
# TypesConfig describes where the mime.types file (or equivalent) is
# to be found.
#
<IfModule mod_mime.c>
```

```
    TypesConfig /usr/local/apache/conf/mime.types
</IfModule>
```

The DefaultType Directive

A client might request a document whose MIME type is not recognized by the server. In such a case, the server responds to the request by using a default MIME type. The DefaultType directive specifies the default MIME type that is used by the Web server.

```
# DefaultType is the default MIME type the server will use for a document
# if it cannot otherwise determine one, such as from filename extensions.
# If your server contains mostly text or HTML documents, "text/plain" is
# a good value.  If most of your content is binary, such as applications
# or images, you may want to use "application/octet-stream" instead to
# keep browsers from trying to display binary files as though they are
# text.
#
DefaultType text/plain
```

This extract indicates that the DefaultType directive is assigned the value text/plain. This means that the default MIME type used by the server is plain text.

The HostnameLookups Directive

This directive is responsible for specifying whether DNS lookups should be enabled. DNS lookups are used to log the names of clients. Enabling this option can slow down the server considerably, however, because every client request initiates a lookup request to the DNS server. As a result, HostNameLookups is disabled by default.

```
# HostnameLookups: Log the names of clients or just their IP addresses
# e.g., www.apache.org (on) or 204.62.129.132 (off).
# The default is off because it'd be overall better for the net if people
# had to knowingly turn this feature on, since enabling it means that
# each client request will result in AT LEAST one lookup request to the
# nameserver.
#
HostnameLookups Off
```

In the preceding extract, the HostnameLookups directive is disabled by specifying the value Off.

The ServerSignature Directive

The ServerSignature directive suggests that a server signature be included at the end of the document when error messages are generated. This happens only when the On value is specified to the directive. If you specify the value Off, the server signature will not be generated.

```
# Optionally add a line containing the server version and virtual host
# name to server-generated pages (error documents, FTP directory listings,
# mod_status and mod_info output etc., but not CGI generated documents).
# Set to "EMail" to also include a mailto: link to the ServerAdmin.
# Set to one of:  On ¦ Off ¦ EMail
#
ServerSignature On
```

The EBCDICConvert and EBCDICConvertByType Directives

The EBCDICConvert and EBCDICConvertByType directives are used to configure *Extended Binary-Coded Decimal Interchange Code* (EBCDIC). EBCDIC is a code used to represent characters as numbers. It is most widely used with IBM architectures. The corresponding entries for EBCDIC in the httpd.conf file are shown in the following code:

```
# EBCDIC configuration:
# (only for mainframes using the EBCDIC codeset, currently one of:
# Fujitsu-Siemens' BS2000/OSD, IBM's OS/390 and IBM's TPF)!!
# The following default configuration assumes that "text files"
# are stored in EBCDIC (so that you can operate on them using the
# normal POSIX tools like grep and sort) while "binary files" are
# stored with identical octets as on an ASCII machine.
#
# The directives are evaluated in configuration file order, with
# the EBCDICConvert directives applied before EBCDICConvertByType.
#
# If you want to have ASCII HTML documents and EBCDIC HTML documents
# at the same time, you can use the file extension to force
```

```
# conversion off for the ASCII documents:
# > AddType          text/html .ahtml
# > EBCDICConvert  Off=InOut .ahtml
#
# EBCDICConvertByType  On=InOut text/* message/* multipart/*
# EBCDICConvertByType  On=In     application/x-www-form-urlencoded
# EBCDICConvertByType  On=InOut application/postscript model/vrml
# EBCDICConvertByType Off=InOut */*
```

Notice that all the lines are commented, which implies that the default configuration doesn't use EBCDIC.

The Alias Directive

The Alias directive enables Apache to store documents in a location other than the directory specified in the DocumentRoot directive. You can specify any number of aliases. The format for specifying an alias is as follows:

```
Alias aliasname actualname
```

Here, the aliasname represents an alias for the file, and the actualname represents the actual location of the file.

The following excerpt displays the corresponding entries related to the Alias directive in the httpd.conf file.

```
# Aliases: Add here as many aliases as you need (with no limit). The format is
# Alias fakename realname
#
<IfModule mod_alias.c>
    #
    # Note that if you include a trailing / on fakename then the server will
    # require it to be present in the URL.  So "/icons" isn't aliased in this
    # example, only "/icons/".  If the fakename is slash-terminated, then the
    # realname must also be slash terminated, and if the fakename omits the
    # trailing slash, the realname must also omit it.
    #
    Alias /icons/ "/usr/local/apache/icons/"
    <Directory "/usr/local/apache/icons">
        Options Indexes MultiViews
        AllowOverride None
```

```
        Order allow,deny
        Allow from all
    </Directory>
    # This Alias will project the on-line documentation tree under /manual/
    # even if you change the DocumentRoot. Comment it if you don't want to
    # provide access to the on-line documentation.
    #
    Alias /manual/ "/var/www/html/manual/"
    <Directory "/var/www/html/manual">
        Options Indexes FollowSymlinks MultiViews
        AllowOverride None
        Order allow,deny
        Allow from all
    </Directory>
    #
    # ScriptAlias: This controls which directories contain server scripts.
    # ScriptAliases are essentially the same as Aliases, except that
    # documents in the realname directory are treated as applications and
    # run by the server when requested rather than as documents sent to the
client.
    # The same rules about trailing "/" apply to ScriptAlias directives as to
    # Alias.
    #
    ScriptAlias /cgi-bin/ "/var/www/cgi-bin/"
    #
    # "/var/www/cgi-bin" should be changed to whatever your ScriptAliased
    # CGI directory exists, if you have that configured.
    #
    <Directory "/var/www/cgi-bin">
        AllowOverride None
        Options None
        Order allow,deny
        Allow from all
    </Directory>
</IfModule>
# End of aliases.
```

The Redirect Directive

The Redirect directive redirects the client to an alternate location. This is useful when you remove certain documents from the site. When this happens, the URLs that point to the document cease to work. To redirect the user to an alternate location, you need to use the old URL, as well as the new URL, with the Redirect directive. The entry for the Redirect directive is as follows:

```
# Redirect allows you to tell clients about documents which used to exist in
# your server's namespace, but do not anymore. This allows you to tell the
# clients where to look for the relocated document.
# Format: Redirect old-URI new-URL
```

Directives Used for Directory Listing

The directives that are used for directory listing occupy a considerable amount of space in the httpd.conf file. You can use several directives to customize the directory listing on your server. The following list discusses some of them:

- **IndexOptions.** This directive specifies the behavior of directory indexing. The IndexOptions directive contains several options, which determine the behavior of directory indexing.
- **AddIconByEncoding.** This directive displays an icon next to files that are MIME encoded.
- **AddIconByType.** This directive displays an icon next to files that are MIME type.
- **AddIcon.** This directive displays an icon next to different files, depending on the type of file.
- **DefaultIcon.** As the name suggests, the DefaultIcon directive specifies the default icon that is used for files whose file type is not recognized.
- **AddDescription.** The AddDescription directive specifies that a description will be displayed for each file that is a part of the indexed directory.
- **ReadmeName.** This directive is used to append a file to the end of the index listing.
- **HeaderName.** This directive specifies that a file will be added to the header of the indexing list.
- **IndexIgnore.** This directive specifies a list of files that you don't want displayed with all the other files in the indexed directory.

Consider the following extract of the httpd.conf file, which generates server-generated directory listings:

```
# Directives controlling the display of server-generated directory listings.
#
<IfModule mod_autoindex.c>
    #
    # FancyIndexing is whether you want fancy directory indexing or standard
    #
    IndexOptions FancyIndexing
    #
    # AddIcon* directives tell the server which icon to show for different
    # files or filename extensions.  These are only displayed for
    # FancyIndexed directories.
    #
    AddIconByEncoding (CMP,/icons/compressed.gif) x-compress x-gzip
    AddIconByType (TXT,/icons/text.gif) text/*
    AddIconByType (IMG,/icons/image2.gif) image/*
    AddIconByType (SND,/icons/sound2.gif) audio/*
    AddIconByType (VID,/icons/movie.gif) video/*
    AddIcon /icons/binary.gif .bin .exe
    AddIcon /icons/binhex.gif .hqx
    AddIcon /icons/tar.gif .tar
    AddIcon /icons/world2.gif .wrl .wrl.gz .vrml .vrm .iv
    AddIcon /icons/compressed.gif .Z .z .tgz .gz .zip
    AddIcon /icons/a.gif .ps .ai .eps
    AddIcon /icons/layout.gif .html .shtml .htm .pdf
.....Many lines deleted.....
```

Directives Used for Document Types

Several directives used in the portion of httpd.conf allow you to configure options for document types. The main directives in this section are discussed in the following list:

- ◆ **AddEncoding.** This directive maps filename extensions to a corresponding encoding type.
- ◆ **AddLanguage.** This directive maps the file extensions to the specified content language.

◆ **LanguagePriority.** This directive specifies the languages that will have primacy over other languages.

◆ **AddHandler.** This directive maps the file extensions to the handler name.

The following extract from the `httpd.conf` file shows the configurable options for the document types:

```
# Document types.
#
<IfModule mod_mime.c>
    #
    # AddEncoding allows you to have certain browsers (Mosaic/X 2.1+) uncompress
    # information on the fly. Note: Not all browsers support this.
    # Despite the name similarity, the following Add* directives have nothing
    # to do with the FancyIndexing customization directives above.
    #
    AddEncoding x-compress Z
    AddEncoding x-gzip gz tgz
    #
    # AddLanguage allows you to specify the language of a document. You can
    # then use content negotiation to give a browser a file in a language
    # it can understand.
    #
    # Note 1: The suffix does not have to be the same as the language
    # keyword —- those with documents in Polish (whose net-standard
    # language code is pl) may wish to use "AddLanguage pl .po" to
    # avoid the ambiguity with the common suffix for perl scripts.
    #
    # Note 2: The example entries below illustrate that in quite
    # some cases the two character 'Language' abbreviation is not
    # identical to the two character 'Country' code for its country,
    # E.g. 'Danmark/dk' versus 'Danish/da'.
    #
    # Note 3: In the case of 'ltz' we violate the RFC by using a three char
    # specifier. But there is 'work in progress' to fix this and get
    # the reference data for rfc1766 cleaned up.
    #
    # Danish (da) - Dutch (nl) - English (en) - Estonian (ee)
```

```
# French (fr) - German (de) - Greek-Modern (el)
# Italian (it) - Korean (kr) - Norwegian (no) - Norwegian Nynorsk (nn)
# Portugese (pt) - Luxembourgeois* (ltz)
# Spanish (es) - Swedish (sv) - Catalan (ca) - Czech(cz)
# Polish (pl) - Brazilian Portuguese (pt-br) - Japanese (ja)
# Russian (ru)
#
AddLanguage da .dk
AddLanguage nl .nl
AddLanguage en .en
AddLanguage et .ee
….·.….·.….·.….·.….·.….··
….·.….·.….·.….·.….·.….··
</IfModule>
# End of document types.
```

The Action Directive

The Action directive is used to specify an action. This activates a CGI script when a request from the client triggers an action-type. The CGI script is a URL path. This path points to a resource that is configured as a CGI script:

```
# Action lets you define media types that will execute a script whenever
# a matching file is called. This eliminates the need for repeated URL
# pathnames for oft-used CGI file processors.
# Format: Action media/type /cgi-script/location
# Format: Action handler-name /cgi-script/location
```

By default, the Action directive is commented.

The MetaDir Directive

The MetaDir directive is used to specify the location for meta information files. Meta information files store information that is hidden from the user. In the Apache context, meta information files are used to store additional HTTP headers that are included in the document before it is sent to the client:

```
# MetaDir: specifies the name of the directory in which Apache can find
# meta information files. These files contain additional HTTP headers
```

```
# to include when sending the document
#
#MetaDir .web
```

The MetaSuffix Directive

This directive is used to specify the suffix for the meta information files. The following is an extract from the httpd.conf file that contains the MetaSuffix directive:

```
# MetaSuffix: specifies the file name suffix for the file containing the
# meta information.
#
#MetaSuffix .meta
```

The value .meta is assigned to the MetaSuffix directive. This indicates that the suffix for the meta information file is .meta.

The ErrorDocument Directive

The ErrorDocument directive is used to specify an action the Web server takes if it encounters a problem or an error. This directive can be configured in a way so that:

- A message appears when an error is encountered.
- Local URL redirection happens. The URL specified by the client is redirected to a local URL, which in turn solves the problem or error.
- The URL specified by the client is redirected to an external URL, which in turn solves the problem or error.

The following extract from the httpd.conf file shows the default options that are set for the ErrorDocument directive:

```
# Customizable error response (Apache style)
#   these come in three flavors
#
#    1) plain text
#ErrorDocument 500 "The server made a boo boo.
#   n.b.  the single leading (") marks it as text, it does not get output
#
#    2) local redirects
```

```
#ErrorDocument 404 /missing.html
#   to redirect to local URL /missing.html
#ErrorDocument 404 /cgi-bin/missing_handler.pl
#   N.B.: You can redirect to a script or a document using server-side-includes.
#
#     3) external redirects
#ErrorDocument 402 http://some.other-server.com/subscription_info.html
#   N.B.: Many of the environment variables associated with the original
#   request will *not* be available to such a script.
```

The ErrorDocument directive is commented by default. However, you should specify suitable values for the ErrorDocument directive. Doing this provides users with a suitable explanation if a server error occurs.

The BrowserMatch Directive

The BrowserMatch directive is used to define environment variables that are based on the HTTP request header field named User-Agent:

```
# Customize behaviour based on the browser
#
<IfModule mod_setenvif.c>
    #
    # The following directives modify normal HTTP response behavior.
    # The first directive disables keepalive for Netscape 2.x and browsers that
    # spoof it. There are known problems with these browser implementations.
    # The second directive is for Microsoft Internet Explorer 4.0b2
    # which has a broken HTTP/1.1 implementation and does not properly
    # support keepalive when it is used on 301 or 302 (redirect) responses.
    #
    BrowserMatch "Mozilla/2" nokeepalive
    BrowserMatch "MSIE 4\.0b2;" nokeepalive downgrade-1.0 force-response-1.0
    #
    # The following directive disables HTTP/1.1 responses to browsers which
    # are in violation of the HTTP/1.0 spec by not being able to grok a
    # basic 1.1 response.
    #
    BrowserMatch "RealPlayer 4\.0" force-response-1.0
    BrowserMatch "Java/1\.0" force-response-1.0
    BrowserMatch "JDK/1\.0" force-response-1.0
```

```
</IfModule>
# End of browser customization directives
```

The preceding extract shows the use of the `BrowserMatch` directive in customizing the behavior of the browser based on its type. The `BrowserMatch` directive helps trigger special responses from the server when accessed by a specific browser.

Allow Server Status Reports

To allow display of server status reports, you need to uncomment the following code lines:

```
# Allow server status reports, with the URL of http://servername/server-status
# Change the ".your-domain.com" to match your domain to enable.
#
#<Location /server-status>
#     SetHandler server-status
#     Order deny,allow
#     Deny from all
#     Allow from .your-domain.com
#</Location>
```

The preceding lines are commented for security reasons by default.

Allow Remote Server Configuration

You need to uncomment the configurable lines from the following extract to allow generation of remote server configuration reports:

```
# Allow remote server configuration reports, with the URL of
# http://servername/server-info (requires that mod_info.c be loaded).
# Change the ".your-domain.com" to match your domain to enable.
#
#<Location /server-info>
#     SetHandler server-info
#     Order deny,allow
#     Deny from all
#     Allow from .your-domain.com
#</Location>
```

Proxy Server Directives

You need to uncomment the configurable lines from the following extract to configure Apache as a proxy server:

```
# Proxy Server directives. Uncomment the following lines to
# enable the proxy server:
#
#<IfModule mod_proxy.c>
#    ProxyRequests On

#    <Directory proxy:*>
#        Order deny,allow
#        Deny from all
#        Allow from .your-domain.com
#    </Directory>

    #
    # Enable/disable the handling of HTTP/1.1 "Via:" headers.
    # ("Full" adds the server version; "Block" removes all outgoing Via: headers)
    # Set to one of: Off ¦ On ¦ Full ¦ Block
    #
#    ProxyVia On

    #
    # To enable the cache as well, edit and uncomment the following lines:
    # (no caching without CacheRoot)
    #
#    CacheRoot "/usr/local/apache/proxy"
#    CacheSize 5
#    CacheGcInterval 4
#    CacheMaxExpire 24
#    CacheLastModifiedFactor 0.1
#    CacheDefaultExpire 1
#    NoCache a-domain.com another-domain.edu joes.garage-sale.com

#</IfModule>
# End of proxy directives.
```

Virtual Host Configuration Options

All other hosts that you can configure on your Apache server, apart from the main server, are virtual hosts. There are various advantages to using virtual hosts. One major benefit is the ability to host more that one Web site, with separate domain names, on a single Apache server. The directives in this category are as follows:

- ◆ <VirtualHost>
- ◆ NameVirtualHost
- ◆ ServerName
- ◆ ServerAlias
- ◆ ServerPath

Apache Modules

Apache has a modular architecture. Various modules are available to implement different functions of the Apache server. You can customize the Apache server, according to your requirements, by using the modules. One of the biggest advantages of Apache, over other Web servers, is that it is easy to write powerful modules for Apache.

Apache has used modules since version 1.0 to implement its functions. Modules need to have access to every stage of serving a client request because Apache itself uses modules for everything. Some of the useful modules provided with Apache are listed here:

- ◆ **mod_dir.** This module enables slash redirection and serving directory index files. A slash redirection is issued when the server receives a request for a URL.
- ◆ **mod_autoindex.** This module enables automatically indexing of directories.
- ◆ **mod_access.** This module can be used to perform access control over clients. The directives provided by mod_access are used in <Directory>, <Files>, <Location> sections, and .htaccess files to control access to particular parts of the server.
- ◆ **mod_auth.** This module enables user authentication by using the text files. The text files contain the text password.

◆ **mod_auth_dbm.** This module enables user authentication based on the DBM files. The DBM files contain the username and the password.

◆ **mod_auth_db.** This module enables user authentication based on the Berkeley DB files.

◆ **mod_auth_anon.** This module enables anonymous to access the restricted data. In addition, it allows access to a user having the anonymous username and the email address as a password.

◆ **mod_auth_digest.** This module enables user authentication based on the MD5 Digest Authentication.

◆ **mod_headers.** This module enables you to customize the HTTP response.

◆ **mod_expires.** This module enables generation of Expires HTTP headers. The HTTP header is generated according to the user-specified criteria. The Expires HTTP header is an instruction to the client about the document's validity and persistence.

◆ **mod_asis.** This module enables you to send files containing their own HTTP headers. This module enables the send-as-is handler that causes Apache to send the files.

◆ **mod_cgi.** This module enables execution of CGI scripts. Any file that has the MIME type application/x-httpd-cgi or the cgi-script handler is treated as a CGI script and is run by the server.

◆ **mod_actions.** This module enables you to execute CGI scripts that are based on media type or request method. This module has two directives, Action and Script. The Action directive enables you to run CGI scripts whenever a file of a specific type is requested. The Script directive enables you to run CGI scripts whenever a particular method is used in a request.

◆ **mod_status.** This module provides information on server status and performance. The Status module allows an administrator to analyze the performance of the server.

◆ **mod_log_config.** This module enables logging of requests that are made to the server.

Virtual Hosts

Apache enables you to run virtual hosts. On a single server, you might need to run multiple Web services, each with different host names and URLs, which appear to be completely separate sites. Virtual hosts enable you to do this. Virtual hosts are used to host multiple sites. There are two types of virtual hosts:

◆ IP-based

◆ Name-based

IP-based Virtual Hosts

In IP-based virtual hosts, each virtual host has its own IP address. Some operating systems allow you to provide multiple IP addresses to a single Ethernet by using the `ifconfig` command.

After selecting the IP address, you should update the DNS so that browsers can convert the hostname to the corresponding address. The entry you need to add to the DNS is an address record pointing at the appropriate IP address. After you have updated the DNS, you need to configure Apache to respond differently to the different addresses. There are two ways of telling Apache which addresses and ports to listen to:

◆ Use the `BindAddress` directive to specify a single address or port.

◆ Use the `Listen` directive to specify any number of specific addresses or ports.

For example, if you run your main server on IP address 172.17.2.3 port 80 and a virtual host on IP 172.17.2.4 port 8000, you can use the `Listen` directives as follows:

```
Listen 172.17.2.3:80
Listen 172.17.2.4:8000
```

Configuring the Virtual Hosts

Next, you need to configure the server so that it responds differently to the requests from the different IP addresses, which you have configured. This is done using `<VirtualHost>` sections in the `httpd.conf` file.

A sample of the virtual host configuration is given here:

```
<VirtualHost 172.17.0.0>
DocumentRoot /www/vhost1
ServerName  www.mywebsite.com
</VirtualHost>
```

The preceding entries should be placed in the httpd.conf file. You need to replace the IP number with the required IP address.

If you do not specify the <VirtualHost> section in the configuration files, Apache will process requests from different addresses and ports identically, as per the default settings. The default behavior for processing the request is specified in the main server configuration section of the httpd.conf file. All virtual hosts inherit the main server behavior unless you override it.

Apache finds a virtual host by using the target IP address and port information whenever a request arrives. If the matching host is found, Apache handles the request as per the virtual host configuration. If no matching virtual host is found, the request is processed according to the main server configuration.

Name-based Virtual Hosts

Name-based virtual hosts are configured in a manner very similar to IP-based virtual hosts. The IP address that the requests reach is specified in the <VirtualHost> directive and the host name is specified in the ServerName directive. There will usually be more than one <VirtualHost> section handling the same IP address. To tell Apache whether name-based requests are supposed to arrive on a particular IP address, the NameVirtualHost directive is used. The ServerAlias directive enables a virtual host to handle multiple non-IP host names.

The VirtualHost directive in the configuration file is used to set the values of ServerAdmin, ServerName, DocumentRoot, ErrorLog and TransferLog, or CustomLog, configuration directives to different values for each virtual host:

```
<VirtualHost www.premierpressbooks.com>
ServerAdmin webmaster@mail. premierpressbooks.com
DocumentRoot /groups/ premierpressbooks /www
ServerName www. premierpressbooks.com
ErrorLog /groups/ premierpressbooks /logs/error_log
```

```
TransferLog /groups/ premierpressbooks /logs/access_log
</VirtualHost>

<VirtualHost www. premierpress.org>
ServerAdmin webmaster@mail. abc.org
DocumentRoot /groups/ premierpress /www
ServerName www. premierpress.org
ErrorLog /groups/ premierpress /logs/error_log
TransferLog /groups/ premierpress /logs/access_log
</VirtualHost>
```

You can include almost any configuration directive in the `VirtualHost` directive. Exceptions are the directives that control process creation, and a few other directives.

 CAUTION

When specifying where to write log files, you should be aware of some security risks. If the directory where the log files are written is made available to users other than the user who starts Apache, security problems can be posed.

You must designate the IP address on the server that accepts requests for the hosts. This is configured using the `NameVirtualHost` directive. In cases where any IP addresses on the server can be used, you can use * as the argument to the `NameVirtualHost` directive. For example, consider that both www.premierpress.tld and www.premierpressbooks.tld point to an IP address that the server is listening to. You should then add the following entry to httpd.conf:

```
NameVirtualHost *
<VirtualHost *>
ServerName www. premierpress.tld
DocumentRoot /www/ premierpress
</VirtualHost>
<VirtualHost *>
ServerName www. premierpressbooks.tld
DocumentRoot /www/ premierpressbooks
</VirtualHost>
```

When a request arrives, the server first checks whether it is using an IP address that matches the NameVirtualHost directive. If it is, the server looks at each <VirtualHost> section with a matching IP address and tries to find a <VirtualHost> section where the ServerName or ServerAlias matches the requested hostname.

If the server finds a matching <VirtualHost> section, it uses the configuration for that server. The first listed virtual host is the default virtual host. The DocumentRoot directive from the main server will never be used when an IP address matches the NameVirtualHost directive. If you would like to have a special configuration for requests that do not match any particular virtual host, simply put that configuration in a <VirtualHost> container, and list it first in the configuration file.

Directory Access Control

Apache enables you to control access to the directories. You can use the <Directory> directive to control the access to the directories, as shown here:

```
<Directory "/var/www/html">
    AllowOverride None
    Options None
</Directory>
```

The advantage of the <Directory> directive is that you need not worry about a user being able to change the settings. No user except the administrator can modify the server configuration files. However, it has a disadvantage that you need to restart Apache every time the config file is changed. Also, adding all the <Directory> containers can be tedious.

.htaccess File

You can use an alternative to overcome the disadvantages of the <Directory> directive. You can use the config file, .htaccess, in each directory with special requirements. An .htaccess file is a text file containing Apache directives. These directives are applicable to the files and subdirectories in the parent directory of the .htaccess file. However, if the subdirectories contain the .htaccess file, the settings in the .htaccess file of the subdirectories are effective on the files in the subdirectory.

The `AccessFileName` directive enables you to change the name of the config files. For example,

```
AccessFileName my.htaccess
```

The preceding statement will cause Apache to look for files named my.htaccess, instead of .htaccess. However, this file will serve the same purpose as .htaccess.

A sample authentication page can be seen in Figure 8-1:

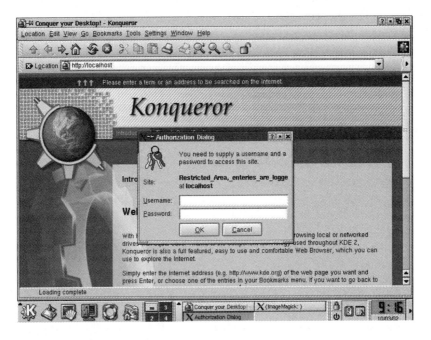

FIGURE 8-1 *An example of an* .htaccess *file based authentication dialog box.*

Working of .htaccess

If the requested resource is a file on the disk, it performs a process known as *directory walk*. Using directory walk, Apache checks its internal list of <Directory> containers. It might also search the directories on the file system for .htaccess files. Directories are included in the settings whenever a set of directives applicable to the request is found during directory walk. Therefore, you get a collection of settings that apply to the final document.

.htaccess files are evaluated for each request, so you don't need to reload the Apache server whenever you make a change. If there's a syntax error in an .htaccess file, only a portion of the server's Web space is affected.

Directives in .htaccess File

Apache directives fall into seven different categories, all of which can appear in the config files. However, only five of the categories can be used in .htaccess files. For Apache to accept a directive in a per-directory file, the settings for the directory must permit the directive's category to be overridden. The five categories of directives that can be used in .htaccess files are as follows:

- ◆ **AuthConfig.** These directives can be used to control directives that deal with Web page security, such as the AuthName, Satisfy, and Require directives.
- ◆ **FileInfo.** These directives control how files are processed.
- ◆ **Indexes.** These directives affect file listings.
- ◆ **Limit.** These directives are related to security.
- ◆ **Options.** These directives support miscellaneous options, such as ContentDigest and XBitHack.

A special directive, AllowOverride, specifies the category to be overridden in a directory tree. This directive is usable only in the server-wide configuration files. The AllowOverride directive accepts the following categories:

- ◆ **All.** This lists all categories. The two statements below are equivalent:

```
AllowOverride AuthConfig FileInfo Indexes Limits Options
AllowOverride All
```

- ◆ **None.** This keyword disables the processing of .htaccess files for a specified directory and its subdirectories. Once this keyword is specified, Apache won't search for the .htaccess files.

These are the two main disadvantages to using .htaccess:

- ◆ Effect on the performance
- ◆ Extending control access to other users

Performance degradation can be managed through judicious use of the AllowOverride directive. This is a matter of establishing trust and performing risk assessment.

Content of a sample .htaccess file is given here:

```
AuthUserFile /Directory1/.htpasswd
AuthGroupFile /dev/null
AuthName "Group is null"
AuthType Basic

<Limit GET>
require valid-user
</Limit>
```

In the preceding sample, AuthGroupFile is null. This directive is used if you have multiple users. AuthName's text is displayed to users when they are prompted for a password. The AuthType directive indicates that Basic authentication will be used.

The password file, .htpasswd, is located in the AuthUserFile directive. This file contains a list of usernames and passwords. Remember that there is no relation between the username and password of your Linux system and the username and password used for the authentication schemes. You can create the .htpasswd file by using the htpasswd command. The syntax of the htpasswd command is as follows:

```
htpasswd -c .htpasswd [username]
```

A sample output of a failed authentication request is shown in Figure 8-2.

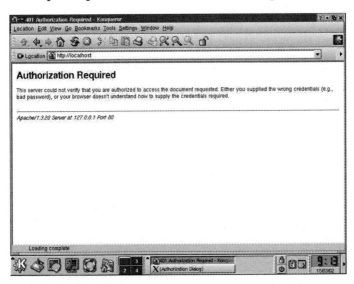

FIGURE 8-2 *An example of an* .htaccess-*based authentication failure.*

Digest Authentication

Two modules provide Digest authentication in Apache:

- **mod_digest.** This module enables user authentication by using MD5 authentication.

- **mod_auth_digest.** This module also enables user authentication by using MD5 authentication. However, it provides more features and is more secure than mod_digest.

Here is an example of a Location directive specifying a URL that is protected with digest authentication:

```
<Location /MyDirectory/>
  AuthType Digest
  AuthName "MyDirectory Digest Authenticated"
  AuthDigestDomain /MyDirectory/ /protected/
  AuthDigestFile /web/auth/.password.md5
  Require group WebAdmins
  </Location>
```

CGI Security

The *Common Gateway Interface* (CGI) acts as an interface between external applications and Web servers. A CGI program is executed on the server during the runtime. The server then sends the output to the client.

Because CGI programs are executed on the servers, and the output of the program depends on the input and request from the client, you need to be careful about the security of the system. You shouldn't let a request pass through that demands to execute a CGI program in a manner that will damage your system.

With every transaction, various components are involved. Some of these components are listed here:

- The client who sends the requests
- The request sent by the client
- The CGI script
- The database, if required

There are two types of security risks involved in using CGI:

◆ At times, CGI programs are executed, and the result is sent to the client. That involves a risk of sending critical information to the client.

◆ CGI programs might take inputs from the client and use those inputs as arguments for executing the CGI program. This is risky, in the sense that a malicious client might send an argument that can cause damage to your system.

Some of the measures you should take to ensure CGI security are these:

◆ Ensure that the CGI script has the required permissions. You do this with the chmod command.

◆ You can place the CGI script inside a wrapper script. Wrappers are capable of performing some critical tasks, such as performing checks on a script and changing the ownership of the CGI prints.

◆ You should check thoroughly all elements of the FORM that is submitted to the CGI program. You also should check the content submitted to the CGI script through the FORM. Checking the content becomes more critical if you use information from the FORM as arguments to a command, which is executed on the server.

◆ You should restrict access to the script to a certain IP address or username. You can ensure that the HTTP_REFERER environmental variable is set to either the server name or the server name from where the CGI script is accessible. The HTTP_REFERER variable isn't always set and it can even be forged. Therefore, you shouldn't rely on it for all your security needs.

The cgi-bin Directory

CGI scripts usually are stored in the cgi-bin directory. Storing the CGI scripts in a central location is more secure and convenient, because you need to apply restrictions only to one directory. You should restrict the accessibility to the cgi-bin directory to only those users who need the information.

The CGI scripts are stored in a file with the extension *.cgi. You should configure the Apache server in such a way that it will not accept any request for documents other than the *.cgi files. You should not leave any important file in the cgi-bin directory.

CGI Applications versus CGI Scripts

CGI applications are binary executable programs that have been compiled using a compiler. These programs are executable from the command line and have execution permissions. CGI programs are less dependent on Apache and its modules. Such programs can be either dynamic applications that require other external libraries for execution or huge static applications that have all the required libraries embedded in them.

CGI applications have a disadvantage in that sometimes the applications can become unstable after the system goes through a library upgrade. Static CGI applications are invulnerable to this problem. However, there's another problem with static CGI applications: because all the required libraries are embedded in static CGI applications, such CGI programs can grow to a huge size after compilation.

CGI scripts are program source codes that do exactly the same job as a CGI application. The only difference is that CGI applications are compiled programs, whereas CGI scripts are source codes of the program. The CGI scripts are compiled every time they are called. CGI scripts are easier to manage, as compared to CGI applications. CGI scripts have a security risk in that if the file permissions are not set correctly, a malicious user can download the script and scan the source code of the file to obtain sensitive data, such as passwords, names of directories, and so on.

Securing Apache Server

You should ensure that the non-root users aren't able to modify Apache. Only the root users should have write permissions. The files, directories, and parents of the directories must be writeable only by the root user. You also should protect the httpd executable in a similar manner. You should prevent users from modifying .htaccess files, which can override security features. Here's one way to do it.

In the server configuration file, make the following entry:

```
<Directory />
AllowOverride None
</Directory>
```

This will prevent the use of .htaccess files in all directories, apart from those specifically enabled.

Securing Server Side Includes

SSI poses several security risks to the system. There is an increased load on the server, and Apache parses all the SSI-enabled files, irrespective of the presence of SSI directives, in those files. This increase in the load is not significant, but it can affect a shared environment significantly.

SSI files pose the same risks as CGI. SSI-enabled files can execute CGI scripts or programs that can prove to be security concerns for the system administrators. Some of the measures to prevent security threats by SSI-enabled files are listed here:

◆ You should use the suEXEC utility provided with Linux. This feature enables you to run CGI and SSI programs under user IDs different from the user ID of the calling Web server.

◆ Enabling SSI for .html or .htm files can be risky. SSI-enabled files should have a separate extension, such as the conventional .shtml. This helps you minimize the server load and manage your files.

◆ Disable the ability to run scripts and programs from SSI pages. To do this, replace Includes with IncludesNOEXEC in the Options directive.

You should consider limiting CGI to specific directories. Doing this enables administrators to control these directories. The users who have write access to these directories should be trusted. In addition, the administrator should test each new CGI script or program for potential security holes.

Default Access

The Apache Web server provides default access. This means that the server can walk through the entire file system to serve a client request. To work around this, add the following entry to the server configuration:

```
<Directory />
    Order Deny,Allow
    Deny from all
</Directory>
```

The preceding entry will forbid default access to the file system. You can add the appropriate <Directory> to allow access only to selective directories. For example, consider the following code:

```
<Directory /usr/users/*/public_html>
    Order Deny,Allow
    Allow from all
</Directory>
<Directory /usr/local/httpd>
    Order Deny,Allow
    Allow from all
</Directory>
```

You should be careful while using the <Location> and <Directory> directives. If specified, the <Location> directive can overwrite the <Directory> directive. If you use Apache 1.3 or above, it is recommended that you include the following line in your server configuration files:

```
UserDir disabled root
```

Summary

The Apache Web server is a popular server that has many advantages, such as advanced features, better performance, and free availability of the source code. httpd.conf, srm.conf, and access.conf are the three configuration files for Apache. However, the srm.conf and access.conf files are no longer in use. All the configuration options of Apache are specified in the httpd.conf file, which contains several directives that determine the settings of the Apache Web server. This chapter covered several such directives in detail.

You can run several virtual hosts on Apache. The concept of virtual hosts enables you to run multiple Web services on the same computer. The two types of virtual hosts are IP-based and Name-based virtual hosts. In this chapter, I discussed both these types in detail. I also explained .htaccess files. An .htaccess file is a text file containing Apache directives. These directives apply to the documents in the directory where the .htaccess file is located, as well as to all the file's subdirectories.

Check Your Understanding

Multiple Choice Questions

1. Which file in the current versions of Apache contains directives for controlling the specification of the documents that are provided by the server to the clients?

   ◆ httpd.conf

   ◆ srm.conf

   ◆ access.conf

   ◆ ftpaccess.conf

2. Which sections are present in the http.conf file?

   a. The Global Environment section

   b. The Main server configuration section

   c. The Main Hosts section

   d. The Virtual Environment section

   e. The Virtual Hosts section

3. The _____ directive is used to specify the location where the configuration, error, and log files are located.

4. The ResourceConfig and AccessConfig directives store the path for the _____ and _____ files, respectively.

Short Questions

1. What is the Listen directive? Discuss the values contained by the Listen directive.

2. Explain the five categories of directives that can be used in .htaccess files.

Answers

Multiple Choice Answers

1. The `httpd.conf` file contains directives that control the specification of the documents provided by the server to the clients.

2. The sections of `http.conf` file are as follows:

   a. The Global Environment section

   b. The Main server configuration section

   d. The Virtual Environment section

3. The `ServerRoot` directive specifies the location of the configuration, error, and log files.

4. The `ResourceConfig` and `AccessConfig` directives store the path for the `srm.conf` and `access.conf` files, respectively.

Short Answers

1. The `Listen` directive is used to specify the IP address on which Apache will listen to the clients. The `Listen` directive can contain any of these three values:

   ◆ This value indicates that Apache will listen to all IP addresses configured on the server machine.

   ◆ **IP address.** This value represents an IP address that is used by the server. You can specify only one IP address.

   ◆ **Domain name.** This value represents a fully qualified domain name, which can be specified in the `BindAddress` directive. This value indicates that Apache will listen only to the Internet domain name specified.

2. The five categories of directives that can be used in .htaccess files are these:

   ◆ **AuthConfig.** These directives can be used to control directives that deal with Web page security, such as the AuthName, Satisfy, and Require directives.

   ◆ **FileInfo.** These directives control how files are processed.

◆ **Indexes.** These directives affect file listings.

◆ **Limit.** These directives are related to security. However, they usually involve involuntary controls, such as controlling access by IP address.

◆ **Options.** These directives support miscellaneous options, such as `ContentDigest` and `XBitHack`.

Chapter 9

Other Network Servers

In Chapter 8, I discussed the Apache Web server in detail. In this chapter, I discuss the following additional network servers:

- ◆ FTP server
- ◆ Sendmail
- ◆ DNS
- ◆ SAMBA

FTP Server

File Transfer Protocol (FTP) is used to transfer files over the Internet. When you download a file from the Internet, you actually transfer the file from a computer on the Internet to your computer.

Wuarchive-ftpd or wu-ftpd, the most popular ftp daemon for Linux systems on the Internet, was developed at Washington University by Chris Myers. While configuring an FTP server, you might need to edit the following files:

- ◆ **/etc/ftpaccess.** This file enables users to access the FTP server. You can configure this file to enable logical groups to access the FTP server.
- ◆ **/etc/ftphosts.** This file enables or disables access to accounts from various hosts.
- ◆ **/etc/ftpusers.** This file contains a list of users who are not allowed to connect to your computer through FTP.

Setting the FTP User Account

FTP has been the target of attacks from hackers. You need to be careful while configuring FTP. FTP users should not be given the shell account for security reasons. You should not allow FTP users to execute all the tasks that normal users on your Linux system can perform. This section provides the steps you need to follow to create new FTP users.

Start by creating new users in the /etc/passwd file. To do this, execute the following commands:

```
# mkdir /home/ftp
# useradd -d /home/ftp/ftpuser2/ -s /dev/null
# passwd ftpuser2
```

The mkdir command creates the /home/ftp directory. This directory will contain all FTP users' home directories. Next, use the useradd command to add a new user ftpuser2 to the server. You set the password for ftpuser2 by using the passwd command.

The next step is performed to limit the access of FTP users on your system. To do this, you need to edit the /etc/shells file as follows:

```
/bin/bash
/bin/sh
/bin/ash
/bin/bsh
/bin/tcsh
/bin/csh
/dev/null
```

Notice the last statement, /dev/null. This statement will add a non-existent shell.

Next, you need to edit the /etc/passwd file. The original entry for the ftpuser2 user is in the /etc/passwd file is shown here:

```
ftpuser2:x:502:502::/home/ftp/ftpuser2/:/dev/null
```

The above entry should be modified as follows:

```
ftpuser2:x:502:502::/home/ftp/./ftpuser2/:/dev/null
```

The preceding modification needs to be done for every user on a system that requires FTP access. After you have the above modifications, a fake shell is created for the FTP users, limiting their access to the system.

Configurations File for FTP Server

The following configurations files are required for the effective functioning of your FTP server:

◆ ftpaccess

◆ ftpusers

◆ ftphosts

◆ ftpgroups

◆ ftpconversion

The next few sections discuss some of these files.

ftpaccess

The ftpaccess file is the main configuration file for the Wu-ftpd server. This file manages the users and other security-related issues of the FTP server. You should place this file in the /etc folder. The default location for this file is /etc/ftpaccess.

The important directives of the ftpaccess file are discussed here:

◆ The deny directive will disallow access to the hosts with the address, <address>. If any specified hosts try to connect, the <message> is displayed:

deny <address> <message>.

◆ The following directives add users and groups as guest user/group or real user/group:

guestgroup <groupname> [<groupname>...]
guestuser <username> [<username >...]
realgroup <groupname> [<groupname>...]
realuser <username> [<username >...]

◆ The tcpwindow directive is used to control network traffic by setting up the TCP window size:

tcpwindow <size> [<class>]

◆ The `timeout` directive is used to specify various time limits:

```
timeout [accept ¦ connect ¦ data ¦ idle ¦ maxidle ¦ RFC931 ] <seconds>
```

◆ The `file-limit` directive limits the number of files a user in the specified class can transfer:

```
file-limit [<raw>] <in¦out¦total> <count> [<class>]
```

◆ The `data-limit` directive is used to specify the limit of the data in bytes that a user in the specified class can transfer:

```
data-limit [<raw>] <in¦out¦total> <count> [<class>]
```

◆ The `limit-time` directive is used to set the time limit for a session:

```
limit-time {*¦anonymous¦guest} <minutes>
```

◆ The `limit` directive is used to limit the class to a specified number of users. The error message `<message>` is displayed when the user is denied access:

```
limit <class> <n> <times> <message_file>
```

◆ The `noretrieve` directive is used to deny the transfer of the specified files:

```
noretrieve [absolute¦relative] [class=<classname>] ... [-] <filename> <filename>
...
```

◆ The `allowretrieve` directive allows retrieval of the specified files:

```
allowretrieve [absolute¦relative] [class=<classname>] ... [-] <filename> <filename>
...
```

◆ The `login` directive is used to specify the number of failed logon attempts that is allowed. The default value is 5:

```
login <fails>
```

◆ The `log commands` directive allows logging of individual commands by users. The `<typelist>` can be anonymous, guest, and `real`:

```
log commands <typelist>
```

◆ The `log transfers` directive enables you to log file transfers for anonymous and real FTP users. `<directions>` can have `TO` value for the
incoming transfer or `FROM` value for the outgoing transfers:

```
log transfers <typelist> <directions>
```

◆ The `log security` directive allows you to log security rules violation by
`real`, `anonymous`, and `guest` users:

```
log security <typelist>
```

◆ The following directives enable or disable the ability to perform the
specified task. The default value for each of these values is `yes`:

```
chmod <yes¦no> <typelist>
delete <yes¦no> <typelist>
overwrite <yes¦no> <typelist>
rename <yes¦no> <typelist>
umask <yes¦no> <typelist>
```

◆ The `passwd-check` directive is used for enforcing the kind of password
checking done for anonymous FTP users:

```
passwd-check <none¦trivial¦rfc822> (<enforce¦warn>)
```

◆ The `upload` directive is used to specify whether the directory, `<dirglob>`,
will allow uploads:

```
upload [absolute¦relative] [class=<classname>]... [-] <root-dir> <dirglob> <yes¦no>
<owner> <group> <mode> [dirs¦nodirs] [<d_mode>]
```

◆ The `throughput` directive is used to restrict the download file transfer
rate for files in a specified directory:

```
throughput <root-dir> <subdir-glob> <file-glob-list> <bytes-per-second> <bytes-per-
second-multiply> <remote-glob-list>
```

◆ The following directives allow specification of UID and GID values that
will be denied access to the FTP server:

```
deny-uid <uid-range> [...]
deny-gid <gid-range> [...]
allow-uid <uid-range> [...]
allow-gid <gid-range> [...]
```

◆ The following directives are used to specify whether real and guest users have access outside their home directories on the FTP server:

```
restricted-uid <uid-range> [...]
restricted-gid <gid-range> [...]
unrestricted-uid <uid-range> [...]
unrestricted-gid <gid-range> [...]
```

◆ The site-exec-max-lines directive is used to limit the number of lines that can be sent to a remote client:

```
site-exec-max-lines <number> [<class> ...]
```

The ftpaccess file specifies which users can access the FTP server. In ftpaccess, you can define the activities that can be performed by a user. The content of a sample ftpaccess file is shown here:

```
class    all    real,guest,anonymous    *
email root@localhost
loginfails 5
readme    README*    login
readme    README*    cwd=*
message /welcome.msg              login
message .message                  cwd=*
compress          yes             all
tar               yes             all
chmod             no              guest,anonymous
delete            no              guest,anonymous
overwrite         no              guest,anonymous
rename            no              guest,anonymous
log transfers anonymous, real inbound, outbound
shutdown /etc/shutmsg
passwd-check rfc822 warn
```

In the preceding extract, you first set the class to allow local and remote access from all addresses. This can be customized depending upon your requirements. You can specify all of your guest groups, one per line. You should log all transfers for security purposes as shown here:

```
log commands real,anonymous,guest
log transfers guest,anonymous,real inbound,outbound
```

The `chmod`, `delete`, `overwrite`, and `rename` directives are set to yes by default. The entries to deny the permissions for anonymous users are as follows:

```
chmod        no            guest,anonymous
delete       no            guest,anonymous
overwrite    no            guest,anonymous
rename       no            guest,anonymous
```

ftpusers

The `ftpusers` file is used to specify the users who are denied access to your FTP server. This file is in the `/etc` directory by default. The `/etc/ftpusers` file allows you to keep certain users from logging into your machine via FTP. When an incoming FTP connection is received, the `/etc/ftpusers` file is read by the FTP daemon program (`ftpd`). The file is a simple list of those users who are not allowed to log on. The content of the file is given here:

```
root
bin
daemon
adm
lp
sync
shutdown
halt
mail
news
uucp
operator
games
nobody
```

ftpconversions

The `ftpcomversions` file contains instructions for compressing files before transfer. The file contains the conversion types and their attributes. The format for entries in the file is given here:

```
%s (field 1): %s (field 2): %s (field 3): %s (field 4): %s (field 5): %s (field
6): %s (field 7): %s (field 8)
```

In the preceding format, field1 and field2 specify the prefix and postfix to be removed. field3 and field4 specify the prefix and postfix to be added. field5 is an external command. field6, field7, and field8 are types, options, and descriptions, respectively.

FTP Administrative Tools

Many tools are available to monitor your FTP servers. Here are two such administrative tools:

- **ftpwho.** This tool displays all the active FTP users and their current processes.
- **ftpcount.** This tool displays only the number of users currently logged on to the FTP server. In addition, it also displays the maximum number of users who are allowed access.

Anonymous FTP

The anonymous FTP service lets anyone in the world have access to a certain area of disk space in a secure way. The connection process involves a remote user creating an FTP connection and logging on to the system. The user logs on with the username anonymous and usually the password is the email-id.

Configuring Anonymous FTP

Setting up anonymous FTP is simple. All you need to do is install the anonftp RPM package. To set up the anonymous FTP, you need to install the anonftp RPM package. Some facts regarding the settings and configuration of Anonymous FTP are discussed in the next section.

Setting up the Anonymous FTP Directories

The anonymous FTP root directory and its subdirectories should not be owned by the FTP account or be in the same group as the FTP account. If you allow the FTP account of any other user in the same group to own the FTP root directory or its subdirectory, an intruder will be able to add or modify files. The FTP account shouldn't own the anonymous FTP root directory. Doing this would enable the intruders to access the FTP server and modify the files in the root directory. You can secure the anonymous FTP server by allowing root to own the FTP root directory and its subdirectories. In addition, you should assign the write permission only to the root.

Using Proper Password and Group Files

Anonymous FTP should not be allowed to use the system's /etc/passwd file as the password file or the system's /etc/group as the group file in the ~ftp/etc directory. Doing so will enable intruders to get a copy of these files. You also should consider using the dummy version of both the ~ftp/etc/passwd and ~ftp/etc/group files. No account name in the ~/ftp/etc/passwd file should be the same as those in the system's /etc/passwd file.

Another risk associated with anonymous FTP is that it allows users to create directories. Users should not be able to automatically create a drop-off directory unless you have analyzed the risks involved. Many cases have been reported where these directories have been used to distribute pirated versions of copyrighted software or to exchange information regarding accounts and password files.

This section discusses three ways to address these problems. The solutions to these problems are listed:

◆ Use a modified FTP daemon

◆ Use protected directories

◆ Use a separate directory

Using Modified FTP Daemon

If you plan to allow a drop-off service, which will enable anonymous FTP users to store files on the FTP server, you should use a modified FTP daemon. This modified FTP daemon should be able to control access to the drop-off directory. Some modifications that you can make to the daemon are as follows:

◆ Implement a policy where any file dropped off can be accessed only after the administrator has examined it and moves it to a public directory. Only the administrator should be able to access the dropped off files. After verifying the content of the file, administrators can move these files to directories accessible to other users.

◆ Limit the amount of data transferred in one session. Anonymous FTP should be allowed to transfer limited data only.

◆ Limit the overall amount of data transferred based on available disk space.

◆ Ensure logging to enable earlier detection of abuses.

Public domain sources for such modified FTP daemons are available from the following sites:

◆ `wuarchive.wustl.edu ~ftp/packages/wuarchive-ftpd`

◆ `ftp.uu.net ~ftp/systems/unix/bsd-sources/libexec/ftpd`

◆ `gatekeeper.dec.com ~ftp/pub/DEC/gwtools/ftpd.tar.Z`

Using Protected Directories

If your site is planning to offer a drop off service and is unable to modify the FTP daemon, it is possible to control access by using protected directories. The protected directories enable you to restrict access to the anonymous FTP users. The protected directories are more useful if you are providing the drop off service to the anonymous FTP users. Although this method cannot guarantee complete protection, it has been used effectively by many sites.

You should protect the top-level directory, `~ftp/incoming`, by giving only execute permission to the anonymous user. This will permit the anonymous user to move to a different directory. By doing this, you can restrict the user's view to the content of the directories.

Using a Single Disk Drive

Consider limiting the amount of data transferred to a single file system mounted as `~ftp/incoming`. If possible, dedicate a disk drive and mount it as `~ftp/incoming`. The `~ftp/incoming` directory should be monitored on a regular basis to ensure that it is not being misused.

Anonymous FTP Warnings

Here are some precautions to take before configuring anonymous FTP:

◆ **Responsibility.** You are responsible for the files that are stored on your domain. This includes files that were uploaded by you as well as by anonymous FTP users.

◆ **Data Transfer.** All the FTP downloads will be used in the calculation of the total data transfer for your account. You might end up spending money if the transferred data exceeds the limit.

◆ **Disk Space.** If you allow people to upload files to your site, you should keep track of the disk space usage.

Securing FTP

The following list provides the measures you can use to secure your FTP server:

◆ Ensure that you have properly configured the `/etc/ftpusers` file. This file should contain the list of users who are not allowed to access the FTP server.

◆ If you need to disable anonymous FTP, you should remove the anonymous user `ftp` from the password file. In addition to this, verify that `anonftp-version.i386.rpm` package is not installed on your system.

◆ Grant upload permissions carefully. Users should not be able to upload into the `dev`, `bin`, `etc`, and `lib` directories. You can edit `/etc/ftpaccess` to modify the upload permissions.

◆ Use the `noretrieve` directive to deny transfer of selected files or directories.

Sendmail

E-mail has become the easiest and fastest way of communication in modern times. On the Internet, the majority of servers run the UNIX operating system or its derivatives, such as BSD, Linux, and SunOS. Sendmail is the program most of these systems use to handle e-mail. To use sendmail, you need to install the `sendmail` and `sendmail-cf` packages.

Sendmail is able to route or deliver mail between a mail *User Agent* (UA) and a *Message Transfer Agent* (MTA). UA is a program you might use to read and send e-mails. MTA is a program that moves mail between hosts using a particular network protocol or language. Sendmail can be easily configured to accommodate new UAs and MTAs, with only minor configuration changes.

When a sender wants to send a message, it issues a request to sendmail. The sendmail program operates in two distinct phases:

- ◆ In the first phase, It collects messages and stores them as requests from the senders.
- ◆ In the second phase, it delivers the messages to the recipients.

If there are errors during processing in the second phase, sendmail creates and returns a message. This mail provides details of the error that occurred and/or the source of the error. When an error is encountered that can be retried, sendmail places the message in a message queue. When an unrecoverable error is encountered, automatic routing happens and e-mail is sent to the sender.

Configuration Files

The sendmail program uses many configuration files. These files are located in the /etc/mail directory. I'll discuss some of these configuration files here:

- ◆ **Makefile.** This file is used when the make command is run. Running make might cause missing database (.db) files to be created with no entries. The make command creates the database files. The content of Makefile is given here:

```
all: virtusertable.db access.db domaintable.db mailertable.db
%.db : %
            @makemap hash $@ < $<
clean:
            @rm -f *.db *~
```

- ◆ **helpfile.** This is the text file sendmail displays when you issue a HELP command.
- ◆ **relay-domains.** This file specifies the domains that the computer will relay.
- ◆ **sendmail.mc.** This file contains the m4 macro preprocessor program. The m4 program is used by sendmail to produce a sendmail configuration file. When run, this macro program produces the sendmail.cf configuration file:

```
divert(-1)
dnl This is the macro config file used to generate the /etc/sendmail.cf
```

```
dnl file. If you modify the file you will have to regenerate the
dnl /etc/sendmail.cf by running this macro config through the m4
dnl preprocessor:
dnl
dnl         m4 /etc/sendmail.mc > /etc/sendmail.cf
dnl
dnl You will need to have the sendmail-cf package installed for this to
dnl work.
include(`/usr/lib/sendmail-cf/m4/cf.m4')
VERSIONID(`linux setup for Red Hat Linux')dnl
OSTYPE(`linux')
define(`confDEF_USER_ID',``8:12'')dnl
undefine(`UUCP_RELAY')dnl
undefine(`BITNET_RELAY')dnl
define(`confAUTO_REBUILD')dnl
define(`confTO_CONNECT', `1m')dnl
define(`confTRY_NULL_MX_LIST',true)dnl
define(`confDONT_PROBE_INTERFACES',true)dnl
define(`PROCMAIL_MAILER_PATH',`/usr/bin/procmail')dnl
define('ALIAS_FILE','/etc/aliases')dnl
define(`STATUS_FILE', `/var/log/sendmail.st')dnl
define(`UUCP_MAILER_MAX', `2000000')dnl
define(`confUSERDB_SPEC', `/etc/mail/userdb.db')dnl
dnl define(`confPRIVACY_FLAGS', `authwarnings,novrfy,noexpn')dnl
dnl define(`confTO_QUEUEWARN', `4h')dnl
dnl define(`confTO_QUEUERETURN', `5d')dnl
dnl define(`confQUEUE_LA', `12')dnl
dnl define(`confREFUSE_LA', `18')dnl
FEATURE(`smrsh',`/usr/sbin/smrsh')dnl
FEATURE(`mailertable',`hash -o /etc/mail/mailertable')dnl
FEATURE(`virtusertable',`hash -o /etc/mail/virtusertable')dnl
FEATURE(redirect)dnl
FEATURE(always_add_domain)dnl
FEATURE(use_cw_file)dnl
FEATURE(local_procmail)dnl
FEATURE(`access_db')dnl
FEATURE(`blacklist_recipients')dnl
dnl We strongly recommend to comment this one out if you want to protect
```

```
dnl yourself from spam. However, the laptop and users on computers that do
dnl not have 24x7 DNS do need this.
FEATURE(`accept_unresolvable_domains')dnl
dnl FEATURE(`relay_based_on_MX')dnl
MAILER(smtp)dnl
MAILER(procmail)dnl
```

◆ **access.** This is the access database. The content of this file is given here:

```
# Check the /usr/doc/sendmail-8.11.0/README.cf file for a description
# of the format of this file. (search for access_db in that file)
# The /usr/doc/sendmail-8.11.0/README.cf is part of the sendmail-doc
# package.
#
# by default we allow relaying from localhost...
localhost.localdomain              RELAY
localhost                          RELAY
127.0.0.1                 RELAY
```

◆ **mailertable.** This database will allow you to specify different routes for e-mail. It allows you to specify domain translation or forwarding to a new domain name.

◆ **virtusertable.** This database allows you to rewrite and redirect incoming mail. It maps virtual domains and addresses to new addresses.

◆ **aliases.** This is the master alias database for the machine. It contains mail aliases. These aliases are used by the system to allow mail sent to one address to be redirected to another recipient. Other uses for the aliases are to allow mail to be piped to a program for additional processing.

Sendmail Security

A mail administrator should ensure that no one should be able to get special permissions or privileges in the mail system. You should carefully consider the read, write, and execute permissions that are assigned. An unauthorized user with write access can cause considerable damage. You should provide the minimum permissions required. There are many more security measures that can strengthen sendmail security. Some of these measures are listed here:

◆ Check the file and directory permissions. You should ensure that users have only the minimal permissions required.

◆ Use the sendmail restricted shell (smrsh) program to limit the programs that can be executed in .forward, aliases, and include files.

◆ Use the SafeFileEnvironment option to limit where the file system mailbox files can be written.

Domain Name Service

You need to identify each computer uniquely when computers are connected to each other in a network. Using IP addresses is the most widely accepted identification system today. Each computer is provided with a unique IP address. You can search for a computer by using its IP address.

I'll discuss IP addresses in detail in the next section of the chapter. However, the drawback of using an IP address is that it is difficult to remember. Consider how difficult it would be if you were required to remember the IP addresses of 50 computers. The alternative is to use the host names, which are easier to remember. For example, remembering www.yahoo.com is much easier than remembering the 32-bit IP address. However, you need a mechanism to convert host names to IP addresses, and vice versa. This mechanism is required because host names are ultimately converted to the IP addresses. The service that implements this mechanism is known as *Domain Name Service* (DNS).

In the early days of the Internet, the responsibility for maintaining unique host names for the computers on the Internet was given to the Stanford Research Institute's Network Information Center (SRI-NIC). Initially, they created a single file called hosts.txt that contained the host name to IP address mappings. All webmasters around the Internet were supposed to regularly update the SRI-NIC about any changes in status of their host names or IP addresses.

This created a lot of problems:

◆ The file grew with the growth of the Internet. After some time, it became extremely difficult to maintain the file.

◆ With the large number of computers connecting to the Internet, it became more impractical to guarantee the uniqueness of a host name.

These shortcomings created a need for things like hierarchical naming structure and distributed management of host names. This led to the evolution of a lookup facility known as DNS. It is a distributed database used for mapping host names to their respective IP addresses. The concept of the distributed database means a single organization will no longer be responsible for host name to IP address mappings.

The next few sections discuss basic concepts of the DNS.

IP Addresses

An IP address is a unique 32-bit name assigned to each computer in a network. A computer with an assigned IP address is known as a host. This IP address is used to identify hosts on a network.

The IP address consists of four 8-bit numbers separated by periods; for example, 172.17.20.10. This technique is known as *dot-notation*. A part of the address is used to identify the network to which the computer belongs. The remainder of the address identifies the system itself. Addresses are categorized under three classes:

- ◆ Class A
- ◆ Class B
- ◆ Class C

Class A is used to address very large networks, whereas class B addresses medium-sized networks. The class C addresses are assigned to small networks, with fewer than approximately 250 hosts.

Domain Name Space

Host names are divided into several pieces called *domains*. Domains are designed in a hierarchical structure. The top-level domains refer to the type of organization to which the network belongs, and subdomains further identify the specific network on which the host is situated.

The domain name space is also a hierarchical tree structure, as shown in Figure 9-1.

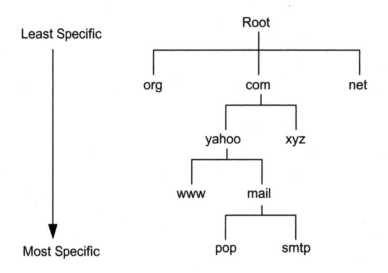

FIGURE 9-1 *An example of a Domain Name Space.*

While searching for a host, the DNS tree is traversed in an ascending order, starting from leaf nodes and moving towards the root. Therefore, the nodes falling on the left side are more specific in contrast to the nodes on the right side. For example, node abc in www.abc.com is more specific than the com node.

In a *Fully Qualified Domain Name* (FQDN), the host name is specified by the leftmost label. The next label to the right defines the local domain to which the host belongs. The local domain also can be a part of or a sub-domain of another domain. Therefore, naming gets less specific while moving from the left to the right. This process is followed until the root of the tree is reached.

The dot (.), which is the root domain, is the starting point of the tree. In DNS, records are specified as the last character in the domain name. A domain is a portion in a domain name space. Consider the following example:

There are four domain names:

◆ abc.com

◆ abc.net

- `xyz.com`

- `pqr.org`

In these domain names, there are only seven domains involved. These seven domains are listed here:

- `abc`

- `abc`

- `xyz`

- `pqr`

- `com`

- `net`

- `org`

A *Top-Level Domain* (TLD) is a domain that directly branches off from the root of the tree. `com`, `net`, and `org` were the top-level domains in the preceding example.

A `subdomain` is a child domain that comes lower in the DNS hierarchy tree. For example, here are three domain names:

- `www.abc.com`

- `pop.abc.com`

- `somethingelse.abc.com`

In these three domain names, `www`, `pop`, and `somethingelse` are the subdomains of the `com` domain. Therefore, it can be concluded that all domains—except the root domain—are subdomains of other domains.

A DNS master name server is a computer that maintains a database of host names and IP addresses for one or more zones. It is advisable to have DNS slave name servers that can be synchronized with the master name server to act as backup name servers in case the primary server fails.

While performing the function of inverse resolution, mapping an IP address to its host name, the DNS moves from the left node toward the right node to deduce the IP address. In contrast to the host name, the dot (.) notation of an IP address becomes more specific while moving to the right. Therefore, the IP addresses in the DNS are represented in reverse order to handle this situation. The Top-Level Domain (TLD) for IP addresses is the `in-addr.arpa` domain. This technique helps in simplifying the process of inverse resolution that now works as a forward resolution process in which the DNS host name finds the corresponding IP addresses.

Services Offered By a DNS Server

The DNS server is a vital component in a network. It is the most popular name resolution service on the Internet. A few functions of a DNS server are given in the following list:

◆ Provides a mechanism for resolving host names into Internet Protocol (IP) addresses. This process is known as *forward lookup*.

◆ Provides a mechanism to find host names from IP addresses. This is known as a *reverse lookup*.

◆ Provides Internet directory-like lookup capabilities to retrieve information concerning other DNS Name Servers, Canonical Names, Mail Exchangers, and so on.

◆ Allows machines to be logically grouped by domains names, and therefore, lead to efficient searching.

◆ Organizes named machines into efficient hierarchies.

◆ Is distributed by nature, which increases its robustness and reliability.

Components of DNS

The DNS implementation in a network has three major components: database, client, and server. These components are discussed in the following list:

◆ **Database.** The database contains the DNS tree and the Resource Records (RR). RR specifies the domain name. The database is distributed in nature and comprises the Domain Name Space, which is basically the DNS tree, and the *Resource Records* (RRs). RR defines the domain names within the Domain Name Space.

◆ **Client.** The client in the DNS contains functions or software routines, which request information from the Domain Name Space on behalf of an application. The clients in the DNS are also known as *resolvers* because they group functions to a resolver library. The resolver library sends query to the name server, accepts answers, and sends it back to the specific application. The client contains methods for gaining information from the DNS. The client is used by the applications.

◆ **Server.** The server in the DNS is called a *Name Server*. These servers manage portions of the Domain Name Space and assist clients in finding information within the DNS tree. In addition, servers can be used as a delegation point to identify other name servers that have authority over subdomains within a given domain.

DNS Transactions

DNS transactions are a regular occurrence over the Internet. The two most common types of transactions are discussed in the following list:

◆ **DNS zone transfers.** In this type of transaction, synchronization of new/updated domains in the backup or secondary DNS server takes place. The secondary DNS server compares its serial number to the serial number of the primary server at regular intervals. If the serial number on the primary server is more recent, the secondary server downloads the new copy of the zone. This is called the *zone transfer*. You will learn more about zones later in this chapter.

◆ **DNS queries/responses.** In this type of transaction, the client sends a DNS query, and the server replies through a DNS response. Clients usually choose three domain name servers to send their queries. These servers are the default servers defined on the client computer that are provided by the ISP. These servers are checked one by one until you obtain the desired result. The query keeps passing through the name servers until a valid response is generated. The name server can also forward the query to another name server if it cannot resolve the query. In this case, the query keeps on passing through the servers and when an answer is found, it is sent back to the original name server. The answer is first cached by the original server and then sent back to the client.

The DNS query and responses that take place between the DNS server and client have five sections. These sections are discussed in the following list:

◆ **Header section.** This section contains information about the type of message and other sections that are present in the message.

◆ **Question section.** This section contains information concerning the object of the query.

◆ **Answer section.** This section contains RRs regarding the answer.

◆ **Authority section.** This section contains either a *Statement of Authority* (SOA) or name server records. These name server records belong to the zone of authority for the owner name of the RR(s) in the Answer section.

◆ **Additional section.** This section contains additional information for the receiver.

Cached answer can be used by that DNS to resolve similar subsequent queries for the same DNS information. Thus, caching increases the efficiency but can lead to security loopholes.

BIND

Berkeley Internet Name Domain (BIND) is an implementation of the DNS protocols on UNIX-based systems, including Linux. The BIND server is the most widely used DNS server on the Internet. It provides a very stable and reliable infrastructure on which the domain's name and its IP address associations are based. BIND is distributed freely. The latest version is available on the Web at the Internet Software Consortium's (ISC) Web site: `http://www.isc.org/BIND`.

BIND Installation

Installing BIND is relatively straightforward. The ISC includes sample definitions in the top-level `Makefile` for most common versions of UNIX, including Linux. The steps for installing BIND are as follows:

1. `untar` the package in a directory.
2. Execute the `./configure` command from the directory where the package was uncompressed.
3. Compile the distribution using the `make` command.

Starting and Stopping BIND

The BIND daemon can be started, stopped, or restarted by using the normal daemon control scripts found in the `/etc/rc.d/init.d/` directory. It is considered a good practice to check the system log for errors and warnings whenever the name server is started or restarted. An invalid directive or option in the daemon control scripts can cause errors in the name server, preventing it from starting or halting abruptly.

To start the named daemon, you can use the following command:

```
/etc/rc.d/init.d/named start
```

Now, to restart a server in RHL, you can use the following command:

```
/etc/rc.d/init.d/named reload
```

To stop an already running named daemon, you can use the following command:

```
/etc/rc.d/init.d/named stop
```

The command to terminate BIND forcefully is as follows:

```
kill -9 `cat /var/run/named.pid`
```

BIND Configuration

BIND's configuration file is stored as named.conf in the /etc directory. It is a text file that you can use to configure various aspects of BIND. BIND also comes with a shell script that can convert older BIND 4 configuration files to the newer format of BIND. This shell script is exceptionally useful while upgrading BIND because the format of the configuration file of BIND 4, which is named.boot, is entirely different from BIND 8 and above.

Global Options

The Global Options section of the named.conf file allows you to configure the following directives:

- ◆ **directory.** This directive defines the base directory for storing all relative paths specified in the named.conf file.
- ◆ **pid-file.** This directive stores the name of the Process ID (PID) file for the named service.
- ◆ **allow-query.** This directive specifies the range of computers that can send DNS queries to a server. The directive accepts individual IPs, IP ranges, and any keyword as valid arguments.

◆ **allow-transfer.** This directive specifies hosts that might copy the database. This option can be used to limit zone transfers in a BIND server. The arguments are similar to those of the Allow-query directive.

An example of the Global Options section of BIND's main configuration file is shown in the following code:

```
options {
            directory           "/var/named";
            pid-file            "/var/run/named.pid";
            allow-query         { any; };
            allow-transfer              { 172.17.100/50; };
};
```

In the preceding code snippet:

◆ The directory directive specifies that the default zone directory for BIND is /var/named.

◆ The pid-file directive specifies that while the named service is running, its ProcessID should be stored in the /var/run/named.pid file.

◆ The allow-query directive specifies that any client can perform a DNS query transaction with the server.

◆ The allow-transfer directive specifies BIND to allow DNS transfer transactions only to the server whose IP address is in the range 171.17.100/50.

Zones

A *zone* is a subset in a domain name space. This subset is maintained in a master name server. It is advisable to have one or more slave name servers also for backup purposes. Depending on ownership or permissions for a domain name, the DNS master server can be configured to manage an entire domain, a domain and all its child domains, or any portion in the domain.

Master Zones

Master zones are used to generate authoritative records for queries on non-cached domain names. The host name given in the query is matched against all configured zones. The file directive specifies the text file that contains the particular zone's database.

An example of an entry for a master zone in BIND is shown in the following code snippet:

```
zone "premierpress.com" IN {
        type        master;
        file        "db.premierpress.com";
};
```

Slave Zones

The slave server, which is the secondary server, loads the zone information from a primary server or another slave server. This server acts as an instantly available backup solution in case the primary name server is down or unreachable. An example of an entry for a slave zone in BIND is shown here:

```
zone "premierpress.com" IN {
        type        slave;
        masters      { 172.17.100.1 }
        file        "db. premierpress ";
};
```

Root Zones

Root zone is the default zone found in every installation. It is used whenever configured zones do not resolve a query. The type here is hint. The file directive contains named.ca, which contains information about root servers on the Internet.

The sample code for the Root zone is shown here:

```
zone "." IN {
        type hint;
        file "named.ca";
};
```

Loopback Zones

Although loopback zones are not strictly required, they are always specified. Many programs in the X Window System use local sockets to emulate IPC queues between cooperating processes. These sockets are bound to host 172.17.0.1, which is the lookup device. Loopback zones should never be slaves.

```
"0.0.172.in-addr.arpa"
```

Resource Records (RR)

A DNS resource record (RR) contains all the information about a domain name system. It defines all the attributes for a domain name such as an IP address or a mail route.

A DNS RR has six fields:

`<NAME>, <TYPE>, <CLASS>, <TTL>, <RD Length>, and <RDATA>`

These fields are explained in the following list:

- ◆ **Name.** This field specifies the DNS name, also known as the *owner name*, to which the RR belongs.
- ◆ **Type.** This field is a 2-byte value that specifies the type of the resource that is defined in the resource record. This field is necessary because a DNS name can have more than one type of RR.
- ◆ **Class.** This defines the protocol family for the RR record. For example, `IN`, which stands for Internet.
- ◆ **Time To Live (TTL).** This field is the time, in seconds, for which a name server can cache an RR. A zero TTL implies that a server should not cache the RR.
- ◆ **RD Length.** This field is the RDATA field's length in octets.
- ◆ **RDATA.** This field is a resource data field and is the value to which the entity specified in the NAME field maps. It is unique for each type of RR.

Table 9-1: Common DNS Resource Records

Record Type	Description	Usage
A	An address record	Maps FQDN into an IP address. For example,
		Mail IN A 172.100.100.1
		Login IN A 172.100.100.2
PTR	A pointer record	Maps an IP address into FQDN. For example,
		1.100 IN PTR mail.premierpress.com.

Record Type	Description	Usage
NS	A name server record	Denotes a name server for a zone. For example, IN NS ns1.abc.com. IN NS ns2.abc.com.
SOA	A Start of Authority record	Specifies many attributes concerning the zone, such as the name of the domain (forward or inverse), administrative contact, the serial number of the zone, refresh interval, retry interval, and so on.
CNAME	A canonical name record	Defines an alias name and maps it to the absolute (canonical) name. For example, POP IN CNAME mail
MX	A mail exchange record	Used to redirect e-mail for a given domain or host to another host. For example, xyz.com IN MX 0 mail.abc.com

Start of Authority (SOA)

The Start of Authority (SOA) record is the first section in every zone. This record contains information about a particular zone. This section also specifies that the server is authoritative for a particular zone. The various attributes that contain information about a zone are discussed briefly in the following list:

- ◆ **Serial number.** Used for controlling versions. Serial numbers represent the full date plus two more digits for sequential revisions during a single day.
- ◆ **Refresh.** This attribute is the delay time that slave name servers should wait before checking the master name server's serial number.
- ◆ **Retry.** This attribute is the delay time that a slave name server should wait before refreshing its database after a refresh has failed.
- ◆ **Expire.** This attribute is the upper limit that a slave name server should use in serving DNS information for a lack of a refresh from the master name server.

◆ **Minimum time to live.** This attribute specifies the number of seconds for which the records in the zone are valid. All cached entries for this record in various DNS servers should expire after this time limit.

An example of an SOA section is shown in the following code sample:

```
@       IN      SOA     xyz.com root.xyz.com  (
                                1997022700 ;        Serial
                                28800           ;               Refresh
                                14400           ;               Retry
                                3600000     ;               Expire
                                86400  )        ;               Minimum time
to live
```

Round Robin Load Sharing

All configurations mentioned in the previous sections are stored in one single database file. If a domain consists of multiple hosts or there is a logical separation between domains, a domain can be divided into multiple domains. Multiple domains can be implemented by performing the following steps:

1. Configure the subdomain as though it were a normal zone in the named.conf file.
2. Specify the main domain in its database file.
3. Create a subdomain database file in /var/named.

In addition, you can use round robin load sharing for heavily loaded servers. This allows duplication of A records to distribute evenly all incoming requests. An example of round robin load sharing is shown in the following sample:

```
www     0       IN      A       192.102.44.1
www     0       IN      A       192.102.44.2
www     0       IN      A       192.102.44.3
```

 NOTE

The Web server traffic is increased depending on the A records duplication. At the same time, the chance of server failure also increases by the same factor.

nslookup

nslookup is a program available in Linux that you can use to send queries to query a DNS. The nslookup program can operate in two modes:

◆ Interactive mode

◆ Non-interactive mode

The syntax for the nslookup program is as follows:

```
nslookup [ -option ...  ] [ host-to-locate ¦ - [ server ]]
```

The two modes are discussed in the following sections.

Interactive Mode

Interactive mode allows a user to query name servers for information about various hosts and domains or to print a list of hosts in a domain. In interactive mode, users can query name servers for information, such as hosts in a domain. Interactive mode is the default mode used when no arguments are given in the command line. This mode allows a user to enter commands while the nslookup program is running. After executing the program in interactive mode, a user can press the Ctrl+C combination keys to enter a number of commands. A few commonly used commands are discussed in the following sections.

host [servername]

If the host command is used without the [servername] parameter, the lookup is done for the default server, as mentioned in the resolv.conf configuration file. Otherwise, the lookup is done using the servername as mentioned in the host command.

If the host is an Internet address and the query type is A or PTR, the name of the host is returned. However, if host is a name and does not contain a trailing period, the default domain name is appended to the name. This behavior depends on the state of the set options domain, srchlist, defname, and search. To look up a host not in the current domain, append a period to the name. The host name returned is an IP address and the query is of either A or PTR type. On the other hand, if only the host name is returned, the domain name is added to the host name.

server <servername>

The server command is used to change the default server to that specified in the command.

finger [hostname]

The finger command is to connect to a finger server on the host computer and retrieve finger information for that host. If a finger daemon is not running, information cannot be retrieved for any other reason and the command returns an error.

ls [option] domainname

The ls command is used to return host names and Internet address information for a particular domain. The command retrieves this information from a DNS server. A few options that you can use with this command are listed here:

◆ -t querytype. This parameter is used to specify that the list information should be retrieved only for a particular type. The types include A, CNAME, HINFO, MINFO, MX, NS, PTR, SOA, TXT, UINFO, WKS, ANY, AXFR, MB, MD, MF, and NULL. The default type is A.

◆ -a. This parameter is used to retrieve alias names for a particular host in a domain.

◆ -d. This parameter is used to list all available records for a domain.

◆ -h. This parameter is used to find hardware and operating system information for a host.

◆ -s. This parameter is used to display all services that are being run in a host. The parameter can list only a limited number of services that are being run in the host computer.

◆ ?. This parameter is used to display help. It also includes sections to display the list of available commands.

◆ exit. This parameter is used to exit the program.

Non-Interactive Mode

In non-interactive mode, the program prints the name and the requested name for a host or domain. The program operates in non-interactive mode when the first argument is the host name to be looked up and the second optional argument is a host name or a name server.

BIND Security

Initially security was not considered a part of DNS because the main purpose of DNS was to help in communication. It was designed to be used by the public, and therefore, restricting users who can query the server was not considered during its design. But with the evolution of the Internet, many applications were developed that used IP addresses and host names as a basis for allowing or disallowing users to access their services. As a result, gradually ensuring correct information to users became very important, and therefore security became a part of DNS. By incorporating security, it has become risky for organizations that rely on the Internet for communicating with clients or other firms to provide false information.

Several problems are faced by the DNS, however. Some of these are discussed in the following sections.

Cache Poisoning

Cache poisoning is one of the main problems faced by the DNS, especially the older versions of BIND. Whenever a DNS server gets a query that cannot be resolved through its cache, it can pass it on to another DNS server. If the DNS server passes its query to another server which contains incorrect information, the original server caches the response from the second server, leading to cache poisoning. The malicious form of cache poisoning is also called *DNS spoofing*.

In spoofing, the users in control of a DNS server try to force the target DNS server to query their server. Once the target server queries, its cache can be easily poisoned. Early versions of BIND were very susceptible to such attacks.

 NOTE

In July 1997, Eugene Kashpureff, while protesting against InterNIC's control over DNS servers, poisoned caches of major servers around the globe, such that all requests going for www.internic.net landed in a site that belonged to the AlterNIC server. This was made possible because BIND cached any response coming from another server without checking its authenticity. A survey carried out in February 1999 showed that around 33 percent of DNS servers were easy targets of such attacks.

Cache poisoning can lead to two major problems, as discussed in the following list:

◆ A request made to a poisoned server for a particular domain name can lead to a failure. This is called *denial of service*.

◆ The person controlling the rogue server can easily poison any server querying it and can act as a trusted source. This can be very harmful, especially for people who give out their credit card numbers and expiration dates on the Internet. This is known as *masquerading*.

Host Name Spoofing

Apart from cache poisoning, a malicious user can give hundreds of DNS responses for a query and the querying server will accept them without authentication. This is termed *cache flooding*.

Other DNS server attacks include leakage of information through zone transfers. Host names can reveal certain things about the host, such as its operating system. This information can be useful to its rival hosts. DNS tools can be used to query a server continuously with different IP addresses of a particular domain. The unused IP addresses can be used to spoof the server and act as a host of that network. If another system is configured to trust the entire IP network, it is vulnerable to attack by an attacker using the unused IP address of the trusted IP network. The way to deal with it is to never configure your machine to trust an entire network; instead, mention explicitly the hosts of the network that can be trusted.

Restricting Queries

As discussed earlier, DNS was designed for public use, and therefore, the earlier versions of BIND did not include any option for restricting querying sources.

Later, when the importance of security was realized, sub-statements like `allow-query` were added from Version 8. The `allow-query` directive can be used both as global option or in particular master/slave section. You learned about `allow-query` in the section, "BIND Configuration," earlier in this chapter.

An example of `allow-query` is shown in the following code:

```
options {
        allow-query { 192.49.49/30; 192.59.59/30; };
};
```

The following code shows a sample of restricting queries in the zone you want to protect:

```
zone " premierpress.com" IN {
        type                    slave;
        masters            { 172.17.100.1 }
        file                    "db. premierpress ";
        allow-query { "XYZ-NET"; };
};
```

Restricting Zone Transfers

Restricting zone transfers is considered more important than restricting queries. If you take another look at the "BIND Configuration" section, you will find an `allow-transfer` statement. The `allow-transfer` statement can limit zone transfers by specifying the hosts allowed to copy the database.

By using the `allow-transfer` statement in the master zone, the number of slaves who can transfer the master can be controlled. An example of the `allow-transfer` statement is shown here:

```
zone "premierpress.com" IN {
        type                    master;
        file                    "db.premierpress.com";
        allow-transfer { 172.32.32.2; 172.42.42.4; };
};
```

The mentioned directives also can be used in slave and global configuration. By using them in slave, you can restrict hackers who can transfer zone in that particular slave.

Running BIND with Least Privileges

BIND should be run under the user or group that has the minimum number of rights or privileges on that system. These rights should just be enough for the name server to run. If a hacker gets into the system running BIND as root, the hacker will get full access to the file system. In addition, the hacker is able to execute any command using the root privileges, which is potentially very dangerous.

Versions 8.1.2 and later of BIND provide the facilities of running BIND under another user or group with less privileges.

BIND Versions

BIND has been constantly evolving. The newer versions are definitely more secure than their earlier counterparts. It is always recommended to install the latest version of BIND. The administrator should keep track of the latest versions available on the Web at www.isc.org/BIND. At this site, you also can find the list of vulnerabilities of various BIND versions.

It is not desirable to let the hacker know which version of BIND you are using. The version number should be removed so that it cannot be revealed using version.bind query. This facility is available in Version 8.2 and later.

Transaction Signatures

Transaction Signatures (TSIG) is a security measure implemented in BIND Version 8.2 and above. This concept provides security with flexibility and without compromising on performance.

TSIG record is added to the DNS message data by the name server. The TSIG is calculated using a one-way hash function. This function computes a hash value based on each and every bit of the message data and a few other fields I will discuss later. The resulting hash function is secure because it cannot be reversed and changes dramatically even with a minor change in the input used for computing it.

The MD5 hashing technique is widely used for storing passwords over the Internet. TSIG uses a modified version of MD5 called HMAC-MD5, which requires a key and computes a 128-bit hash value using the message data and the key as input.

First a secret code is decided between the sender and the receiver, which is keyed with the hash value. This secret key has two advantages, as discussed in the following list:

◆ It ensures that the message originates from a reliable and expected source.

◆ It ensures that the message was not altered after the time it was signed by the sender.

Once the TSIG record and message is ready, it is sent by the signer. After receiving the signed message, the receiver first removes the TSIG record and checks it. At this point, no data is cached; caching is done only when it is confirmed that the message is genuine. These security measures help in combating hackers who try to attack by capturing authorized (signed) messages and then sending them again at their own convenience.

TSIG is used for securing zone transactions, queries, responses, and dynamic updates. In BIND 8, the TSIG key is created using the dnskeygen program included in it.

DNS Security Extensions (DNSEC)

DNSEC are the DNS security extensions provided by the *work group* (WG) formed in 1994 by IETF. This was done because of the security issues haunting DNS servers.

The primary aim of this WG was to provide the information in DNS zones with authentication and integrity. This was achieved through the use of public key technology and is based on the use of cryptographic signatures like the TSIG concept. The need for public key cryptography arises due to the problems faced by the TSIG. Some of these problems are listed here:

◆ Trouble in maintaining too many keys at a time.

◆ Once somebody gains access to the server, the keys can be easily retrieved.

Public Key Encryptography

Public key encryptography is used for safe transactions between two computers. A computer first creates a key pair. This key pair is generated using an asymmetric cryptographic algorithm where one key is used to decrypt the data and the other key is used to encrypt the data.

After a key pair is made, the public key can be placed for anyone who wants to communicate with that computer. To communicate with the computer, the message is encrypted using the public key of the receiving computer. When the message is received, the computer decrypts it using its private key. Therefore, if the private key is saved securely, the genuine computer will only read the message.

Signing and verification of a message also is possible by using digital signatures. In this process, first the hash value of the message is calculated and then it is encrypted. This encrypted hash value is called a *digital signature*, which is then sent along with the message. The receiver can authenticate it by first decrypting the digital signature and then by computing the hash value of the message. The message is considered genuine if the two hash values match.

Signing and Verification of a Message

The process of signing and verifying a message is used because asymmetric algorithms for encryption usually take more time to encrypt, and therefore, encrypting the whole message can be really time-consuming. Some resource records also were created with DNSSEC to assist it. These records are discussed in the following sections.

KEY Record

Key record or key RR is a general record used for storing various public cryptographic keys. It stores information like the public key, protocol type, algorithm type, and flags for various purposes.

SIG Record

SIG RR is used to store the digital signature of the private key. It also provides the signature's validity time and authentication. If more than one algorithm for encryption is used to sign the resource records, more SIG RR will be required.

NXT Record

All records in a zone are sorted in alphabetical order. Whenever a request generates a negative response, it implies that the query has no corresponding RRSet. RRSets that are not present also are given signatures to authenticate their absence. This is done using NXT RR. NXT RR indicates the following:

- ◆ The range of unavailable DNS names
- ◆ The list of absent RRSets for an existing DNS name

SAMBA

SAMBA is open source software used to provide Windows-like network services, such as file and printer sharing. SAMBA makes the UNIX-based box act like a Windows NT server, providing many services that an NT server provides over a network.

SAMBA is basically the UNIX version of *Common Internet File System* (CIFS), which is used by Microsoft to induce compatibility between the Windows NT and Windows 98 operating systems. SAMBA was originally designed and developed by Andrew Tridgell in 1992. It was called SAMBA because the name contained SMB, which is the underlying protocol it uses. SAMBA is now developed and maintained as an open source project under the guidance of Andrew Tridgell. The official Web site of SAMBA is `www.samba.org`.

The goal of the SAMBA project is to monitor the changes done by Microsoft in CIFS and to provide the same services and features in SAMBA. Over the years, as has been proved through various real-world tests, SAMBA performs significantly better than Microsoft's CIFS implementations.

SAMBA Services

The various services provided by a SAMBA server are given in the following list:

- ◆ **File and Printer Sharing.** File and printer sharing are the most widely used SAMBA services. These services make it very easy to retrieve files over the server or print through any printer attached to the network.

- ◆ **WINS Server.** WINS server is a *NetBIOS Name Server* (NBNS) for Windows networks.

- ◆ **User Authentication and Authorization.** Authentication of the user is done via passwords or domains. This is explained in detail later in this chapter.

- ◆ **Browsing Support.** NetBIOS Name Server is used by SAMBA, which gives the browsing support. SAMBA also can act as LAN's Master Browser.

- ◆ **FTP-like Options.** Various resources from other operating systems can be accessed through its FTP-like SMB client feature.

Apart from these features, there are various administrative functions that can be performed by SAMBA, using tools discussed later in this chapter. All communication in SAMBA is done primarily with the *Server Message Block* (SMB) protocol.

SAMBA Servers

Two main servers are used by SAMBA:

◆ **nmbd.** This server is the NetBIOS name server. The purpose of this server is to help in browsing resources over the network. The nmbd server also can act as a WINS server if required.

◆ **smbd.** This server is the SMB server that is used mainly for user authentication and authorization and file- and printer-sharing. This is done using the SMB protocol.

SMB Protocol

The SMB protocol is a server client request-response protocol. All Windows operating systems that can be used for networking—such as Windows 3.11, Windows 95, Windows 98, Windows ME, Windows NT, Windows 2000, and Windows XP—can run SMB as server, client, or both. This protocol is used mainly to connect systems with different operating systems, such as Windows, Linux, and so on.

SAMBA runs SMB over TCP/IP, with NetBIOS under it. Whenever an SMB client starts and needs to know the IP address of a specified host, it broadcasts its query over the network. It gets replies from the nmbd server in the form of clients' NetBIOS information. In this case, nmbd acts as a WINS server and keeps a record of all hosts connected in the network. This keeps the network safe from saturation caused by the broadcasts made by the SMB clients.

SAMBA Installation

SAMBA supports a variety of Linux distributions and other UNIX variants like Solaris, NetBSD, UNIXWARE, HP-UX, Digital UNIX, SCO Open Server, IRIX (SGI), SunOS, AIX, ULTRIX, BSDI, and so on.

You can download the latest version of SAMBA from www.samba.org. Installation manuals and other documents also are available with the SAMBA distributions.

SAMBA Configuration

The main configuration file of the SAMBA server is `smb.conf`. By default, this file is located in the `/etc/samba` directory. This file is huge and provides a number of directives that you can set to enable or disable various features of SAMBA. The same configuration file also allows users to add new and shared directories in SAMBA.

`smb.conf` is divided into sub sections, each headed by a caption enclosed in square brackets ([ ]). The parameters contained in the sections are in the form of `name = value`.

An example of a portion of the `smb.conf` file is shown here:

```
[global]
 workgroup = domain_name
 [share1]
comment = Linux SAMBA Server
path = /users/smbuser1
read only = yes
```

The preceding lines are the minimum lines required in the `smb.conf` file for the server to work. The options in the `smb.conf` file are discussed in the following list:

- ◆ **[global].** This option describes the global settings for controlling the server.

- ◆ **[share1].** This option is used when you need to define a new share that the SMB clients can access.

- ◆ **comment.** The label specified in the `comment` directive is shown in the users network neighborhood folder as the share name.

- ◆ **path.** This directive specifies the name of the directory that will be shared.

A few other directives that are important from the security point of view are discussed in the following list:

- ◆ **public.** This is a Boolean directive and can accept arguments in `yes` or `no`. If this directive is set, guest level users are able to access the share.

- ◆ **browsable.** This also is a Boolean directive and if it is set, network users are able to see the share in the network browse list.

◆ **printable.** This Boolean directive tells SAMBA that the device is a printer.

◆ **users.** This directive accepts user names as parameters. The users listed in this list are allowed to access the shared resource.

◆ **group.** This directive stores the group names that are allowed to access this particular shared resource.

Printer Sharing

All installed printers are defined in the /etc/printcap file. Only valid SAMBA users are allowed to use these printers. All printers in the /etc/printcap file are shared as resources by default. However, this can be changed to allow sharing of only specific printers. The following code shows the sample of the global printer option:

```
[printer]
            comment = printer x
            path = /var/spool/samba
            browsable = no
            public = yes
guest ok = yes
writable = no
printable = yes
```

You can define a specific printer by using the statement public = no and add another option, valid users, as shown in the following code:

```
valid users = userX userY userZ
```

Mounting the SMB File System

Linux exclusively supports mounting of the SMB file system. This is due to the support that Linux enjoys from its kernel. The mounted SMB file system can be used just like a normal network file system. The command used for mounting file system is as follows:

```
submount //server1/share /mnt/SMBfs mountpoint -o username=userx
```

In the preceding example, share is connected to host server1.

Mounting also can be done automatically at system boot. This is done by adding the following line in the `/etc/fstab` file:

```
//server1/share /mnt/SMB SMBfs defaults,username=userx 0 0
```

SAMBA Client Tools

Some tools used by SAMBA clients are useful and easy to use. These tools are discussed in the following sections.

nmblookup

The `nmblookup` tool is used to query a WINS server. In addition, it is used to list machines and works similarly to `nslookup` in DNS. To list specific machines, use the following statement:

```
nmblookup -U server -R 'machine_name'
```

To list all machines on the network, use the following statement:

```
nmblookup \*
```

The preceding statement uses * to query by broadcasting, but a \ (backslash) should precede it to protect it from shell expansion.

smbclient

The `smbclient` tool is used for retrieving files during a normal FTP operation. The `smbclient` tool uses the following command:

```
smbclient //machine1/share
      > cd directory123
      > get file123
```

To view shared services, you can use the following command:

```
smbclient -L hostx
```

You also can specify the `username` and `password` by using the `-U` option, as shown in the following example:

```
smbclient -U user1%unsafepassword
```

As you can see, the username and password fields are separated with a%. It is unsafe to mention password like this because anyone who can retrieve previous commands will be able to access the password easily.

SAMBA Security

Security has been a major concern with the SAMBA server. SAMBA has several options that allow an administrator to set up file sharing safely. SAMBA security can be learned in four levels:

◆ Share-level security
◆ User-level security
◆ Server-level security
◆ Domain-level security

I now discuss each of these options in detail.

Share-Level Security

Every share that is set up in a network workgroup can be either a free share or a share that requires an access password. SAMBA supports both such shares. When a user needs to access a share that requires no password, only the share needs to go with the connect request. However, if a share name requires a password before it allows access, a client would be required to send the sharename and a password.

Note that no username is associated with such a share. There are the two types of share-level security options in SAMBA. Each share requires independent authentication. Therefore, if there are 10 shares set up in a particular server and a single client needs to access them, the client computer must authenticate itself 10 times.

These shares are similar to those in Windows 98 that can be associated with a password. The only difference is that SAMBA uses UNIX authentication of a username and password instead of the Windows authentication combination of a sharename and password. One main advantage of this security mode is that, in order to connect to a SAMBA server, no UNIX accounts are needed for every corresponding Windows account.

User-Level Security

This is a user-based authentication scheme. In this security level, when the user connects to the server, the server has no idea which share the user wants to access. Therefore, no share names are involved until the user is successfully authenticated into the server. The authentication is done only on the basis of a username and password. With user-level security, each client needs to authenticate itself only once, irrespective of how many shares the person wants to access. After logging in, all the shares with required permission become accessible to the user. The SAMBA server verifies each user using the standard authentication with /etc/passwd files. If the shadow suite is installed and enabled, /etc/shadow also is used in addition to /etc/passwd file.

Alternatively, if the encrypt password = yes is set in the smb.conf file, SAMBA uses the smbpasswd file to authenticate users.

An administrator can reduce some workload by keeping /etc/passwd synchronized. However, this should be done only if all users have shell access and shadow suite is not being used. If any users on the computer do not have shell access, this would prevent all those users from also accessing SAMBA share. This is due to the presence of a * in place of the hashed password. Similarly, if the shadow suite is being used, the hashed password field is replaced by a * in the /etc/passwd file.

Server-Level Security

Server-level security mode is almost identical to the user-mode security mode. The only exception is that the authentication is not performed within the same server. A separate SMB server is used to authenticate the users. This server can be a Windows NT computer, a SAMBA server, or any other server that is fully compatible with the SMB protocol. The server that is used to perform this authentication can be specified in the global section in the smb.conf file with the following directive:

```
server = <SERVERNAME>
```

The <SERVERNAME> should be a valid Netbios name of the SMB computer.

The server-level security has a major disadvantage, however. SAMBA is used mainly to support Windows file-sharing features with Linux computers. When SAMBA connects to a remote server, the connection doesn't close down after the authentication is complete. The connection remains active until either the

SAMBA daemon that requested authentication sends a close connection request or the requesting daemon is dead. In both cases, long active connections are required. If the authenticating server is a Windows server, the limited simultaneous license restraint in some versions of Windows, such as Windows 2000 and Windows NT server, can be a hindrance.

Domain-Level Security

If domain-level security is set in SAMBA, it needs to perform all authentications from the *Primary Domain Controller* (PDC). Before SAMBA can send authentication requests to the PDC of the network, it must be added in the NT domain using Server Manager for domains. An important thing to note here is that the SAMBA server should not be made the PDC of the network.

Unlike the share-level security, once a user has been authenticated with domain level security, the user is not asked for individual passwords for shares. After authentication, the user is granted a ticket that can be universally used to access all permissible shares.

Because the authenticated user already has a session ticket to access all information, domain-level security mode doesn't require the SAMBA server to maintain a continuous connection with the PDC of the network.

Summary

In this chapter, I discussed the important network servers that are used in Linux. I also explained the methods to secure these servers. In the first half of the chapter, I discussed the concepts and options that are used to configure FTP and sendmail. In the latter half, I explained servers like DNS and SAMBA.

Check Your Understanding

Multiple Choice Questions

1. Why do you need a DNS server?

   a. It allows a computer to be recognized based on names.

   b. It allows a computer to shares files with another computer on the Internet.

   c. It allows transfer of files from one computer to another.

   d. It provides username- and password-based authentications to many computer zones single-handedly.

2. Which of these services allows a Linux user to participate in a Windows network?

   a. Apache Web Server

   b. Sendmail Server

   c. ICMP Server

   d. SAMBA Server

3. File Transfer Protocol sends all data in an encrypted format.

   a. True

   b. False

4. Sendmail is _____ :

   a. A server that collects e-mails for every user in a Linux server.

   b. A server that is used as needed to accept e-mails in a Linux network that originated from a Windows computer.

   c. A server that broadcasts instant messages or e-mails to all users in a server who are currently connected.

   d. An implementation of a Simple Mail Transfer Protocol in Linux.

5. An alternate to a DNS server for Internet in Linux is

_____:

  a. Writing the names and IP addresses of every computer on the Internet in the /etc/hosts file.

  b. Writing the names of every server on the Internet in the /etc/host.allow file.

  c. Installing a SAMBA server in your Linux computer.

  d. Computers on the Internet can interact with each other as they do with a DNS server. DNS isn't really required, but it has been added for security reasons.

6. The SMB protocol was initially developed for _____:

  a. Windows Networks

  b. UNIX networks

  c. Linux Networks

  d. ISO Reference Model Specifications

Answers

Multiple Choice Answers

1. A DNS server is needed because it allows a computer to be recognized based on names.

2. A SAMBA server allows a Linux computer user to participate in a Windows network.

3. File Transfer Protocol doesn't send all data in an encrypted format.

4. Sendmail is an implementation of a Simple Mail Transfer Protocol in Linux.

5. An alternate to a DNS server for Internet in Linux can be writing the names and IP addresses of every computer on the Internet in the /etc/hosts file.

6. The SMB protocol was initially developed for UNIX networks.

Chapter 10

In this chapter, I discuss network defense and intrusion detection. These are the primary and critical tasks of the network administrators. I also discuss various Linux services, monitoring tools, secure protocols, and some security tools you can use. These tools and services help you in detecting intrusion and protecting your networks. At the end of this chapter, you will find a security checklist.

Linux Services and Monitoring

Linux provides several programs for monitoring the services running on a Linux system. I discuss the following programs in this section:

◆ netstat

◆ ps

◆ lsof

Netstat

Netstat prints information about the Linux networking subsystem. The netstat command is used to view the network connections, routing tables, interface statistics, masquerade connections, and multi-cast memberships.

The different syntax of the netstat command is shown here:

```
netstat [address_family_options] [−tcp¦-t] [−udp¦-u] [−raw¦-w] [−listen-
ing¦-l] [−all¦-a] [−numeric¦-n] [−symbolic¦-N] [−extend¦-e[−extend¦-e]]
[−timers¦-o] [−program¦-p] [−verbose¦-v] [−continuous¦-c]
```

The [address_family_options] argument in the preceding syntax can have the following values:

```
[−protocol={ inet,unix,ipx,ax25,netrom,ddp}[,...]] [−unix¦-x]  [−inet¦−ip]
[−ax25]  [−ipx]  [−netrom]  [−ddp]
```

Descriptions of the arguments of the netstat command follow:

◆ —**route, -r.** This option is used to display the kernel routing tables.

◆ —**groups, -g.** This option is used to display the membership information for IPv4 and IPv6.

◆ —**interface=iface, -i.** This option displays the network interface tables of either all the interfaces or a specified interface.

◆ —**masquerade, -M.** This option is used to display a list of masqueraded connections.

◆ —**statistics, -s.** This option displays summary statistics of the protocols.

◆ —**verbose, -v.** This option is used to switch on the verbose mode.

◆ —**numeric, -n.** This option is used to display the addresses in the numerical form.

◆ —**continuous, -c.** This option prints information that is refreshed every second.

◆ —**timers, -o.** This option displays the information regarding the networking timers.

◆ —**program, -p.** This option displays the program name and the PID to which the socket belongs.

◆ —**listening, -L.** This option shows only the listening sockets.

◆ —**all, -a.** This options displays all the sockets.

◆ -**F.** This option is used to print the routing information from the FIB.

◆ -**C.** This option prints the routing information.

If no argument is specified, netstat displays a list of open sockets. A sample output of the netstat command without any argument is displayed here:

```
Active Internet connections (w/o servers)
Proto   Recv-Q Send-Q Local Address          Foreign Address        State
tcp       0          126 premier.ltb.in.ni:telnet 172.17.65.103:2018   ESTAB-
LISHED
tcp       0            0 premier.ltb.in.ni:telnet 172.17.65.103:1389   ESTAB-
LISHED
Active UNIX domain sockets (w/o servers)
Proto RefCnt Flags      Type      State      I-Node Path
unix  1      [ ]        STREAM    CONNECTED  1461   @0000007b
 _ _ _ _ _ _ _ _ _ _ _ _ _ _ _ _ _ _ _ _ _ _ _ _ _ _ _

 _ _ _ _ _ _ _ _ _ _ _ _ _ _ _ _ _ _ _ _ _ _ _ _ _ _ _
```

```
unix   1      [ ]           STREAM    CONNECTED     1170   @00000062
unix   13     [ ]           DGRAM                   475    /dev/log
unix   0      [ ]           DGRAM                   2297
unix   0      [ ]           DGRAM                   2126
unix   1      [ ]           STREAM    CONNECTED     1465   /tmp/orbit-root/orb-
8930230691780337123
- - - - - - - - - - - - - - - - - - - - - - - - -
- - - - - - - - - - - - - - - - - - - - - - - - -
unix   1      [ ]           STREAM    CONNECTED     1406
unix   1      [ ]           STREAM    CONNECTED     1404   /tmp/orbit-root/orb-
18701168241899746813
- - - - - - - - - - - - - - - - - - - - - - - - -
- - - - - - - - - - - - - - - - - - - - - - - - -
unix   1      [ ]           STREAM    CONNECTED     1171   /tmp/.X11-unix/X0
unix   0      [ ]           DGRAM                   1169
unix   1      [ ]           STREAM    CONNECTED     1131   /tmp/.ICE-unix/1022
- - - - - - - - - - - - - - - - - - - - - - - - -
- - - - - - - - - - - - - - - - - - - - - - - - -
unix   0      [ ]           DGRAM                   531
unix   0      [ ]           DGRAM                   490
```

ps

The ps command is used to obtain the status of the currently running processes. The syntax of the command is as follows:

```
ps [options]
```

The options of the ps command can be categorized into the following five groups, based on the output produced:

- ◆ **Simple process selection.** Enables you to view simple listing of the running processes. The options in this category are -A, -N, -a, -d, -e, -T, -a, -g, -r, -x, and –deselect.

- ◆ **Process selection by list.** Enables you to view output based on the different selection criteria provided as the argument. The options in this category are –C, -G, -U, -g, -p, -s, -u, -U, -p, -t, -Group, -User, -group, -pid, -sid, -tty, -user, and -123.

◆ **Output format control.** Enables you to view output in different formats. The options in this category are -0, -c, -f, -j, -l, -o, -y, -O, -X, -o, -s, -u, -v, and –format.

◆ **Output modifiers.** Enables you to view the output in a customized way; for example, you can set the number of rows and columns to be displayed. The options in this category are -H, -m, -n, -w, -C, -N, -O, -S, -c, -e, -f, -h, -m, -w, -cols, -columns, -cumulative, -forest, -html, -headers, -lines, -rows, -nuls, -nulls, -sort, -width, and –zero.

◆ **Information.** Enables you to view information, such as the version number and help. The options in this category are –V, L, -help, -info, and –version.

lsof

The lsof command is used to list open files. An open file could be a regular file, a directory, a block special file, or a character special file. You also can specify an executing text reference, a library, or a stream or network file. The syntax of the lsof command is as follows:

lsof [options]

The options of the lsof command are discussed here:

◆ **-a.** This option adds the list selection options.

◆ **-b.** This option prevents execution of kernel functions that might block command, such as lstat, readlink, and stat.

◆ **-C.** This option disables display of path name from the name cache of the kernel.

◆ **-d.** This option selects files having comma-separated sets.

◆ **-D.** This option enables lsof to use the device cache file.

◆ **-g [s].** This option displays files having Process Group Identification (PGRP) numbers in the comma-separated sets.

◆ **-i [i].** This option selects files with the specified Internet address.

◆ **-k.** This option specifies a file with kernel name.

◆ **-l.** This option disables conversion of user ID to the login names.

◆ **-m.** This option specifies a kernel memory file instead of /dev/kmem or /dev/mem.

◆ **+|-M.** This option can allow or disable the display of information regarding portmapper registrations for TCP and UDP ports.

◆ **-nThis.** This option disables the conversion of the network numbers to host names. Inhibiting conversion may make lsof run faster.

◆ **-N.** This option displays a list of NFS files.

◆ **-o.** This option displays the file offset. It changes the SIZE/OFF column to OFFSET. The -o and -s options are mutually exclusive. That is, you cannot specify both of them together.

◆ **-o.** This option enables you to specify the number of digits that will be printed after the 0t for a file offset. The 0 value directs lsof to use the 0t form for all offset output.

◆ **-O.** This option can be used to avoid blockade of lsof by kernel operations.

◆ **-p.** This option selects the files whose ID numbers are in the comma-separated set.

◆ **-P.** This option disables the conversion of port numbers to port names. It is useful when host name lookup is not working properly.

◆ **-R.** This option is used to display the Parent Process IDentification (PPID) number.

◆ **-s.** This option is used to display the file size. It changes the SIZE/OFF column to SIZE. If the file size is 0 byte, nothing is displayed.

◆ **-S.** This option is used specify the timeout limit in seconds. It also can be used to specify value for kernel functions, such as lstat, and readlink. These kernel functions are capable of causing deadlocks. The minimum value is two and the default is 15.

◆ **-t.** This option displays the process identifiers.

◆ **-u.** This option lists the files owned by those users who have login names and user ID numbers in comma-separated sets.

◆ **-U.** This option lists the UNIX socket files.

◆ **-v.** This option displays the version information. In addition, it displays other information such as revision number, time of construction of lsof binary, and so on.

◆ **+|-w.** This option can be used to enable or disable warning messages.

Secure Protocols

In the Internet age, when business transactions are happening increasingly over the network, you need to secure your data that is being transmitted. Hackers and unauthorized users keep attacking the network. One way you can discourage hackers from doing so is to use secure protocols. The following two secure protocols are commonly used today:

◆ Secure Socket Layer (SSL)
◆ Secure Shell (SSH)

SSL

The SSL protocol was developed by Netscape. SSL provides privacy and reliability between communicating applications and prevents unauthorized access to data over the network. It provides encryption for the server and client, as well as message authentication services. SSL is a layered protocol. It runs above the TCP/IP protocol and below the higher level protocols, such as Telnet, FTP, or HTTP.

Some of the features of SSL are as follows:

◆ **Cryptography security.** SSL establishes a secure connection between the communicating parties. A symmetric encryption is used after an initial handshake to define a secret key.

◆ **Reliability.** SSL establishes a reliable connection. Message transport includes a message integrity check using a keyed *Message Authentication Code* (MAC). Secure hash functions are used for MAC computations.

◆ **Interoperability.** SSL enables different applications to exchange cryptographic messages successfully.

◆ **Extensibility.** SSL provides a framework that allows new public-key and encryption methods to be incorporated whenever necessary.

◆ **Relative efficiency.** Cryptographic operations tend to be highly CPU-intensive. For this reason, the SSL protocol includes options, such as caching and compression, that allow a reduction in the number of connections that need to be established from scratch and a reduction in network activity.

The SSL protocol supports different ciphers. It uses symmetric cryptography—such as DES, RC4, and Triple DES—for data encryption and also supports public-key cryptography, such as RSA, DSS, and KEA.

SSL is located above a reliable transport layer, such as TCP, and below an application layer. It takes the data of the application to be sent, fragments it into manageable blocks, compresses it, applies a MAC to the data, encrypts it, and transmits the result. When data is received, the reverse process occurs: the data is decrypted, verified, decompressed, reassembled, and delivered to the application layer.

SSL protocol has two important states:

◆ SSL session state

◆ SSL connection state

An SSL session state has the following parameters:

◆ **Session ID.** An arbitrary byte for identifying the session state.

◆ **Peer certificate.** An X509.v3 certificate of the peer.

◆ **Compression method.** Definition of compression algorithm.

◆ **Cipher spec.** Definition of cryptography and MAC algorithms to be used when application data is to be transmitted.

◆ **Master secret.** A secret shared value between client and server.

◆ **Is resumable.** Flag for indicating whether the session can be used for other connections.

A connection state consists of the following components:

◆ Server and client random numbers

◆ SERVER-MAC-WRITE-SECRET

◆ CLIENT-MAC-WRITE-SECRET

◆ SERVER-WRITE-KEY

◆ CLIENT-WRITE-KEY

◆ Initialization vectors

◆ Sequence number

Every connection is associated with one session only, but one session may include different connections. The connection state defines the MAC parameters, while the session state defines a set of cryptographic parameters that can be used for various connections. Each session has the following four states:

◆ Current operating states for read

◆ Current operating states for write

◆ Pending operating states for read

◆ Pending operating states for write

When the handshake protocol is done, the pending state becomes the current state. You will look at the handshake protocol in the next section.

SSL has two major layers:

◆ The SSL handshake protocol

◆ The SSL record protocol

The SSL Handshake Protocol

The SSL handshake protocol, also called the *key-exchange protocol*, is responsible for creating secure communication between client and server. It authenticates both the client and the server and negotiates the encryption algorithm and cryptographic keys.

Communication through SSL handshake protocol is divided into several stages:

◆ Authentication of the server to the client.

◆ Negotiation of cryptographic algorithms between the server and the client.

◆ Authentication of the client to the server.

◆ Exchange of cryptography parameters by using public-key encryption.

◆ Establish an encrypted SSL connection.

Different types of SSL handshake protocol messages are exchanged between a server and a client:

◆ `client_hello`

◆ `server_hello`

◆ `server_certificate`

- server_key_exchange
- certificate_request
- server_hello_done
- client_certificate
- client_key_exchange
- certificate_verify
- change_cipher_spec
- finished

Each of these messages is discussed in the next few sections.

client_hello

The client sends the client_hello message to the server when it first tries to establish a session with the server. This message includes the following parameters:

- **Version.** This is the client version of SSL.
- **Random.** This is a random data value generated by the client.
- **Session ID.** This is the session identifier. This ID can be used by a client to establish a new connection in the session.
- **CipherSuite.** This is a list of key-exchange algorithms supported by the client.
- **Compression Method.** This is the list of compression algorithms that the client supports.

server_hello

The server sends the server_hello message in response to the client_hello message. The parameters of the server_hello message are the same as that of the client_hello message. The version field includes the version suggested by the client and the highest versions supported by the server. The server searches a match for the client's given session ID. If the session ID is found, the handshake process is carried out. If it is not found, the server creates a new session ID, and the client and server perform a handshake.

server_certificate

The server authenticates itself to the client by using the `server_certificate` message. The server sends its certificate to the client immediately after the `server_hello` message.

server_key_exchange

The `server_key_exchange` message is sent when the server has no certificate or has a certificate that contains only a signature of its public key. Usually, the public key is taken from the certificate itself. In case the certificate does not contain the public key, the `server_key_exchange` message is sent. SSL 3.0 supports the following algorithms:

- ◆ RSA
- ◆ Fixed Diffie-Hellman
- ◆ Ephemeral Diffie-Hellman
- ◆ Anonymous Diffie-Hellman
- ◆ Fortezza

certificate_request

The server uses the `certificate_request` message to authenticate clients. The server gets a certificate from the client and establishes the identity of the client.

server_hello_done

The `server_hello_done` message is sent to indicate that the server has finished its part in sending its identification parameters. After sending this message, the server waits for the client's response.

client_certificate

When the server requests a client certificate, the client sends the `client_certificate` message to the server. If no certificate is available with the client, the `no_certificate` alert message is sent.

client_key_exchange

The client_key_exchange method is based on the key-exchange algorithm specified by the server:

- ◆ If the RSA algorithm is used, the secret key generated by the client is encrypted with the server's public key.
- ◆ In case the Ephemeral or Anonymous Diffie-Hellman algorithms are used, the Diffie-Hellman public key parameters of the client are sent.
- ◆ If the Fixed Diffie-Hellman algorithm is used, this message will have no content, because the Diffie-Hellman parameters are already sent in a certificate message.
- ◆ If Fortezza algorithm is used, the Fortezza parameters are sent.

certificate_verify

The certificate_verify message is sent to provide verification of a client certificate. This message is sent after receiving all client certificates except those including Fixed Diffie-Hellman parameters.

Change_cipher_spec

Both the server and the client generate the session keys that are symmetric keys. These keys are used to encrypt and decrypt data exchanged during the SSL session. The change_cipher_spec message is exchanged by the server and client to indicate that the future messages will be encrypted by using the session keys.

finished

The finished message is sent immediately after an SSL change_cipher_spec message is sent by the client to indicate that the communication setup is successfully done. After this, the client waits for the server to send its SSL change_cipher_spec and finished messages.

After the server and the client send the finished messages to each other, SSL handshake protocol is completed and the application data can be transferred through the secure channel that is established.

The SSL Change Cipher Spec Protocol

The SSL Change Cipher Spec protocol is used in the last stage of the SSL hand-shake protocol. This protocol moves the communicating servers and clients from the pending state to the current state. Therefore, the clients and servers will now use the encryption and the MAC algorithms.

The SSL Alert Protocol

This protocol tells you about errors that occur during the connection. There are two levels of alerts:

◆ Fatal alert

◆ Warning alert

If a fatal alert occurs, the connection is terminated immediately. Other connections of the same session may continue, but this session ID will be marked as invalid so that no new connections can be established on this session.

The SSL Record Protocol

The SSL record protocol is responsible for encapsulating data that is transmitted in the higher level protocol above the base TCP/IP protocol. In SSL, all transmitted data is encapsulated into an object called a *record*. A record consists of a *header* and the *data*. The header includes information about the record and is transmitted before the data. The record header is discussed in the next section.

SSL Record Header

Each SSL record has a header that is five bytes long. The header fields are as follows:

◆ **Type (8 bit).** This field indicates the data type of the record. In addition, the header specifies that higher level protocol will handle the record data. The different types are these:

- change_cipher_spec
- alert
- handshake
- application_data

◆ **Version (16 bit).** This field specifies the SSL version protocol.

◆ **Length (16 bit).** This field specifies the record data length.

SSL Record Data

The record data part of the SSL record contains the actual data that will be transmitted through SSL. Before being transmitted, the record data passes through four stages:

◆ Fragmentation

◆ Compression

◆ Applying MAC

◆ Encryption

Fragmentation

The data is first fragmented into small pieces. In this phase, the data is fragmented into SSLPlaintext records of 2^14 bytes or less.

Compression

In this phase, the compression algorithm defined in the handshake stage compresses the given `SSLPlaintext`. No data is lost during compression. The resultant compressed data is called *SSLCompressed*. The `SSLCompressed` length must not exceed 2^14 + 1024.

Applying MAC

In this phase, a MAC is attached to the `SSLCompressed` data. MAC is an authentication tag or checksum obtained by applying an authentication scheme to the data. MACs can be generated and verified by using the same key. Therefore, it is ensured that only the intended recipient can verify MAC. The hash algorithm used to compute the MAC is derived from the cipher suite. SSL supports two hash function algorithms:

◆ MD5, a 128-bit hash

◆ SHA, a 160-bit hash

Encryption

Two types of encryption algorithms can be used in this stage:

♦ Stream encryption
♦ Block encryption

When a *stream encryption* algorithm is used, no padding is required. While using *block encryption*, the data block needs to be a multiple of the block size. If the data block is not a multiple of the block size, padding is used to pad the length of the data block.

Advantages of SSL

Some of the advantages provided by SSL are given here:

♦ Prevents identity fraud
♦ Prevents garbling attacks
♦ Prevents replaying of messages
♦ Prevents cut and paste attacks
♦ Prevents CipherSuite rollback attacks
♦ Prevents version rollback attacks
♦ Prevents dictionary attacks
♦ Prevents traffic attacks
♦ Prevents short block attacks

SSH

SSH secures connections over the Internet by encrypting all transmitted confidential data, including passwords, binary files, and administrative commands. SSH enables secure remote management of network hosts over the Internet.

SSH offers the following types of security:

♦ Data security
♦ Network security

Data Security

SSH encrypts data during transmission. It can be used with POP3/IMAP3/SMTP clients and servers. If a user is using packet sniffers, he can catch the data during transaction in a Telnet session. SSH provides a solution to this by transferring the data in encrypted form. In addition, SSH provides security against unauthorized access to your data. It provides a strong means of user authentication.

Network Security

Network security involves protecting network devices, which includes securing routers, firewalls, switches, and any computer connected to the network. SSH secures connections over the Internet by encrypting passwords and other data. It provides strong authentication and secure communications over insecure networks.

The SSH protocol consists of three layers:

◆ Transport layer
◆ User authentication layer
◆ Connection layer

Transport Layer

This layer runs over insecure TCP/IP networks. The transport layer provides server authentication, data confidentiality, and integrity.

The SSH transport layer provides the following services:

◆ Encryption
◆ Host authentication
◆ Data integrity protection

SSH might also provide data compression. The encryption mechanism as well as a key is negotiated during the establishment of the connection. The following encryption algorithms are currently supported:

◆ 3DES in CBC mode
◆ Blowfish in CBC mode

◆ IDEA in CBC mode

◆ CAST-128 in CBC mode

The transport layer protects data integrity by including a MAC with each message, computed from the contents of a packet.

Public key algorithms are used for server authentication. The following public key formats are currently defined:

◆ Simple DES

◆ X.509 certificates

◆ SPKI certificates

◆ OpenPGP certification

User Authentication Layer

The user authentication layer runs over Transport layer protocol. This layer authenticates a client to a server. SSH user authentication protocol relies on the transport layer for data integrity. It also assumes that the transport protocol already has authenticated a server machine, established an encrypted communication channel, and computed a unique session identifier for that session.

SSH supports the following authentication methods:

◆ No authentication

◆ Public key authentication

◆ Password authentication

◆ Host-based authentication

Server initiates the authentication process, which goes through the following stages:

◆ Server sends a list of supported authentication methods to the client.

◆ Client chooses the most convenient method for the current application and returns its name to the server. Further exchange of messages depends on the authentication method chosen.

◆ If the server accepts the authentication request, it sends a message to the client and starts the requested service.

Connection Layer

The connection layer runs over the user authentication layer. This layer allows opening secure channels over a single SSH connection. These channels can be used for a wide variety of services, such as transparent tunneling of existing protocols and new ones. It provides interactive login sessions, remote execution of commands, forwarded TCP/IP connections, and forwarded X11 connections.

Although this protocol is used mostly as a replacement for RSH command, it is much more flexible. It can wrap and forward any other protocol, for example X11, making it secure. X11 protocol has its own means of data protection, but SSH tunneling or forwarding is much more secure.

A single secure connection can hold multiple sessions. These sessions are called *channels*. The connection layer creates multiple channels using time multiplexing. Therefore, opening many connections is not recommended unless there is enough bandwidth. SSH protocol suite is designed in such a way that new protocols can be added any time and will coexist with those listed previously.

Intrusion Detection

Intruders attack and harm your system, data, and business interests. As system administrator, it is your duty to be able to detect such intrusion attempts and avoid them. You should be aware of the security measures that you can take to protect your system and data. The process of identifying attack from users is known as *Intrusion Detection*. There are various tools and software available in the market that enable you to catch intrusion and prevent it. In addition, you can take some security measures to avoid intrusion. The collection of such intrusion detection tools and security measures is called *Intrusion Detection System* (IDS).

There are various types of mechanisms available for intrusion detection:

- ◆ **Network Based Intrusion Detection.** This mechanism consists of tools that search for patterns indicating attempted intrusion in the network.
- ◆ **Host Based Intrusion Detection.** This mechanism involves performing intrusion detection checks on each host on your network. You need to look for signs of intrusion, such as suspicious entries in the log file. This mechanism involves lots of overhead. Therefore, the administrators do not prefer it.

◆ **Log File Monitoring.** This mechanism involves checking of log files for events that indicate intrusion.

◆ **File Integrity Checking.** This mechanism involves checking file integrity. This is helpful in cases where intruders have modified your files. There are some viruses that lead to the presence of suspicious files on your computer and modification of other files.

The next section lists some signs that indicate intrusion.

General Indications of Intrusion

Intruders usually leave behind some signs of intrusion attempts that can be tracked. Some of the intrusion signs are listed here:

◆ Failed logon attempts and logon attempt at unusual time and to unusual accounts.

◆ Presence of accounts not created by the administrators.

◆ Failed su attempts.

◆ Modified timestamp of files and software. Unexpected change in the file size. Presence of unusual files in on your disk. Change in file permission.

◆ Attempt to logon to an account that has not been used in a long time.

◆ The unexpected deterioration in the performance of your system.

◆ Modified log in your system. The log contains suspicious entries.

◆ Some processes running unexpectedly on your system. Repeated probes of the available services on your machines.

◆ Some unknown computer tries to connect to the hosts and servers on your network. Repeated logon attempts from remote hosts.

General Methods for Detecting Intrusions

Some of the intrusion detection methods you should be familiar with are listed here:

◆ Analyze the log file for unusual entries.

◆ Use the `last`, `lastcomm`, and `netstat` commands to get the information about the users and computers connected to your system.

◆ Make sure that the tools you use for intrusion detection have not been modified. Use the latest version of the tools.

◆ Check the file and data integrity on the servers and remote hosts.

◆ Check the hardware that is attached to your system. Presence of suspicious devices connected to your computer could be a sign of intrusion.

There are various tools available to help you detect intrusion. Some of these tools are available free of cost, while some developers charge for their tools. In the following sections, you will look at some of these tools.

Intrusion Detection Tools

Usually the intrusion detection is done by checking files, such as the log files. The intrusion of the virus attacks lead to modification in file size and timestamp. The first step towards intrusion detection is to look for the presence of suspicious files on your system. You should even look for the system files that are missing or that might have been tampered with. The following enables you to search for files that have been modified recently:

```
/usr/bin/find / -ctime -1 -print
```

Checking local files for possible Trojan horses, missing files, and files that have unexpected increase or decrease in size is the easiest way to detect intrusion. There are several tools that can verify file integrity:

◆ Tripwire

◆ Red Hat Package Manager (RPM)

◆ Packet Sniffers

Tripwire

Tripwire is a tool that performs integrity checks on binaries and config files. Tripwire compares these files against a database of known good values as a reference. Therefore, any changes in the files will be detected.

Tripwire requires less space than other tools. You can store it on a floppy disk. Therefore, to avoid any tampering with Tripwire itself, you should store it on a floppy disk. After you have set up Tripwire, you should run it regularly. You also can add a crontab entry to run Tripwire from your floppy disk every night and mail you the results in the morning.

You should keep a track of the files on your system that are modified. Many files could be modified as a result of hacker activities.

Using RPM

The RPM program can be used to verify packages installed on your system. By using RPM, you can ascertain whether the package has been corrupted or any component of it is missing due to intrusion. In such cases, RPM will report a verification failure.

The following command can be used to verify the files on your system:

```
root# rpm -Va
```

You also must be sure that unauthorized users have not altered RPM binary. You can use RPM with PGP to check the signature of a package. Therefore, every time a new RPM is added to the system, the RPM database will need to be re-archived.

Packet Sniffers

Intruders can easily gain access to the hosts on your computer by using a packet sniffer on a compromised host. The packet sniffers listen on the Ethernet port for information such as password and login in the packet stream. The packet sniffer creates a log of the traffic on the network. Therefore, critical information like passwords are logged by the packet sniffers. Intruders can use these logs to gain entry into your system. You can avoid this by encrypting passwords using methods such as SSH. If you are using `syslog` to send your data to a central log server, consider using a secure implementation of `syslog`, which encrypts and compresses the data before it is sent.

Network Security Tools

There are various tools available to assist you in detecting intrusion in your network. These tools also help you in ensuring security in your network. I'll now discuss the following network security tools:

◆ Snort

◆ nmap

- ◆ spidermap
- ◆ Firewalk

Snort

Snort is a network intrusion detection system developed by Martin Roesch. Snort can be used to notify an administrator of an intrusion attempt. Snort is easy to use and there are many command line options available. Snort can be configured in three main sections:

- ◆ Sniffer
- ◆ Packet logger
- ◆ Network intrusion detection

Sniffer Mode

Sniffer mode reads the packets off the network and displays them on the console. The following command is used to print the TCP/IP headers:

```
./snort -v
```

The preceding command will run Snort and display only the IP and TCP/UDP/ICMP headers. If you also need to see the application data in transit, execute the following command:

```
./snort -vd
```

The preceding command displays the packet data as well as the headers. If you need to obtain more information, such as the data link layer headers, execute the following command:

```
./snort -vde
```

Packet Logger Mode

Packet logger mode is used to log the packets to a log file. To log the packets, you need to specify a logging directory, and Snort will automatically switch to the packet logger mode:

```
./snort -dev -l ./log
```

The preceding command assumes that you have a directory named log in the current directory. If the specified directory does not exist, Snort exits with an error message. In this mode, Snort collects and places the packets in a directory hierarchy.

If you are on a high-speed network or you want to log the packets into a more compact form for later analysis, you should log it in binary mode:

```
./snort -l ./log -b
```

In binary mode, the entire packet is logged, not only sections of it. Therefore, when in binary mode, you need not run in verbose mode or specify the -d or -e switches. To Snort into logger mode, you need only to specify a logging directory at the command line. The default output format is plain ASCII text. However, you can specify a different output format with the –b option.

Sniffers that support the tcpdump binary format can be used to read binary file packets. Two such sniffers are tcpdump and Ethereal. You also can use Snort to read packets. To read packets, you need to put Snort in playback mode by using the –r switch.

Network Intrusion Detection Mode

Network intrusion detection mode allows Snort to analyze network traffic for matches against a user-defined rule set and perform actions. To enable *Network Intrusion Detection System* (NIDS) mode, execute the following command:

```
./snort -dev -l ./log -h 172.17.1.0/24 -c snort.conf
```

Here, snort.conf is the name of the rules file. Doing this will apply the rules specified in the snort.conf file to the packets. The rules in the snort.conf file are used to determine the action to be taken on the packets. If no output directory is specified, the default is taken as /var/log/snort.

If you are using Snort as your Intrusion Detection tool, you shouldn't use the -v option. Doing this decreases the speed of the system.

The data link headers need not be recorded for most applications. Therefore, it also is not necessary to specify the -e switch.

In the NIDS form, Snort logs packets as specified in the snort.conf file to the directory structure. To run the Snort in the NIDS form, execute the following command:

```
./snort -d -h 192.168.1.0/24 -l ./log -c snort.conf
```

nmap

The nmap program is a network exploration tool and security scanner. Following is the syntax of the nmap program:

```
nmap [Scan Type(s)] [Options] <host or net #1 ... [#N]>
```

nmap is designed to allow system administrators and users to scan large networks to determine which hosts are running and the services running on the hosts. nmap supports a number of scanning techniques, such as, UDP, TCP connect(), TCP SYN, ftp proxy, Reverse-ident, ICMP, FIN, ACK sweep, Xmas Tree, SYN sweep, IP Protocol, and Null scan.

nmap also offers advanced features, such as:

◆ Remote OS detection via TCP/IP fingerprinting
◆ Stealth scanning
◆ Dynamic delay
◆ Retransmission calculations
◆ Parallel scanning
◆ Detection of down hosts via parallel pings
◆ Decoy scanning
◆ Port filtering detection
◆ Direct RPC scanning
◆ Fragmentation scanning

nmap should be run as root whenever possible. Many critical kernel interfaces require root privileges. A number of ports on the computer are scanned. nmap provides service name, number, state, and protocol of the port. The state can be one of the following:

◆ **Open** means that the target machine will accept connections on that port.

◆ **Filtered** means that the port is secured by firewall, filter, or any other means. These filtering activities prevent nmap from determining whether the port is open.

◆ **Unfiltered** means that the port is closed and no firewall or filter will be able to determine the port.

Options of the nmap command can be combined. Some options are specific to certain scan modes. nmap tries to catch and warn the user about unsupported option combinations. Some of the options of the nmap command and their explanations are given here:

◆ **-P0.** Enables scanning of the networks so that the ICMP echo requests or responses through the firewalls are not allowed.

◆ **-PT.** Uses the TCP ping to determine the hosts that are running. This option preserves the efficiency of the scanning hosts that are running while still allowing you to scan networks/hosts that block ping packets.

◆ **-PS.** Uses SYN connection request packets instead of ACK packets for root users.

◆ **-PI.** Uses the ICMP echo request packet. It finds the hosts that are running and also looks for subnet-directed broadcast addresses on your network.

◆ **-PB.** Uses both the ACK and ICMP packets. Therefore, you can get firewalls that can filter either one. This option is the default ping type.

◆ **-O.** Activates remote host identification via TCP/IP fingerprinting. The fingerprinting mechanism is used to determine the type of system you are scanning.

◆ **-I.** Switches on TCP reverse scanning by ident protocol. The ident protocol allows disclosure of the username that owns any process connected via TCP, even if that process did not initiate the connection.

◆ **-f.** Causes the requested SYN, FIN, XMAS, or NULL scan to use tiny fragmented IP packets. The TCP header is split over several packets to make it difficult for intrusion detection.

◆ **-v.** Provides information about the activities that are going on.

◆ **-h.** Displays a quick reference for nmap usage options.

◆ **-p <port ranges>.** Specifies the ports you want to be scanned.

SpiderMap

Spidermap is a collection of perl scripts. Spidermap provides you with a set of tools for scanning networks. The tools have features such as custom packet rates and scan types for each network with increased efficiency.

Components

There are three major components of the SpiderMap toolkit:

◆ Breakdown

◆ Spidermap

◆ nlogdb

Breakdown

This script takes a list of IP addresses as input and then prompts the user for specific information about each network. This allows scans to be predefined for specific tasks.

SpiderMap

This script reads in a configuration file generated by breakdown, performs the scans, and dumps the raw output to a file for use by the createdb script.

nlogdb

The nlogdb script reads in the nmap output from spidermap and copies it to the Nlog file. Nlog is a log file that can be used for various purposes, such as scheduled network analysis and providing input for another set of tools.

Firewalk

Firewalk is a network-auditing tool. This tool determines the transport protocols that a specific gateway will let through. Firewalk sends out TCP or UDP packets with an IP Time-To-Live (TTL) one greater than the targeted gateway. If the gateway allows the traffic, it will forward the packets to the next hop. In the next hop, the packets will expire and the "TTL exceeded in transit" message is sent. If the gateway host does not allow the traffic, it will drop the packets. You can determine the access list on the gateway by sending and recording packets.

Firewalk has two phases:

◆ A network discovery phase

◆ A scanning phase

In the network discovery phase, the IP TTL is obtained. To get the correct IP TTL, you need to determine the hop counts. You do this by sending out packets with incremented IP TTLs toward the destination host. After determining the gateway hop count, you can move to the next phase: the scanning phase.

In the scanning phase, Firewalk sends out TCP or UDP packets and sets a time-out. If it receives a response before the timer expires, the port is considered open. If no response is received, the port is considered closed.

Although scanning is necessary to detect intrusion, you need to protect your network from the external threats. Scanning is of no use until you take action to safeguard your networks. Exposing your network to the outside world will certainly encourage hackers to attack your network. One way to prevent external users from accessing your internal resources is to use firewalls.

Firewalls

A *firewall* is a set of related programs located at a network gateway server that protects the resources of a private network from the outside world. For example, an enterprise with an intranet that allows its employees to access the Internet can install a firewall to prevent outsiders from accessing its internal resources. Firewalls also control the outside resources that a user within the network can access.

The most basic operation in the firewall technology is packet filtering. Routers can be configured to examine and filter the incoming packets to the network. The packets can be filtered based on various criteria, such as IP addresses or subnets, particular TCP or UDP port numbers, or combinations of these properties.

IP packet filtering is designed to do three things:

◆ **IP Filtering.** This involves consulting a set of rules to determine whether to pass each IP packet. Undesirable or potentially unsafe packets can be blocked.

◆ **Network Address.** This involves assigning new IP addresses according to mapping rules and translating IP packets between old and new addresses. This can be useful in an environment that has a large number of hosts.

◆ **IP Accounting.** This involves recording the number of input and output bytes.

There are rules that determine the entry and exit of packets from a network through a firewall. These rules are designed to check the packet headers of the packets. A collection of rules is called a *chain*. Normally, checks during the packet filtering are performed based on the rules in the chains. There are three basic chains:

◆ **Input chain.** The rules in this chain are used to perform checks on the incoming packets.

◆ **Output chain.** The rules in this chain are used to perform checks on the outgoing packets.

◆ **Forward chain.** The rules in this chain are used to perform checks on the packets that are meant for another computer.

Two firewall subsystems available with Linux are `ipchains` and `IPtables`. These are discussed in detail in the next few sections.

ipchains

You can use ipchains to set up, maintain, and inspect IP firewalls rules specified in the Linux kernel. These rules can be divided into four different categories:

◆ The IP input chain

◆ The IP output chain

◆ The IP forwarding chain

◆ The user defined chains

For each of these categories, a separate table of rules is maintained.

The syntaxes for using the `ipchains` command are as follows:

```
ipchains -[ADC] chain rule-specification [options]
ipchains -[RI] chain rulenum rule-specification [options]
ipchains -D chain rulenum [options]
ipchains -[LFZNX] [chain] [options]
```

```
ipchains -P chain target [options]
ipchains -M [ -L ¦ -S ] [options]
```

A firewall rule specifies criteria for a packet to pass through. If the packet does not match, the next rule in the chain is examined. If the packet matches the rule, the next rule is specified by the value of the target. The value of the target can be the name of a user-defined chain or one of these special values:

- **ACCEPT.** This value lets the packet pass through.
- **DENY.** This value drops the packet.
- **REJECT.** This value is same as the DENY value. However, it is easier to debug because an ICMP message is sent back to the sender indicating that the packet was dropped
- **MASQ.** This value is applicable only for the forward and user defined chains. MASQ can only be used when the kernel is compiled with CON-FIG_IP_MASQUERADE defined.
- **REDIRECT.** This value is applicable to the chains. It can be used only when the Linux kernel is compiled with CONFIG_IP_TRANSPARENT_PROXY defined.
- **RETURN.** This value is the target value of a rule.

Some of the options that you can use with the ipchains program are as follows:

- **-A.** This option is used to append rules at the end of the selected chain. A rule is added for each address combination when the source and/or destination names resolve to more than one address.
- **-D.** This option is used to delete rules from a chain.
- **-R.** This option is used to replace a rule in a chain. The command will fail if the source and/or destination names resolve to multiple addresses.
- **-I.** Insert one or more rules in the selected chain.
- **-L.** This option is used to list the rules in a chain.
- **-F.** This option is used to delete rules in a chain.

IPtables

You can use iptables to set up, maintain, and inspect the tables of IP packet filter rules as specified in the Linux kernel. Tables contain two types pf chains:

◆ Built-in chains

◆ User-defined chains

Each chain is made up of a set of rules. These rules match a set of packets. The rules determine the actions to be taken when a packet is found that matches the rules. The usage of the IPtables is given here:

```
iptables -[ADC] chain rule-specification [options]
iptables -[RI] chain rulenum rule-specification [options]
iptables -D chain rulenum [options]
iptables -[LFZ] [chain] [options]
iptables -[NX] chain
iptables -P chain target [options]
iptables -E old-chain-name new-chain-name
```

A firewall rule specifies criteria for a packet to pass through the firewall. If the packet does not match the rule, the next rule in the chain is examined. The target value can be one of these:

◆ ACCEPT

◆ DROP

◆ QUEUE

◆ RETURN

There are three tables, filter, nat, and mangle. The tables present at any time depend on the kernel configuration options and modules present. These tables are described here:

◆ **filter.** This is the default table and contains three built-in chains:

- **INPUT.** This chain is used to perform checks on the incoming packets.
- **FORWARD.** This chain is used to perform checks on the outgoing packets.
- **OUTPUT.** This chain is used to perform checks on the packets that are meant for another computer.

◆ **nat.** This table is used in situations when a new connection is found. It consists of three built-in chains:

- **PREROUTING.** This chain is used for altering incoming packets.
- **OUTPUT.** This chain is used for altering outgoing packets.
- **POSTROUTING.** This chain is used for altering packets that are scheduled to go out.

◆ **mangle.** This table is used for specialized packet alteration. It has two built-in chains:

- **PREROUTING.** This chain is used for altering incoming packets before routing.
- **OUTPUT.** This chain is used for altering locally generated packets before routing.

The options of the `iptables` command are listed here:

◆ **-A.** This option is used to append rules in the end of a chain. A rule is added for each address combination when the source and/or the destination of the packets maps to more than one address,.

◆ **-D.** This option is used to delete rules from a chain.

◆ **-R.** This option is used to replace a rule in a chain.

◆ **-I.** This option is used to insert rules in a chain.

◆ **-L.** This option lists the rules in a chain.

Even if the firewall allows a connection to establish, you need to ensure that the clients are allowed access to the service they are requesting. The level of trust is different for different clients. Every client has different requirements. You need to analyze the trust and requirements of clients before providing them the access to your resources. A mechanism to do this is to use TCP wrappers.

TCP Wrappers

The TCP Wrapper can be used to provide services, such as access control, restrictions, and requests logging. TCP wrappers check the access control list to determine whether a connection should be allowed. It also submits a log entry to the daemon `syslogd`. The `tcpd` invokes a suitable list if a service is not restricted. The access list is used to determine the restricted services. The invoked daemon authenticates the service and writes an entry in `syslogd`.

TCP wrappers implement access control through the use of two files:

◆ **/etc/hosts.allow.** This file contains the allow list.

◆ **/etc/hosts.deny.** This file contains the deny list. The `/etc/hosts.allow` file is an allow list, while the `/etc/hosts.deny` is a deny list. The allow and deny lists in these files determine the set of restrictions imposed on all services that are imposed through `tcpd`.

You can use TCP Wrappers for UDP and TCP services. However, these services should be invoked through a central daemon.

Routing Security

Routers are the computers that let the packets flow between the source and destination hosts. Routers identify the destination of the packets by reading the packet headers. The router refers to a configuration table to decide where the packets should go. A configuration table is a collection of information:

◆ The connections that lead to a particular address

◆ Priorities for the identified connection

◆ Rules for handling traffic

There are various routing packages available for Linux. I discuss a few in the following sections.

routed

routed is one of the standard routing packages available for Linux. It supports only the RIP protocol, the simplest of all the routing protocols. In RIP, the routers simply broadcast their routing tables to neighboring routers. The broadcasting of routing tables results in a routing table that contains entries for every destination on the Internet. This method is insecure and inefficient outside small secure networks. Securing it is not possible. You can firewall ports 520 and 521, which RIP uses to transfer data. However, doing so might result in blocking the routes you want and the hackers can still spoof routes. Therefore, it is not recommended to run this service.

GateD

You can use GateD software to manage interior as well as exterior protocols. GateD is more advanced routing software than routed. It supports the following:

- RIP versions 1 and 2
- DCN HELLO
- OSPF version 2
- EGP version 2
- BGP versions 2 through 4

The routing protocols are divided into two general groups:

- **Interior protocols.** These protocols are used to exchange information within an autonomous system.
- **Exterior protocols.** These protocols are used to exchange routing information between different autonomous systems.

GateD supports the following interior protocols:

- RIP
- OSPF
- ISIS

RIP

The Routing Information Protocol (RIP) is the most commonly used interior protocol. RIP selects the route that has the lowest hop count. The longest path that RIP accepts is 15 hops. If the hop count is greater than 15, the destination is considered unreachable and GateD discards the route. GateD discards a route with hop counts greater than 15.

OSPF

Open Shortest Path First (OSPF), is a routing protocol used to determine the shortest and the fastest route for packets within IP networks. It was designed by the Internet Engineering Task Force to serve as an *Interior Gateway Protocol* (IGP), replacing RIP.

The advantages of OSPF are listed here:

◆ Any change in an OSPF network can be incorporated quickly.

◆ OSPF has a hierarchical structure. It uses area 0 as the top of the hierarchy.

◆ OSPF is a Link State Algorithm and supports *Variable Length Subnet Masks* (VLSM).

◆ OSPF uses multicasting within areas.

◆ OSPF sends only the updated routing table sections upon initialization. OSPF does not send the entire routing table.

◆ OSPF networks can be logically segmented to decrease the size of routing tables. This is possible by the use of areas. Using route summarization can further reduce table size.

◆ OSPF is not related to any particular vendor. It is an open standard.

ISIS

Intermediate System to Intermediate System (ISIS) protocol is a protocol similar to OSPF. ISIS uses the state-link algorithm and short-path-first algorithm. The components of the ISIS network are as follows:

◆ **End systems.** These are typically the user devices.

◆ **Intermediate systems.** These are the routers.

◆ **Areas.** These are a set of users organized in a local group.

◆ **Domains.** These are a set of the areas taken together.

ISIS is an IGP originally developed for routing International Organization for Standardization/Connectionless Network Protocol (ISO/CLNP) packets. The ISIS version distributed with GateD can route IP packets as well.

Exterior protocols exchange information between autonomous systems. The gateways between two autonomous systems communicate by using an exterior routing protocol. GateD supports two exterior protocols:

◆ Exterior Gateway Protocol (EGP)

◆ Border Gateway Protocol (BGP)

EGP

The EGP protocol is used for exchanging routing information between two gateways in a network of autonomous systems. It is used to exchange routing table information. The routing table contains the following:

◆ A list of known routers

◆ The addresses they can reach

◆ A cost metric associated with the path to each router

The entries in the routing table determine the selection of the best available route. The router polls its neighbor at regular intervals between 120 and 480 seconds. The neighbor responds by sending its complete routing table.

BGP

BGP is replacing EGP as the exterior protocol. Like, EGP, BGP also exchanges reachability information between autonomous systems. However, BGP provides more capabilities than EGP. It uses path attributes to provide more information about each route. These path attributes help in selecting the best route. BGP supports non-hierarchical topologies. It can be used to implement a network structure of equivalent autonomous systems.

BGP hosts communicate through TCP protocol. These hosts send an updated part of the routing table. BGP communicates with autonomous networks by using IBGP. The autonomous networks maintain two routing tables:

◆ One table for the interior gateway protocol

◆ One table for IBGP

MRT

The *Multi-threaded Routing Toolkit* (MRT) toolkit can be used to build a wide variety of tools, ranging from routing daemons to BGP fault-injection and traffic generation test packages. MRT provides features such as the following:

◆ Parallel lightweight processes

◆ Multiple processor support

◆ Shared memory

The MRT software facilitates adding and prototyping experimental routing protocol and inter-domain policy algorithms. This is possible due to the object-oriented and modular design of the software.

You can use MRT applications and libraries to do the following :

◆ Serve as the backbone routing software for your network connection.

◆ Simultaneously handle tasks, such as:

- Routing policy communication
- Routing policy calculation
- Maintenance of a RIB

◆ Generate and analyze route statistics

◆ Generate real-time graphical maps of Internet routing

◆ Capture a BGP peering session and monitor it in real time

◆ Record and replay sequences of events, such as routing failures

MRT first reads a configuration file to configure routing protocols, route peering, and routing policy. By default, the configuration file is /etc/mrtd.conf. MRT reads the configuration file and scans the kernel for existing routes. MRT then scans the kernel interface list and initiates routing protocol communications. In addition, MRT listens to the mrt service port, mrtd, for users using the Telnet connections.

The MRT toolkit includes two main categories of tools:

◆ Routing tools

◆ Network performance measurement tools

Routing Tools

The components of the routing tools are listed here:

◆ **MRTd.** A routing daemon that supports RIPng, BGP4+, multiple RIBs, and RIP1/2. MRTd reads router configuration files and supports a router-like Telnet interface.

◆ **BGPsim.** A BGP4+ traffic simulator.

◆ **SBGP.** A simple BGP4+ speaker and listener.

◆ **Route_BtoA.** Converts binary MRT messages to ASCII.

- ◆ **Route_AtoB.** Converts ASCII descriptions of MRT messages to binary MRT message format. Binary MRT messages can be piped into other MRT programs, including SBGP and BGPSim.

You can invoke MRT programs either from the command line or from the Linux boot/startup script. After MRT programs are invoked, the MRT-based tools listen for user Telnet connections on the TCP port. The TCP port is specified in /etc/services. The configuration file or utility can be used to configure MRT programs. The configuration file can also be used to specify passwords. An extract of a configuration file is given here:

```
>telnet 172.17.0.0 mrtd
MRT version 1.5.2 ALPHA June 10, 2002
User Access Verification
[71] password> ***
[71] MRTd>
```

By default, MRT programs restrict Telnet to the loopback address or the interface address of the local machine.

There are various commands available for user management and configuration. Some of these commands are listed here:

- ◆ **show config.** View the configuration file.
- ◆ **show version.** Show the current version.
- ◆ **show threads.** Show the status of application threads.
- ◆ **config.** Enter configuration mode.
- ◆ **enable.** Enter enable mode.
- ◆ **write.** Save volatile memory configuration to disk.
- ◆ **reboot.** Restart the application.
- ◆ **help.** Show all commands available.
- ◆ **exit.** Leave the UII interface.

The syntax of using the mrtd program is given here:

```
mrtd [-v] [-n] [-f] [-l rib file] [-r] [-m]
```

The options of the mrtd program are as follows:

- ◆ **-v.** This option is used to turn on the verbose mode. The output is displayed on the standard output device.
- ◆ **-n.** This option specifies that the MRT tools will not be able to modify the kernel routing tables.
- ◆ **-f.** This option is used to read the configuration file.
- ◆ **-l.** This option is used to obtain routes from the routing tables.
- ◆ **-m.** This option is used to enable MRT to use new dump format.

Zebra

When you connect to the Internet, your data packets pass through many routers. These routers have TCP/IP routing functionality. Zebra is a routing software package that provides TCP/IP based routing services with routing protocols support.

You can use a system with Zebra installed on it as a router. Zebra uses the routing table information to ensure data delivery. You can view the routing table information from a Zebra terminal interface.

Some of the routing protocols supported by Zebra are listed here:

- ◆ RIPv1
- ◆ RIPv2
- ◆ RIPng
- ◆ OSPFv2
- ◆ OSPFv3
- ◆ BGP-4
- ◆ BGP-4+

The advanced software architecture of Zebra enables it to provide a high-quality and multi-server routing engine. This enables you to add new protocols to daemons. Zebra provides different user interfaces for each protocol. Zebra also supports common client commands

Zebra has a different system administration method. The types of users supported by zebra include these:

- **normal mode users.** These users are able to view the system status.
- **enable mode users.** These users are able to modify Zebra configuration.

Each routing protocol is handled by a corresponding daemon. It is easy to add a new routing protocol daemon to the entire routing system without affecting any other software. You need to run only the protocol daemon associated with routing protocols in use. The Zebra daemon is responsible for changing the kernel routing table and redistributing routes between different routing protocols. Therefore, users can run a specific daemon and send routing reports to a central routing console.

Linux Security Checklist

System administrators need to perform some tasks regularly in order to protect their systems. In this section, you look at some checklists for securing Linux. Here are some tasks you can perform to reduce your risk:

- Keep up with software patches
- Comb through your log files and investigate any entry that is out of the ordinary.

Here are some tasks you can perform to reduce the risk for the Linux system:

- Check network integrity
- Turn off your unessential services

Unused running services are the prime target of the hackers. You tend to forget about the services that are running and not often used, and those are the services that get attacked by the hackers. There are some easy ways to guard against this. You can move to the directory where the init files are stored and add an `exit 0` line at the beginning of the scripts for the services that you do not want to use. An easier and more secure way to accomplish this task is to use the `chkconfig` and `ntsysv` utility. These utilities don't involve editing the script. As a result, it is less error-prone to use them. The init files are usually stored in the `/etc/rc.d/init.d` directory. Services you might want to turn off include these:

◆ identd

◆ lpd

◆ linuxconf

◆ netfs

◆ portmap

◆ routed

◆ rstatd

◆ rusersd

◆ rwalld

◆ rwhod

◆ sendmail

◆ ypbind

◆ yppasswdd

◆ ypserv

You also can turn off some unnecessary inetd services from your /etc/inetd.conf file. You can comment a line by putting a # at the beginning.

Summary

In this chapter, you learned various aspects of network defense and intrusion detection for the Linux environment. I discussed tools such as netstat, ps, and lsof. Secure protocols play a vital role in securing your networks. SSL and SSH are protocols most commonly used to ensure security. I talked about these protocols in depth in this chapter.

Detecting intrusion attempts on host computers is the primary task of system administrators. I listed some indications of intrusion attempts and gave you some commonly used methods to detect intrusion. Apart from this, intrusion detection tools, such as Tripwire, RPM, and packet sniffers, were explained in detail in this chapter. I also covered various network security tools, such as Snort, nmap, Spidermap, and Firewalk in this chapter.

You can secure your network from the outside world by using firewalls. Firewalls restrict the movement of packets in and out of a network. You looked at ipchains and IPtables programs that perform packet-filtering checks in the Linux environment. Routers are the devices that ensure delivery of packets to the destination. Routing security tools such as routed, GateD, MRT, and Zebra were discussed in detail in this chapter.

Additionally, this chapter provided you with a Linux security checklist. The checklist includes steps you can take to secure your Linux environment.

Check Your Understanding

Multiple Choice Questions

1. Which command is used to view network connections, routing tables, interface statistics, masquerade connections, and multi-cast memberships?

    a. netstat

    b. ps

    c. lsof

2. Which command is used to list the open files?

    a. netstat

    b. ps

    c. lsof

3. Which of the following components is responsible for encapsulating information of higher level protocols?

    a. SSL handshake protocol

    b. SSL record protocol

    c. SSH handshake protocol

    d. SSH record protocol

4. Select the header fields of an SSL record:

    a. Type

    b. Version

    c. Length

    d. Protocol

5. Arrange the following stages in the order in which a record data passes through before being transmitted.

   a. Applying MAC

   b. Fragmentation

   c. Encryption

   d. Compression

6. SSH protocol consists of which three layers?

   a. Transport layer

   b. User authentication layer

   c. SSH handshake layer

   d. Connection layer

Short Questions

1. Edward, the system administrator, has decided to use Snort as the network intrusion detection tool in his network. Explain to him the modes in which Snort can be configured. Execute the command to display the packet data as well as the headers. Edward needs to specify the log directory as snort_log in the current directory. You also need to explain to him how to enable Network Intrusion Detection System (NIDS) and specify the snort_rules as the rules file. Help him do all these.

2. Stephen, the network administrator, is consulting with management in favor of using the SSH protocol in the network for security reasons. He needs to explain to them the different layers of the SSH protocol. Help him do so.

Answers

Multiple Choice Answers

1. The `nestat` command is used to view network connections, routing tables, interface statistics, masquerade connections, and multi-cast memberships.

2. The `lsof` command is used to list the open files.

3. The SSL Record Protocol is responsible for encapsulating information of higher level protocols.

4. Type, version, and length are the header fields of an SSL record.

5. The sequence of stages record data passes through before being transmitted is as follows:

   1. Fragmentation
   2. Compression
   3. Applying MAC
   4. Encryption

Short Answers

1. Snort is a network intrusion detection system used to notify an administrator of an intrusion attempt. Snort is easy to use and many command line options are available. There are three main modes in which Snort can be configured:

   ◆ **Sniffer.** This mode reads the packets off the network and displays them on the console. The command to display the packet data as well as the headers is as follows:

   ```
   ./snort -vd
   ```

   ◆ **Packet logger.** This mode is used to log the packets to a log file. You need to specify a logging directory and Snort will automatically switch to the packet logger mode. The command to specify the directory as snort_log is as follows:

   ```
   ./snort -dev -l ./snort_log
   ```

◆ **Network Intrusion Detection.** This mode allows Snort to analyze network traffic for matches against a user-defined rule set and perform actions. To enable Network Intrusion Detection System (NIDS) mode, execute the following command:

```
./snort -dev -l ./log -h 172.17.1.0/24 -c snort_rules.conf
```

2. The SSH protocol consists of three layers:

◆ **Transport Layer.** This layer provides server authentication, data confidentiality, and integrity. SSH transport layer provides various services, including encryption, host authentication, and data integrity protection.

◆ **User Authentication Layer.** This layer runs over Transport layer protocol and authenticates a client to a server. SSH user authentication protocol relies on the transport layer for data integrity. It also assumes that the transport protocol has already authenticated a server machine, established an encrypted communication channel, and computed a unique session identifier for that session. It supports different authentication modes.

◆ **Connection Layer.** This layer runs over the user authentication layer. The connection layer allows opening secure channels over a single SSH connection. These channels may be used for a wide variety of services, such as transparent tunneling of existing protocols and new ones. It provides interactive login sessions, remote execution of commands, forwarded TCP/IP connections, and forwarded X11 connections.

Chapter 11

The Linux Kernel

The kernel is the core of the Linux operating system. It controls the basic services offered by the Linux operating system. The kernel is responsible for the following:

◆ CPU resource scheduling

◆ Process management

◆ Memory management

◆ Device control, as well as the device-file and device-driver interface

◆ Security at the device, process, and user level

◆ Accounting services including CPU usage and disk quotas

◆ Inter process communication

The kernel acts as an interface for your programs and system hardware. It performs memory management tasks for all the running processes and ensures that each process gets the required amount of processor time.

Linux comes with the source code of the kernel. The source enables the system administrators to customize the kernel according to their requirements. You might need to customize kernel for reasons such as these:

◆ Modification in the system hardware

◆ Optimization of memory usage

◆ Improvement in the speed and performance of the system

A naming convention is followed for Linux kernel sources. A version with an even number is stable, and odd numbered kernels are unstable. The Linux kernels that are being developed support all the available functionalities of the existing kernels. These kernels are sometimes unstable. You should always make backups of your data if you intend to use such developing kernels.

The kernel is stored in the /usr/src/linux directory. The source code of the kernel is spread across various subdirectories of /usr/src/linux. Descriptions of some important subdirectories of /usr/src/linux are as follows:

- **arch.** Contains all of the architecture-specific kernel code. The subdirectories of arch are based on the architectures supported by the Linux platform.
- **include.** Contains the include files. These files are needed to build the kernel code. Like the arch directory, it has various subdirectories. There's a subdirectory corresponding to each supported architecture.
- **init.** Contains the initialization code for the kernel.
- **mm.** Contains the memory management code. The architecture specific memory management code is stored in this directory.
- **drivers.** Stores the device drivers. Device drivers are an interface between the operating system and the hardware devices.
- **ipc.** Stores kernel's inter-process communications code.
- **modules.** Stores the built-in modules.
- **fs.** Stores the file system code. The subdirectories within this directory represent a supported file system.
- **kernel.** Stores the main kernel code.
- **net.** Stores the kernel's networking code.
- **lib.** Contains the kernel's library code.
- **scripts.** Contains the scripts that are used to configure the kernel.

As you can see from the preceding listing, the directory structure for kernel is very complex. Here are guidelines for searching for a specific subject in the kernel tree:

- **System Startup and Initialization.** During system startup, the boot loader loads the kernel into the memory. The control is passed over to the kernel. The commands for loading are located in the arch/i386/kernel/head.S file.
- **Memory Management.** The code for memory management can be found in the mm directory. The mm/memory.c file contains the code for handling page fault. You can find the memory mapping and page cache code in mm/filemap.c. The mm/buffer.c file implements the buffer cache.
- **Kernel.** You can find the relevant generic code in kernel. The architecture-specific code is available in arch/*/kernel. The kernel/sched.c file implements the scheduler.

- ◆ **PCI.** The PCI pseudo driver can be found in the `drivers/pci/pci.c` file. You can find the system-wide definitions in the `/linux/pci.h` file.

- ◆ **Interprocess Communication.** The System V InterProcess Communication (IPC) objects include a data structure, called `ipc_perm`. This data structure can be found in the `include/linux/ipc.h` file. The `ipc/msg.c` file implements the System V messages.

- ◆ **Interrupt Handling.** The code for handling kernel's interrupt is often platform specific. For example, the Intel interrupt handling code is available in `arch/i386/kernel/irq.c`.

- ◆ **Device Drivers.** Linux's device driver sources can be categorized as follows:

  - • **/block.** These are the block device drivers, such as IDE and SCSI. To view how all devices are initialized, you should look at the `device_setup()` method in `drivers/block/genhd.c`.

  - • **/char.** The character-based devices, such as serial ports and mice, are available here.

  - • **/cdrom.** The CDROM devices, such as Soundblaster CDROM, can be found in this directory.

  - • **/pci.** This directory contains the source for the PCI pseudo-driver. The PCI subsystem mapping and initialization can be viewed here.

  - • **/scsi.** You will find all the SCSI code here. In addition, you will find the drivers for the SCSI devices supported by Linux.

  - • **/net.** You will find the network device drivers, such as the DECChip 21040 PCI ethernet driver, in this directory.

  - • **/sound.** The sound card drivers are stored in this directory.

- ◆ **File Systems.** The `fs/ext2/` directory contains the sources for the EXT2 file system. The data structure definition is available in the `include/linux/ext2_fs.h`, `ext2_fs_i.h` and `ext2_fs_sb.h` files. `include/linux/fs.h` describes the Virtual File System data structures, and `fs/buffer.c` implements the buffer cache.

- ◆ **Network.** The networking code is located in `include/net make`. The BSD and the IP version 4 INET socket code are located in `net/socket.c` and `net/ipv4/af_inet.c`, respectively. `net/core` provides the generic protocol support code. The network device drivers can be found in `drivers/net`.

◆ **Modules.** The Linux module code is available in the kernel and modules package. The `kernel/modules.c` file contains the kernel code. The `include/linux/module.h` file contains the data structures. The `include/linux/kerneld.h` file contains the `kerneld` daemon messages.

Kernel has a modular structure. Various functions and features of kernel are made available through the use of modules. I discuss modules in the next section.

Modules

A *module* is an object file containing functions for interfacing with a particular device or performing particular tasks. The use of modules makes kernel smaller and keeps only the bare basics compiled into the kernel. Modules have also revolutionized the kernel compilation. You no longer need to compile every device driver into kernel. You can simply enable or disable the modules, as per your requirements.

The functionality of modules is used by the kernel while communicating with a program called `kerneld`, which is run at boot time. When the kernel receives a request for use of a module, kernel checks whether the module is loaded in memory. If it is not loaded, the `kerneld` loads the module into memory. `kerneld` also can remove a module if it has not been used for a specific period of time, which is configurable.

The concept of modules is advantageous, but you should be aware of the following:

◆ Frequently used devices and the devices required during boot process, should not be used as modules. These devices must be compiled into the kernel.

◆ If you compile a module into the kernel, it might use more memory. However, this is better than a system that uses its CPU and IO resources to constantly load and unload modules.

◆ You should modularize devices, such as the floppy disk, CD-ROM, and parallel port. Either these devices are not used very often, or they are used only for a short period.

◆ You should not modularize frequently used modules.

After learning about the kernel compilation and how useful modules can be, it's time to discuss how to build kernels.

Building Kernel

The Linux kernel contains the drivers for various hardware and file systems. Each hardware component on a Linux system has its own module. If you add hardware to your computer, you need to add the corresponding module to the kernel. You also might want to enable or disable a module. You can do this by using the `modprobe` command.

Making changes to the kernel is a three-step process:

- ◆ Editing the kernel, which includes adding or removing modules
- ◆ Building or compiling the kernel
- ◆ Installing the kernel

Before reconfiguring the kernel, you should save the current settings. This will enable you to recover your settings, just in case you make mistakes while reconfiguring kernel.

Obtaining Kernel and Module Information

The kernel configuration is determined by the modules that are available. To view the list of currently loaded modules, execute the following command:

```
modprobe -l
```

The sample output of the preceding command to view the list of modules is given here:

```
/lib/modules/2.2.16-22/fs/autofs.o
/lib/modules/2.2.16-22/fs/binfmt_aout.o
/lib/modules/2.2.16-22/fs/binfmt_java.o
/lib/modules/2.2.16-22/fs/binfmt_misc.o
/lib/modules/2.2.16-22/fs/coda.o
/lib/modules/2.2.16-22/fs/fat.o
/lib/modules/2.2.16-22/fs/hfs.o
/lib/modules/2.2.16-22/fs/hpfs.o
/lib/modules/2.2.16-22/fs/lockd.o
```

```
/lib/modules/2.2.16-22/fs/minix.o
```

....

....

....

You might want to obtain the version of the kernel you are using. The command to do so is as follows:

```
uname -r
```

Preparing to Build a Kernel

Before you actually start building the kernel, you should perform the following steps:

◆ Prepare a bootable recovery disk. This will be helpful if the kernel doesn't work properly after you build it. By using the recovery disk, you can restart the system and rectify the problem.

◆ Make a backup of the kernel. After you have done this, provide an entry for the backed up kernel in the boot manager.

Selecting Modules

Next, you need to select modules to be enabled or deselect modules to be disabled. The steps to do this are these:

◆ Log on as root user and move to the /usr/src/linux directory.

◆ Open a kernel-editing tool. Two commonly used editing tools are as follows:

• **menuconfig.** The interface of the menuconfig tool is displayed in Figure 11-1.

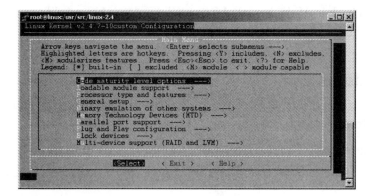

FIGURE 11-1 *The menuconfig tool.*

- **xconfig.** This is a desktop tool. The xconfig tool is displayed in Figure 11-2.

FIGURE 11-2 *The xconfig tool.*

Once you invoke the editing tool, edit the kernel as per your requirements.

◆ Exit the editing tool. When you do this, the file /usr/src/linux/.config is created. The /usr/src/linux/.config file contains the configuring options for the kernel.

Building the Kernel

Next, you need to build the kernel. The steps to build the kernel are as follows:

◆ Select the modules to enable and then generate the dependency files. The command to generate the dependency files is as follows

```
make dep clean
```

◆ Create the kernel image. If you want the image file to be compressed using gzip, type the following command:

```
make zImage
```

Otherwise, if you want the image file be compressed by using bzip2, execute the following command:

```
make bzImage
```

◆ Install kernel modules. To do this, you need to execute the following command:

```
make modules modules_install
```

After you perform these steps, you can install the kernel. To install the kernel, perform the following steps:

◆ Rename the `zImage` and `bzImage` to `vmlinuz<version>`. Move this file to the root partition. Usually, the kernel is stored in the `/boot` directory.

◆ Add the new kernel to the boot manager.

◆ Create a bootable recovery disk.

 NOTE

The kernel package enables you to automate the kernel building process. After you have installed the kernel package, you need to execute this command:

```
make -kpkg kernel_image
```

The next section discusses the kernel security.

Recompiling Kernel

You might need to recompile kernel after you've added some hardware to your Linux system. You also should recompile your kernel after the installation process for your Linux system is complete.

Another reason to modify the kernel is to customize some of its data structures for your system. Some modifications that you need to perform are increasing the number of processes the kernel can support and modifying the size of certain buffers. To modify the kernel, you need the kernel source code. You can obtain the source code from various sites on the Internet. For users who installed Linux from CD-ROM, the source code can be found as part of the distribution.

Some guidelines to remember while recompiling the kernel are as follows:

◆ You should check the directory where the kernel will be installed. Some sources install kernel to directories given by the kernel version and not to the linux directory. You can check the directory where the kernel will be installed by issuing the following command:

```
tar -txvf source_filename
```

The preceding command will list all the files and directories that are contained in source_filename. If they are to be installed into a directory other than Linux, you must make a symbolic link, called linux, in the /usr/src directory. This link should point to the directory containing the new source.

◆ Never delete the old source. You might need it to recompile your old kernel version if the new version doesn't work properly.

Kernel Security

You can secure kernel by configuring various options during the kernel configuration process. Some of these options are discussed here:

◆ **CONFIG_FIREWALL.** This option should be set if you intend to run any firewall on your Linux computer. If the computer will be used just as a client computer, you should specify the no value. If you specify the yes value here, you'll get a packet filter. A packet filter can block network traffic based on type, origin, and destination.

- ◆ **CONFIG_IP_FORWARD.** This option effectively makes your computer a router. This option is enabled if you specify the yes value. IP forwarding is not secure if your computer is on a network because the data will be directly forwarded from one computer to another. If enabled, this option might subvert the firewall on your network.

- ◆ **CONFIG_SYN_COOKIES.** This option, if enabled, allows a legitimate user to connect by using a challenge protocol known as SYN cookies. TCP/IP networking is vulnerable to an attack known as SYN flooding. SYN flooding prevents legitimate remote users from connecting to your computer during a session.

- ◆ **CONFIG_IP_FIREWALL.** This option enables you to filter packets for the local network. You need to assign the value yes to this option to be able to use IP masquerading, IP packet logging and accounting, and IP transparent proxying.

- ◆ **CONFIG_IP_TRANSPARENT_PROXY.** This option enables you to redirect local network traffic.

- ◆ **CONFIG_NCPFS_PACKET_SIGNING.** This option enables you to secure packets.

- ◆ **CONFIG_IP_FIREWALL_NETLINK.** This option enables you to use the ipchains tool to copy packets reaching the Linux firewall to optional user space monitoring software. The monitoring software then detects attacks and takes appropriate actions.

- ◆ **CONFIG_FILTER.** This option enables programs to attach a filter to a socket. This will enable the kernel to determine whether it should allow or deny data through the socket.

Applying Kernel Patches

Incremental upgrades of the kernel are available as *patches*. Patches are basically text files containing a list of differences between two versions of kernels. A kernel patch file contains the differences between all files in one version of the kernel to the next. The benefit of using patches is that they reduce download time and space.

To apply a patch, you can use the patch command. The patch command expects a file as a parameter to which the patch should be applied.

The patch Command

The `patch` command is used to apply a different file to an original file. The syntax of the patch command is shown here:

```
patch [options] [originalfile [patchfile]]
```

The `patch` command takes a patch file called `patchfile`, which contains a list of differences. The differences in the listing are applied to one or more original files, producing the patched versions. The patch file contains the file names that need to be patched. You also can specify the files to be patched on the command line. However, only one file can be specified at a time.

For example, to patch `original_file` with `patch_file`, use the following command:

```
patch original_file patch_file
```

The preceding command applies the `patch_file` patch to `original_file`. After the command, a file called `original_file.orig` is created as a backup of the original file. Before proceeding further, I'll discuss the patch command in detail.

The various options of the `patch` command are listed here:

◆ **-b or –backup.** This option specifies that, during the patch operation, the original should be backed up. When you backup a non-existent file, an empty and unreadable backup file is created.

◆ **—backup-if-mismatch.** This option instructs the `patch` command to back up a file if the patch does not match the file exactly. This is the default, unless `patch` conforms to POSIX.

◆ **—no-backup-if-mismatch.** This option instructs the `patch` command to not back up a file if the patch does not match the file exactly. This is the default if `patch` conforms to POSIX.

◆ **-B pref or —prefix=pref.** This option specifies the prefix `pref` to be added to a file name when generating its simple backup.

◆ **—binary.** This option instructs the `patch` command to read and write all files in binary mode, except for standard output and `/dev/tty`.

◆ **-d dir or —directory=dir.** This option instructs the `patch` command to change to the directory `dir` immediately.

◆ **-D define or —ifdef=define.** This option uses the `#ifdef ... #endif` construct to mark changes.

◆ **—dry-run.** This option prints the results of applying the patches, without actually changing any files.

◆ **-e or –ed.** This option interprets the patch file as an ed script. ed is a text editor utility.

◆ **-E or —remove-empty-files.** This option deletes the empty files and directories.

◆ **-g num or —get=num.** This option determines the action to be taken for RCS and SCCS controlled files. In addition, it also controls the patch's actions when a file is read-only and matches the default version.

◆ **-i patchfile or —input=patchfile.** This option reads the patch from patchfile.

◆ **-l or —ignore-whitespace.** This option matches the patterns loosely, ignoring the whitespaces.

Another drawback is that you need to apply all the patches to upgrade. For example, to upgrade a kernel version that is three versions behind the required version, you need to obtain and apply three patches. It is often much easier and quicker to obtain the entire kernel source again than it is to upgrade.

Summary

In this chapter, we looked at the various aspects of kernel. Kernel is the core of the Linux operating system and provides the mechanism for interaction between the OS and the underlying hardware. The kernel source code is freely available. You can modify and customize the kernel to meet your requirements. Modules provide the various functionalities for kernel. You can add or remove modules depending on your need. In this chapter, I discussed the procedure for upgrading and building kernel. I also discussed the patches in detail. Patches are incremental upgrades of the kernel.

Check Your Understanding

Multiple Choice Questions

1. What is the command to enable or disable a module?

   a. patch

   b. modprobe

   c. modAdd

   d. moduleprobe

2. Arrange the following steps involved in making changes to the kernel in the proper sequence.

   a. Build or compile the kernel.

   b. Edit the kernel.

   c. Install the kernel.

3. What is the command to generate the dependency files?

4. Which of the following configuration options for kernel enable you to effectively make your computer a router?

   a. CONFIG_IP_FORWARD

   b. CONFIG_FIREWALL

   c. CONFIG_SYN_COOKIES

   d. CONFIG_IP_FIREWALL

5. Which option enables you to configure your Linux box as a packet filter firewall for a local TCP/IP based network?

   a. CONFIG_IP_FORWARD

   b. CONFIG_FIREWALL

   c. CONFIG_SYN_COOKIES

   d. CONFIG_IP_FIREWALL

Short Questions

1. Briefly discuss the following kernel configuration options:

   ◆ `CONFIG_FIREWALL`

   ◆ `CONFIG_IP_FORWARD`

   ◆ `CONFIG_SYN_COOKIES`

   ◆ `CONFIG_SYN_COOKIES`

2. Discuss the following subdirectories of the `/usr/src/linux` directory.

   ◆ `arch`

   ◆ `include`

   ◆ `mm`

   ◆ `drivers`

   ◆ `fs`

   ◆ `scripts`

Answers

Multiple Choice Answers

1. `modprobe` is the command to enable or disable a module.

2. The correct sequence for making changes to the kernel is as follows:

   b. Edit the kernel.

   a. Build or compile the kernel.

   c. Install the kernel.

3. The command to generate the dependency files:

   ```
   make dep clean
   ```

4. The option to enable you to effectively make your computer a router is `CONFIG_IP_FORWARD`.

5. The option to enable you to configure your Linux box as a packet filter firewall for a local TCP/IP-based network is `CONFIG_IP_FIREWALL`.

Short Answers

1. The kernel configuration options are explained here:
   - ◆ **CONFIG_FIREWALL.** This option should be set if you intend to run any firewall on your Linux computer. If the computer will be used only as a client computer, you should specify the no value.
   - ◆ **CONFIG_IP_FORWARD.** This option effectively makes your computer a router. This option is enabled if you specify the yes value. IP forwarding is not secure if your computer is on a network because the data will be directly forwarded from one computer to another.
   - ◆ **CONFIG_SYN_COOKIES.** This option, if enabled, allows a legitimate user to connect by using a challenge protocol known as SYN cookies. TCP/IP networking is vulnerable to an attack known as SYN flooding. SYN flooding prevents legitimate remote users from connecting to your computer during a session.

2. Descriptions of some of the subdirectories of /usr/src/linux directory are given here:
   - ◆ **arch.** This directory contains all of the architecture-specific kernel code. It has further subdirectories, one per supported architecture; for example, i386 and alpha.
   - ◆ **include.** This directory contains most of the include files needed to build the kernel code. Like the arch directory, it has various subdirectories.
   - ◆ **mm.** This directory contains the memory management code. In this directory, the architecture-specific memory management code is stored.
   - ◆ **drivers.** This directory stores the device drivers. Device drivers are an interface between the operating system and the hardware devices.
   - ◆ **fs.** This directory stores the file system code. The subdirectories within this directory represent a supported file system.
   - ◆ **scripts.** This directory contains the scripts that are used when configuring the kernel.

Chapter 12

System Logs

In the aftermath of an attack, nothing can prove to be more revealing than a comprehensive log accounting the complete chronology and description of the attack. This information is recorded and updated regularly in the system logs.

Logs are an efficient and easy way to track down past intruders and manage your system so that these "break-ins" are not repeated. They provide accountability and traces that would keep any future hacker from remaining anonymous. Apart from assisting in tracking down intruders, logs also have intrinsic functions, such as keeping track of jobs run regularly on the system, backups, booting information, and other important tasks.

As major archives of sensitive data, these logs automatically are the prime targets of any intelligent hacker who wants to cover his trail of intrusion in the system. Assuming that any hacker would not consider meddling with these files would be underestimating the hacker's ability, which in recent times has showed great acumen for innovative damage and stealth.

The greatest challenge faced by any system administrator is the segregation of information in the logs and deciding which information is important enough to be logged and which is to be discarded. The system administrator should take great care that these files are inaccessible to the majority of users and remain untraceable.

What Are Log Files?

Log files are activity recorders. Every operation that is done in a computer, irrespective of whether it was successful or resulted in an error, is recorded in a log. This sequential recording is known as *logging*.

In any computer, the operations or activities can be general system activities or service specific. Similarly, logs can be general system logs or service specific logs. A few uses of logs are listed here:

- ◆ Help in intrusion detection
- ◆ Create demographic statistical reports
- ◆ Create system summary reports

The log files in any Linux system reside in various directories. By default, most important log files are stored in the /var/log directory. If some packages were customized during installation time, the logs files also may be present in other directories. The access to all important system logs is reserved with the system administrator unless indicated otherwise. All user logs are modifiable by the owner of the respective log and by the super user. In addition, service-specific logs can be written or appended by respective service daemons.

Important Log Files

As already discussed, log files can be general activity logs or service-specific logs. A few important log files that reside in your Linux system and are important from the network security aspect are discussed in detail in the subsequent sections:

- ◆ System Logs
- ◆ Kernel Logs
- ◆ Apache Web Server Logs

System logging in a Linux box is done by the *system logging daemon* (syslogd) and *kernel logging daemon* (klogd). The log configuration, which includes the parameters and the basic rules for logging, is stored in the /etc/syslog.conf file. All log messages are typically redirected and stored in the /var/log directory. Some of the common systems log files in Linux are listed here:

- ◆ **boot.log.** This file contains all messages and relays generated for the services starting and stopping during system startup and shutdown, respectively.
- ◆ **cron.** This file is used to store messages generated by the cron daemon. We can see the start time of each job as well as information about any errors that may have occurred during execution of the job.

NOTE

Cron jobs are specific processes that are scheduled to run at regular intervals in the system.

- **error_log.** This file contains information about error messages generated by processes running in the system.
- **dmesg.** This file contains messages that are generated during system startup regarding hardware initialization. It is particularly useful for debugging hardware failures.
- **maillog.** This file records the messages and activities of the sendmail daemon.

 NOTE

Sendmail daemon is a service used to send and receive e-mail messages. This service has been discussed in greater detail in Chapter 9, "Other Network Servers."

- **messages.** This file stores the messages generated by the various daemon processes in the system, such as apmd and xinetd.
- **secure.** This file is one of the most important log files that can aid you in cracking down attackers on your system. It contains all data about remote hosts logged into your system, including attempts to log into your system. Any discrepancy in the secure file indicates a breach in security.
- **xferlog.** This file stores the files that have been transferred, uploaded, or downloaded to and from your ftp server.
- **wtmp.** This file contains information about those who are currently logged on to your system and what each one of them is doing.
- **lastlog.** This file contains the latest login time and date for each user logged on to your system.

In addition to these files, there are other logs present in the system; these also are stored in the /var/log directory. A few of them are listed here:

- **httpd.** All messages from Apache are stored in this file. This file is created only if Apache Web server is installed in your system.
- **news.** Messages from Internet news service are stored in this file.
- **samba or log.smb.** The messages that are generated by the SAMBA server are stored in this file.

> **NOTE**
>
> SAMBA is a server that enables Linux computers to masquerade as a Windows computer and access all shared files and printers using the SMB protocol. SAMBA has been discussed in greater detail in Chapter 9, "Other Network Servers."

- **uucp.** Status messages from the UNIX-to-UNIX copy protocol daemon are stored in this file.

General System Logs

General system logs mainly constitute the System activity logs and the Kernel logs. Both these logs are managed by two daemons that come with the `sysklogd` package. The two daemons have been listed below:

- `syslogd`
- `klogd`

Almost all log files in the `/var/log` directory are maintained and updated by `syslogd`. The function of `syslogd` is to accept messages from other processes, sort them by their type and priority, and write the information to the respective log file.

`sysklogd` provides the following advantages:

- Provides a centralized logging facility instead of a distributed logging system in which each program writes the log independently.
- Saves much needed system resources and also provides ease of use because anyone can configure `syslogd` according to their own priorities.
- Logs can be maintained on remote computers. This feature is particularly handy for system administrators who are handling a vast network of computers. It also provides a major security advantage because if any hacker breaks into a system, he cannot change or delete any log files because the log files are not stored in the same computer.

Besides handling messages generated locally within a system, the `syslog` daemon also can accept messages from other computers connected to the system via LAN or the Internet.

sysklogd Installation

Before you begin installation, it is important to check for an already installed version of `sysklogd`. To verify this, type the following command at the command prompt:

```
# rpm -q sysklogd
```

If it is not installed, you can download the `sysklogd` rpm file for your Linux distribution from either **www.rpmfind.net** or from the home site of your Linux distribution.

 TIP

The `syslog` daemon and the `klog` daemon are automatically started during system boot up if they have been installed from the `/etc/init.d/syslog` script.

The `syslog` script also can be executed manually to perform operations, such as starting, stopping, restarting, or finding out the status manually. The command to do this is as follows:

```
/etc/rc.d/init.d/syslog start ¦ stop¦ restart ¦ status
```

Configuring Daemons

Each system has its own needs and requirements. As a result, the levels and priorities of logging might vary from system to system. By default, the `syslog` daemon works according to the configuration file `/etc/syslog.conf`. However, this file can be edited to suit specific requirements.

To edit the `syslog.conf` file, you need to be logged in as the superuser. Therefore, if you are already logged into the system, type **su** to become the root user. Then open the configuration file `/etc/syslog.conf` using any text editor, such as pico or vi.

To view the entire set of commands related to editing of the `syslog.conf` file, type the following command:

```
man sysklogd
```

The `sysklogd` manual will be displayed on the screen.

To write to the `syslog.conf` file, you will have to understand and then appropriately modify two fields:

◆ **The `selector` field.** Defines which information is to be logged.

◆ **The `action` field.** Defines where that information is to be logged.

The selector Field

The `selector` field specifies the type and priority of the message to be logged as well as other characteristics that might pertain to selective logging. Therefore, the selector field must contain at least one of the two sub-fields listed here:

◆ The message type

◆ The message priority

Message Type

The message type is also called a *facility* and can be one of the following:

◆ **kern.** This facility tracks kernel messages.

◆ **cron.** This is a daemon, which can be used to schedule jobs to be run at specific time periods. The cron facility in the selector field tracks messages from the cron system.

◆ **daemon.** This facility is used to track messages from additional system daemons.

◆ **auth.** This facility is used to track authorization messages from the system. It is essentially a security feature that can track every program that uses the Linux authentication scheme.

◆ **lpr.** This facility is used to track printer system (`lpd`) messages.

◆ **authpriv.** This is a security feature that tracks security and authorization messages.

◆ **mail.** This is used to track all mail system messages.

◆ **news.** This is used to track the Internet news service messages.

◆ **uucp.** This tracks UNIX-to-UNIX copy protocol messages.

Message Priority

This part of the field is not required unless you want to segregate the output from the other messages. It proves useful in situations where a large number of messages are generated in the system.

The types of priority parameters are as follows:

◆ **alert.** This is used to indicate a serious malfunction, which requires immediate attention by the user.

◆ **crit.** This indicates a fatal problem and demands quick action.

◆ **debug.** This provides debugging and the output information of the debugging on the processes currently running.

◆ **emerg.** This indicates an emergency condition.

◆ **err.** These messages consist of errors committed on the system; typically, STDERR.

◆ **info.** This provides information (text messages) about any program that you specify.

◆ **notice.** This is used to generate standard messages.

◆ **warning.** This provides standard warning messages if a function could not be completed.

The action Field

The `action` field specifies the task that the system logging should do with the information gathered by the first field, the `message type`. The output target can be anything from a file to a user message. The various choices are as follows:

◆ **To a file.** The target name contains the target filename; for example, `/var/log/kern.log`.

◆ **To the console.** The target contains `/dev/console`.

◆ **Through targeted pipes.** The target is a named pipe that can be created using the `mkfifo` command; for example, `./file1 > /var/log/output.log`.

◆ **To a remote system.** The target contains the ID of a remote system, such as a dedicated logserver; for example, `@loghost`.

◆ **To a group or to users.** The target contains the UID, GID, or a * (indicates that the message to be sent to all the users).

Some Examples of Writing to syslog.conf

Below is an example of the `syslog.conf`.

In the following listing, lines beginning with a # indicate a comment.

```
# Log all kernel messages to a kernel log file
kern.*                          /var/log/kernlog
#Log all mail authpriv messages to the screen
authpriv.*              /dev/console
#log all cron messages to a log file
cron.*                          /var/log/cron
#Emergency messages are sent to all plus they are logged on another system
*.emerg                 *
# Till now all these messages did not have a priority field
#In case of news or mail errors
news.=crit              /var/log/newscrit.log
news.=err               /var/log/newserr.log
mail.=crit              /var/log/mailcrit.log
mail.=err               /var/log/mailer.log
#(message type and priority)            (target file or action field)
```

In the preceding listing, notice that the lines containing the rules for logging have two fields, the `selector` and the `action` field, which are separated by colons.

Redirecting Log Messages to a Dedicated Loghost or Logserver

To send messages to a loghost or a logserver, simply replace the `action` field with the symbol @ and the identifier or name of the loghost. A sample is given here:

```
#Log anything (except mail) of level info or higher
#Don't log private authentication messages
*.info;mail.none;news.none;authpriv.none;cron.none    @loghost

#The authpriv file has reserved access rights
authpriv.*          @loghost

#log all mail and news messages to the loghost in one place
mail.*;news.*           @loghost
```

```
#log all kernel messages to the loghost
kern.*                  @loghost
```

Using the preceding configuration will enable the syslogd of one system to export its log messages to another loghost or remote system for better security. After the logs are sent, they will be handled by the system-logging daemon, which is running on the target system.

This also provides easy portability and transfer of the loghost. If you ever want to change the loghost, simply replace the loghost alias with the name of the new loghost system instead of editing each computer's syslog.conf individually.

Apache Server Logs

Apache Web server logs are written by the httpd daemon. The default directory for storing apache logs is /var/log/httpd/apache. Two important logs files are generated by Apache:

- ◆ access_log
- ◆ error_log

access_log

This file stores the general access activity handled by the Apache server. The apache configuration file provides several directives and sections that can be modified to store more or less information in the log files. The default columns in a particular row of the access_log file contain the following information:

- ◆ **Visitor's IP address.** This is the IP address of the client machine that made a request to the browser.
- ◆ **Time and date of event.** This column specifies the time and date of the event. The time and date mentioned in the log is according to the system clock settings of the server.
- ◆ **Commands and requests.** This column logs the type of request, the document that was requested, and the content type header that was sent by the server.
- ◆ **Status code.** This is the result code for the logged event. The server according to the result of the event generates these codes. Result codes have been discussed in detail later in the chapter.

A typical example of an apache access log file is listed here. This is only part of the file:

```
203.94.248.151 - - [01/Apr/2002:00:56:53 -0600] "GET / HTTP/1.1" 200 -
203.94.248.151 - - [01/Apr/2002:00:56:54 -0600] "GET /pc_header.css HTTP/1.1" 200 -
203.94.248.151 - - [01/Apr/2002:00:56:55 -0600] "GET /fws.gif HTTP/1.1" 200 -
203.94.248.151 - - [01/Apr/2002:00:56:56 -0600] "GET /pc_header.css HTTP/1.1" 304 -
203.94.248.151 - - [01/Apr/2002:00:56:57 -0600] "GET /fws1.gif HTTP/1.1" 203
203.94.248.151 - - [01/Apr/2002:00:56:58 -0600] "GET /pc_header.css HTTP/1.1" 304 -
203.94.248.151 - - [01/Apr/2002:00:56:59 -0600] "GET /fws.gif2 HTTP/1.1" 204
203.94.248.151 - - [01/Apr/2002:00:57:00 -0600] "GET /pc_header.css HTTP/1.1" 303 -
203.94.248.151 - - [01/Apr/2002:00:57:01 -0600] "GET /fws1.gif HTTP/1.1" 303
203.94.248.151 - - [01/Apr/2002:00:57:02 -0600] "GET /pc_header.css HTTP/1.1" 303 -
203.94.248.151 - - [01/Apr/2002:00:57:03 -0600] "GET /fws3.gif HTTP/1.1" 303
203.94.248.151 - - [01/Apr/2002:00:57:04 -0600] "GET /pc_header.css HTTP/1.1" 303 -
203.94.248.151 - - [01/Apr/2002:00:57:05 -0600] "GET /fws4.gif HTTP/1.1" 300
203.94.248.151 - - [01/Apr/2002:00:57:05 -0600] "GET /pc_header.css
```

In the preceding extract, you can see that the output of the access_log file is composed of the fields discussed previously. If you break up and analyze a particular row in the preceding log file, you can find out a lot of detail about the system, such as those listed here:

```
203.94.248.151 - - [01/Apr/2002:00:56:53 -0600] "GET / HTTP/1.1" 304 -
203.94.248.151              =  the visitor's IP address
01/Apr/2002:00:56:53 -0600 =  time and date of event
GET / HTTP/1.1             =  the command or request
304                         =  the status code
```

As discussed earlier, the apache server generates status codes and logs them into the access_log file. A complete list of http status codes follows:

◆ **200.** Indicates a successful operation.

◆ **201.** Indicates that a POST command was issued and completed successfully.

◆ **202.** Indicates that the server accepted the visitor's command.

◆ **203.** Indicates that the server could only partially satisfy the client's request.

◆ **204.** Indicates that the client's request was accepted but the server could not return any data.

- ◆ **300.** Indicates that the client's requested data had been moved recently.
- ◆ **301.** Indicates that the client's requested data was found at an alternate URL.
- ◆ **302.** Indicates that the server suggested an alternate location for the client's requested data.
- ◆ **303.** Indicates that the server could not modify the data concerned.
- ◆ **400.** Indicates a flawed request that could not be processed.
- ◆ **401.** Indicates an attempt by the client to access data that he was not authorized to have.
- ◆ **402.** Indicates that a payment process has been set up.
- ◆ **403.** Indicates that the access is altogether forbidden.
- ◆ **404.** Indicates that the document was not found at the requested location.
- ◆ **500.** Indicates that an internal server error and the server could not recover.
- ◆ **501.** Indicates that the client requested an action, which the server does not support.
- ◆ **502.** Indicates a server overload.
- ◆ **503.** Indicates that `httpd` was waiting for another service to return information, but the external application did not return any data.

Access logs can play an important role in data security. An administrator can extract much useful information about a Web server from these logs and make appropriate changes in the server to correct issues. For example, by analyzing access logs, an administrator can find out when all pages of a Web site were indexed by search engines. If the logs show access to pages that were not meant for public use, an administrator can add relevant directives in the `robots.txt` file. This file is present in the root directory of every Web site and most search engine and Web crawlers follow the guidelines mentioned in this file. Apache access logs also can be used to generate statistical reports of visitors; for example, a script that can analyze popular user trends, most visited pages, never accessed pages, etc. Such reports are useful for Web masters and can help fix many logical errors in their Web sites.

error_log

The `error_log` file stores all activities handled by the Apache server which resulted in error responses. These errors could be due to several reasons. A few commonly encountered errors are shown here:

◆ Buggy scripts that were executed by Web site visitors

◆ Links to missing files, also known as *broken links*

◆ Internal server errors that could occur due to erroneous modules

◆ Access denied errors that could be due to links to files that the apache daemon cannot read or furnish

The default error logs for Apache contain the following fields:

◆ **Date and time.** This is the time and date of the host server, when this error occurred.

◆ **Type of message.** This column specifies the type of error that was generated; for example, a message could be a notice or error.

◆ **Reason for this error.** This is generally a phrase or sentence that explains the cause of the error.

◆ **Service name.** This is the name of the service that resulted in the error. This is generally Apache followed by the version number or the daemon name that halted the proceedings of this activity and generated an error response.

◆ **Apache response.** This column specifies the corrective action or the reciprocated response that was performed by the Web server.

An extract from an Apache log can be seen in the following example:

```
[Fri May 17 19:53:55 2002] [alert] mod_unique_id: unable to gethostbyname("big.big-
gerlinux.com")
[Fri May 17 20:00:45 2002] [notice] Apache/1.3.24 (UNIX) configured — resuming
normal operations
[Fri May 17 20:08:42 2002] [error] [client 272.13.68.143] user superbeast: authen-
tication failure for "/": password mismatch
[Sat May 18 16:07:49 2002] [notice] SIGHUP received.  Attempting to restart
[Sat May 18 16:07:50 2002] [notice] Apache/1.3.24 (UNIX) configured — resuming
normal operations
[Tue May 21 21:12:37 2002] [crit] (98)Address already in use: make_sock: could not
bind to port 80
```

```
[Tue May 21 21:18:30 2002] [crit] (98)Address already in use: make_sock: could not
bind to port 80
```

I will pick a particular row in the error log to discuss each of the columns.

```
[Fri May 17 20:00:45 2002] [notice] Apache/1.3.24 (UNIX) configured — resuming
normal operations
```

In the preceding row,

- ◆ `[Fri May 17 20:00:45 2002]` is the date when the event occurred.
- ◆ `[notice]` is the message type that Apache generated.
- ◆ `Apache/1.3.24 (UNIX) configured` is the name of the service that produced a response.
- ◆ `Resuming normal operations` is the response that was taken by Apache.

Configuring Apache Logs

Apache logs can be configured to store selective information. This feature can be used to remove unnecessary information from logs or produce more detailed log files. The Apache server provides the `LogFormat` directive for this purpose, and it can be specified in the main configuration file `/etc/httpd/conf/httpd.conf`.

The following parameters can be used with the `LogFormat` Directive:

- ◆ **%b.** This adds number of bytes, which were sent as a result of a request. This size does not include the size of headers.
- ◆ **%f.** This adds a column that stores the filename, which was requested.
- ◆ **%h.** This specifies that the client computer's address should be stored in each request row.
- ◆ **%l.** This is used if the server uses the `inetd` service. It records the username in a column with every row in the log file.
- ◆ **%P.** This adds the Process ID of an external service, if it was used to extract any information for the client.
- ◆ **%p.** This adds the port number to which Apache server directed the response.
- ◆ **%r.** This records the first row of the client's request.
- ◆ **%s.** This stores the status code of the client's request

- ◆ **%t.** This stores the time when the request was made according to the server system clock.

- ◆ **%T.** This stores the response time of the server to complete a request.

- ◆ **%u.** This stores the remote username of the client computer when the auth module is used.

- ◆ **%U.** This records the original URL that was requested by a client computer. The parameter is important when URL mapping is implemented in the Apache Web server.

- ◆ **%v.** This adds the virtual host name that was requested for information.

The LogFormat directive can be used in the main section of the Apache configuration file or can also be used inside a <VIRTUALHOST> </VIRTUALHOST> section to record all transactions for a particular host.

sendmail Logs

Sendmail service is used to handle e-mails in a Linux system. I have already discussed this service in great detail in Chapter 9. This service also generates log data regularly in a log file called maillog that can be found in the default log directory /var/log. All the sendmail logging is done according to the directives set in the sendmail's main configuration file, sendmail.cf. This file can be modified to change the current level of logging by configuring sendmail on the system. It is preferable, however, to let the program keep its default values because it provides adequate coverage of mail and error messages.

Whenever sendmail is started, log entries, such as those listed here, are generated and entered into the /var/log/maillog file:

```
Jun  3 20:39:06 localhost sendmail[853]: alias database /etc/aliases rebuilt by
root
Jun  3 20:39:06 localhost sendmail[853]: /etc/aliases: 40 aliases, longest 10
bytes, 395
```

Log Filtering

Log filtering is a process that is used to remove junk data from a log file. Such junk data can come because of inadvertent recursive operation, hack attempts, or improperly configured cron jobs. Such accidents can cause log files to become extremely large with useless data. This data can cover a majority portion in log files and can significantly affect statistics that are extracted from these logs.

Log filtering can be done on the basis of the following criteria:

◆ **Pattern matching.** This involves removal of rows from a log that have a common pattern. An example could be too many users with spurious IP addresses trying to access a particular non-existent file.

◆ **Time period based filtering.** This process involves removal of particular sets of records that were recorded in a particular time frame. For example, when some tests were being performed on the server, a lot of data might get recorded in the logs. This data is useless once the testing is complete. If an administrator knows the time frame of this period, such entries can be safely removed from the main logs.

◆ **Source based filtering.** Source based filtering is done by removing all log entries that originated from an identified client source. Such filtering is done generally after remote brute force attack attempts.

Tools for Managing Log Files

In a single computer or a very small network, the amount of log generated is mostly intrinsic, and therefore, very small in size. You won't have any problems handling the small quantity of logs; however, in a large network or in a Web server that is publicly accessible over the Internet, massive logs are generated because of heavy traffic to and from the system. Any adept system administrator should sort, backup, and rotate the logs regularly. There are various methods of log rotation; the one discussed in the following section is called `logrotate`.

logrotate

`logrotate` is a package that allows an administrator to manage log files on a system. The `logrotate` program can perform various functions of system logs such as those listed here:

◆ **Rotating log files.** This is a process in which log files are copied to a new location and a blank file is left in the original location. This process helps in dividing log files into smaller chunks.

◆ **Compressing log files.** This process involves compressing old log files that were copied during the rotate process. This compression saves disk space on servers, which is a limited resource.

◆ **Taking backup of log files.** This is a process that gathers all the logs from original locations or from the files that were created during the rotation phase. These files then are put together separately in a sequential format, which can be later used to restore original logs or be analyzed for attack pattern matching.

◆ **Exporting system logs.** This is a process of freeing disk space from the main server and storing the logs in cheaper backup mediums or those servers that have ample disk space. This process is a critical need and is a very good asset at times when the server crashes. Exported logs are not affected by any problems in the original server; therefore, to a certain extent they can be used to find the cause of the problem.

logrotate has been specially designed to facilitate the task of system administrators who manage systems related to a fairly large amount of traffic. *logrotation* is a critical process in administrating a Linux server because log files are ever growing in nature. Servers with high traffic activity can choke themselves if the log files become too large. In addition, for every periodic log analysis, it is better to analyze a log file that was created only during the fixed time period. Extracting period information from a single massive log file is a wasteful activity and can increase the load on the server unnecessarily.

Maintaining a single huge log file also has some other disadvantages that might not be easy to see. In a single huge file, every time the log is analyzed, the log file needs to be locked by the software. This means that the log-writing daemon will have no write/append access to the log for that period, which could mean loss of important information. If logs are rotated at regular time intervals, older logs can be analyzed safely while the log recording daemons can continue to write to fresh log files.

The logrotate package itself is very flexible and allows any chronology or parameter for execution. You can run logrotate as a daily, weekly, or monthly job or specify other parameters as log file sizes for its execution. logrotate is run according to a user-specified configuration file. This file can be modified to suit any particular purposes of the user.

The logrotate configuration file

Each time `logrotate` is run, the program reads its options from a configuration file, which is created and modified by the user. Following is a typical `logrotate` configuration file:

```
errors webmaster@localnetwork.net
            compress
/var/log/messages {
            rotate 3
            daily
            notifempty
postrotate
                /sbin/kill -9 syslogd
            endscript
}
```

The first two lines are the global parameters for the configuration file. They specify that all error message logs are to be mailed to `webmaster@localnetwork.net` and that all the logs should be compressed for export.

The rest of the lines are a set of rules for the respective log file; in this case, the `/var/messages` file. These rules are written using a directive based language.

The section begins with the filename of the log file, and then lists all the lines based upon a set of directives enclosed within an opening brace({) and a closing brace (}). Consider this:

```
/var/log/messages { # work on the log file /var/log/messages
            rotate 3 # rotate the log file 3 times before removal
            daily     # rotate the log file daily
            notifempty # do not rotate the log file if it is empty
            postrotate  # indicates that the file has been rotated and do the
following things..
                /sbin/kill -9 syslogd # run after rotation basically kill the
syslog daemon
            endscript #  indicates end of script
} # closing brace
```

A list of important logrotate configuration file directives is as follows:

- ◆ **compress.** This keyword, if present in a set, tells the logrotate program that the old log file is to be compressed using gzip.

- ◆ **nocompress.** This keyword indicates to logrorate that the final log files need not be compressed

- ◆ **create mode owner group.** When logrotate rotates an old log file, it creates a new one in its place. The create command is used to specify the new file's mode, owner, or group rights.

- ◆ **nocreate.** This directive is used to specify that logrotate should not create a new log file.

- ◆ **daily.** The daily directive is used to specify that logrotate should rotate the logs daily.

- ◆ **weekly.** The weekly directive specifies that logrotate should rotate the logs weekly.

- ◆ **monthly.** The monthly directive specifies that logrotate should rotate the logs monthly.

- ◆ **errors <e-mail address>.** This directive is used to indicate that all error logs should be sent to the specified e-mail address.

- ◆ **mail <e-mail address>.** This directive is used to specify the e-mail address to which logrotate will mail the final files (after rotation and compression).

- ◆ **nomail.** This directive is used to indicate that logrotate need not mail the final files anywhere.

- ◆ **ifempty.** This directive is used to indicate that logrotate should rotate the specified log files even if they are empty.

- ◆ **notifempty.** This directive is used to indicate that logrotate should not rotate the specified log file if it is empty.

- ◆ **noolddir.** This directive is used to indicate that logrotate should rotate the log file in the same old directory where they are currently present.

- ◆ **olddir <directory>.** This directive is used to declare that logrotate should move the rotated log files into the specified directory.

- ◆ **rotate n.** This directive is used to specify the number of times logrotate should rotate the specified file before mailing or removing it.

◆ **size [size Mb/Kb].** This directive is used to specify the maximum permissible limit for the size of the file specified before `logrotate` should rotate it. The value can be expressed in megabytes or kilobytes.

◆ **endscript.** This directive is used to declare the end of a particular section for a specified log file in the configuration file.

The `logrotate` program is a vital package that must be installed on every Linux server that has significant traffic activity. Once the `logrotate` configuration is complete, the program can be used in two ways:

◆ **Manual execution.** Manual execution has only one advantage that comes into play when the activity on the server is exceptionally low or high. The administrator can manually execute the program as per the requirements of the server. But when the server activity is normal, this can become a difficult option because manual operation would be required each time, even if the job can be easily automated.

◆ **Automatic execution as a cron job.** This form of operation should be preferred in normal circumstances. Automating a logrotation process can be of great help to the administrator because the administrator does not have to do the job manually. On a single server this might not seem like much, but with a data center that manages many servers at a time, this can be a crucial cost-cutting and security-enhancing factor.

Summary

In this chapter, you learned that log files are powerful assets that can help system administrators detect many problems in a server. You also learned that if logs are not managed properly, these very helpful assets can easily overwhelm you with data. When this overflow of data happens, it can cause many problems with the server apart from creating a possible security hole. Exceptionally large logs are difficult to analyze. "Lazy" administrators who ignore such large files can miss important information that can cause problems later. Automating the filtering of such logs solves the problem. These automated filters do the work for you, alerting you in real time with the information you need.

Check Your Understanding

Multiple Choice Questions

1. The default log file for `sendmail` is

    a. `/var/log/sendmail.log`

    b. `/etc/sendmail/sendmail.log`

    c. `/var/log/maillog`

    d. `/var/sendmail/sendmail.log`

2. Which of the following is true for Apache error logs?

    a. After every entry in the Apache error log, Apache is either restarted or halted.

    b. Every error reported in the error log is caused by the Apache daemon.

    c. Every entry in the Apache error log contains an error code from 200 to 503, inclusively.

    d. Apache error log cannot be rotated using `logrotate`.

3. State which of these statements about `logrotate` are true:

    a. `logrotate` can change the default value for log files for most daemons in Linux.

    b. `logrotate` can compress log files after rotating them.

    c. `logrotate` cannot be used with kernel logs.

    d. `logrotate` should not store the backup files in the boot partition of Linux.

4. Which of these statements are true about FTP logs?

    a. If a client accesses an FTP server using the web browser by typing `ftp://ftp.sitename.com`, FTP logs are not generated for these transactions.

    b. There are no FTP logs generated for anonymous FTP downloads or uploads.

    c. FTP logs can be generated by the `syslogd` daemon.

5. Apache access logs store events that resulted in errors, along with the error code.

a. True

b. False

Short Questions

1. Write a brief description of the Apache error log.
2. Write a brief description of log filtering.

Answers

Multiple Choice Answers

1. The default log file for `sendmail` is `/var/logs/maillog`.
2. None.
3. b and d.
4. c.
5. Apache access logs store events that resulted in errors, along with the error code: True.

Short Answers

A. Apache error logs are used to store all the errors that occurred during any events that were handled by Apache. These error logs contain many fields including a field that tells the level of error. The other fields stored in the error logs are date/time, the reason for the error, the name of the service that caused the error, and Apache's response action to this error.

A. Log filtering is a process that removes data from log files. Log filtering is done on three criteria, such as pattern-based matches, time-based matches, and source-based matching.

Chapter 13

In the last few chapters, I discussed various aggressions that can be targeted against your online server, taking preventive measures, and hardening services in Linux to defend against such attacks. An equally important part of Linux security is data backup, which is an integral part of any security policy. If you have a very important piece of information in a document that you want to preserve at all costs, a logical solution would be to keep another copy of it! This is exactly what data backup is all about. *Data backups* are copies of original data that can be used later as a part of a disaster recovery operation. A good data backup arrangement can save an organization lots of time and money.

Overview

Data losses can occur for a number of reasons and not just due to network attacks. Here are a few possibilities:

- **Hardware failure.** Hardware devices, including your storage devices, are prone to failure, either due to manufacturing defects or irregular power supply. Such failures can cause data losses.
- **Unintentional data deletion.** Administrators or other privileged users or a system might inadvertently modify or delete critical data.
- **Erroneous software.** Wrongly configured software or buggy applications can cause data loss.
- **Natural disasters.** Natural disasters such as floods, earthquakes, and so on can cause damage to network centers and vis-à-vis the stored data.

Many reasons exist for backing up your data. These include the nature of the Linux operating system itself. Linux is a multiuser and multitasking operating system. Therefore, many system files can be open at any given moment and data is written to the disk every millisecond. In addition, Linux also maintains information about its current state and file systems. When the system comes to an unexpected halt, system files and tables can be lost from memory. Therefore, these files should be written to the disk frequently.

Data backups are possible in a variety of ways. An administrator should choose a backup plan according to the requirements of the organization. For example, an administrator in the computer lab of a computer institute wouldn't need to backup all the sample database, but he would need to back up uniform configuration files of different nodes so that he can reset computers to their initial stages if needed. Similarly, an administrator managing a Web hosting server would be required to make backups of not only the configuration files but also the home directories of the users, databases, and other related files.

Types of Backups

The backup should be taken at regular intervals. Obviously, the very purpose of the backup will be lost if you do not do them regularly. The interval at which you will make backups depends on your requirements. For example, if you use a Linux machine for your own purposes, you can make a backup when you feel it is important. If the system is used by many users, it should be decided when and where the backups will be made on a regular basis. Based on the requirements, backups are of two types:

- ◆ **Full backup.** This type of backup copies everything on your file system, including all files, to the backup media. It does not keep any record of past backups. The backup media required for full backups is usually equal to the total size of the file system.

- ◆ **Differential backup.** This type copies only those files that have been modified since the last full backup.

- ◆ **Incremental backup.** This type copies only the files that have been modified or created since the last full or incremental backup. This type of backup is advisable for most systems that have few users, constant Internet access for e-mail or newsgroups, and similar changes to file systems.

Backup Media

Similarly, you can choose from a variety of backup media. The media ranges from magnetic tapes to removable hard disks, from CD-ROM drives to WORM drives (write once, read many), and from cartridge systems to floppy disks. All of these backup media offer their own advantages. You can choose the one that is best suited to your requirements.

When you are connected on a network, the first and foremost backup medium that comes to mind is any another system on the network. You also can add another hard disk to your system and use it as the full backup.

The most common medium for backups is tape because it is low cost, easy to store, portable, and fast. However, its limitation is that you need a tape drive to be able to use a tape for taking backup. Alternatively, you can use a removable hard disk—for example, Iomega Bernoulli or ZIP drives. These disk platter systems, which are kept inside a protective cartridge, can be removed from the main system and stored in another location. Many removable cartridges can cost less than the tape cartridges. The cost of removable cartridges varies depending on the capacity, manufacturer, and technology.

Magneto-optical cartridge systems are 3.5-inch cartridge systems that fit into a small drive unit. These systems provide more security and some of them might even cost less than some tape drives. Magneto-optical cartridge systems have a potentially longer life. Some of the costlier but higher capacity systems approaching 2.4GB are also available these days.

The CD-ROM and WORM drives also are quite popular but cannot be reused and are only used for archival purposes. CDs are used for permanent storage of important files. They can hold up to 750MB of data. Finally, you also can use a floppy disk to back up small files. The drawback of using floppy disks is that the media is not reliable and has very small capacity. You need to handle floppy disks extremely carefully because they get corrupted very easily.

Automating Backups – Cron

In systems that support multiple users and where data changes frequently, you should schedule the backups after fixed intervals. This scheduling of repetitive tasks at a certain time can be done manually by an administrator by maintaining manual backup logs for future and history backups. The backup scheduling can be automated using the `cron` facilities to set the exact backup time.

The `cron` facilities in Linux place scheduling information in the system `crontab` file in the `/etc` directory, using the following format:

```
minute hour day month weekday command
```

The minute, hour, day, month, and weekday components of the preceding format can be assigned numerical values. For example, day can have values from 1 to 31. You also can use wildcards, such as *. Consider the following example:

```
00 15 u u u echo 'Time to make backup and log off'
```

The preceding statement will display the message, Time to make backup and log off, every day at 3 P.M. The content of a sample crontab file is given here:

```
SHELL=/bin/bash
PATH=/sbin:/bin:/usr/sbin:/usr/bin
MAILTO=root
HOME=/


# run-parts
01 * * * * root run-parts /etc/cron.hourly
02 4 * * * root run-parts /etc/cron.daily
22 4 * * 0 root run-parts /etc/cron.weekly
42 4 1 * * root run-parts /etc/cron.monthly
# sysstat
0 * * * 0,6 /usr/lib/sa/sa1 600 6 &
5 19 * * * /usr/lib/sa/sa2 -A &
```

Apart from the crontab file, Red Hat adds other subdirectories in the /etc directory. Some such subdirectories are listed here:

```
drwxr-xr-x    2 root     root          4096 Feb 27 21:45 cron.daily
drwxr-xr-x    2 root     root          4096 Feb 27 21:20 cron.hourly
drwxr-xr-x    2 root     root          4096 Aug  8  2000 cron.monthly
drwxr-xr-x    2 root     root          4096 Feb 27 21:24 cron.weekly
```

These directories contain executables that can be executed on a daily, hourly, monthly, or weekly basis. The directory name where the executables are placed suggests when it will be executed. For example, an executable placed in the /etc/cron.daily directory will be executed daily.

Backup Tools

Linux supports many tools to backup your data; each one has its advantages and disadvantages. These are noncommercial tools, which are available in any Linux distribution, and they include various command line tools, such as tar and cpio and text-based tools such as Amanda.

Non-Commercial Backup Tools

The following tools can either be downloaded freely from the Internet or are available by default with Linux:

◆ tar and gzip

◆ cpio

◆ AMANDA

◆ rsync

◆ Burt

The following sections elaborate on these tools.

tar

tar is a command used to save files and directories to an archive medium which can be recovered later. As the name indicates, tar (tape archiver) creates an archive file, which is a single large entity that holds many files within it. The syntax of the tar command is as follows:

```
tar switch modifiers files
```

In the preceding syntax, files are the files or the directories that you need to archive. You can archive files, directories, or an entire file system. The switch in the preceding syntax determines the way the tar reads or writes to the backup media. You can specify only one switch at a time. Table 13-1 explains the switches used with the tar command.

Table 13-1 tar Switches

Switch	Description
c	This switch creates a new archive file.
r	This switch is used to append to an existing archive.
t	This switch is used to list the content of an archive.
u	This switch adds files that are not already archived or modified.
x	This switch is used to extract content from an archive.

Modifiers in the tar command control the archive and how tar uses it. Table 13-2 explains the modifiers used with the tar command.

Table 13-2 tar Modifiers

Modifier	Description
A	This modifier suppresses the absolute file names.
b	This modifier specifies the blocking factor.
e	This modifier prevents files from splitting.
f	This modifier specifies that the argument is an archive file or a device.
F	This modifier is used to specify a filename for tar.
k	This modifier enables you to specify archive volume size in kilobytes.
l	This modifier displays an error message for unresolved links.
n	This modified indicates that the archive media is not a tape.
p	This modifier stores the permissions of files while archiving.
v	This modifier lists files in an archive.
w	This modifier waits for user inputs after displaying archive actions.
z	This modifier specifies the backup media that needs to be compressed with gzip.
j	This modifier specifies the backup media that needs to be compressed with bzip2.

In addition to the switch and modifiers, you can specify some options with the tar command. Table 13-3 explains the options used with the tar command.

Table 13-3 tar Options

Option	Description
—directory	Indicates the directory path to which the tar command should first switch before starting the backup.
—exclude	Allows you to specify the directories that should not be backed up by tar.
—label	Specifies some information about the backup set into the archive file itself.

I will now discuss some examples to help you understand the usage of the tar command. Consider the following command:

```
tar -cvpf /dev/tape /
```

The preceding command creates a new archive in the tape drive called /dev/tape and copies the entire root file system into it, provided the size of the file system is less than the tape's capacity. The switch and the modifiers specified create a new archive file, list the files while archiving, preserve file permissions, and allow you to specify the archive media device name.

The following command restores an entire file system from an archive:

```
tar -xvpf /dev/nst0 /
```

The preceding command restores all files because no specific file is indicated for restoring. If you want to restore the specific file /usr/moo1/myfile, issue the following command:

```
tar -xvpf /dev/nst0 /usr/moo1/myfile
```

The following command can perform a backup of your entire Linux system on to the /archive file system, excluding the /proc pseudo-file system, any mounted file systems in /mnt, the /archive file system, and Squid's rather large cache files (these files are not required to back up):

```
tar -cvpf /archive/backup-`date '+%d-%B-&Y'`.tar —directory / —exclude=mnt —
exclude=proc —exclude=/archive —exclude=var/spool/squid .
```

Apart from the familiar switch and modifiers, the preceding command specifies the name of the archive in which the current date is derived by enclosing the data command in two reverse quotes. .tar is the common naming convention for tar files. Notice how the —directory option is used to switch the current directory to /

before beginning to create the archive. The −exclude options tell tar not to back up the files and directories specified. Finally, the dot (.) character specifies that tar should back up everything in the current directory.

 NOTE

When backing up your file systems, you should not include the /proc pseudo-file system. The contents in /proc are not files but file-like links that point to kernel data structures. Therefore, backing up these is waste of the space in backup media.

If you want to specify a label for the backup set on a tape drive, you can use the −label option, as in the following command:

```
tar -cvpf /dev/tape −label="Backup created on `date '+%d-%B-&Y'`." −directory /
−exclude=mnt \
            −exclude=proc −exclude=var/spool/squid
```

When writing on tapes, most tapes require the blocking factor to be specified. The blocking factor determines the amount of data that will be written on the tape. As specified in Table 13-2, you can specify the blocking factor by using the b modifier, as in the following command:

```
tar -cvfb /dev tape 20 /www
```

The preceding command creates an archive of the /www directory in the tape drive with a blocking factor of 20. Maximum tapes have a blocking factor of 20. However, you can modify this value.

The tape you are using for archiving might not be large enough for holding the entire archive. In this case, you will have to specify the size of each tape by using the k modifier. This argument specifies the size of the tape in kilobytes. For example:

```
tar --c -v -b fk 20 -f /dev/nst0 -k 122880 /www
```

In the preceding example, the capacity of the tape drive is specified as 122880KB.

Using tar with gzip

In order to conserve space used by the archived file on the backup media, you can compress the archive by using the gzip command. The syntax of the gzip command is as follows:

```
gzip -9 archive-name.tar
```

In the preceding command, `archive-name.tar` is the name of the archive with the `.tar` extension. You also can compress the archive with the `tar` command itself by issuing the following command:

```
tar -zcvpf /archive/backup-`date '+%d-%B-%Y'`.tar.gz —directory / —exclude=mnt —
exclude=proc —exclude=var/spool/squid .
```

The preceding command creates the compressed archive because of the z modifier specified. The common naming convention for the compressed archives is `tar.gz`.

 NOTE

You should not use the z modifier when archiving to a tape because if data on one portion of the tape gets corrupted, you will lose your entire archive.

In order to decompress and extract the files from the compressed archive (compressed using the preceding command), you can use the following command:

```
tar -zxvpf /archive/backup-07-June-2002.tar.gz
```

The preceding command extracts all files contained in the compressed archive, preserving the original file permissions and ownership. If you don't want to extract all files contained in the archive, you can specify the files you want to restore, as in the following command:

```
tar -zxvpf /archive/backup-07-June-2002.tar.gz etc/profile usr/usr01
```

The preceding command restores the `etc/profile` and `usr/usr01` files from the archive.

Cpio

cpio enables you to copy files to and from a cpio archive. This command supports the following three modes:

◆ **Copy out mode.** In this mode, cpio creates an archive by reading files from standard input device. The archived files are written to the standard output device.

◆ **Copy in mode.** In this mode, cpio reads the files from an archive created by using copy out mode.

◆ **Pass mode.** In this mode, cpio copies files from one location to another. The files are read from a standard input. The files are written to a directory as specified in the directory argument.

The following sections discuss these modes in detail.

Copy Out Mode

Copy out mode is specified by using the -o option with the cpio command. The syntax of copy out mode is as follows:

```
cpio -o [ aABcLPvV ] [ -C bufsize ] [ -H header ] [ -O file [ -M message ] ]
```

Table 13-4 describes the options used with copy out mode.

Table 13-4 Options for Copy Out Mode

Option	Description
-a	This option is used specify the access time of archived files.
-A	This option is used to add files to existing archives.
-B	This file is used to set block sizes to 5120 bytes.
-c	This option writes the cpio header information in ASCII format.
-L	This option follows the symbolic links.
-v	This option enables verbose output.
-z	This option compresses the archive by using the gzip format.
-Z	This option compresses the archive by using a compressed format.
-C bufsize	This option sets the block size as specified by the bufsize parameter.
-H header	This option is used to write header information.
-O file	This option prints the output in a file specified by the file argument.
-M message	This option can be used to specify the messages that will be printed when the archive media changes or the end of an archive media is reached.

Consider an example to understand the usage of cpio -o. When standard input is directed through a pipe to cpio -o, it groups the files to direct (>) them to a single file (../myfile). The -c option ensures that the file will be portable to other machines (as would the -H option):

```
# ls ¦ cpio -oc > ../myfile
```

You also can use find, echo, cat, and so on, to pipe a list of names to cpio. You also can direct the output to a device instead of a file.

Copy In Mode

Copy in mode is specified by using the -i option with the cpio command. The syntax of this mode is as follows:

```
cpio -i [ bBcdfkmPrsStuvV6 ] [ -C bufsize ] [ -E file ] [ -H header ] [ -I file [
-M message ] ] [ -R id ] [ pattern ... ]
```

Some of the options used with -i are similar to the ones used with the -o option, except that here they are used to read from the archive. For example, the -z option is used to uncompress the file archive when specified with -i. Table 13-5 describes the other options used with copy in mode.

Table 13-5 Options for Copy In Mode

Option	Description
-b	Swaps the order of bytes within each word.
-d	Creates any intermediate directories as needed during restore.
-E file	Reads list of file names to extract from the archive from an input file (file).
-f	Restores all files except those matching the patterns given on the command line.
-I file	Uses the contents of the specified file (file) as the input for the archive.
-m	Retains modification times on files.
-r	Renames restored files interactively.
-s	Swaps bytes after reading data from the archive.
-S	Swaps words after reading data from the archive.
-t	Lists the contents of the archive (no files or directories are created).
-u	Copies unconditionally.
-6	Processes old-style cpio format archives.

In addition to the options described in Table 13-5, the -I option supports the patterns operand.

Consider an example to understand the usage of cpio -i. cpio -i can use the output file of cpio -o directed through a pipe with cat, as follows:

```
# cat myfile ¦ cpio -icd "direc/a1" "direc/c?"
```

Notice that Cpio extracts the files that match the patterns (direc/a1, direc/c?). The -d option creates directories and places the files in those directories.

Pass Mode

Pass mode is specified by using the -p option with the cpio command. The syntax of pass mode is shown here:

```
cpio -p [ adlLmPuvV ] [ -R id ] directory
```

Again, some of the options used with -p are similar to the ones used with the -o and -i options. Table 13-6 describes the other options used with pass mode.

Table 13-6 Options for Pass Mode

Option	Description
-d	This option creates directories to store files.
-l	This option creates links to the files.
-u	This option copies files without any condition.
-R id	This option sets the ownership to the files to a user identified by the id argument.

In addition to the options described in Table 13-6, the cpio -p also has the directory operand, which is the path name of an existing directory to be used as the destination directory for cpio -p.

Consider the following command that uses the cpio -p option:

```
# find . -depth -print ¦ cpio -pdlmv mydir
```

In the preceding command, cpio -p takes the file names piped to it and copies or links (-l option) those files to another directory (mydir) and creates the directories as needed (-d option). The -m option retains the modification time. The -depth option can be used to specify path names for cpio. By doing this, you can eliminate the problems that cpio can face while creating files under the read-only directories.

AMANDA

Advanced Maryland Automated Network Disk Archiver (AMANDA) is a client/server based network backup program with support for most UNIX and Windows hosts. AMANDA allows you to set up a single master backup server to back up multiple hosts to a single backup drive. AMANDA is usually used with tape drives. It also can be used with an optical or CD-ROM drive.

AMANDA instructs each client backup program to write to standard output, which is collected and transmitted to the tape server. This allows AMANDA to add compression and encryption to the data. Multiple clients are simultaneously backed up to files in one or more areas on the disk. A separate process writes this data to the tape for maximum throughput.

AMANDA supports a variety of tape storage devices. It also supports several tape changers, stackers, and robots to provide unattended operation. Clients that go into a hang during backup are noted and bypassed. If errors occur on the tape, backups are still performed, but only to the holding disks. After the errors are handled, the backup can be transferred to the tape.

AMANDA supports both hardware and software compression. Software compression can be performed by either the tape server or the client server. Software compression on the client side reduces network traffic and on the server side reduces the client CPU load. If the backup files need to be kept in an encrypted format, clients can use Kerberos for authentication. Using Kerberos, dump images also can be encrypted. If Kerberos is not available, .amandahosts authentication can be used, which is similar to .rhosts authentication, or AMANDA can be configured to use .rhosts. AMANDA is compatible with security tools such as TCP Wrappers and firewalls.

Because AMANDA uses standard tools to create dump images and software compression, normal UNIX tools—such as mt, dd, and gzip—can be used to recover a dump image in case AMANDA software is not available. If AMANDA is available, it first locates the tapes needed on the tape server and then locates the dump images on the tapes.

AMANDA can be configured to control all aspects of the backup operation and provides many scheduling options. A typical configuration performs periodic full backups with partial backups in between. Some of the other features of AMANDA configuration include these:

◆ **Periodic archival backup.** AMANDA allows you to make full backups on a site away from the primary site.

◆ **Incremental-only backups.** AMANDA can be configured to perform incremental backups where full backups are performed outside AMANDA, such as crucial areas that must be taken off the network, or no full dumps at all for areas that can be easily recovered from vendor media.

◆ **Full-only backups.** AMANDA can be configured to perform only full backups for areas that change completely with each run, such as databases or critical areas, which can be dealt with easily during an emergency, if they are stored in a single archive.

◆ **Support for multiple configurations.** AMANDA also can support multiple configurations on the same tape server if there are multiple tape drives. For example, a periodic archival backup configuration can run simultaneously with a normal daily full backup configuration. The configuration files will be stored under `/var/amanda/etc/amanda/normal/` and `/var/amanda/etc/amanda/archive/`, respectively.

Obtaining and Installing AMANDA

You can obtain AMANDA from the `www.amanda.org` Web page or with anonymous FTP at `ftp.amanda.org/pub/amanda/`. A typical release of AMANDA is a `gzip` compressed `tar` file, which can easily be downloaded and installed. After downloading, you must read the `README`, `docs/INSTALL`, and `doacs/SYSTEM.NOTES` files to gather the latest information on how to set up AMANDA.

You also might require several other packages for installing AMANDA. You should locate and install the packages listed in Table 13-7.

Table 13-7 Related Packages

Package	Available at	Description
GNU tar 1.12 or later	**www.gnu.org**	This is the GNU version of the standard tar program that can be used to perform partial backups and skip selected files. This is one of the client backup programs supported by AMANDA.
Samba 1.9.18p10 or later	**www.samba.org**	This contains a tool, smbclient, that AMANDA can use to back up Windows clients.
Perl 5.004 or later	**www.perl.org**	This scripting language is used for a few AMANDA reporting tools and by some tape changers.
GNU readline 2.2.1 or later	**www.gnu.org**	The GNU readline library provides command-line history and editing ability.
GNU awk 3.0.3 or later	**www.gnu.org**	The GNU version of the awk programming language is used for the optional AMANDA amplot statistical tool.
gnuplot3.5 or later	**ftp.Dartmouth. edu/pub/gnuplot**	This gnuplot library is a graph plotting tool and is used for the optional AMANDA amplot statistical tool.

A typical AMANDA configuration runs as a user other than root, such as backup or amanda, given just enough permission to do backups. AMANDA users should have read access to the disk devices. You can create a group of such users who have the read access to the disk devices. You should add members to this group judiciously.

Use the AMANDA user for the —with-user option and the AMANDA group for the —with-group option to ./configure. For example, to specify user1 for the user and user_backup as the group, do the following:

```
# ./configure —with-user=amanda —with-group=backup
```

The default security mechanism uses a file formatted in the same way as .rhosts but called .amandahosts.

If the hosts are separated by a firewall, the TCP ports used for data transfer also can be controlled by using —with-portrange while configuring AMANDA. For example, for allowing ports 50000 and 50100, the entry would be as follows:

```
# ./configure —with-portrange=50000,50100 …
```

The UDP requests from the tape server are not affected. The firewall should allow traffic through the AMANDA UDP port, which is normally 10080.

After configuring the ./configure file, you can run the make command to build AMANDA. The make install command can then be used to install AMANDA. The make install command should be executed by the users having root privileges.

Table 13-8 AMANDA Setuid-root Programs

Program	Description
usr/local/sbin/amcheck	This is the AMANDA sanity checker.
usr/local/libexec/dumper	This performs client communication.
usr/local/libexec/planner	This gathers the estimates.
usr/local/libexec/killpgrp	This kills vendor dump programs that run as root.
usr/local/libexec/rundump	This is the setuid wrapper for systems that need to run the vendor dump program as root.
usr/local/libexec/runtar	This is the setuid wrapper to run GNU tar as root.

The first group (amcheck, dumper, and planner) run on the tape server machine and need a privileged network port to communicate securely with the clients. As you can see, other programs are utility routines optionally used on the clients, depending on the dump program used and the type of operating system.

You need to make some changes to the network services and inetd configuration files to be able to use AMANDA properly. For example, add the specified entries to the /etc/services file or YP/NIS map in case the client-src/patch-system script does not work. The client-src/patch-system is used to set up systems.

```
Amanda 10080/udp
Amandaidx 10082/tcp
Amidxtape 10083/tcp
```

An entry for each client should be made to the /etc/inetd.conf file.

```
amanda dgram udp wait Amanda /PATH/libexec/amandad amandad
```

The amanda service is used by all AMANDA controlling programs to perform functions on the clients. You need to add entries as follows in the tape server host if you want to use the amrecover tool:

```
amandaidx stream tcp nowait Amanda /PATH/libexec/amindexd amindexd
amidxtape stream tcp nowait Amanda /PATH/libexec/amidxtaped amidxtaped
```

The amandaidx service enables you to access catalogs. The amidxtape service enables remote access to a tape device.

Configuring AMANDA

After installing, you need to configure AMANDA for use. The first thing you should decide is which machine will be used as the tape server. If you want to perform server compression, the tape server machine should be able to take that much load. The machine should have a direct access to a tape device that supports media with enough capacity to handle the unexpected load.

You should first estimate the size of the backups based on the total disk usage and the frequency of full dumps to calculate the tape capacity. AMANDA must be configured with non-rewinding tape devices.

You can establish a link between AMANDA and the tape device group using one of these methods:

◆ Make the AMANDA user a member of the group owning the tape devices.

◆ Create a new group for AMANDA users. The ownership of the tape devices should be passed to this group.

As stated earlier, you can choose to use software compression on the client or the tape server. Alternatively, you can choose to compress dump images on the tape device hardware. Software compression allows AMANDA to track usage and make better estimates of image sizes. However, hardware compression is more efficient than CPU resources.

If possible, you should allocate some holding disk space for AMANDA on the tape server. The holding disk space allows AMANDA to take several dumps at the same time when the tape is being written. This reduces the backup time by a great deal. For efficient backup, there should be enough holding disk space for two large dump images so that, while one image is being dumped on the holding disk, the other can be dumped on the tape.

There are three user-editable files that control the behavior of Amanda and are stored in a config directory under /var/Amanda/etc/Amanda. These include:

◆ **amanda.conf.** This is the main configuration file. It contains parameters to customize Amanda for your site.

◆ **disklist.** This file lists hosts and disk partitions to back up.

◆ **tapelist.** This file lists the tapes that are currently active.

amanda.conf file has a number of parameters that control the behavior of AMANDA programs. All of these parameters have default values. You can change these default values if they are not suitable. Some of the parameters that you might need to change are listed in Table 13-9.

Table 13-9 Parameters in the amanda.conf **File**

Parameter	Description
org	This parameter specifies the subject line text of AMANDA e-mail reports.
mailto	This parameter specifies the recipients of the AMANDA reports that are sent through e-mail.
dumpcycle	This parameter specifies the days after which full backup is to be made.
runspercycle	This parameter specifies the number of times AMNADA is to be run in the dump cycle.
tapecycle	This parameter determines the tape cycle.
runtapes	This parameter specifies the number of tapes to be run per run. The value that you specify here should be one more than the number of runs during dumpcycle.
dumpuser	This parameter specifies the username that'll be used by AMANDA to run backups.
tapetype	This parameter specifies the tape media type.
netusage	This parameter is used to specify the network bandwidth allocated to AMANDA.
labelstr	This parameter specifies the expression format to be used to label tapes.

Each holding disk is to be configured in the `holdingdisk` section in the `amanda.conf` file. Each option in the section is explained in Table 13-10.

Table 13-10 Options in the `holdingdisk` Section

Option	Description
comment	This option contains details of the holding disk.
directory	This option contains the path to the holding area. The default value is `/dumps/Amanda`.
use	This value contains the amount of space that can be used in this holding disk area. If partitions are dedicated for AMANDA, you can set this value as negative. This instructs AMANDA to use all available space minus that value.
chunksize	This value contains the holding disk chunk size. If the value is negative, the dumps larger than the size of the holding disk will be written directly to the tape. Positive number values cause the dumps in the holding disk to split into chunks of the size of the `chunksize` value.

The backup options can be specified in the `config` file. The `dumptype` section of the `config` file contains the backup options. The options might be used to configure various settings, such as using compression, recording results of backups, and so on.

The `amanda.conf` file can define multiple types of tape media. The characteristics of the tape media can be set in the `tapetype` section in the `amanda.conf` file. After setting the `tapetype` definition, set the `tapetype` parameter to reference it.

If you are not using any special hardware to mount tapes, such as a robot or stacker, you should either set the `tapedev` parameter to `no-rewind device name` or set up the AMANDA `chg-manual changer` script. This script prompts for tape mounts, when required, usually on the terminal of the person running AMANDA. Other popular tape changers are `chg-multi` and `chg-scsi`. Both these changers have configurations files. You can specify your settings for the changers in these files and specify the path to the configuration file in the `amanda.conf` file. There are samples in `example/chg-multi.conf` and `example/chg-scsi.conf`, respectively.

To configure the backup clients, start with the tape server host itself. Use either the vendor dump program or GNU `tar` to take client backups. Choose the type of compression for each area. GNU `gzip` might be used for compression to allow both for fast and slow compression.

The `disklist` specifies the disks that Amanda will back up. The file has an entry for each available disk. Table 13-11 describes the fields in the line.

Table 13-11 Fields in the `disklist` File

Field	Description
hostname	This field specifies the host to be backed up.
diskdevice	This field specifies the disk to be backed up.
dumptype	This field specifies the dump type. The dump type is obtained from the `amanda.conf` file.
spindle	This a number that is used to balance the load on a host.
interface	This field specifies the interface that will be used to balance network load. The network interfaces are defined in the `config` file.

To set up a Windows client, set the host name in the `disklist` file to the name of the UNIX machine running SAMBA and `diskdevice` to the Windows share name, such as `//win-client/C$`.

You can allow clients to access AMANDA from the tape server host. This can be done either by editing `.amandahosts` in the AMANDA user home directory or by modifying `.rhosts`. You should ensure that AMANDA is the owner of the file and no other user has access to it. Whenever required, you need to provide fully qualified tape server host names and the AMANDA username.

Running AMANDA

After configuring, you can run AMANDA completely hands-free. The `amdump` command takes care of the normal AMANDA backup runs. `Amdump` can be run completely in an automated mode `cron`. You should run `cron` as the AMANDA user, not root or the installer. The `amdump` command performs the following tasks:

◆ amdump logs an error and terminates if another copy of amdump is running or a previous run is aborted. If an earlier run is aborted, the amcleanup command must be run.

◆ The areas to be backed up and when the backup should be performed is determined by the AMANDA planner.

◆ The backup schedule is available to the driver program. The driver programs perform the backup based on the schedule.

The driver instructs the dumper to start backups. In addition, the driver provides each dumper with dump information, such as its client, area, and options, such as compression and whether the dump should go to the holding disk or directly to tape. The dumper requests amandad on the client to run dump programs. Along with the requests, options to run the programs are also passed. The client sends the dump image back to the dumper who writes it through the server compression program, into the holding disk, or directly to a taper connection.

The amreport command can be used to generate backup reports. The report is sent as e-mail. Complete information about the backups can be gathered from AMANDA reports obtained from the amreport command. It gives all details about the failed dumps, file systems dumped, the dump rate, the number of dumps made daily, partial dumps, and so on. The following are additional commands used by AMANDA:

◆ **amflush.** Used to flush backups from the holding disk to tape. When amdump reports an error while writing backups to tape, backups stay in the holding disk. After resolving the tape problem, you can run amflush to write backups from the holding disk to the tape.

◆ **amcleanup.** Used to clean up after an interrupted amdump. At times, the amdump command is interrupted for reasons like the crashing of taper server hosts.

◆ **amrecover.** Enables you to search for index files of AMANDA. It also enables you to select the backup tape from which the files will be restored. It also can run amrestore and the system restore program, such as tar, in some cases.

◆ **amrestore.** Used to read an AMANDA tape, searching for requested backups. It provides an interactive interface to restore single files as well as partitions on a failed disk.

◆ **amlabel.** Used to write an AMANDA format label on a tape. All Amanda tapes are supposed to be labeled with `amlabel`.

◆ **amcheck.** Used to verify the tape in the tape drive. It also verifies whether the file systems are ready to be backed up. `Amcheck` can optionally be run by `cron` before `amdump` to issue a mail warning for backup failure unless corrective action is taken.

◆ **amadmin.** Performs administrative tasks, such as determining which tapes are needed to restore a file system, forcing hosts to do full backups of selected disks, and looking at schedule balance information.

◆ **amtape.** Performs tape changer control operations, such as loading particular tapes, ejecting tapes, and scanning the tape rack.

◆ **amverify.** Used to check AMANDA backup tapes for errors. `Amverify` is provided for GNU `tar` format backups only.

◆ **amrmtape.** When a tape is completely damaged, `amrmtape` can be used to delete a tape from the `tapelist` and AMANDA database.

◆ **amstatus.** Gives the status of a running `amdump`. `Amstatus` also may be used after an `amdump` run to generate statistics on how many dumpers were used, what delayed the process, and so on.

rsync

Rsync is a utility that enables you to perform faster file transfers. This utility uses the `rsync` remote-update protocol to increase the speed of file transfer. It performs the incremental file transfer. Therefore, only the differences between two sets of files are transferred across the network link, using an efficient checksum-search algorithm. Some of the additional features of `rsync` taken from the manual page are as follows:

◆ Support for copying links, devices, owners, groups, and permissions

◆ `Exclude` and `exclude-from` options similar to GNU `tar`

◆ A CVS `exclude` mode for ignoring the same files that CVS would ignore

◆ Can use any transparent remote shell, including `rsh` or `ssh`

◆ Does not require root privileges

◆ Pipelining of file transfers to minimize latency costs

◆ Support for anonymous or authenticated `rsync` servers (ideal for mirroring)

Burt

Burt, the backup and recovery tool, is an extension of Tcl/Tk 8.0 designed to perform backups and recoveries for a wide variety of data sources. It provides an interactive user interface built using Tcl, which provides greater flexibility for administration. The main feature of Burt is that it provides an I/O engine built in a powerful scripting language that solves many problems related to backups of large installations.

Most of today's network installations run a wide variety of operating systems. Most users want to store data on their hard disks. In addition, in our fast-paced world, network administrators are under constant pressure to increase backup speeds. Burt is made to address these issues. The main features of Burt are as follows:

◆ Allows you to store and track data on long term media, such as tapes

◆ Allows maximum integrity and reliability of stored data on the backup medium

◆ Provides a mechanism to run backups unattended

◆ Allows the administrator to create a completely custom interface

◆ Allows parallel streams of data backup to run directly to the tape providing faster backups

Commercial Backup Tools

Apart from the tools freely available, certain backup tools are available commercially. These include the following:

◆ BRU

◆ Backup Professional

◆ CTAR

◆ Arkeia

◆ Legato NetWorker

◆ EssentialServer

The following sections elaborate on these tools.

BRU

Backup and Restore Utility (BRU) is quite an old backup tool. This tool provides a variety of features with a flexible format, available both in command-line and GUI interface. The graphical interface allows easier administration and can easily be automated. It supports full, incremental, and differential backups, as well as catalogs, and can write both to a file or a tape drive.

Backup Professional

The Backup Professional tool is a client/server backup tool server that allows for both manual and automated backups. It is an enterprise backup and disaster recovery software solution. It supports more than nine servers and over 20 operating systems. When running manually, Backup Professional allows registered clients to be backed up by a request from the *backup user agents* (UAs). Backup UA can exist on both the client and the server. The backup UA on the client can request a backup for itself. On the other hand, the server UA can request backup for itself as well as a client.

When a client sends a backup request to the server, the server reads the request and places it into the task table. The backup is performed based on the availability of the resources needed for the backup.

There are three types of backups that can be performed:

- ◆ **Master Backup.** This backup archives the complete data on a specified client.
- ◆ **Incremental Backup.** This backup archives data that has been modified after the last master backup was performed.
- ◆ **Selective Backup.** This backup specifies only the selected files.

Backup Professional file recovery/verification utility is used to restore files and directories to client machines and verify previous backups. Documentation and other information about Backup Professional is available on the Web at **www.unitrends.com**.

CTAR

Compressing Tape Archiver (CTAR) provides a rock-solid backup and recovery solution for UNIX systems and UNIX-only networks. It allows you to backup and restore files from a variety of storage media, such as tape, floppy disk, or add-on hard disks. A key argument controls the actions performed by CTAR. The key contains the function names and modifiers. Like Backup Professional, CTAR is available at **www.unitrends.com**.

CTAR can be used to archive or restore all the files and directories in a file system. The crash recovery features of CTAR enable it to recover data from archive files. CTAR enables you to split files across multiple media. CTAR also supports faster backups. The double buffering feature enables it to do so. During double buffering, shared memory buffers, semaphores, and dual processes increase the backup speed. Shared memory buffers play a critical role in this. While one CTAR process is reading data from the hard disk and writing it to the shared memory buffers, the other process writes the data from the shared memory buffer to the tape drive.

Arkeia

Arkeia is another backup tool that greatly simplifies data protection by providing automated backup and recovery. Available at **www.arkeia.com**, Arkeia supports a wide variety of computers, operating systems and storage devices. Arkeia is easy to install and configure. It is suitable for any kind of network, simple or complex. Other features of Arkeia include these:

◆ **Speed.** Arkeia uses a multi-flow technology and client-side compression provides a high speed to Arkeia operations. You can perform several backups and restore operations at the same time.

◆ **Reliability.** If network and system errors halt the backup process, Arkeia is designed to recover and restart the backup process. Arkeia uses a catalog to track the data and metadata. In case of backup server failure, Arkeia recovers the data by using the catalog. The fail-safe restore utility enables Arkeia to do so.

◆ **User-friendly.** The software is based on three components: a server, a client, and a graphical user interface (GUI). This kind of architecture offers an exceptionally easy installation and management of any backup. Arkeia's architecture and GUI enables easy deployment of Arkeia and makes it user friendly. It also allows the administration to remotely manage backup and restore operations virtually from any computer where the GUI is installed, including via the Internet.

Arkeia can be used to perform full and incremental backups. You can schedule the backups to be performed.

Legato NetWorker

A number of enterprise customers worldwide use Legato NetWorker to protect critical business data and to simplify, centralize, and automate backup and recovery operations across different platforms. These platforms include UNIX, Windows, Linux, and NetWare platforms in DAS, network attached storage (NAS), and SAN storage environments. Built on open and flexible client/server architecture, NetWorker reduces management overhead by providing strong protection of files in different fields, from the largest corporate data centers to the smallest satellite branch offices.

NetWorker allows companies and organizations to standardize on one application that is used to provide complete, fast, and reliable protection of business-critical information across a heterogeneous enterprise. This results in lower downtime costs, less management overhead, and greater ROI of storage resources. Legato Networker documentation, software, and other details can be obtained from **www.legatonetworker.com/products/networker**.

EssentialServer

The EssentialServer is a device that enables you to perform data backup, storage, and recovery in your network. It provides you a solution to add 80GB to 960GB data storage capacity and file sharing across various platforms in your network. EssentialServer's browser-based interface allows it to be easily set up. An easy-to-understand installation wizard guides you through the process of installation. EssentialServer has a robust, reliable, and scaleable architecture, fast network performance, and efficient multiplatform file sharing. In addition, it is easy to manage via a Web-based interface. It also provides fast and easy disaster recovery. Some of its features, as listed on **www.merlintechnologies.com/ partners/index.html,** include:

- ◆ **Backup support for non-Linux clients.** EssentialServer includes client-side backup software to enable Windows and Macintosh users to backup their local files to EssentialServer automatically.

- ◆ **Fully integrated backup.** The backup capabilities are fully integrated in EssentialServer hardware. The tape drive, CD-RW drive, and backup software are easy to manage and use.

- ◆ **Fast, easy restore.** EssentialServer enables you to restore and recover complete data from the backup media. It also provides a user-friendly interactive interface for restoring files.

◆ **Reliable NAS storage.** EssentialServer's NAS models provide fast and economical data storage and multi-platform file sharing. You can configure EssentialServer as per your requirements.

◆ **Four levels of protection and security.** EssentialServer provides different levels of protection. Thus, enhanced security is available when you use EssentialServer. The data to be backed up is stored on the user's computer. This data is copied to the EssentialServer. Next, they are either mirrored or striped across RAID drives; and finally, they are backed up to tape or CD.

Summary

One of the top priorities of the system administrator should be making regular backups. A powerful operating system, such as Linux, also can face disasters in the form of hardware failures, power failure, natural disasters, or other unforeseen problems. These problems might be caused by human error resulting in undesired changes to files or cause deletions of crucial files in certain cases. Regular backups save you from such calamities. In this chapter, you learned about various commercial and non-commercial tools available for taking backups. You must intelligently choose a backup mechanism that provides maximum security of data on individual workstations as well as on servers.

Check Your Understanding

Multiple Choice Questions

1. Which of the following is a client/server-based network backup tool?

   a. AMANDA

   b. `tar`

   c. `rsync`

   d. `cpio`

2. Which program in AMANDA provides you with an interactive interface to browse the AMANDA index files?

   a. amrestore

   b. amrecover

   c. amcheck

   d. amverify

3. Which types of backups are supported by Backup Professional?

   a. Selective backups

   b. Master backups

   c. Incremental backups

   d. All of the above

Short Questions

1. What is the difference between selective and incremental backups?
2. How can backup logs be helpful in managing backups?
3. Name a commercial backup tool that is a hardware device.

Answers

Multiple Choice Answers

1. a, c. Both AMANDA and rsync are client/server-based network backup tools.

2. b. amrecover provides you with an interactive interface to browse the AMANDA index files and allows you to choose the tape from which files will be recovered. It also can run amrestore and the system restore program, such as tar, in some cases.

3. d. Backup Professional allows you to take three types of backups. A master backup archives the complete data on a specified client. An incremental backup archives data that have been modified after the last master backup was performed. A selective backup archives only the selected files. Backup Professional file recovery/verification utility is used to restore files and directories to client machines and verify previous backups.

Short Answers

1. Selective backups can be a form of incremental backups. When making incremental backups, you back up the areas that have modified since the last backup. You can do this manually or automate it by using a backup tool that allows automation of incremental backups. Selective backups are backups in which you back up the selected files. Obviously, these files would be the ones that change frequently.

2. Backup logs help an administrator keep track of various details regarding backups. These might involve writing the details of the contents of a tape on the tape itself, maintaining a register for the date of backup, name of the backup tape used, the file system being backed up, the type of backup performed, and so on.

3. EssentialServer.

Appendix A

Linux—Best
Practices

Linux Partitions

You need to set up Linux partitions during Linux installation. Be sure to take proper care while partitioning the hard disk. You should ensure that no components of Linux are installed in the boot partition of Linux. No file systems containing files that can be modified by ordinary users should reside on the boot partition of Linux. Here are a few guidelines about file systems or directories that should not be present in the boot partition:

◆ You should not place user logfiles in the boot partition. These logfiles are sometimes so huge that they can consume all the space on the system. This might cause Linux to crash.

◆ File systems with critical system components and configuration should be stored on separate partitions. Then if a user data partition gets corrupted, the rest of the system remains safe.

◆ Partitions with system binaries should be mounted as read-only to prevent anyone from modifying them. A possible disadvantage of doing this is that more effort is required at the time of upgrading.

◆ The root directory requires extra care. It should be modifiable by users other than the root. You need to restrict users' access to the directory completely.

◆ All backup files should reside on a separate partition, or if enough resources are available, on a separate partition.

The /home Directory

The /home directory contains users' home directories, and users have write permissions to these directories. E-mail client programs also store their e-mails in this directory. This file system can grow huge very rapidly. If any users have limited disk quotas, space overuse can cause a lot of problems.

Here are some of the precautions you should take while dealing with the /home directory:

◆ Store the /home directory on a partition separate from the boot partition. User directories can grow huge and storing them in the boot partition can cause damage to the Linux system.

◆ Storing the /home directory on a separate partition restricts users from creating hard links to the /home directory and other files inside the /home directory. Hard links are links that point to the actual INODE of the files.

◆ The /home directory should be mounted in nosuid mode.

◆ If possible, also mount the /home directory as noexec. Although this is a good security measure, it can put many restrictions on the users.

General Best Practices

A few best practices are listed here:

◆ Ensure that the software is downloaded from secure and authentic Web sites. As an added precaution, validate the installation file checksums like PGP or MD-5 signatures before installation is done.

◆ Ensure that the partition sizes are set according to the data that will be stored in them. Partitions that contain user writable data should have extra space beyond their expected use.

◆ Ensure that the partition scheme and security policies are well documented and are kept in safe custody. After reading the documentations, a new administrator should be able to restore a damaged system without much effort. The document should specify the details of the services that are needed, storage location of all configuration files, important directives in all running services, authentication schemes in use, details of backup server, and restore procedures.

Stop All Unused Services

In a Linux system, services that are running are the only ones that can be attacked. Other services that are installed on the server but have not been started either at boot time or manually are not vulnerable to network attacks. An administrator should analyze closely all the services that are required on the server and stop the rest of the services. Apart from these services, an administrator should try to avoid running services that can be remotely utilized in any way and that do not use any kind of encryption. The following list provides a few services that are not recommended on a Linux computer unless they are critically required:

- ◆ **rlogin.** This service allows remote terminal sessions.
- ◆ **rstatd.** This service serves kernel performance statistics.
- ◆ **rusersd.** This service provides information on users that are currently logged on to the system.
- ◆ **tftpd.** This service is used to transfer files between computers. tftpd doesn't support any authentication mechanisms; therefore, it can be used to transfer only those files that are publicly accessible.
- ◆ **talkd.** This service allows remote users to communicate with each other. This program allows two or more remotely logged on users to copy and paste data from the terminal screen of one user to that of another user.
- ◆ **fingerd.** This service provides an interface to the finger program at most network sites. The program displays a user-friendly and detailed status report on either the system at the moment or a particular user.
- ◆ **uucp.** This service copies files between systems.

To stop services that are not required, you need to make changes in the /etc/inetd.conf file. You can turn off a service by placing a # symbol in front of it. This stops the service from starting during the next system reboot.

Not all services that run in Linux systems are controlled by the inet daemon. Therefore, in addition to commenting out services from the inetd, check /etc/inittab to look for other programs that are being executed at boot time.

Use Secure Protocols for Remote Administration

Administrators should avoid using remote terminal protocols such as rlogin and telnet. Instead, use encryption-based protocols, such as SSH. SSH protocol ensures that the information you type at your local computer is not sent across a network in plain text. Data is encrypted using dual key encryptography before it is transmitted over an unreliable network.

Choosing Your Passwords

Passwords should be strong enough that they won't be guessed by anyone. The only way to crack your password is using a brute force attack. Brute force attacks can be made impractical by choosing longer passwords and using wider character sets in your passwords. Here are a few guidelines you can keep in mind while choosing your passwords:

- ◆ Your login name should not be related to your password in any way. Other common mistakes are reversed, capitalized, doubled, and numbered forms of your login name.

- ◆ Your password should not contain your first, last, or middle name in any form. Neither should it contain names of your spouse, child, dog, license plate numbers, telephone, home addresses, or any other information about you that can be easily guessed.

- ◆ Your passwords should not be all letters or all numbers. Passwords that contain combinations of mixed-case letters, numbers, and punctuation marks are difficult to guess or crack.

- ◆ Do not use words listed in language directories. Brute force attacks are often based on language and name databases.

- ◆ Choose longer passwords. Passwords should be longer than six characters.

- ◆ Choose a password that is easy to remember and you don't have to write it down. The first character of each word from a line in one of your favorite songs can be a good password.

- ◆ Choose passwords that you can type very quickly without looking at the keyboard.

Apart from these guidelines, passwords should be changed at regular intervals. Some security advisory boards encourage you to change your passwords every 30 days.

Regular Updates

All services running in your system should be updated regularly. Administrators should subscribe to popular security advisory lists, such as www.cert.org, to keep themselves updated about all version updates and security patches. All running services in a system must be updated as soon as the upgrades are available.

Running an older system is an open invitation to attackers. A hacker can easily know the version you are using because most services display version numbers in the output of various commands.

Make Backups

You should make regular backups of your critical files. No security software or policy is 100 percent safe. If a system is compromised, the only means to restore the system is to use backups. Every storage media has a limited lifetime. Older backup media should be verified at regular intervals and replaced with newer media.

Enable Shadow Suite

Shadow Suite is a good security tool that can discourage attackers from trying to download your password files. You should use Shadow Suite to protect your password-related information.

BIND

Here are the guidelines regarding BIND:

◆ If a master server is maintained in a server, ensure that /etc/named.conf is modified suitably to restrict zone transfers. The allow-transfer option should explicitly mention the IP address of the master server.

◆ If a Slave or Secondary is running on your system, all zone transfers should be restricted. The allow-transfer option should not have anything next to where the directive is placed in the file.

◆ Ensure that named is chrooted.

◆ Ensure that all events in the DNS server are being properly logged by syslogd. The /etc/rc.d/init.d/syslog should contain the following line:

```
daemon syslog-a /home/dns/dev/log.
```

Sendmail

Here are some guidelines regarding `sendmail`:

- ◆ Permit only fully qualified domain names and subdomains for mail relays. The `/etc/mail/access` file should be modified to include valid networks to mail relaying.

- ◆ Review the `/etc/sendmail.cf` file to ensure that the SMTP `vrfy` and `expn` have been turned off.

- ◆ Ensure that the POP/IMAP servers are of the latest stable version available.

- ◆ Set up TCP wrappers in `/etc/hosts.allow` to allow mail deliveries only to authorized networks.

- ◆ Set up domain name masquerading by modifying the `/etc/sendmail.cf` file.

- ◆ Set up SSL wrapper to secure POP/IMAP connections.

Appendix B

Linux FAQs

Q. **Briefly discuss the security of Linux.**

A. Security is ensuring the availability, integrity, and confidentiality of your systems. In Linux, chances of a security breach increase with the increase in the number of services that your server offers. The best way to tackle this threat is to install Linux with minimum packages and then add the required services. Any services that are no longer needed should be removed from the system. Linux is very secure if it is implemented properly. The administrator should also keep track of the security updates and patches released by various Internet Linux communities.

Q. **How can I protect my system from hackers?**

A. You can use these security measures to protect your system from hackers:

◆ Turn off the services not required and protect the other services by implementing TCP wrappers.

◆ Keep track of the latest security updates and install new security patches regularly.

◆ Replace unencrypted services, such as ftp and Telnet, with more secure equivalents, such as SSH and SCP.

◆ Always maintain backup copies of the important resources. Having backup copies helps in recovery. If possible, you also should back up all files that were created or modified by either the administrator or any user.

◆ Go through security manuals to read updated information about all security measures.

Q. **Why do I always fail while trying to login as root through Telnet?**

A. Many Linux distributions don't allow you to login as root through Telnet as an added security feature because the password will travel in a plain text format through the network. You should first login as a normal user and then use the su command to work as root. You can change this option from /etc/securetty, although it is not recommended.

Q. Is Linux vulnerable to viruses?

A. Linux is to a great extent safe from viruses due to the following reasons:

◆ First, it is very difficult for a virus to activate itself on a Linux machine because Linux does not run programs automatically in the form of mail attachment scripts.

◆ In Linux, every piece of code needs permission to run. This means that the virus has to find a code in which it can insert itself and get executed. For this, the virus code needs a certain degree of privilege, which is not easy to acquire.

Q. Why is using SSL considered safe?

A. Secure Socket Layer (SSL) protocol was created to provide reliable and secure transfer of data over an unreliable network. This is done by utilizing encryption and authentication features that make SSH more reliable than other protocols, unlike the Telnet protocol in which data and commands are transmitted and received in plain text. The SSH protocol encrypts every piece of data before transmitting it and decrypts it before the data is put in use. This ensures that network traffic sniffers are unable to collect any unauthorized information during data transits.

Q. How can I detect whether my system has been hacked?

A. To check whether your system has been intruded, you should search for various signs that the hacker may have left behind. Here are some common signs of intrusion:

◆ Failed logon attempts

◆ Change of password

◆ Sudden degradation in system performance

◆ Strange and unexpected entries in log file

◆ Missing files

◆ Change in file organization

Q. **I want to shut down all unused services, but how do I find out which services are already running?**

A. You can use the `ps auxw` command to get a list of processes that are currently running. You also can use variations such as `ps, auxf, or ps auxfw` for a better output in tree format. Using `netstat` also is a good option for listing services.

Some of the options of `netstat` that you can use are these:

◆ - **a.** This option lists the services listening for connection.

◆ - **ltp.** This option lists services listening to well-known ports.

Q. **Why is connecting to a computer using Telnet considered unsafe?**

A. Telnet is a very unsafe means for communication. The data is not encrypted and any hacker listening to your connection can retrieve important information, such as password. This is possible because all data is sent as plain text. Therefore, using a secure method like SSH is recommended. In SSH, the transfer of the data is encrypted, which makes it more secure.

Q. **My computer has been hacked. What do I do now?**

A. After your computer has been hacked, your aim should be to minimize the damage that could be done to your system and draw a safe recovery chart. First remove your computer from the network. This can protect the system from any further damages by the hacker. Check your log files to determine the method of attack. If your data is severely damaged, you should use the backup to replace the data with a correct copy. You also should try to find the vulnerability in your system which led to an attack. This loophole should be immediately removed in order to safeguard your systems from similar threats in future.

Q. **How can I use TCP wrappers to enhance security?**

A. TCP wrappers are used to provide access control for services. They can be used to mention explicitly the hosts who can use a service. It controls access through two lists:

- **/etc/hosts/allow.** This file contains a list of users who are allowed access to the service.

- **/etc/hosts/deny.** This file contains a list of users who are denied access to the service.

  These configurations are used to accept or drop a requested connection. TCP wrapper also provides you with the additional function of writing logs for all activities that take place.

Q. **I want to test my computer for vulnerabilities. Are their any tools available for this purpose?**

A. Plenty of tools are available for this purpose and it is considered a good practice to use these tools to check your system, both from inside and outside your network. Here's a list of such tools:

- **SATAN (System Administrator's Tool for Analyzing Networks)**

  This tool is available from `http://www.porcupine.org/satan/`.

- **SAINT (Security Administrator's Integrated Network Tool)**

  This tool is available from `http://www.wwdsi.com/saint/`.

- **Nmap**

  This tool is available from `http://www.insecure.org/nmap/`.

- Other tools like Nessus also are available.

Q. **Are Trojans viruses? Is my system vulnerable to them?**

A. Trojans are different from viruses. Trojans are harmful programs that try to act like friendly and useful programs. Unlike viruses, trojans do not replicate by themselves. Their aim is to create a security loophole in your system, which can give the hacker access to it.

Q. **How does Linux manage passwords?**

A. In Linux, passwords are not encrypted. They are hashed using hashing algorithms like MD5, etc. These hash values are unique and cannot be reverted back to the original text. When you enter your password in Linux, its hash value is generated and is compared to the hash value of the stored password. If the values match, access is given; otherwise, access is denied.

Q. **How can I make my Linux kernel more secure?**

A. The Linux kernel can be configured in a number of ways to make it more secure. A few of these configurations are listed here:

◆ **CONFIG_FIREWALL.** This option enables a kernel-based firewall. If you use the intended host on which this configuration will be done as a client machine, this option is not needed.

◆ **CONFIG_IP_FIREWALL.** Use this option to enable kernel support for a packet filter-based firewall. This option allows you to use features such as IP masquerading, IP transparent proxying, and IP packet logging. Packet filtering is done in the network layer. Therefore, packet filtering uses only the source address, destination address, type and protocol used, and the port information in the IP packet header to decide whether to let a packet through.

◆ **CONFIG_IP_FORWARD.** This option enables IP forwarding on the host machine, thus enabling it to act as a router. If used according to the planned security architecture of a network, this option enables you to avoid the need for a hardware router. But if this is enabled on a secured network that depends on firewall security, it can become the biggest loophole in the security of the network because this host can then forward IP packets to external networks without going through the firewall.

◆ **CONFIG_SYN_COOKIES.** This option is used to protect the system from a SYN flooding attack. When enabled, the TCP/IP stack uses a SYS cookie protocol to establish connections. Although this challenge protocol is very effective against a SYS flooding attack, it can cause erroneous reporting at the client machine if the server is actually busy. SYN cookies are not enabled by default.

◆ **CONFIG_IP_MASQUERADE.** Use this to enable masquerading for TCP and UDP packets. Masquerading is basically Network Address Translation in which the firewall changes the source IP address of outgoing packets to its own address and the destination IP address of the incoming packet to the actual destination address of the internal network host. You need to enable IP forwarding in order to use this option.

Q.   **Does disabling incoming or outgoing pings make my Linux more secure?**

A.   Although rejecting incoming pings doesn't make your system invisible, it can certainly work against ping sweeps and certain denial-of-service attacks. Incoming pings can be used to flood your network or simply to detect your presence.

Outgoing pings can be exploited by certain Trojans to broadcast their presence in a host to the base. Although outgoing pings are useful in some cases, they should be disabled if not needed.

Q.   **How can Identd affect security?**

A.   Identd is used to identify a user in your own network who is creating trouble in an external network. It is not of much use for a very small network. When a user initiates a TCP/IP connection to a remote host, the identd of the remote host replies to port 113, asking the identity of the initiator. Identd at this time replies with the username of the owner of the process that initiated the connection request.

If a user misuses the system to launch an attack targeted at another network, the victim can identify the defaulter and report to the system administrator of the first network. This can be very helpful in keeping the network from becoming a launch pad of attacks.

Identd should never be used as an authenticating service because anyone with root privileges or on a Windows system can tamper the Identd response.

You can block access to identd by commenting out the auth line in /etc/ identd.conf or by using tcpwrappers and/or firewalling software to disable or restrict access. If you need to enable identd in order to connect to a certain server, you might want to consider allowing access to it only from that server. If you choose to firewall the identd port, consider using a reject policy rather than a deny policy. Using deny may greatly increase the time it takes you to connect to servers that use identd.

Appendix C

Future of Linux

inux's growth has been exponential for the past seven years. In 1995, an estimated 500,000 computers used Linux. This figure tripled the next year. In 1997, 3.5 million were using Linux. The growth is continuing. Several factors, such as its open source nature, efficiency, portability, and flexibility have contributed to its popularity. In this appendix, I discuss some products for the Linux platform that are expected to be catalysts in continuing to boost the popularity of Linux. Specifically, I'll talk about Bastille Linux, Apache 2.0 Web server, and `qmail`.

Bastille Linux

The Bastille Linux project was started in April 1999 with the goal assisting system administration in the Linux environment. It was initially released for the Red Hat distribution but later versions were compatible with the other distributions as well. Bastille Linux is freely available under the GNU General Public License (GPL). Jay Beale is the lead developer of the project.

A few of the scripts that manage Bastille Linux are listed here:

- ◆ `InteractiveBastille.pl`. This script prompts users for various options during configuration. The options selected by the user are stored in a `config` file.
- ◆ `BackEnd.pl`. This script takes care of systems modification.
- ◆ `Undo.pl`. This script enables you to undo any modification in case of trouble. The backup copies of configuration files are placed at `/root/Bastille/undo` directory.

Features of Bastille Linux

Some features of the Bastille Linux are listed here:

- ◆ Bastille provides support for various distribution of Linux.

◆ The GUI interface installation makes Bastille user friendly for users new to Linux.

◆ It supports the Linux 2.4 kernel and enhanced firewall features.

Apache 2.0

Apache 2.0 is the latest version of Apache. Apache 2.0 has improved significantly from its previous versions. Some of the new features of Apache 2.0 are listed here:

◆ The scalability of Apache has increased. Apache now runs in a hybrid multiprocessing and multithreaded mode on systems with POSIX support.

◆ Apache 2.0 supports multiple protocols.

◆ Apache 2.0 is now faster and stable on platforms such as OS/2 and Windows. This became possible due to the implementation of Multi-Processing Modules (MPM) and Apache Portable Runtime (APR).

◆ Apache 2.0 API has been significantly enhanced as compared to previous versions. New calls in the API provide enhanced functionality.

◆ Apache 2.0 can be used to filter the incoming and outgoing data traffic to the server.

◆ IPv6 socket is now available by default for Apache. This socket is required for systems where IPv6 is supported by the underlying Apache Portable Runtime library.

◆ Multilingual error responses can now be displayed to the client. This is done by using the Server Side Includes (SSI).

◆ The directives have been simplified. Some directives from previous versions are now deprecated. For example, the `BindAddress` directive is dropped.

◆ Apache 2.0 uses utf-8 for all filename encoding on Windows NT.

New Modules in Apache 2.0

Apache 2.0 has introduced some new modules in the latest release. Some new modules in Apache 2.0 are these:

◆ **mod_ssl.** This module provides an interface to the SSL/TLS encryption protocols provided by OpenSSL.

◆ **mod_dav.** This module implements the HTTP Distributed Authoring and Versioning (DAV) specification for posting and maintaining web content.

◆ **mod_charset_lite.** This experimental module allows for character set translation or recoding.

◆ **mod_file_cache.** This module adds further caching abilities to the functionality of mod_mmap_static in Apache 1.3.

Enhanced Modules

Here are some improved modules in Apache 2.0:

◆ **mod_auth_digest.** This module provides additional support for session caching across processes using shared memory.

◆ **mod_headers.** This module can be used to modify request headers used by mod_proxy. This module is much more flexible in Apache 2.0, as compared to previous versions.

◆ **mod_proxy.** The proxy module has been completely rewritten to take advantage of the new filter infrastructure and to implement the HTTP/1.1 compliant proxy, which is very reliable.

◆ **mod_autoindex.** This module is used to configure autoindexed directory listings to enable it to use HTML tables for cleaner formatting. Autoindexed directorys allow finer control of sorting, including version sorting and wildcard filtering of the directory listing.

◆ **mod_include.** This module contains directives that allow the default start and end tags for SSI elements to be changed. It also allows for error and time format configuration to take place in the main configuration file.

◆ **mod_auth_dbm.** This module provides support for multiple types of DBM-like databases by using the AuthDBMType directive. This directive sets the type of database file that is used to store the passwords. The default database type is determined at compile time.

qmail

`qmail` is a secure and reliable Message Transfer Agent (MTA). According to a survey conducted in October,. 2001, `qmail` is the second most popular SMTP server after `sendmail`. This information is available at `http://cr.yp.to/qmail.html`. In recent times, it is fast catching up with `sendmail`. Here are the advantages provided by `qmail`:

◆ Secure
◆ Reliable
◆ Efficient
◆ Simple

The mailing list management feature is one of the strengths of `qmail`. It enables you to do the following:

◆ Handle your own mailing lists as you wish.
◆ Setup mailing list owners easily.
◆ Deliver messages at twice the speed of `sendmail`.
◆ Prevent mailing list loops.
◆ Build huge mailing lists. No limit whatsoever has been put on the number of users in the mailing list.
◆ Handle aliasing and forwarding easily.

Some fundamental precautionary measures have been taken to ensure `qmail`'s security. Some of these measures are listed here:

◆ `qmail` doesn't treat programs and files as addresses. In `qmail`, the `qmail-local`, which is a delivery agent, runs programs or writes to files as directed by `~user/.qmail`. However, the local delivery agent always runs as a user.
◆ `qmail` restricts the `setuid` programs to a minimum. In `qmail`, only one program, the `qmail-queue`, is `setuid`. The `qmail-queue` program adds a new mail message to the outgoing queue.
◆ `qmail` restricts the activity of the root to the minimum. In `sendmail`, the entire `sendmail` system runs as root. However, in `qmail`, only two programs, `qmail-start` and `qmail-lspawn`, are run as root.

◆ qmail distributes functions in different programs, which don't trust each other. As a result, even if an intruder gets access to some of the programs, he would not be able to gain complete control over the system.

◆ qmail has been kept as simple as possible. The more features a system has, the more vulnerable it is to attacks. Therefore, only the minimum required features have been provided with qmail.

sendmail vs. qmail

sendmail has some security problems. It has been the target of hackers and many security holes have been detected. Users often configure sendmail with minimal security, making it vulnerable to attacks. qmail is more secure and efficient than sendmail. Fewer security-related problems have been reported by qmail users.

sendmail has a plethora of features. As a result, a user uses barely 30 to 40 percent of the features. Many of the services provided by sendmail remain unused and they continue to consume your system resources. qmail, on the other hand, is less complex and all its features are more or less frequently used. In addition, the qmail documentation is simpler and easy to understand compared to the sendmail documentation.

Index

Symbols

@ symbol, 56

` (back ticks), 201

3DES (Triple Data Encryption Standard), 137

A

access
  evaluating, 15
  users, 15

access control lists. *See* ACL

access file, 291

access_log file, 392-394

AccessConfig directive, 232

AccessFileName directive, 246, 266

accessing (Apache)
  default configuration, 272
  directories, 265-271
    directives, 267-268

account security, 16, 30-40. *See also* accounts; users
  devices, 32
  file permissions, 39-40
  file systems, 37-39
  manual page commands, 34
  passwd command, 31-32
  passwords, 31-33
  root accounts, 33-34
  Shadow Suite, 31
  SUDO command, 34

user accounts, 35-40
  default users, 34
  logs, 36
  user IDs, 33
  write permissions, 33

accounts. *See also* account security; users
  adding, 103-104
  deleting, 104-105
  FTP servers, 278-279
  guest, 35
  root, 33-34
  users, 35-40
    file systems, 37-39
    logs, 36

ACL (Access Control Lists)
  firewalls, 25-26
  TCP wrappers, 353-354

Action directive, 255

actions (log files), 390

adding accounts, 103-104

AddModule directive, 238-239

add-on modules (Apache), 228

administration, 88
  daemons, 107-109
  FTP servers, 285
  Linuxconf, 109-111
    configuring, 112-118
    control panel, 118
    status, 119
  managing users, 101-106
    groupadd command, 105
    groupdel command, 105